In the Midnight Hour

IN THE MIDNIGHT HOUR

The Life & Soul of Wilson Pickett

Tony Fletcher

OXFORD
UNIVERSITY PRESS

Oxford University Press is a department of the University of Oxford. It furthers
the University's objective of excellence in research, scholarship, and education
by publishing worldwide. Oxford is a registered trade mark of Oxford University
Press in the UK and certain other countries.

Published in the United States of America by Oxford University Press
198 Madison Avenue, New York, NY 10016, United States of America.

Library of Congress Cataloging-in-Publication Data
Names: Fletcher, Tony, author.
Title: In the midnight hour : the life & soul of Wilson Pickett / Tony Fletcher.
Description: New York : Oxford University Press, [2017] |
Includes bibliographical references and index.
Identifiers: LCCN 2016014880 (print) | LCCN 2016015915 (ebook) |
ISBN 9780190252946 (hardcover : alk. paper) | ISBN 9780190252953 (updf) |
ISBN 9780190252960 (epub)
Subjects: LCSH: Pickett, Wilson. | Soul musicians—United States—Biography.
Classification: LCC ML420.P5256 F64 2016 (print) | LCC ML420.P5256 (ebook) |
DDC 782.421644092 [B] —dc23
LC record available at https://lccn.loc.gov/2016014880

9 8 7 6 5 4 3 2
Printed by Edwards Brothers Malloy, United States of America

To Holly George-Warren,
For ensuring this book is in your hands,
And to the Catskill 45s
For being soul brothers and sister.

CONTENTS

PREFACE

He was the Wicked Wilson Pickett, the Midnight Mover, the Man and a Half. He was the soul man behind an incomparable series of classics that spanned the breadth of the 1960s and early 1970s: "In the Midnight Hour," "634-5789," "Land of 1000 Dances," "Mustang Sally," "Funky Broadway," "I'm in Love," "Engine Number 9," and "Don't Let the Green Grass Fool You," to name just a few of his forty-five hits. He was impossibly handsome ("You end up loving him," said one of the many female associates who did just that), a shamanistic stage presence whose thunderous live performances were given to repeated stage invasions by men and women of all colors, eager to bask—and dance—in his radiance. In an era graced by so many epic voices, each with their own distinct personalities, Wilson Pickett was in many considered opinions the greatest, the most visceral and sensual—and as a man who turned screaming into an art form, surely the most forceful. He served as the very embodiment of soul music.

Fifty years on, his longevity is evident. Somewhere right now, a Wilson Pickett song is playing on the radio. Somewhere right now, a band is playing a Wilson Pickett song on stage. Indeed, so ubiquitous is his music that it can be difficult to date one's introduction to it. For my part, I believe it was at the end of 1977 when, aged thirteen, I heard British punk-mod band The Jam covering "In the Midnight Hour"—at such breakneck speed that they shaved fifty seconds off a song that was only one hundred and sixty seconds long to begin with! Similar contemporary interpretations of classic soul songs soon had me searching out the originals, and by my mid-teens, I was among the thousands of Londoners jumping around at house parties every weekend to Pickett's immortal "Land of 1000 Dances," a song equally dominant on the live scene at the time.

Still, while writing and researching this book I was frequently asked *Why Wilson Pickett?*—as if a white Englishman born the same year the twenty-three-year-old Pickett signed to Atlantic Records, a writer generally known for his coverage of rock music, would or could have no cultural connection to a black soul singer from the cotton fields of Alabama. The short answer, as confirmed by the punk originators and mod revivalists of my own youth, is that a love of American soul music runs deep through British veins, even among those who were too young to enjoy it the first time around. The longer answer includes my emigration to the United States in the late 1980s, and an ongoing immersion in a music I believe to be one of America's most important contributions to global popular culture. That immersion has included copious reading, the collecting of box sets and scratchy old 45s alike, and making the Stax Museum of American Soul Music in Memphis a compulsory stop on our family's cross-American road trip in 2012.

Several months after that trip, listening to Pickett's music, it suddenly occurred to me I had never come across a biography of the man, and I sought to understand why, especially as my shelves contained so many books on his peers. Perhaps his story was simply not that interesting? Cursory research immediately indicated otherwise: his tale might lack the alluring drama of a premature death, such as befell his great influence Sam Cooke, his good friend Otis Redding, and his fellow emigrant to Detroit Marvin Gaye, but from a purely rags-to-riches perspective Pickett's story quickly reveals itself as having all the hallmarks of great fiction, with even his cruel decline meeting some blessed redemption toward the end.

Yet it is from a more historical viewpoint that Wilson Pickett's story proves *truly* remarkable, for it turns out that he was not just at the vanguard of his generation; Wilson Pickett effectively *was* the vanguard. Joining the Great Migration of blacks out of the rural south, he settled in Detroit as a teen in the mid-fifties, where he experienced the waning years of the Gospel Highway with the Violinaires, and witnessed the birth of Motown while in R&B vocal group the Falcons, scoring big with his prototype soul anthem "I Found a Love." Striking out solo and moving to New York City, he hit the charts on a label run by rock 'n' roll pioneer Lloyd Price, before embarking on a tempestuous but highly productive relationship with legendary Atlantic Records soul man Jerry Wexler. Pickett became the first Atlantic singer to record at both Stax in Memphis *and* Fame in Muscle Shoals, the label's first male singer to work with Gamble and Huff at Sigma in Philadelphia. Along the way, he turned "Hey Jude" *and* "Sugar Sugar" into soul songs, rehabilitated an exiled Bobby Womack, and introduced Duane Allman to the world. He was the first to take the word "funk" into the charts, the first to headline a black American music package in Africa. He achieved all of this before his thirtieth birthday. Even in the manner by which he reluctantly—and embarrassingly—jumped on the disco bandwagon, he served as a weather vane for his generation of gospel-raised shouters left directionless as soul softened throughout the 1970s. His journey, I therefore came to conclude, personified nothing less than that of black American music through the second half of the twentieth century, and it is that wider context I hope to bring readers over coming pages even as I focus most closely on the life and music of Pickett himself.

It is, to be sure, a hard story at times. The "Wicked" Wilson Pickett was born into the deprivations and segregation of the Jim Crow Deep South, and this biography delves frequently, and deeply, into the painful ongoing narrative of race and racism in America. After all, for many listeners, soul music is the sound of black emancipation, and while Pickett never made color an issue in his music (much of which he recorded with white musicians), nor did he hide away from it. His brother Maxwell wrote to me, "Wilson was not only black, he was a dark skinned black man, and . . . I believe it probably mattered in his life." Given the reaction of the other Falcons when bass singer Willie Schofield introduced Pickett to them as a prospective new tenor in 1960—that he was "*too* black"—there is little doubt that Maxwell's observation bears merit.

Wilson Pickett demanded the best from his associates, in no small part because he knew how good he was himself. Any number of musicians told me that working with him was the highlight of their professional lives; it would be hard to overemphasize his charisma, the easy manner in which he could energize a studio, dominate a gathering of his supposed peers, and bring tears of joy and laughter to anyone in his vicinity with his quick wit, ready rap, and brilliant smile. But just as one of his long-term stage partners described him as a "quarterback," so other musicians used the term "drill sergeant" and even "slave driver," a man as likely to settle an argument or confirm a directive with his fists as with reason. In this readiness to aggression, he was hardly unique—it is one of the many characteristics that links him to James Brown, for example—and though it could make him difficult to get on with, I have done my level best to explain, if not excuse, such behavior.

For, as often the case with such great talent, Wilson Pickett suffered from demons. Those demons led him, belatedly, to drink and drugs, inevitably escalating his violent tendencies and eventually bringing him to prison—twice. As such, it's surely no surprise that the expression I heard most frequently used to describe Pickett was that "he was his own worst enemy." Unable to trust those who loved him, unwilling to take advice from those who sought to help him, he simply refused to let people in on his troubled soul. It's no coincidence that the word applied to the music of Wilson Pickett's generation is that which we typically use to define our emotional personalities, the part of our body that we can't physically identify but all fully acknowledge as real. As such, the subtitle to this book—*The Life & Soul of Wilson Pickett*—has a deliberate double meaning.

Perhaps the most poignant summary of such a supremely talented yet ultimately conflicted personality came from one of his peers, the great, late Ben E. King, with whom Wilson shared a lengthy stint at Atlantic Records, many a concert stage, the short-lived dream of the Soul Clan, and a few insults and contretemps along the way.

"I wish the world would have known him better as a person," the mild-mannered King told me shortly before he passed away in 2014, "because he let out the rough side of him, and there was a gentle side that I knew, that he would only give to you for a split second. But in that second, you'd learn there's a fighter in there and there's a person that's likable. There was a sweet gentle person in there for that time that you could talk to him—had he not been Wicked."

Tony Fletcher, Mount Tremper

ACKNOWLEDGMENTS

On my initial flight to Montgomery, Alabama, where I was meeting with Maxwell Pickett in Prattville to discuss this book, I found myself seated next to a garrulous salesman who, upon concluding his preflight cell phone call, insisted on knowing my reason for travel. "Wilson Pickett?" he exclaimed when I warily told him. "I saw him with the Falcons at Charlotte Coliseum, 1962; I was one of the only white kids in the audience!" For the rest of the flight, he proceeded to engage me in positive conversation about soul music and race in America, and I would like to thank him for being a good omen, given that this book has proven relatively painless, at least by the standards of my previous projects.

I then have to thank the aforementioned Maxwell Pickett, keyholder to his brother's estate. He was not only receptive to my approach, but was willing to get out of the way and let me write Wilson's story without any preconditions, all while standing by to provide me with contact information and introductions, and being there as I came back to him with increasingly personal and (for me) sometimes uncomfortable questions. I'd also like to thank his wife Brenda for sharing the welcome mat during that first visit in Prattville.

In alphabetical order, my thanks to all the following for consenting to be interviewed: John Abbey, David Akers, Joe Arnold, Herb Boyd, Charlie Chalmers, Dan Cipriano, Dennis Coffey, Paddy Corea, Don Covay, Steve Cropper, Elcanon Dubose, Bobby Eli, Eddie Floyd, Roger Friedman, Dovie Hall, Bertha Harbison, Nona Hendryx, Ronnie Hinton, Ricardo Holmes, David Hood, Wayne Jackson, Eddie Jacobs, Jerry Jemmott, Jimmy Johnson, Ben E. King, Margo Lewis, Johnny Long, Chris Lowe, Tami Lynn, Bobby Manriquez, Robert Margouleff, Robert Martin, Joyce McRae-Moore, Carlton McWilliams, Mario Medious, Sam Moore, Otis Myers, Floyd Newman, George Norris, Danny O'Donovan, Spooner Oldham, David Panzer, André Perry, Jack Philpot, Helen Pickett, Maxwell Pickett, Saphan Pickett, Veda Pickett-Neal, Curtis Pope, Lloyd Price, Marc Ribot, Willie

Schofield, Terry Scott, Brad Shapiro, Bunny Sigler, Ernest Smith, Marvell Thomas, Robert "Mousey" Thompson, Jon Tiven, Chris Tuthill, Lee Wade, Kevin Walker, Danny White, Elbert "Woody" Woodson, Earl Young, Reggie Young, Paul Zamek.

I prefer not to pull favorites from such a long list, but I must make two exceptions. Pickett's final producer, Jon Tiven, turned out to be my first interview, and while I was concerned at starting the book from the "wrong end," so to speak, his wealth of contacts and enthusiasm for the project helped speed up the interview process quite considerably. He also established a positive pattern of people who didn't just work with Pickett, but clearly cared for him.

On that note, Curtis Pope was also among my first interviewees, and played a similarly vital role in connecting me with the vast network of Pickett's former stage musicians, many of whom he additionally helped identify in photographs and videos. Although most of these musicians have no financial choice but to gig until they drop, I found them, almost without exception, an extraordinarily friendly group of people, largely devoid of the bitterness and cynicism I have encountered in other genres. More power to all of you—and for the two or three people listed above whose memories have not made it into the text of this book, please know that your words nonetheless helped shape the overall picture.

Special thanks to all those who responded to my follow-up calls and e-mails with such patience and enthusiasm. In seeking as much accurate information from our sources as they will deign to give us, obsessive biographers like myself walk a perpetual tightrope between persistence and pestilence, and I would like to believe that I generally pick up the warning signals that I might be pushing too hard. In any case where I crossed that line, and I'm aware of at least one, I offer my apologies, and my gratitude that you indulged me up to your breaking point!

My thanks to all the family members, managers, publicists, and friends who put me in contact with my interview subjects and otherwise helped facilitate our meetings. You are too numerous to mention; you are all greatly appreciated.

On my major three-week, 3,750-mile, cross-American research road trip during the winter of 2015, I encountered many wonderful people. My especial thanks to Katy Kattelman (for whom "I Found a Love" is still her going-out song) and "King" Curtis (though obviously not *that* King Curtis) for their unexpected and delightful hospitality in Nashville; to Bob Mehr for the night out in Memphis; to Gordon Alexander and Rob Gordon additionally in Memphis; and to my Mini Countryman for keeping me going through snow in every one of the thirteen states I visited, as far south as

Mississippi! Thanks also to Chris and Linda Boyle for hosting me in Florida, and to Mellow Mushroom, for keeping me sated with vegan food and craft beer throughout the South.

Thanks to Tim Sampson at the Stax Museum of American Soul Music in Memphis; Jennie Thomas and Andy Leach at the Rock and Roll Hall of Fame and Museum's Library Archives in Cleveland; Bonnie Bak at Muscle Shoals Music Foundation in Sheffield, Alabama; Dixie Griffin at the Alabama Music Hall of Fame in Tuscumbia; Michael Gray at the Country Music Hall of Fame in Nashville; Michael Perry at the Schomburg Reference Library in New York. The Detroit Historical Museum, the Charles H. Wright Museum of African American History in Detroit, the National Civil Rights Museum at the Lorraine Motel in Memphis, the Liberty Bell Center in Philadelphia, the Rock and Roll Hall of Fame Museum in Cleveland, and the various Smithsonian Museums in Washington, DC all additionally informed my research.

My gratitude to fellow authors Robert Bowman, Robert Gordon, Jonathan Gould, Gerri Hirshey, and David Ritz for sharing notes, conversations, and more. Additional nods to Gerri, John Abbey, Sue C. Clark, Ted Drozdowski, and Michael Lydon for enthusiastic permission to quote at will from their interviews with Wilson Pickett.

Thanks to Barney Hoskyns at *Rock's Back Pages*, Keith Rylatt, Bob Fisher, Opal Nations, Audrey Johnson, Michael Johnson, Ken Hall, Anthony Roman, Deane Rink, Amy Jackson, Real Gone Music, and everyone I else I have surely left out, for miscellaneous correspondence, music, suggestions, and facilitations.

Thank you to the late Fergus McGovern for offering to read and revise.

Thank you to Michael Harriot at Folio for selling this book; to Suzanne Ryan at Oxford University Press for buying it, and for her patience with deadlines and initial overwriting; to Eden Piacitelli for staying on top of editing and production issues, and, in advance, everyone else at OUP engaged in further work on it.

Thank you so very much to my Catskills neighbor, good friend and fellow author Holly George-Warren. Holly pushed me to pursue this project beyond the original idea stage, provided me with several key initial introductions, helped make my road trips more comfortable via further contacts, and was generally there for me at all times, despite a schedule that makes my own look rather lazy. Her husband Robert and son Jack are damn good people too.

As always, an enormous debt of gratitude to my wife Posie Strenz for her forbearance and support. To my children Campbell and Noel for being who they are.

And finally, to fans of soul music in general, and Wilson Pickett in particular, for surreptitiously supporting this project all along.

In the Midnight Hour

PART I

Rise 1941–1972

CHAPTER 1

It should always be remembered that soul music in all of its forms is the aesthetic property of a race of people who were brought to this country against their will and were forced to make drastic social adjustments in order to survive in a hostile environment.

Phyl Garland, *The World of Soul*

The two-room wooden shack in which Wilson Pickett Jr. was born, on March 18, 1941, lay tucked away on a dirt track, above a creek, behind a cemetery, on a part of the sprawling McQueen Smith lands off the meandering Washington Ferry Road, in an area of Prattville, Alabama known as Washington Hill. Even by the rural standards of the era, when Prattville contained just 2,500 people, Washington Hill was the backwoods.

The shack is long gone, as is the dirt track. The Prattville of the twenty-first century presents itself as a model of small-town values and large-scale expansion, a place "where progress and preservation go hand in hand."[1] Progress, of a sort, can be measured by seemingly ceaseless growth: the population has increased more than a dozenfold in just seventy-five years, with generic strip malls and suburban housing developments encroaching ever closer on the state capitol of Montgomery, just a few miles to the southeast. Preservation, meanwhile, at least in its standard definition, can be found in the historic buildings scattered around town, and at an Autauga County Heritage Center, where genteel volunteer ladies offer an echo of the social decorum once prevalent across the antebellum South.

Just across the road from the Heritage Center, in between the Prattville Police Department and the Prattville Creative Arts Center, close to a Heritage Park that extends briefly out to and alongside the Autauga Creek, there stands a historical marker in the name of Wilson Pickett Jr. It seems an obscure location at which to celebrate the city's most famous musical son, its most illustrious person of color, its most instantly recognizable voice. And it was only erected in 2009, a few years after the singer passed away, following considerable lobbying from some of his siblings. As such, its obscure placement perhaps reflects the difficulties inherent in *truly* reconciling progress and preservation in America's Deep South. For what goes unstated on the marker is that Wilson Pickett Jr. had little positive to say about Prattville, that his father left it behind when the younger Wilson was a boy, that his elder sisters followed as soon as they married, that Wilson did likewise before he finished his schooling, and that he pulled his mother out once he acquired the wealth to do so.

Several miles to the west, just beyond the village of Autaugaville, where Wilson attended a segregated school in the 1940s and 1950s, there stands another historical marker in the name of a Pickett. This one is for a Colonel Albert J. Pickett, Alabama's first historian, and again, it's what is *not* stated about the life of this Pickett that provides the awkward contemporary context. Arriving in 1818 to what was then known as the Alabama Territory, Albert Pickett eschewed a family call to law and politics and aspired instead to the life of a writer. He sat with the indigenous Creek tribespeople in their wigwams, and transcribed their verbal histories. This friendship did not prevent him participating as an aide-de-camp to the state's governor in the Creek War of 1836, a conflict that concluded the tribe's enforced ceding of land to the white settlers, and forced their expulsion to modern-day Oklahoma along the Trail of Tears.[2] Similarly, in his *History of Alabama*, published in 1851, this early Pickett displayed an empathy for the bravery of certain "Negro" slaves in defending the early European settlers against their Indian attackers, but as a man of inherited means as well as leisure, he lived according to the era's conventions. Upon his death in 1858, Albert Pickett owned two plantations among his five properties in the counties of Montgomery and Autauga, his holdings of 4,500 acres serviced by 162 slaves.[3]

Deprived of their own ancestry, American slaves were often assigned the last name of their owner, and there were nearly two hundred such Picketts (or Pickettes) listed in Autauga and Montgomery Counties in the Census of 1860.[4] As Civil War broke out a year later, fully 45 percent of Alabama's 964,000 inhabitants remained enslaved, the fourth highest figure in the nation in both physical presence and relative percentage,[5] accounting for almost one-tenth of the country's entire black population. And in Alabama, they served largely in support of a single crop: cotton.[6]

Wilson Pickett's ancestors were sharecroppers as far back as any of them could recall. Theoretically, this put them a step up from the tenant farmers: sharecroppers were supplied with accommodations and the means by which to farm the land, in return for a portion of the crop; tenant farmers, in broad terms, paid rent on the land for the right to farm it, which carried greater risk.[7] In reality, though, the Picketts around the dawn of the twentieth century were not far removed from their former existence as slaves.

Major Pickett and his wife Minnie—the singer's paternal grandparents, both born in the early 1890s—resided mainly in Spring Hill, a rural black neighborhood just south and west of downtown Prattville, where a Pickett Street may have been named for the many members of the family that (still) live there, though more likely for the former historian and plantation owner.[8] Major and Minnie had several children, including sons Roosevelt, Grace, and Major Jr., and Wilson, born on February 9, 1917, just as the American president of that name was leading the United States into the Great War. Minnie passed on, Major subsequently remarried, and he and his younger wife Polly had several children of their own. Almost all of them grew up working on land belonging to the McQueen Smith family.[9]

The maternal side of Wilson Pickett Jr.'s family came together when, in those years of considerable rural migration directly prior to the Great War, a young itinerant passing through the area on foot stopped to ask for sustenance. The man, one Shepherd Jackson, born in 1891, was taken in by a Clara Presley, born in 1893, whose husband had passed. Clara had been left with a son, Tom Daniel, to raise on her own, and had she been thinking primarily of her future security when she first welcomed Shepherd, she chose well. In addition to joining Clara on the McQueen Smith land, he worked as a freewheeling Baptist Minister, preaching in churches as far afield as Selma, to which he would journey at weekends by wagon. Greatly admired and equally feared, Shepherd was rarely seen without a Bible, which doubled up as a frequent and effective tool of admonishment for his own four children and, especially, for the children of his and Clara's second daughter, Lena Jackson.

Shepherd and Clara made for a contrasting couple. He was a strong, big-boned man, with an equally commanding presence; Clara was petite, by all accounts attractive, with what her children recalled as "beautiful" hair, and for all that she had to work the fields, a dedicated and gentle homemaker. Their daughter Lena, born in 1918, took more from her father in terms of build, and outdid him in temper. She gave birth to the first of her dozen children, Catherine, at the age of fifteen; the father, a J. C. Woods, quickly drifted up to Birmingham and out of their lives. In 1935 Lena became pregnant by her fellow sharecropper, one Wilson Pickett, and they married. Lena gave birth to twins, of whom only Bertha survived infancy; William James (often referred to as Willie James, but more typically just as James), the first of three boys, came along in 1937.

Four years later, in that two-room shack in Washington Hill, Wilson Pickett Jr. was born. He proved so restless as a baby that his oldest sister Catherine, the most likely to watch him when Lena was unavailable, called him "Wiggly" for his slippery nature; the name "Wiggy" would stick until it was replaced in his mid-twenties, at which point he was an established singer, by "the Wicked."

The boy was only six weeks old when his father was sentenced to a year in the penitentiary for selling moonshine whiskey, a crime not uncommon in the old dry South, where poor blacks had little recourse if caught. The old cliché states that the apple does not fall far from the tree, and Wilson Pickett Jr. would inherit his father's tendency to drink—and eventually, like at least one of his brothers, he would tumble into full-blown alcoholism. Likewise, he adopted his mother's temper, her quick resort to anger and even violence; he also carried many a chip on his shoulder about her hardships, for which he may have come to blame his father for getting caught and leaving them to fend alone for his first year.

By the time Wilson Jr. came along, Catherine had been out in the fields for a couple of years already, and Bertha had just about joined her. It was common to start chopping and picking cotton at the age of five or six, for as little as seventy-five cents a day. Few among their parents' generation had progressed beyond a fourth-grade education before heeding to the call of full-time field work. Being sharecroppers, the family additionally lived where directed, so that when Wilson Sr. came out of the penitentiary and managed to resume employment, tending hogs on the McQueen Smith Farms, they moved from Washington Hill to the area around Cooters Pond, just off Highway 31 that ran on down to Montgomery. The house was shared with another family, just two rooms apiece, and the kids would have to cross the highway to run errands to the store. It was in the midst of doing so one day that a speeding car took the life of the neighbor's girl, Maddie Pearl, and badly injured Catherine, who was relocated to live with Shepherd and Clara Jackson. Catherine would subsequently credit her grandparents with raising her—as would, to varying extents, all the children, their numbers joined in October 1943 by another daughter, Emily Jean.

Like most people of color around him, Wilson Sr. had little by way of education, but he still set his sights on escaping the sharecropping life. He took a job at the Gin Company factory (built by Prattville's founder Daniel Pratt a century earlier, it had long served as the largest manufacturer of cotton gins in the region), just over the creek from Main Street. With it, the family moved up to a neighborhood known locally as Duncan Quarters. Ostensibly this was Prattville proper, though it was still woods enough that Wilson Sr. was able to resume his moonshine ways. "They didn't give them but a year and a day in the penitentiary, and they'd be back doing the same thing," observed Catherine, whose future father-in-law, also from Prattville, did similar time for exactly the same crime.

But Wilson Sr. knew well enough from past experience to keep the still's whereabouts hidden, and he only entrusted one child with that knowledge. "Wilson was the one kept watch over the distillery while Daddy Wilson was at work," said Catherine. Yet any bond that appeared to be now building between father and son was soon to be broken. What came to be known as the Second Wave of the Great Migration, during which fully five million blacks over a three-decade period would move from the mostly rural South to the industrial cities of the North, picked up right around the time of Wilson Jr.'s birth, prompted by the boom in the war economy. Roosevelt Pickett, Wilson Sr.'s elder brother, was at its vanguard.

The paths north tended to follow those of the former Underground Railroad that had provided an escape passage for runaway slaves, some of whom had established communities en route, if and where they had secured their freedom. Blacks from Louisiana, Texas, and Arkansas traditionally gravitated up through Kansas City and Memphis (where the more musically minded were waylaid, some for years or a lifetime) toward Minneapolis and environs, and in the Second Wave out west to Los Angeles, too. Those born in Mississippi made their way through St. Louis to Chicago, in such numbers that by the end of the 1940s they accounted for one in three black Illinois residents.[10] Blacks from Florida, the Carolinas, and Georgia generally went on up the Eastern Seaboard toward Washington DC, Baltimore, Philadelphia, New York, and Boston.

The path out of Alabama, meanwhile, typically stopped by way of Louisville, Kentucky, on its way up to the factories of Cleveland, Pittsburgh, and, most desirably, Detroit. Being on the border of Canada, Detroit had established a small but socially and politically vibrant black community as the last American stop on the Underground Railroad, and with the rise of the car manufacturing industry and the businesses that had grown up around it, attracted immigrants from the South in unprecedented proportions. The city's population increased almost fourfold between 1910 and 1940, to 1.6 million; the percentage of blacks during that period rose more dramatically, some 2,600 percent.[11]

Even with such growth, blacks still accounted for less than one in ten Detroiters, and were subject to all manner of discrimination at work, in school, and especially by the restricted covenants that prevented them from purchasing property beyond their existing, crowded communities. This did not prevent Detroit erupting in a race riot in 1943: a term that was accurate insofar as it described another episode in the periodic violent reaction of white people to black encroachment on their lives, although with unprecedented results, leaving thirty-four people dead, six hundred injured, and 1,800 arrested, the vast majority of them black. The ongoing tensions failed to deter Wilson Pickett Sr. from following in his brother's footsteps as soon as Roosevelt secured a foothold: it was commonly stated that the lowliest of jobs in Detroit still paid four times that of a solid share-cropping existence on the farm down south, and that was reason enough to leave one form of second-class citizenry behind for another.

By all accounts, Wilson Sr. had no intention of deserting his children. "I never thought it was a separation," said his oldest daughter, Bertha. "I thought he was leaving to go north and get a better job so he could see about his family better than he was." Still, his absence was felt more keenly than when he had been jailed. Lena took ill and couldn't work, Bertha was put off from starting school to stay home and help look after her mother and her three younger siblings, and the family found itself without the resources to get by. The sickly Lena finally got word to her own parents ten miles away, and Shepherd Jackson came to the rescue, literally, retrieving his daughter and her five younger children to rejoin Catherine on what they all referred to as the Rice Place, a wooden house on the McQueen Smith Farms, out the far side of cotton fields accessed only via a dirt road from County Road 29, a couple of miles south off the old Selma Highway.

At Rice Place, once Lena recovered, the family, young Wilson included, enjoyed a semblance of what passed for normal plantation life. The wooden house, one of four that formed a protective near-circle, had a kitchen big enough to store the meat from a slaughtered hog down at one end, a bench with room for all seven to eat at the other, and a cook stove in between. Across a platform from the kitchen stood one bedroom, with access from there to two more. The wooden floors were routinely scrubbed so clean, "you could do whatever on them," said Catherine. There was no running water or electricity, but what you'd never had, you couldn't miss. Besides, the pump out back was a vast improvement on the old bucket-and-well of Washington Hill.

Those children of age took to attendance at Jericho Elementary, a two-room schoolhouse further down Route 29 that doubled up as the Baptist Church. Bertha learned to cook from her grandmother, she and Catherine generally looked after the younger ones, and Shepherd engaged everyone, regardless of enthusiasm, in evening Bible study. Those who could run far enough played in the woods and the fields, and down at Dry Creek, Bertha would fish and Wilson Jr., in particular, would watch and learn.

It could be inferred that the family was finally coping without the presence of Lena's husband. But then a letter arrived from Detroit, and with it everything changed. Roosevelt had taken Wilson Sr. under his wing at his home on Livingston Street, to the northern end of the downtown Detroit neighborhood known as Black Bottom, where the migrant population from the South had mostly settled, and where Roosevelt and his partner Alberta lived, each with offspring from previous relationships. This made it an act of great generosity that they allowed Wilson Sr., now that he had secured a job on the Dodge assembly line, to send home for his family, or at least the part of it that took up the least space. For Lena, eager to heed the call of the big city up north, that meant leaving Catherine, Bertha, and James behind with her parents at Rice Place. She packed up baby Jeannie and her youngest boy, Wilson Jr., and boarded the Greyhound bus for Detroit.

CHAPTER 2

He said, "When I leave here I'm not coming back and one day you're all going to be buying my records." And I said, "Yeah, sure." But it really happened. It really did.

Otis Myers, cousin, Prattville, Alabama

Helen Walker was living on Brady Street, a block south of Livingston in Detroit's Black Bottom, just off the black community's famed commercial thoroughfare of Hastings Street, when she first met her future stepson. The local kids were playing in the backyards and alleyways as always, when she noticed a boy, maybe six years old, "get into it" with another, whom he hit with a stick before running down the alley and sitting himself down in her backyard. He knew, said Helen, "that the other boy wasn't going to come up to where grown people was, to fight him." The boy with the stick was Wilson Pickett Jr.

"His mama came out the door," recalled Walker. "She said, 'What's the matter *now*, Wilson?' He said 'Nothing.' And the other little boy was standing there on the corner of the house, peeping, waiting for him to come out. And Wilson kept looking at him, wouldn't move."

Wilson, Helen learned quickly enough, "was a mean little boy," a description not intended as much as an insult, perhaps, as a note of his tough spirit. He would "never take nothing off the other kids—and if they jumped on him, he would fight."

Helen would have expected to meet Lena Pickett and her children soon enough. She knew Roosevelt Pickett's partner, Alberta, through church, had occasionally seen Roosevelt's brother, Wilson Sr., who was lodging with them, and had heard that Wilson had sent for his wife and a couple of the younger kids from Alabama, the latest new arrivals from the South. Only a few years ago Helen had been one of them—marrying, at the age of sixteen, a near stranger in her hometown of Gould, Arkansas just to get out from under the feet of her grandmother and mother, only thirteen years her elder. That was in 1941, and now six years on it was evident that her husband was a ne'er-do-well, staying out all night and often all week. He was gone beyond that frequently enough that Helen had taken a job of her own to guarantee an income for when he didn't come back at all.

It wasn't uncommon for families to room together, but the Picketts' accommodations at 642 Livingston were especially tight, the family living together in one of three bedrooms. When Lena became pregnant again, she returned to Prattville with Wilson and Jeannie in tow to give birth, to another boy, Hezekiah, in 1946. She then came back to Detroit to the same, now even more cramped quarters with all three of these children.[1] Given Wilson Sr.'s job at Dodge, the family should have been able to afford a place of their own—and in Lena's absence Helen Walker, proclaiming only to be helping her church friend Alberta regain her living quarters, posed as Wilson Sr.'s wife to make the rounds of available rooms.

But the landlords, Helen recalled, "didn't want too many kids." With new immigrants from the South arriving thick and fast, landlords could choose who they wanted, charge more or less what they liked. Complicating matters further, when Lena did return to Detroit she became pregnant *again*, heading back down to Prattville to give birth to Maxwell in February 1948. A couple of weeks later, Wilson Sr. took a rare trip south to see the whole family. Considerable discussion about their future concluded with the understanding that while it was impossible to raise all six of Wilson's children in Detroit on his salary, Shepherd and Clara Jackson were no longer willing to accept full-time rearing responsibilities for anyone left behind. (Catherine, fifteen now, was setting to marry a local boy, Tommy Williams, and escape the cotton fields by moving to Louisville, Kentucky). Wilson Sr. returned to Detroit and worked through the kind of decision frequently faced by menfolk up from the South. He put his family first, quit his job at Dodge, and prepared to return home.

Then he received news that Lena was pregnant yet again. Based on the due date, the child wasn't his, and the betrayal ruined the marriage. Whatever excuse the children in Prattville may have been given, the result was the same: "Daddy Wilson" was not coming back, and the long-term trips to Detroit for the younger kids were over. Lena and her children, under the guidance of Shepherd and Clara, moved to a new four-room cinderblock home the McQueen Smiths built for them just across the cotton fields from Rice Place. It was smaller and lacking in character, but presumably safer and sturdier, on Route 29 itself, where a bus now came by each morning to take the children to the Autauga County Training School, about ten miles down the old Selma Highway. Modernization—of a sort—was working its way through rural Alabama, and the Jackson/Pickett family's move represented their own small part in it.

This was a major change of environment for Wilson Jr., who until this point had spent almost his entire life in Prattville or Detroit with his father, and it likely had a significant impact on the young boy. In Detroit he had lived within a self-sufficient—and segregated—black community that by necessity assembled its grocery stores, churches, nightclubs, barbershops, restaurants, funeral parlors, banks, community centers, schools, and record stores alongside each other.[2] The northern city was not the Promised Land: there was too much poverty and overcrowding for that. But compared to what Wilson Jr. was coming back south to in Alabama, it must have looked like it. At the age of seven he would be living once more on the farm, where the term "neighbor" meant someone perhaps three miles away, where the local store was a five-mile round trip by foot, and where many of the other facets of the urban black lifestyle that he'd known in Detroit simply did not exist. He was now expected to work for a living: planting, chopping, and picking cotton and corn in the fields, through the hard cold of winter and the harsh heat of summer, all for the ultimate benefit of the white man.

For now, though, Prattville was home. As Bertha put it, "We was poor but didn't know we was poor, because we always had plenty to eat." The family, like most on the plantation, lived a largely agrarian, self-sufficient lifestyle. Shepherd and Clara raised hogs and kept two milk cows. They tended a garden out back of the "block house," as it came to be known, where they grew white potatoes, sweet potatoes, corn, tomatoes, and peas. They produced their own meal, flour, sugar, syrup, and butter. After the harvest each year, they erected a tent to preserve the root vegetables through the winter.

Then there were the communal slaughters. "Every year a family would butcher a hog and share the meat, they would butcher a cow and share meat," said Maxwell. "There was a lot of sharing that was going on to make sure everyone was sufficient. During the Thanksgiving season, the plantation owner would make sure that all the families would receive free turkeys, as many as they needed based on size of family." And when nonagrarian items were required, such as shoes or tools, the family could get them on credit from the company supply store up in Prattville—the cost to be held against their income from the forthcoming crop. Compared to the sharecropping lifestyle of twenty years earlier, there simply *was* no comparison.

As a small boy Wilson played regularly with one of the white supervisors' sons, Charles "Hutt" Hall—but only outside, in the country, where there were no parks with enforced segregation, and not at either family's house. As recently as 1930, Alabama had passed a law forbidding adult blacks and whites from playing billiards or pool together, and for as long as that system endured, integrated childhood friendships on the farm were always likely to be short-lived. "For me, Catherine, James, Wilson, we didn't think about [segregation]," said Bertha. "We only lived."

Wilson Jr. took to hunting and fishing with boundless enthusiasm. He would head down to the swamp creeks that meandered through the woods into small ponds, and muddy the waters to bring the fish to the surface where they could be caught by hand or knocked out by pole. He used a similar method when hunting rabbits: "I couldn't understand how they did it, but Wilson and his friends used to kill rabbits with a slingshot," recalled Bertha. "He was doing it so much that mama decided to buy him a rifle." Shepherd and Clara vociferously expressed their opposition, but Wilson was persistent, and as tended to be the case, he eventually got his way. Armed with a weapon more powerful and as deadly as his slingshot, his zeal for hunting grew even more. He would often stay out for a couple of nights in the woods and return home with a sack full of rabbits, which he would skin perfectly so that not a hair could be found.

Later in life Wilson would talk of having run away from home following a particularly savage beating from his mother. She had told him to walk the several miles up to the company store on the Selma Highway to get "dipping snuff" for his grandma. "I'd done worked my ass off ... I said, 'Mama, I'm so tired, why don't you ask one of the others.' *Whoaaa*, she almost killed me." As he told author Gerri Hirshey, "I cried for a week, me and my little dog," that being Tag, formerly his sister Bertha's dog who had attached itself to Wilson. He claimed to have lived off fresh fish and corn for those many days in the woods, before eventually coming home, "'Cos I got scared. Too many hoot owls out there."[3]

In Wilson's mind, disappearing overnight into the woods with his rifle or fishing rod might well have *felt* like running away. The irony is that nobody seemed to recall worrying about him in the meantime. "Down there in the country," said Bertha, "those boys just went out in the woods like they wanted to, and they come back when they got ready." Wilson Jr. was a study in contrasts, and for all that he thrived on attention, he was also something of a loner. A part of him genuinely sought escape from the confinements, the chores, the arguments, and the "whuppins" back at the block house, where as many as seven children at any one time were living with three adults in a four-room house comprising all of about two hundred and fifty square feet. (The family grew extensively in the absence of Lena's husband, with the additions of Louella, born 1949; Linda, 1950; and Lillie, 1952. All three took the name of Pickett, given that their biological father, a share-cropper named Anderson Thomas, did not live with them.)

Everyone around Wilson recognized that that he was special. "Wilson was a highly energetic person," said Maxwell. "He always had to be doing something. And whatever he engaged in doing, it involved him doing it quickly, energetically. He was not the type of person that you would have to worry about laying about the house being lazy. That was not in his blood. And when he decided to put his mind, take an interest in something, and he decided he wanted to do it, then he would pursue it in such a way that he would get very good at it." The obvious manifestation of this would be his musical talent, which he would soon come to identify in his voice. But his perfectionist trait applied also to athletics. Wilson ran track at school, and was soon part of the relay team. He loved to wrestle—and win, and then challenge his victims to another bout, only to gleefully pin them again. The same determination to succeed was noted in an ability with mechanics. In his early teen years he put a bicycle together from spare parts, some procured from the plantation supervisors, inspiring one of them to give him a couple of inner tubes as a bonus and observe, presciently, "You gon' be somebody."[4]

The one area where Wilson was not inclined to succeed was in the cotton field. He understood instinctively the inequities of the sharecropping system, and had a vivid sense that he was destined not to live by them. And so although he was quite capable of picking a few hundred pounds of cotton in a day, he would just as likely risk cheating the system as succumbing to it. This might involve putting "rocks and dirt in our bags to make it heavier," said his close cousin and frequent coconspirator Otis Myers. Or, at the weighing truck, diverting the foreman's attention so that an accomplice could throw his bag back out the other side, at which Wilson would, in his own words, "go out in the field and mess around long enough to make it look good, and then bring the same bag of cotton back to get it weighed again."[5]

"Sometimes we got caught," said Myers. "Sometimes we didn't." Punishment for cheating would usually be administered by the parents—an improvement, of sorts, from the old slavery days when engaging in such antics would have meant a lashing from the white man. Most of the time, however, Wilson would do his best to avoid working in the fields at all. "He would be walking around that field with that rifle on his shoulder," said Bertha. "He wouldn't really be doing nothing. He wasn't picking no cotton worth wanting. He would leave the fields and go in the woods to go hunting. I'd say 'Wilson, why aren't you in the fields?' 'Well, I don't feel like it.'"

He inherited his insolence from Lena ("Mama would speak out," said Catherine, "she didn't care"), as he did his penchant for fighting: Wilson Sr. carried a scar on his forehead from the time Lena threw a bowl of beans at him in the Livingston Street, Detroit kitchen. Wilson Jr., meanwhile, had his arm fractured by his mother after arguing back about his chores. "In a fit of rage," recalled Maxwell, "Mama just grabbed this piece of stove wood and went to hit him with it—and Wilson raised his arm up in defense and she hit it." The limb was put in a makeshift sling—doctors weren't called out for a perceived minor injury like this—but hung loose for a long time afterward. "It wasn't uncommon for that type of thing to happen in the South," said Maxwell. "Not only for our family, but for a lot of families. They was under so much stress and it builds up and every now and then it would just release, in fits of rage and anger."

For most southern blacks of the era, harsh physical discipline was accepted as a rite of passage. Rage and anger aside, the parents beat their children to keep them in line because their own parents had beaten *them* to keep them in line. Few considered that the routine violence, the use of the switch and the whip, had been introduced and imposed on them through slavery. And punishment for disobedience or lack of respect was often administered out of perverse parental mercy—because if a black child, a boy in particular, proved similarly insolent in front of a white person, and especially a white woman, the end result could be something *far* worse. "One thing our parents always told us," said Otis Myers. "Do not talk back to a white man, a white person, and do not associate with white women, or white girls. That was a danger for us. Whatever they wanted to call you, they did. And you had to say, 'yes, sir.'"

The whuppins, then, were a necessarily painful part of what one writer called "steeling against the pure meanness that waited out there,"[6] and as such it was common practice for *any* black adult within a close—and often closed—community to administer the punishment. Maxwell Pickett recalled a particularly harrowing example:

The Studemeyer family was a prominent and a very high producing family. The daddy, we called him Deacon S because he was a permanent Deacon. One day, all three of the Studemeyer boys and James and Wilson was together and they decided that they would delay for their convenience the taking care of their chores. And you was meant to take care of your chores before the sun went down, because after the sun go down you can't see. Ain't no light anywhere. So this day, the Studemeyer boys didn't get the chores done. Deacon decided that they was in for punishment because when you didn't get your chores done, something got to be done. He had two mules and he had a wagon, and he had become very efficient with a whip. He had all the boys line up, and he said "If anybody gets by me, that means the blessing of God is upon you and I got no problem with that." And Wilson, because he was always swift of foot, the fastest one, he always wanted to go first. He's thinking "I'm gonna make it and I'm gonna be done with it and I can sit back and laugh at the rest of them." So Wilson lines up, and he takes off and he's running like a bat out of hell, and at a certain point I guess he thinks he's made it, but then that whip comes out of nowhere and cracks him across the back. And without exception, whenever they would get hit, they would fall down on the ground, and because it hurt so much, they would be rubbing themselves on the ground. But it's in the backyard and it's all dirt and it would be kicking up all this dirt. They had to go twice. Go by one way and then come back again. None of them made it [without catching the whip].

The older sisters considered the physical punishments normal, even healthy. "We are thankful for the whuppins we got, because it made us like we are today," said Catherine. Maxwell viewed it as an effective deterrent. "I witnessed Wilson getting beat two or three times a day, I witnessed Jeannie getting beat. Somewhere down the line I got to have just a little common sense. If they do it and they get their butt beat I got to know that if I do that I get my butt beat too. So I'm not gonna do it. If Mama say, 'Get your wood brought in and stack it,' I'm not gonna wait till after sundown."

But then Maxwell was *always* seen as the sensible sibling. When it came to Wilson, the whuppins proved entirely counterproductive. The boy seemed not just unwilling, but un*able* to tow the line. And because his stubborn resistance provoked ever more harsh lashings, and because these *still* failed to deter him, it created an especially vicious cycle. The excessive violence Wilson later perpetrated on his male children, his female partners, even his band members and business associates represented a continuation of the way he had been raised: doing unto others as had been done unto him. And the fact that he had braved his whuppins and was willing to brave more of them rather than bow to authority may only have proven to Wilson that he was stronger than others, in whom he then could instill fear and acquiescence—because, after all, that's the way the world worked.

This cycle began early. Not just in confrontations with his brother James, which at one point involved Wilson pointing his loaded rifle at his sibling in the backyard, but on his sister Jeannie, who shared his rebellious streak: "Anything I wanted to do, I did it, and I don't care who told me not to," she told her sister Louella for a posthumous book on their famous brother. The day after Wilson had got his bicycle in working order, he went to school leaving strict instructions for Jeannie not to touch it. She disobeyed, and promptly rode the bike into a ditch. On coming home and seeing it busted up Jeannie recalled seeing Wilson cry for the first time—after which Wilson administered an official whuppin' to which Jeannie formally submitted. "I think he gave me eight licks, and they was hard licks too."[7]

Strict discipline went hand-in-hand with strict adherence to church. Twice a month, the entire Pickett family (excluding Shepherd Jackson, out preaching on the road) would attend Jericho Baptist. For the younger children, the day would start with Sunday school; then there was morning service, a lunchtime picnic on the church grounds, and afternoon Bible teaching. By the time the families had communed again and taken the walk back home, it would be evening already. Attendance was not optional.

The southern blacks were largely left alone to practice their devout Christianity by their white overseers, and the churches were the one institution black people were allowed to build and own. As a result, they became the most important of *all* institutions. At church they received both education and entertainment in the form of the theatrical sermons, especially if the preachers were visiting from out of town; they experienced social interaction by way of the groups who would be "outside partying," as Bertha recalled of a significant part of the Jericho community; and the boys and girls whose hormones were just beginning to kick in were able to observe the opposite sex in their finery. Church provided schooling not just on Sundays, but at places like Jericho in the early years, as an elementary schoolhouse for the local black children. It provided charity and community outreach, and it preached social and economic betterment.

As much as anything, it provided the congregation an opportunity to listen to and participate in music. Indeed, for the younger churchgoers, especially those in strict religious households like the Picketts, this was the only music they were exposed to. No surprise, then, that for a young Wilson Pickett, gospel music became everything.

For sure, the brand of Baptist faith practiced at Jericho was markedly more restrained than that of the increasingly widespread Pentecostal church, where the Sanctified were given to "falling out" and speaking in tongues, and this would be reflected in Pickett's subsequent performance style, foot-stomping rather than convulsing, as distinct a mark of his roots as his accent. But that's not to say that it wasn't fervent. "When I was a young 'un, you'd see these big ole girls just getting carried away by it all and hollerin', lettin' it all loose," Pickett told the writer Nick Kent in 1979. "I used to watch 'em, then I joined in and then I got the sound that I would use as the basis for my whole style of vocalizing."[8]

The whole family sang—Lena was particularly well known for it—but it was Wilson's voice that stood out from the beginning. Such was its power that Lena frequently called upon him to lead the singing in the cotton fields (on those occasions he deigned to work them), and the others would quickly fall in behind him. He was recruited into the church choir, along with younger sister Jeannie. On Sunday mornings the pair would break into gospel hymns as they wended through the woods on a short cut down to Jericho Baptist, provoking holy shouts from the porches of the other sharecropping shacks where folk were busying readying themselves for the Sunday service.

Wilson soon focused his love of gospel music away from church choirs and into quartet singing. Male quartets exclusively sang religious music and were named for their four-part harmonies rather than the number of singers (typically capped at six). The genre had grown out of the Jubilee and barbershop styles prevalent earlier in the century and influenced the development of vocal R&B groups that were starting to come together on the street corners and in the community centers of northern cities. Yet in a country obsessed not only with segregation between the races but also with compartmentalization within the races, these connections have been historically underplayed or obscured. Even as the music industry magazine *Billboard* changed its popular black music charts from "race" to "rhythm and blues" in 1949, the quartets were confined to a separate "spiritual" listing until that term was replaced by "gospel" in 1960. (White spiritual music was ascribed its own chart under the listing of "sacred.") Some of this division came down to the gospel community's self-imposed isolation, its refusal to serve both sacred *and* secular. On the occasion that Wilson Pickett blurted out the chorus to Louis Jordan's 1947 early rhythm and blues smash "Ain't Nobody Here But Us Chickens," his grandfather beat him across the head with the Bible. (As Wilson later recounted, with a sense of amusement, "You know the Bible weigh a *lot*."[9])

Still, such was the power and presence of the young Wilson's voice that at a young age he was invited to join a quartet alongside his older brother James, and Anderson Thomas, the sharecropper father of their youngest siblings. The group sung its way from church to church, as was the fashion of the day.[10] Along the way, Wilson "got so good that eventually he took over," James told Louella of his brother's capabilities.[11] This might have presented a further challenge in their long-established sibling rivalry, but in 1953 James graduated from Autauga County Training School at the age of sixteen—and promptly left Alabama to join his father in Detroit.

A thousand miles north, events had unfolded according to predictable script. Helen Walker's husband had left her at almost exactly the same time that Wilson Sr. found out Lena was pregnant by another man, and the couple had started dating around the end of 1948. Having picked up construction work where he could in the meantime, Wilson had finally secured another job on the assembly line, this time at Ford, where he would stay for the rest of his life.

At Ford, Wilson Sr. was making two dollars an hour at a time that picking cotton brought two dollars for every hundred pounds; by Alabama standards, he was rich. Wilson and Helen, without children to tend to in Detroit, sent some of the earnings back to Prattville. On one occasion, recalled Helen, she sent $75: "a mansion to them." It seemed a better use of Wilson Sr.'s wages than the alternatives. "When he was drinking, you would have to be careful with his money," said Helen. "Because he would gamble and wouldn't know what he was doing. So I would take his money off of him, seal it in an envelope and send it to Lena."

Wilson Sr. took a trip back south to see the family in 1950, around the time his oldest daughter Bertha got married, at fifteen. (She eventually followed Catherine up to Louisville.) In 1953, Wilson Sr. and Helen returned to Alabama, driving down together for James's graduation in a shiny new Ford that Wilson had acquired at the employees' discount.

For the younger among Wilson Sr.'s own six children, this visit was a rare encounter with a father they barely knew: Maxwell reckoned that he only saw his father maybe four times in his entire life. For the older boys, it was the start of a belated reunion. James, his schooling complete, accompanied his father and Helen on their drive back to Detroit, moving in with them on Brady Street. That left Wilson Jr., at twelve, as the oldest remaining child, the "man" of the house.

This change, right as he was reaching adolescence, sent Wilson Jr.'s rebellious streak into overdrive. At school, he was frequently sent to the principal's office to receive a beating for his behavior. On the bus there and back, he took it upon himself to physically protect his siblings and any girlfriend from perceived threats, and sometimes from each other. "Every day, without exception," recalled Maxwell for a BBC Radio documentary on his brother, "going to school, Wilson would fight somebody, and coming back home, he would fight somebody."[12] On several occasions the driver, Mr. Albright, forcibly ejected him from the bus by prodding him up the aisle and out the doors with a stick. Wilson was left on the side of the road somewhere along the old Selma highway and down Route 29, to travel the remaining distance home on foot.

The Autauga County Training School was firmly rooted in the Jim Crow doctrine of "separate but equal," which emphasized the former and scoffed at the latter. The budgets were miniscule, the classrooms overcrowded, and the textbooks overused hand-me-downs from the white schools, all of which only served to confirm the obvious: by their very name, the schools were designed to prepare young blacks for their place at the menial base of the segregated economic system. Agriculturally focused 4-H youth clubs sought, at least, to ensure a sense of pride and ownership in the agrarian lifestyle, and the teachers did what they could, stressing the importance of education for those who would listen.[13] Still, many local parents, deprived of much more than a fourth-grade education themselves, couldn't wait to get their children out of school and into the fields. For the many male children who could not get into a college or migrate north, the best way to evade this bare subsistence lifestyle of the Old South was to join the military—finally desegregated in the Korea War, and an institution ideally suited for young men already hardened by years of physical labor in the field and fierce discipline in the house. In time, all three of Wilson Pickett Jr.'s brothers would follow this path.

For Wilson, it became ever more about the music. Until now Shepherd Jackson had jealously guarded the lone radio of the house, which he typically restricted to news and religious programming. (Jackson's deep faith was such that he built his own church, True Vine Methodist, in the woods off Gin Shop Hill Road, just across the water from downtown Prattville.) But around the time that James left home Wilson was allowed to buy himself a transistor radio, on condition that he confine its musical broadcasts to gospel. There was no lack of choice in this regard, given the number of AM radio stations with powerful 50,000-watt transmitters covering large parts of the country. It's quite possible that Wilson was able to connect with Detroit's own WJLB, on which "Senator" Bristol Bryant, with whom he would soon become personally acquainted, broadcast the best in quartet singing. From Nashville, he could have heard gospel on WLAC. And from 1954, when Memphis station WDIA, the self-proclaimed "Mother Station of the Negroes" (despite its white ownership), upgraded to a 50,000-watt transmitter, he could hear gospel music in two lengthy blocks daily.[14] That meant not just the weekly live broadcasts by resident local groups but also the stars of the "Gospel Highway," those who had a recording career, too: the Five Blind Boys of Alabama, their namesakes the Five Blind Boys of Mississippi, the Fairfield Four, the Dixie Hummingbirds, the Soul Stirrers, the Swan Silvertones, the Sensational Nightingales, and more. Wilson inhaled every one of them. "Anyone cried to the Lord so's He could hear, I got down there," he later told Gerri Hirshey.[15]

Still, everyone has a preference, and two lead singers in particular would have a profound impact on Wilson. Archie Brownlee had been part of the Mississippi Blind Boys since their inception as the Jackson Harmoneers, singing in the clearly enunciated, tight-harmony style that was common in schools for the blind. When they joined the Great Migration, moving to Chicago during the war years, they teamed up with another Mississippi native, Percell Perkins, who had developed a fierce holler in the cotton fields down south and who pushed Brownlee to match him, shout for shout, until Brownlee overtook him in presence and prominence. It was Brownlee, said the Dixie Hummingbirds' revered leader Ira Tucker down the line, who "started that scream you hear all of the soul singers do."[16] Indeed, listen to Brownlee's lead on "Will My Jesus Be Waiting," recorded in 1952, and hear how, following the familiar introductory build-up verse with its tight accompanying harmonies, it suddenly leaps into another dimension, unleashing a blood-curdling yelp that Pickett later cloned in his own screams of spiritual ecstasy.[17] Brownlee was also known as the "baddest man on the road," given to running up and down the aisles in displays of wanton abandonment, and matching this wild athleticism with a hard-drinking lifestyle that would bring him, in 1960, that much closer to Jesus, at the age of just thirty-five.

By that point, Brownlee's reputation had already been superseded by the Reverend Julius ("June") Cheeks, of the Sensational Nightingales. Born in Spartanburg South Carolina, Cheeks was one of thirteen kids living with a widowed mother, and raised hard. "All us kids worked the cotton fields. Mama would whip me every day. I'd look for it, it was signed. When I was eight, I worked in the cotton fields and mama told me, you take one row of cotton, I'll take another. If I catch you, I'll hit you." Leaving school in the second grade, Cheeks was working in a hobo "shanty car" by age twelve, but his love of the Bible and exposure to gospel music on the radio brought him to a group called the Baronets. They made it to a local stage in 1946 alongside the Sensational Nightingales, who, the next day, as often the case when a supporting act's voice impressed, invited Cheeks to join them. He likened his subsequent training regimen to "gettin' out there, plowin'," but the hard work paid dividends, especially when Cheeks spent a transitional period with the legendary Soul Stirrers, where he claimed to have given a teenage Sam Cooke his "first shout," pushing him harder just as Percell had done to Brownlee. Cheeks was back in the Nightingales by the time Pickett acquired his radio, challenging Brownlee's reputation both as the most overt entertainer on the gospel highway ("I was the first to cut the fool," he told author Anthony Heilbut), and as its loudest voice. His hollering on "God's World Will Never Pass Away," recorded in 1953, doesn't quite match Brownlee's for sheer exuberance, but he holds his scream longer, and with more evident control. Again, comparison with the voice of the adult Wilson Pickett is unavoidable.[18]

It wasn't just gospel that Wilson heard. Listening to his radio "around the side of the house, out in the field, along the road," as Maxwell recalled his obsession, "he was sneaking in a lot of the secular music, no doubt about it." The fact that Wilson acquired a harmonica around this period, and was frequently heard by his younger siblings making sweet sounds on it, further indicates that Shepherd Jackson was gradually losing control of Wilson's musical habits.

Besides, with his good looks, athletic grace, and easy charm, Wilson had no trouble attracting girls. A first girlfriend, Audrey, moved away to New York, giving way to Clara Kate Williams, who lived around the loop that the school bus took on its route back up to the Selma Highway, and was just far enough removed from the direct Pickett blood line to make dating acceptable. "Wilson would sleep, eat, and drink Clara Kate," said his brother Maxwell, and the two were so close, recalled Otis Myers, that "we always thought they were going to get married someday."

Wilson had other plans. By the mid-1950s, word got back to his mother and grandparents that he was regularly missing school and not focusing on his classwork when he did attend. Meantime, his reputation for fighting and physical violence only increased—it has even been suggested that he kept his girlfriends in line with his fists. He didn't always win these fights, though. When James came back for a rare visit, wearing a Marines uniform, he described the use of deadly force in which he had been trained to a group of Wilson's peers. Wilson refused to believe that he would no longer be able to get in a first punch. He came at his brother and was promptly put out cold with two fingers to a pressure point.

It was all bound to come to a head, and for a profile in *Ebony* magazine in 1968, Wilson described it happening in an especially dramatic style. He had grown increasingly frustrated with what *Ebony*'s David Llorens called "the white folks' custom of walking into the homes of black people without knocking at the door." According to Pickett, "One day I asked this white cat, 'Why don't you knock? Don't you know how to knock on a door?' "[19]

Such righteousness indignation, or perceived "uppity-ness," would have been in keeping with his character. It would also have been appropriate within the context of the times. In 1954 Dr. Martin Luther King Jr. took over as Pastor at the Dexter Avenue Baptist Church, fifteen miles away in Montgomery. His presence as a politically motivated preacher led directly to the bus boycott the following year spearheaded by Rosa Parks, which in turn ignited the whole civil rights movement. Meanwhile, in the midst of the landmark *Brown v. Board of Education* decision of 1954, in which the Supreme Court ruled that segregated schools were unconstitutional, Autherine Lucy had sued for admission to the University of Alabama, and the Alabama Attorney General responded by shutting down the State's National Association for the Advancement of Colored People.

The Pickett family was not so much disinterested in all this statewide upheaval as profoundly uninformed—only Shepherd Jackson routinely travelled beyond downtown Prattville—but any white boss Wilson may have dissed would likely have been all too aware of the growing sense of equal entitlement among blacks who had long toiled under white rule. As Wilson admitted to *Ebony*'s Llorens, "When I was growing up down south, the young people didn't have respect for whitey that a lot of the old folks used to have."[20] But there is no hard evidence that Wilson Jr.'s insolence led to him leaving Prattville. His frequent insistence to his siblings that, as Catherine recalled it, "he didn't want to work and make money for the white man" was not so much a reflection of a racial bias (he would end up making plenty money for the white men of the music industry) as much as that "he wanted to make his *own* money." On the plantations of rural Alabama, that was all but impossible.

His move north came down to a general understanding that he was as gifted and ambitious a talent as he was unmanageable and recalcitrant a personality. Unlikely to ever finish his schooling at Autauga, with too great a voice for the church choirs and gospel quartets of Prattville, and lacking for the discipline of a father figure, especially as his grandfather got older and Wilson increasingly stood up to his mother (who in 1955 gave birth to her last child, Vanessa, by another father), it made sense to let him go. In 1956, at the age of fifteen, Wilson Pickett Jr. left Alabama to live with his father and Helen Walker in Detroit.

His final Sunday, Wilson Jr. took a solo at Jericho Baptist as his send-off. He chose a classic example of the eternally popular "Mother" songs that played off the dynamic between the selfless family matron and her ungrateful and unruly children, an especial calling card of the great Archie Brownlee.[21] The stately sixteen-bar blues song in question had the mother talking to her child from her deathbed, but Wilson turned the title line around to offer it as Christian assurance from a wayward, departing son. It was called "I'm Going To Leave You In The Hands of the Lord."

CHAPTER 3

Detroit was a real music town. You heard it everywhere, from radios and record players, outside the doors of the clubs that kids like us were too young to enter legally, from guys and girls standing out on the street singing. It sounds like a scene out of a musical, but that's truly how it was.

Otis Williams, *Temptations*

Wilson Pickett could not have landed in a better place at a better time than Detroit, 1956. Just two years after the *Detroit Tribune*, the city's major black newspaper, lamented how "very few local entertainers or musicians have hit the big time," and three years before Berry Gordy established a record label called Tamla, Pickett arrived to find several now nationally successful rhythm and blues heroes serving additionally as local musical role models.

Hank Ballard, for one, confirmed that a childhood of church singing in Alabama did not forestall finding fame as a young adult in Detroit. Ballard's song "Work With Me Annie" had topped the R&B charts through the summer of 1954, and with their sexually charged singing, his group the Midnighters ensured that it acquired iconic status among early rock 'n' roll records, giving vent to all manner of other "Annie" songs (by the Midnighters and other acts alike) with even more blatant sexual references.

Jackie Wilson, for another, showed that you could be raised singing gospel with your mother, fall sideways into a street gang and a juvenile corrections center as a teen, take up boxing as an outlet for your aggression, avoid having your pretty face pummeled despite a losing record, and go on to find a mentor in a be-bop bandleader searching out new talent (such as, perhaps, the legendary Dizzy Gillespie). Given that lucky break, your keening tenor, your magnetic sexuality, and your bewitching stagecraft could then land one of the the most coveted gigs in all of rhythm and blues: a replacement for the Dominoes' lead singer Clyde McPhatter.

And the emerging stardom of Little Willie John proved that you could be an enthusiastic gospel-singing Arkansas boy, and that your God-fearing parents could forbid you to tour with Dizzy Gillespie (him again!)—merely because you should have been home in bed when you were instead winning the amateur night at the local Paradise Theater. But you could nonetheless go on to hit the road with Detroit big-bandleader Paul Williams ("The Hucklebuck," 1949) and land a recording contract with Cincinnati's King Records. You might even score a top five R&B hit with "All Around the World" at your first solo session, announcing your talents in just six introductory seconds of astoundingly accomplished and unaccompanied vocals, before going several better by topping the charts with the inaugural recording of the soon-to-be-classic "Fever."

At just eighteen years old, Little Willie John was the golden boy of the Jeffries Homes, the new public housing high-rise on Detroit's west side. Built to cater to the overflow of black families still flooding up from the South, the massive complex also took in those displaced by the "urban renewal" (which many translated as "black removal") that demolished the southern end of the thriving Black Bottom community in order to make way for integrated housing in Lafayette Park, and several large medical institutions that civic leaders thought a more fitting use of prime downtown real estate.

Everywhere the young Wilson turned on his arrival in Detroit, there was music. His father and Helen Walker, having moved out of Black Bottom themselves, and living now on 14th Street and Calvert, enrolled Wilson at the local Northwestern High School, where Mary Wells, Norman Whitfield, Florence Ballard, Melvin Franklin, and other future Tamla and Motown players all formed part of a thriving singing scene that reverberated through the city's high school halls, recreation centers, parks, and housing projects.

Any vocal hopeful with a dollar or two, meantime, could head down to Fortune Records, recently relocated to Third Avenue on the west side opposite Central High School, and record a demo on the label's one-track tape recorder, knowing there was every chance that Jack and Devora Brown, the white couple who had established the label in the late 1940s, would release the results. Fortune's catalogue of over four hundred singles reflected an anything-goes mentality that allowed for some of the most wondrously unpolished and underproduced vocal harmony on record.[1] Then again, Fortune also had on its roster the respected bandleader Joe Weaver, the mercurial Andre Williams and his Don Juans, and Nolan Strong and the

Diablos, widely considered the sweetest of all Detroit singing groups and those most revered by fans of of the style later termed "doo-wop."

Over on Hastings Street, Joe Von Battle and his eponymous record shop herded acts of all stripes into the back of his store for recording sessions that made those at Fortune seem positively professional by comparison. Battle, up from Macon, Georgia, had added the Teutonic prefix to his name partly as a sign of aspiration but also to confuse record buyers of his Negro roots: like 125th Street in Harlem, Hastings Street had still been very much a Jewish business area in the 1940s, when Battle was the first black businessman to set up shop. With business savvy, relentless enthusiasm, and the advantage of prime real estate, Battle cornered the market on the big city blues that had been all the rage that past decade. He recorded the Clarksdale, Mississippi pioneer John Lee Hooker alongside Boogie Woogie Red, Washboard Willie, One String Sam, and the Detroit Count, whose "Hastings St. Opera" offered up a salacious tour of the street's many dive bars and shady night clubs.

Seeing no particular distinction between Saturday night sin and Sunday morning salvation, Battle likewise recorded much of the best in Detroit gospel. Gracing his studio were the great Della Reese's group the Meditation Singers, the Spiritual Wonders, and the Violinaires, whose single "Another Soldier Gone"/ "Joy In The Beulah Land" balanced a delicately crooning A-side against a surprisingly rhythmic vocal assault on the flip. To further expose this rougher side to their music, the Violinaires also recorded as a secular group. Calling themselves the Gales, they released a couple of crossover singles in 1953 that featured the lead talents of the high-pitched Isaiah Jones and the more conventional tenor Calvin Fair. The Gales might have had a problem had their singles sold well, given that the gospel legends the Sensational Nightingales were better known by this abbreviated name, but the singles did not take off and the Gales returned to their previous identity as the Violinaires.

Battle also recorded and released Baptist preachers, and in 1951 he was delivered a glorious gift when the New Bethel Baptist Church moved into its new 2,500-capacity location a few blocks to his north. Its pastor, the Reverend C. L. Franklin, a native of Mississippi who had first made a name for himself in Memphis before moving up to Detroit via Buffalo, delivered legendary sermons, equal parts musical performance, theatrical eloquence, Biblical profundity, and civil rights radicalism. At New Bethel, Battle preserved aural evidence of these sermons, as mastered on "The Eagle Stiret'h Her Nest"—in which Franklin likened the Great Migration to the exodus of the Israelites under Moses, and which became a bestselling record among black Baptists on Battle's Von label in 1953. Indeed, the Reverend's sermons proved such a draw that Joe Von Battle made Franklin's name as prominent as his own on both his business cards and his record shop awning. Given Franklin's Memphis roots, and the fact that he broadcast on Detroit's powerful station WJLB, it's entirely possible that Wilson Pickett Jr. had heard the famous sermon in Alabama.

Reverend Franklin was a blues man at heart and was frequently seen at club shows in Detroit—often enough with the great gospel singer Clara Ward, not his wife, on his arm. "He was one of us," guitarist B. B. King told author David Ritz. "He let us know that he admired what we were doing. He called us true artists and had no qualms about telling the world just how he felt."[2] That feeling was mutual: the great blues singer and soul pioneer Bobby Bland claimed to have been inspired by Franklin's delivery style way back in Memphis. In 1956, just as Pickett hit town, Joe Von Battle brought his recording equipment back up the block to Bethel, to record the Reverend singing - with Franklin's fourteen-year-old daughter Aretha as a featured performer.

Aretha Franklin had been part of her father's preaching caravan since she was ten; she had given birth to her first child at age thirteen. Her voice was already imbued with soulful gravitas, whether from her experiences, genetics, or pure genius. Aretha could hear a song once and promptly play it on piano, perfectly, and she could take a gospel song like the Thomas Dorsey standard "Precious Lord," turn it inside out, and render it a moaning blues. Her singing that day at New Bethel prompted an astonished congregant to call "Listen at her!"—an exclamation preserved on the album of "spirituals" (still not referred to as "gospel" even by the black community itself) Battle released from those recordings, the first ever musical artifact of the future Queen of Soul.

Wilson Pickett Jr. would form a friendship with the young Aretha Franklin in Detroit—and he would soon get to sing at New Bethel for himself. It was at Franklin's church that he heard the Soul Stirrers just as the pop success of lead singer Sam Cooke's solo single "You Send Me" ripped the young star away from his mentors, helping clear a path from sacred music to secular that both Wilson and Aretha would later follow. "Them sisters fell like dominoes when Sam took the lead," Pickett told Gerri Hirshey of the female church members' response to Cooke's vocal presence. "Bang. Flat-out. Piled three deep in the aisles."[3] He would also witness his idol the Reverend Julius Cheeks leading the Sensational Nightingales, and he claimed to have seen Archie Brownlee and Clarence Fountain, of the Blind Boys of Mississippi and Alabama respectively, "team up." Evidently, and despite the temptations around him, Pickett remained dedicated to the music on which he had grown, and which he felt destined to sing: gospel.

He joined, first, by some accounts, a group called the Pearly Gates, and then the Sons of Zion, which quickly brought him to the attention of the Violinaires.

The lineup of a semiprofessional gospel group was no more fixed than that of a street singing group, dependent on members' day jobs and whatever factions were vying for control of the group at any time. But the Violinaires had by this point solidified around founding singer, guitarist, and manager Wilson DeShields (a former member of Spartanburg's Baronets, providing a direct connection to Julius Cheeks), Isaiah "Lil Shot" Jones, Calvin Fair, Leo Coney, Robert Gandy, and Elcanon Debose. "We had the best group in Detroit," recalled Debose, another native of Alabama, though born a decade earlier than Pickett. "We already had what we needed. Everywhere we went we had big crowds." But as the Violinaires performed in Detroit's churches and at gospel music gatherings through 1956 and 1957, the sight and sound of a young Wilson Pickett in the Sons of Zion increasingly threatened to upstage them. "He went right behind us and had the same big crowds. He was pretty tough around Detroit. We couldn't necessarily beat him, so we had him join us. We stole him from the other group." If the Violinaires felt any guilt for stealing the star singer from the Sons of Zion, Pickett quickly allayed their fears. "He admitted that's why he was doing what he was doing," said Debose. "He wanted to get with us all the time—because we were the best group. And after he got with us, it made us better than what we were."

Pickett had barely been in Detroit a year. Compared to the other kids at school and their endless rotation among harmony groups that rarely made it to a recognized stage, he must have figured he had found his career already. Not surprisingly, then, especially given the precedent he had set back in Prattville, he soon stopped showing up at Northwestern High. But that was not the agreement he had struck with his father and Helen, whose lives were additionally complicated by the arrival of their own first child, Audrey, born in 1957. As far as they were concerned Wilson Jr. either attended school, got a job, or found somewhere else to live. He had no particular interest in any of these options, so while Helen played the role of a supportive stepmother, driving Wilson to gospel group rehearsals, the father and son frequently butted heads—and quite likely, the collision was physical. "Supposedly, he picked our father up and threw him on the other side of the bed or something, against the wall," recalled Maxwell.[4]

The payback was drastic. "He put Wilson out," recalled his sister Bertha of their father, "and Wilson was sleeping in the theaters." It was around this time that his oldest sister Catherine received a letter from their mother Lena, down in Alabama, telling her to collect Wilson Jr. from Detroit and bring him to Louisville to live with her. Evidently, Lena no more wanted the responsibility for her wayward son's well-being than did her former husband. The instruction came as a shock for Catherine, and not only because she now had two small children of her own; she didn't even know Wilson had moved to Detroit to begin with.

Catherine and her husband Tommy Williams nonetheless drove north, collected Wilson Jr. from his father, and briefly became his surrogate parents. It was the same old song. "In Louisville, he wouldn't go to school," said Catherine. "He sung on weekends, that's all he wanted to do." Williams had a group called the Golden Echoes along with Wilson's uncle, Albert Jackson (another member of the extended family who had moved up from Prattville), and for the next several months their performances were graced by one of the better young gospel voices to ever pass through town.

Recognizing that she could no more win the schooling battle than anyone else in the family, Catherine employed Wilson to sit her own children while she went to work. On her return home, Wilson would complain about having had to change their diapers. "What do you think you're supposed to do if you raise kids?" she would ask him. Similarly, Wilson would express dismay at the mere fifteen dollars he'd receive for his weekly babysitting duties—even though Catherine made it plain that's all that it cost to drop the kids at daycare. But the relationship was essentially positive. "He weren't nothing but a big playful kid," said Catherine. Wilson eventually found himself a job at a brick company—at the same point as a letter arrived from the Violinaires seeking his return. He replied, the next letter came with a bus ticket, and Catherine found herself mailing Wilson's first paycheck to Detroit.

On arrival back in the Motor City, Wilson Jr. discovered that his father, Helen, and baby Audrey had again relocated, this time to Merrick just off 12th Street (the main thoroughfare of the now predominantly black west side), and Wilson would spend much of the next two years bouncing from place to place in between road trips with the Violinaires. Elcanon Debose stated that he and Leo Conroy paid Wilson's rent on a cheap hotel room for a while. Pickett would often recall this period of desperate existence later in life when justifying his unwillingness to give others a financial hand; here and there, however, he could reflect on it with humor. "When I hit Detroit, I was eatin' nothin' but beans and rice, rice and beans," he told Gerri Hirshey. "Maybe once a month I come up with a chicken liver to throw in it. And pancakes. Aunt Jemima done saved *my* starvin' ass."[5]

His suffering was rewarded in November 1957, when the Violinaires included him in a recording session conducted by Joe Von Battle in the back of the Hastings Street store. Wilson Pickett is likely the second tenor on the full-throttled "Sign of the Judgment," making his recording debut. But just about nobody heard it at the time. The song was pressed up in limited quantities as part of a promotional single by the Philadelphia-based Gotham label to which Battle often sent myriad (and sometimes unlabeled) recordings, but it was held back from commercial release. It was probably the right move given the quality of the recording; "Sign of the Judgment" was never going to stand out in the marketplace.[6]

(A myth created on the internet, and cemented by a BBC Radio documentary on Pickett's life, claims that the young Wilson made his recording debut singing lead with a gospel group called the Spiritual 5, instead, on their Peacock Records single, "Christ's Blood." He did not. The single was released in 1963 with no reference to it being an older recording. Pickett was an R&B star by then, and Don Robey's Peacock label would surely have made a point of this being a valuable early find—and Pickett made no reference to such a recording either.[7])

Though they never enjoyed an official record release during Pickett's tenure, the Violinaires busily rode the gospel highway north and south, around the midwest and along the east coast, in an eight-seater Chrysler station wagon. Their travels took them back down to Alabama, where they sang in Birmingham, Montgomery, Selma—and at the Spring Hill AME Zion church right there in Prattville. For brother Maxwell, sister Jeannie, and for his cousin and friend Otis Myers, this was confirmation of their belief in Wilson's talents, proof that he had done right by leaving the family behind, however much he might have been hurting financially.

"He was just a star," said Debose of Pickett. "We didn't make him a star. He was a born star. He put fear into a lot of the groups. Because he was just that good. I mean, he was *good*." Discovering that he could hold his own against some of the more established names in gospel, Pickett proved unforgiving when it came to singers from his own generation. Of David Ruffin, up from the backwoods of Mississippi and recording independently before his career with the Temptations launched, "Pickett used to pick at him: he'd be like, 'Oh you're never going to do nothing.' Pickett would say 'I'm the best.'"

Without a doubt, the regular competition with his fellow shouters paid off. "It definitely helped me," Pickett told Sue C. Clark in 1969. "Because it developed the kind of voice that I wanted to have. A real hard-type drivin' voice. And I think if I hadn't've been a gospel singer all those years, I couldn't last singing like I do." Indeed, Pickett was always clear that the strength of his voice—the ability to hold that tuneful scream, to split the notes of an octave like a mystical throat singer, and to do so without damaging the vocal cords as happened to Julius Cheeks—was due to consistent and constant training over the years. As he responded to an interviewer a decade down the line, at the peak of his popularity, and with perhaps unintentional dismissiveness of contemporary soul music, "The gospel sound is much more powerful than the stuff I'm doing now."[8]

Pickett remained devout during this period. "When I was in the church, I was sincere," he told Clark. "I wouldn't dance or do nothing. Wouldn't drink. Wouldn't smoke. Just sing." Elcanon Debose confirmed that: "None of us ever drank." Helen Walker insisted, "He never clowned around, never run with no bad crowd," and in the house, at least, "you never heard him cuss." The latter virtue was not exactly upheld on the road, where gospel music promoters were no more scrupulous than those in other genres. Wilson DeShields, said Debose, "was the brain of the group. But when it came to getting the money, Wilson [Pickett] was the brain of the group. He'd say 'Motherf---er, you'd better come up with our god---n money, or I'm kicking your god---n ass.' And they would come up with the money."

Inevitably, Pickett's powerful presence and natural good looks made for a regionalized version of the Sam Cooke phenomenon. At New Bethel, "Aretha would scream every time we come on," said Debose. The two future stars were only a year apart in age, and rumors would circulate about the nature of their friendship—as they tended to with almost any female singer within Wilson Pickett's orbit, which during those formative years in Detroit included most of the future Motown roster.

Pickett would soon leave the ranks of the eligible young bachelors in town. In the spring of 1959, just as he turned eighteen, his steady girlfriend, seventeen-year-old Bonnie Covington, became pregnant with a son. A migrant from Pickett's home area of Montgomery, Alabama, Bonnie was an aspiring church singer and familiar face on the Detroit gospel scene, well known to the Violinaires even before they acquired Pickett. According to Wilson and Bonnie's daughter, Veda Neal Pickett, the couple met "singing gospel at Aretha Franklin's father's church." Bonnie, said Veda, was "a low-key person, very quiet." Her own mother, the youngest of thirteen children, had given birth to Bonnie at the age of fifteen, and Bonnie had been raised primarily by her grandmother and aunts. She was eager to provide traditional parental love for her own children, and that required the presence of a father. Before their child, Lynderrick, was born on December 26, 1959, Bonnie dropped out of school in her senior year, and the pair quietly wed. It would be Wilson's only marriage.

Now that the younger Wilson had a wife and child to feed, Wilson Sr. and Helen welcomed him and his new family back into their home. The elder pair and their own baby had recently returned from the west side to a four-room apartment back on Brady Street, between Hastings and St. Antoine. They were able to secure a lot of space in this new home, while the bulldozers were busy making their way up from Paradise Valley, clearing out the last of Hastings Street to replace it with the Chrysler Freeway (subsequently acknowledged as a travesty of urban planning). For Wilson Jr. the location provided an additional boon: he now found himself two blocks from Joe's Record Shop in one direction and just four or five from New Bethel in the other. And the presence of an upper porch, accessible from the street, afforded him a space to practice the guitar he had acquired—and to reflect on the limitations of a career in gospel singing.

"You'd sing all day and you pass around the basket and the sisters would put a dime in a piece, and say 'Y'all boys sure did sing,'—and you couldn't get your shirts cleaned or nothing," he told Sue C. Clark. "And then you begin to grow to have a family. And you say, 'Well, if entertainin' going to be my life, I got to do somethin' now to try to make a living, y'know?'"⁹

Helen placed him and Bonnie on welfare. The poverty was such that his brother James recalled a brief period of helping Wilson Sr. strip carpeting from abandoned houses to use in their own. Wilson remained without a job, claiming that would have interfered with his own singing ambitions; the closest he ever got to regular employment was delivering groceries on Dexter Avenue. The pressure gradually closed in—until one night, Helen Walker heard a fight break out from the room next door.

"Bonnie was hollering, 'And don't bother my baby.... Ow! You hit me!' That's when I broke the door down, and said, 'You fighting her?' He said, 'No, I didn't hit her' and she said, 'Yes you did, you slapped me.'" Rather than throw Wilson Jr. out on the street (again), Helen called Bonnie's mother to collect her to keep her safe from her young husband. The couple would soon reconcile.

Meantime, he persisted with the Violinaires. The group did not lack for respect. "Senator" Bristol Bryant regularly brought them in on Sunday mornings to sing on WJLB, they were frequent guests of honor at New Bethel, and they continued to tour. But without a recording contract, or at least a proper release, they were never going to ascend to a higher level. And Wilson knew it.

CHAPTER 4

You couldn't fight the power in his voice. Wilson was so aggressive, he wasn't gonna be denied.

Eddie Floyd, singer.[1]

The story of the Falcons—often tagged "The World's First Soul Group"—started just down the road from Prattville, in Montgomery, Alabama. It was there that a teenage Eddie Floyd, born in 1937, begged to be allowed to follow his uncle, Robert West, to Detroit. His wish granted, in 1955 Floyd recruited a couple of white boys from the jewelry store where he worked to form a vocal harmony group. His uncle, who was in his forties, came on as manager and quickly solidified the lineup, luring bass singer Willie Schofield from a Drifters cover group, then hiring a vocal coach, Bob Hamilton, to knock the boys' voices into better shape.

Donning their showy stage uniforms—the required fashion for all vocal groups of the time—the Falcons ventured to Chicago, where they passed an audition at Mercury Records. The professional coaching likely helped them pass, but their novel integrated lineup probably explained why they got the audition in the first place—they had arrived right as the mixed-race Frankie Lymon & the Teenagers set the vocal group scene on fire. Still, their 1956 debut single, a jump tune written and led by the silver-toned Floyd and backed by Willie Dixon's band, stirred little national interest and the group's two white members promptly left for the armed services. Floyd and Schofield, however—and especially Robert West—had the bug. They secured Joe Stubbs, a teenage wonder who had already toured Canada alongside the Five Dollars, as one of the replacements. Stubbs brought with him a talented guitarist, Lance Finney, a popular addition to any vocal group with one eye on the R&B charts. The other vocal replacement came in the form of Mack Rice. Born 1933 in Clarksdale, Mississippi, Rice was known on the circuit from his lead on a local hit single for the Five Scalders (so named because they considered themselves "hot"). The reconstituted Falcons quickly established themselves as one of the city's revered vocal groups in supper clubs such as the 509 Downtown, the Woodward, and the Congress—clubs they as black men could only enter as performers, never as customers.

The Four Aims, led by Stubbs's older brother Levi, were more popular in the clubs. But, said Floyd, referring to that group's sweeter style of singing, "We weren't really trying to do doo-wop. We did the rough and tough." Either way, the Falcons were dropped by Mercury when they couldn't score a hit. Manager West promptly founded three different independent labels of his own, putting out three different singles by the Falcons in a short span of time, one of which, "Sent Up,"—a skit about a guy getting sent to jail for what would today be called date rape, as written by guitarist Finney— perhaps verified Floyd's statement of intent. All three singles flopped. In 1959 the Falcons finally found the right formula with "You're So Fine," a spritely number with Joe Stubbs on lead, that pulled out all contemporary commercial tricks—from the descending bass vocal at the end of each verse to the wailing sax solo in the middle.

Originally released on yet another of West's growing collection of independent record labels, "You're So Fine" was soon picked up by United Artists. At about the same time, "Come To Me" by Marv Johnson—catalog number Tamla 001—served as the debut release on another new Detroit label, this one established by the thirty-year-old Berry Gordy. A failed pugilist, pimp, and record store proprietor, Gordy had finally redeemed himself by writing songs for Jackie Wilson. From Wilson, he learned the hard way that you needed to own the publishing if you expected to get paid for composing. He learned much the same about the label business by producing the hit "Get a Job" for the Miracles, and from various production and writing around Bob West's multiple enterprises, he learned the importance of quality over quantity. "Come To Me" was recorded in Detroit's premier independent studio, United Sound, around the corner from the office Gordy established for his label on West Grand Boulevard; by stark comparison, recalled Floyd, "You're So Fine" was recorded "in a bathroom around a commode at three a.m."

Backed by United Artists, which picked up Gordy's debut Tamla release as well as "You're So Fine," the Falcons and Marv Johnson hit the road together. By the end of their tour the Falcons had scored the bigger hit: "You're So Fine" had reached number two on the R&B charts, and was a top twenty smash on the pop charts. Featured on Dick Clark's *American Bandstand*, the Falcons were stars now, but public recognition and adulation would be short-lived without a follow-up, and Bob West flooded the market with an almost comical number of releases by a variety of labels, including two commercially oriented singles for United Artists on which Stubbs sang lead, "the Teacher" and "I + Love + You." When the royalty checks came in for "You're So Fine" and the song's composers, Schofield and Finney, received just $500 each, Schofield realized, like Gordy before him, that the real money was clearly to be made on the other side of the microphone. He set about scouring the Detroit streets for prospective artists of his own.

That same summer of 1960, Willie Schofield was on his way back to his car after a doctor's appointment on Hastings Street when he was stopped short by someone singing "The Sky Is Crying," a major urban blues hit for Elmore James at the time. The voice belonged to Wilson Pickett, accompanying himself on acoustic guitar on the upstairs balcony of 653 Brady Street.

"Still to this day I can hear it," recalled Schofield over half a century later. "What caught my attention was him hitting those notes, the clarity and the strength." Schofield started up his car, but then paused and thought better of it. "I let the window down and listened some more and said, 'Hey, I've got to hear who this is.'" When the song was over, he walked up the outer steps to the balcony and introduced himself.

"Have you ever sung professionally?" he recalled asking the stranger.
"Well no . . . I sung with a gospel group," replied the nineteen-year-old.
"Would you be *interested* in singing professionally?"
"Well yeah, I would love that."

Wilson Pickett's version of this event differed only in that he recalled Schofield requesting that he sing the song a second time, to which he responded with his typical attitude: "Why should I do it for you? Who are *you*?" Either way, Schofield introduced himself as a member of the Falcons, handed Pickett his business card with the address of the studio the group shared with Bob West on East Forrest, and agreed on a time and date for Pickett to come by.

Pickett showed up for the audition as planned. "I played the piano for him," recalled Schofield, "and when he started that squalling, people started coming out of the other offices. 'Who in the world is singing like that? 'Wilson Pickett, a new artist I'm auditioning.' 'Sign him, sign him.' 'I intend to.'" And he did.

Still, Schofield refused to lay claim to "discovering" Pickett. "I always feel it was going to happen for him. He was, for me, that kind of a singer.

He had so much self-confidence." And if Schofield hadn't have found him, it may otherwise have been Berry Gordy, or one of his producers or groups—perhaps the Temptations, then named the Distants, who had shared roots in the churches of Alabama and were still assembling their permanent lineup. But musically, joining up with Gordy at this point would never have worked: Pickett was always first to insist that the Tamla/Motown aesthetic, once it took shape, was too "pop" for his personal singing style.

Besides, although Pickett had jumped at the invitation to audition, he had considerable doubts about abandoning his gospel aspirations. It was, he believed, the music best suited to his voice, and he did not want to turn his back on three years' hard work with the Violinaires. More so, he was faithful enough to his Baptist upbringing that he questioned the morality of singing secular music for a living. When he sought Helen Walker's opinion, she took the equivalent of the Fifth, responding, "Why don't you ask your mother?" To which Wilson replied, "You know what mama going to say: 'You just going to hell.'"

Many of the churchgoers he was singing to appeared to be headed that way themselves, the most prominent coming from New Bethel. The Reverend C. L. Franklin was carousing around the blues clubs at night—and on one occasion, according to the reputable Reverend James Cleveland, was seen slapping Clara Ward around in public.[2] Franklin had fathered an illegitimate daughter with a twelve-year-old, something Wilson may not have been aware of—but he did know that Aretha had given birth to her second child already, at the age of sixteen (she never disclosed the father of either child). And in a world where the Franklins' sermons and singing sat cheek by jowl at Joe's Record Shop alongside heartfelt urban blues and bawdy street party music, it was perhaps no surprise that the church people of Detroit saw no reason to show up for church on Sunday morning sober from Saturday night.

Pickett unloaded his conflicted thoughts on his new mentor, only two years his elder. "He was disillusioned," said Schofield, "'cos he thought the church was full of godly people. And he found out they was just like everybody else out there." Schofield had long ago figured as much from his own experiences in church. "I told Wilson, 'You're dealing with people—so you might as well just come out here in the real world where you'd expect that from them.'"

Eventually, Pickett agreed. The deciding factor, ultimately, was financial. "He wrote Mama a long letter, that he was going to make some money," said his sister Bertha. "He said he had been visiting C. L. Franklin's church and he had sung there and he was singing to a drunken audience. And he said, 'I might as well be singing rock 'n' roll as singing to a drunken audience.

I might as well make me some money.' And that's when he stopped singing gospel."

It was never the original plan for Pickett to join the Falcons; indeed, he was never featured in an official group photograph. But his entry into the orbit of Schofield and Bob West coincided with the Falcons' frustrations with Joe Stubbs. As the lead voice on their hits, Stubbs had attracted significant attention—and developed the ego to match. He was now insisting that his name prefix that of the group—like, say, Nolan Strong and the Diablos, or Hank Ballard and the Midnighters. Given the depth of singing and songwriting talent in the Falcons and the close ties between manager West and founding member Floyd, the others were not inclined to agree. When Stubbs called their bluff on the eve of a major tour, the Falcons called it back on him. That left them three weeks to find a new lead singer. No problem, thought Schofield, who promptly brought Pickett to a rehearsal—but the response of the other Falcons was not the one he had expected.

"First thing come out their mouths: 'He's too black.' I said, 'What the hell you mean he's too black?' 'Well, you know . . .' I said, 'Well what about me?' they said 'No it's different with you.'" (Schofield had darker skin than the others, though not as dark as Pickett.) "That pissed me off to no end: 'He's too black.' Prejudice within your own people like that? And I thought Pickett had the prettiest smile, beautiful teeth, personality . . ."

The group's reaction likely reflected a black aspiration to white cultural ideals of beauty that was prominent at the time, along with a desire to "pass" as white. This desire extended back to the promoters' insistence on employing "high yaller" girls—those who looked white from a distance—at the Cotton Club in 1930s New York, and no doubt at corresponding venues in Detroit. It could be found every day in barbershops across America where young black men subjected themselves to an uncomfortable hair straightening process so they could imitate the hairstyles of a white man. And it played out most visibly, if subtly, in the common desire among black entertainers to "cross over"—to reach the lucrative white audience that, it was always presumed, wanted its black music delivered milky and its singers the same. How were the Falcons to know that in only eight years, James Brown would be sporting an afro, singing "Say It Loud (I'm Black and I'm Proud)," and taking it to the top ten of the pop charts?

Of course Floyd and Rice, and Finney perhaps and West, may have in fact *heard* Pickett as "too black." Gospel music was ingrained in the Falcons (they'd often end a rehearsal with a quartet song just for the hell of it), but Pickett was so deeply immersed in the culture of church singing that in his audition with the same "The Sky Is Crying" that Schofield had heard out on

Brady Street, his voice would have ripped the roof off the studio had it not been located in the building's basement. Gospel's commercial decline was already starting to take effect around 1960, and the Falcons had to consider whether the nineteen-year-old vocal dynamo with the coal-black features and stiff church presentation represented a link to the future—or a chain to the past.

Pickett had reservations of his own. "They were singing this 'peanuts and popcorn' type music back then," he told Michael Lydon of the *New York Times* in 1977, in a recorded interview on which he then derisively mimicked the chorus from "the Teacher." "I call it corny music: pop pop doo-doo-da-doo. I couldn't relate to that."[3]

An aggrieved Schofield suggested the group find their own lead singer, and they obliged with a request to Marvin Gaye, a new arrival to town alongside Harvey Fuqua of the freshly dissolved Moonglows. But Gaye declined. His wagon was already hitched to the growing Gordy enterprises, and not just because Berry had bought out his contract from Fuqua: Gaye was also dating Gordy's sister, Anna. Mack Rice suggested the grandiloquently named Don Juan Mancha, who had sung with Tamla's hit artist Barrett Strong in the Delrays, and would remain within Robert West's circle. Ultimately, they came back to Pickett. Whatever other reservations they might have, there was no doubt that he could sing. Still, it was a hint of troubles to come that a bill for Detroit's 20 Grand club in 1960 advertised the Falcons *and* Wilson Pickett.

As for the Violinaires, DeShields heard a rumor on the street and called a meeting, where Pickett admitted that he was leaving for the Falcons—that same weekend. There was disappointment, even anger, that the Violinaires hadn't been approached for permission (despite the fact they had done the same thing in poaching Pickett in the first place). They had given Pickett the foothold in gospel music that he had so desperately desired, and some of them had dug deep in their own pockets to supply him with food and housing at a point when he had neither. However, most of them held down day jobs and were none so desperate as Pickett for income or fame. "He had a legitimate reason to go over and work in that field, because he had a family," said Debose. And, good as the Violinaires were, the Falcons represented something bigger. "It was like he got out of a Cadillac with us and got into a limousine with them."

The Violinaires would bounce back. Recruiting Robert Blair, a singer of no ill repute himself, they went on to make records for Chess in the 1960s, even as gospel was marginalized in the wake of the soul music phenomenon. When all was said and done, the Violinaires recognized that they had been blessed just to share in Pickett's talent. "The guy was great," said Debose. "The only thing about him is that he just made his greatness famous after he left us. But he was just as great when he was with us. He was the show. Believe me."

Wilson Pickett endured a baptism of fire with the Falcons. At his inaugural show with the group, in Kansas City, the sound of girls screaming was so loud that he couldn't hear Lance Finney play the opening chord to the first song, the current Jackie Wilson hit "Doggin' Around." Pickett promptly started singing in the wrong key. That, at least, was Schofield's memory. Mack Rice remembers the show in Des Moines, Iowa, where Pickett froze on the opening chord, the audience heckling him in response.

In addition to these early vocal foibles, the Falcons soon discovered that Pickett did not know how to *move*. The singer readily admitted as much. "I would trip up, fall on the stage and the group would rehearse me in the dressing room after every show," he told Lydon. "I would get mad, 'cos I wanted to go out and look at the girls as well! They said, 'No, you got to rehearse, Oscar.' They called me Oscar." He let his tough veneer disappear for a moment. "I don't know why they called me Oscar, I didn't like that very much."[4]

"They'd pick on him, call him little off-the-wall names," confirmed Schofield. The mild hazing increased when Stubbs, possibly repentant and otherwise unemployed, returned to the group, swelling its size to five singers and at least that many large egos. Eddie Floyd confirmed that he thought Stubbs was "phased out by the group" and that Pickett "was a replacement, as far as I was concerned," but that once Stubbs returned "there were two leaders" (it says much for the shifting dynamics of the group Floyd had founded that he no longer included himself among them).

The primary conflict between Pickett and Stubbs was ultimately settled in the studio. While on tour with Marv Johnson in 1959 the Falcons had appeared on a bill coheadlined by Sam Cooke, who, taking a liking to Stubbs's voice and noting the Falcons' current popularity, offered them an exclusive composition, "Pow! You're in Love."[5] When it came time to record the song, however, it was Pickett who was chosen to sing lead. For someone who had grown up on the Soul Stirrers, had seen Cooke sing in church, and watched him take that path from sacred to secular, weathering the storm of discontent from the faithful to emerge the other side, with reputation intact and bank balance and fame enhanced—for Wilson Pickett to be offered the opportunity to sing an unreleased composition by Cooke for his first professional studio session must seemed too good to be true.

And it was. "Pow!" was a jaunty pop tune, but that's all it was: Cooke had become so watered down by his own crossover aspirations that his compositions were now largely devoid of gospel roots. The big band accompaniment, courtesy of United Artists' Artist & Repertoire chief, Don Costa, ended up overwhelming the inexperienced studio singer, who was kept low in the final mix, equal prominence given to the other Falcons falling into chorus alongside him. Other than a cute modulation and a promising squall or two from Pickett in the second verse, the sole musical interaction between Cooke and Pickett, released at the start of 1961, was a creative and commercial flop.

It may have been simply a sign of the times, of those musical dark ages between the initial burst of rock 'n' roll and the coming surge of rock and soul. Elvis Presley, Chuck Berry, Little Richard, Richie Valens, Buddy Holly, Jerry Lee Lewis—all these pioneers had been neutered or silenced in recent years, by conscription, religion, scandal, jail, or early death. Meanwhile, a growing furor over radio "payola" had reached the US Senate, and the fallout created a barrier between the independent labels and the disc jockeys they had previously bought off with liquor, women, and cold cash. This suited the likes of United Artists, ABC-Paramount, and other labels born out of movie and TV money, who transformed the newly populist strain of ex-rock 'n' roll into an appropriately Hollywood-esque assembly line of acquiescent "talent" to be produced, arranged, and otherwise molded according to time-honored Tin Pan Alley standards. Under such circumstances, even the icons of R&B and rock 'n' roll toed the line. At the time that "Pow!" was released, "the Genius" Ray Charles was crooning "Georgia On My Mind" accompanied by full orchestra; Elvis Presley was howling a rewrite of "O Sole Mio" as if he'd never sung in an Assembly of God church choir; and the Drifters had grafted their gospel voices onto the newly ubiquitous *baion* rhythm. Back in Detroit, Berry Gordy had yet to lock into the house style that would make Motown an assembly line of a very different hue and grace, and as Hank Ballard was (hopefully) getting rich on the success of Chubby Checker's smash version of his composition "The Twist," so too was every record label, big and small, that came up with ever weaker imitations. Wilson Pickett had made the right move in leaving the Violinaires just as gospel was getting cold, but he was so late jumping into rock 'n' roll that, for now, he found himself competing in the pop marketplace instead.

Several further recording sessions followed for the Falcons, most taking place at United Sound in Detroit, where they were often backed by future Motown "Funk Brothers" Richard "Pistol" Allen on drums, Joe Hunter on piano, and, on one occasion, James Jamerson introducing them to the sight and sound of an electric Fender bass (as opposed to the stand-up acoustic variety that had long been the studio staple). The lead vocals were largely assumed by Pickett, and the results rose and fell according to his comfort level with the material. Ultimately, United Artists declined to release any of it and let the Falcons go.[6]

In the absence of record releases, the Falcons toured extensively. The shows provided valuable experience and visibility for Pickett, they introduced him to the availability of women on the road, and, just as importantly, they gave him some form of income, greatly needed once he discovered that Bonnie was pregnant again. (Their daughter Veda was born in July, 1961.) That income was not always guaranteed, however; the promoters on the chitlin' circuit of backwoods clubs and urban bloodbuckets had a tendency to make those on the gospel highway seem saintly by comparison. Often times they'd be out the back door before the Falcons had left the stage. A group's reputation—as much as its career—was dependent on getting paid, and it was partly for this reason that Schofield, Rice, and Floyd all took to packing guns on the road. They carried them occasionally on stage too, as additional and preemptive defense against the inevitable jealous boyfriends in the audience. And there was also the need to be armed as defense against racial attacks down south—carrying a gun potentially raised the stakes to a deadly level, but many black groups believed it was worth the risk in the event of a showdown.

The Falcons didn't seek out trouble: "We made it a point never to play Mississippi," said Schofield, though Rice hailed from there, and Floyd and Pickett from neighboring Alabama. (On their way to Baton Rouge, the two Alabama natives took the opportunity to surprise their moms, in Montgomery and Prattville, respectively. The other Falcons' suspicions of Pickett's country roots were duly confirmed when they saw the "block" house.)

But trouble found them anyway. There was the occasion they were heading down the highway, the band members mostly asleep, when a pickup truck pulled alongside them and its white passenger pointed a gun at the Falcons' driver. The truck pulled back, and pulled up again, repeating the threat. The nervous driver woke the group, and the next time the truck pulled alongside, the Falcons pulled down the windows and fired shots into the air. "They went off in the corn field somewhere," recalled Schofield. "Pickett just loved that." It was only a matter of time before Pickett, already a marksman, was packing heat too. "He was real green when he came to us," said Mack Rice, referring to Pickett's devout Gospel group lifestyle compared to various Falcons' fondness for drinking and smoking weed—although, like Debose in the Violinaires before him, Rice noted that Pickett had no qualms about swearing.[7] "Once he started knowing the ropes, *he* was the man."[8] Pickett would often talk of the occasions that the station wagon's "six-dollar tires" would blow out under the pressure of heavy luggage above and hot tarmac below, sending their vehicle spinning across the highway, through oncoming traffic, and oftentimes into the ditch on the other side. It was enough to make Pickett look back on his experience with amazement: "We should have been dead long ago."

The touring travails were compensated for Pickett by the reaction to that glorious scream of his. On one memorable occasion the Falcons found themselves on a theater revue, apparently at the Uptown in Philadelphia, second on the bill to James Brown. "We set the stage on fire with Pickett," said Mack Rice, who at one point during the first evening's show came over to his fellow singer to let him know that he was perhaps getting a little *too* close to the headliner's style:

> "Pickett, man, you singing James Brown shit now."
> "Yeah, I know," said Pickett between breaths, and he carried right on screaming.[9]

Accordingly, they received a formal visitor in the dressing room. James Brown wanted the Falcons moved down the bill—or off it entirely. Pickett recalled it as the latter: "James Brown fired us off his tour 'cos I was screaming a little too loud," he told Lydon. "I had the girls grabbing my leg and everything."[10] Mack Rice remembered that the Falcons volunteered to open the revue instead. The incident was but the first of many between Pickett and Brown, who endured and eventually enjoyed a relationship built upon professional rivalry and begrudging personal respect.

On their travels, the Falcons came into contact with the Ohio Untouchables. A fully contained group based out of Dayton, their numbers included a two-person brass section and an electrifying guitarist, Robert Ward, schooled in Georgia by his gospel-singing father and guitar-playing mother. A working relationship was initiated between the two groups, and when in February 1962 Bob West launched yet another new label, Lu Pine, he did so with a song that combined the Untouchables' instrumental talents with the vocal qualities of the Falcons.

That song was "I Found a Love," sung and primarily written by Wilson Pickett, who based it on the Pentecostal hymn "Yes Lord."[11] Over fifty years later, "I Found a Love" has lost none of its capacity to surprise, thrill, and astound: while so many of its contemporaries are buried in the cultural graveyard, their passing dated by the times and values—the fads—to which they subscribed and competed, this song remains very much alive, born out of the musical intercourse between its gospel, rhythm and blues, doo-wop, and rock 'n' roll influences.

The recording is all the more important because no major label would ever have sanctioned its release. The levels peak way above all acceptable production norms from the moment, just three seconds in, that the assembled chorus of Falcons shout a victorious "yeah . . . yeah," by which point an initial upward piano scale has already introduced the bass, drums, piano, and sax, and Robert Ward is about to flex his lead guitar licks through his distinctive Magnatone amp. Before the listener has time to recoil from the voluminous attack, the vocal chorus subsides, Ward briefly steps back, bass singer Ben Knight sets the foundation for the verse, Don Juan Mancha on piano hammers out a simple syncopation to emphasize the 6/8 rhythm, and Wilson Pickett steps forward, singing—the churchgoers would know it as shouting—the title three times over with passion, power, and precision that could only have come from years of intoning a similar refrain in service of the Lord. This time, however, his subject is of a most assuredly earthly nature: Wilson Pickett has a found a *love*, a kiss that he can't resist, and he is quite happy—ecstatic would be the right word—for the whole world to hear about it.

The performance gains confidence as it progresses. Drummer Cornelius Johnson steadily lightens his grip on the group in front of him; within a minute, the harsh snare fill that had dictated the introduction has relaxed into a marching band shuffle. Marshall Jones on electric bass similarly breathes relief in the knowledge that the bass singer is providing plenty enough bottom end for the both of them, while pianist Mancha, and Untouchables' sax players Pee Wee Middlebrook and Clarence Satchell, all step back to let the real stars of the show take over. As Eddie Floyd and Mack Rice temper the verses with the reassuring strains of a fading doo-wop era, Robert Ward and Wilson Pickett duel it out in a delightful game of musical call-and-response. Pickett delivers the decisive blow at the end of the second verse when, his voice straining in a key far too high for common sense, he lets out an arguably superfluous "whoaah" that rises briefly up, then dips briefly deep down below, giving way to the resounding "yeah . . . yeah" chorus before the others can even grasp what he's done. Ward wisely doesn't threaten him again, but rather offers his flirtatious guitar licks in pure devotional support of Pickett's commanding voice, which duly gains volume and character in a third verse of carnal bliss, the final syllable this time engaging in a dozen or so notes before Pickett takes a quick breath, observing of his love that "Sometimes I call her in the midnight hour." And at that he lets rip at the top of his lungs, capturing for the first time on vinyl that future trademark scream. Over the final "yeah . . . yeah" chorus that has already pushed the decibel level into the distortion zone, he repeats the scream once more for good measure, and this time more tenaciously, floating upward to a note beyond the reach of most mortals, holding it . . . and then signing off by somehow pitching it briefly higher—concluding the most shatteringly exhilarating ballad in all of black music since James Brown's "Please, Please, Please" six years earlier.

The Falcons knew they had a hit on their hands the moment they brought test pressings to the local disc jockeys. In a city so deeply immersed in the black musical melting pot, "I Found a Love" broke out immediately, and copies soon found their way to Atlantic Records, as all happening black music had a tendency to do.

    The famed American independent record label had staked its early post-war reputation, and made an initial fortune on recording, releasing, and then properly promoting and distributing what it considered to be "authentic" black music of all strands. This included a great deal of jazz—and a staggering amount of rhythm and blues talent, including Ruth Brown, Big Joe Turner, and Ray Charles. What really distinguished Atlantic from its equally hungry rivals, though, was how it handled that talent: Atlantic required extensive rehearsals, written arrangements, proven producers, and established session musicians, all of which afforded its finished masters a gloss at distinct odds with other independents of the era, and all the more likely to gain airplay as a result. Of course success brought a different set of challenges, and in recent years, as its artists had crossed into the pop mainstream, some had left for more lucrative contracts—most notably Ray Charles, to ABC-Paramount, and Bobby Darin, Atlantic's first white pop star, to Capitol. At the same time, the Coasters had reached the end of a long run of amusing R&B hits, mostly penned and produced by the duo Leiber and Stoller, who were themselves in the midst of a falling-out with Atlantic over its accounting practices. Although the Drifters and their former lead singer Ben E. King were continuing to place singles in the higher reaches of the charts—the latter, most recently, with a reworking of the old gospel standard "Lord, Stand By Me"—the music no longer contained the urgency that had marked Atlantic's earliest successes.

    The label had reached a point of creative stasis. Cofounder and President Ahmet Ertegun, the cultured son of a Turkish diplomat, had long given up his "slumming" trips to the Deep South, where he had ferreted out poor black artists of merit, and had instead taken to ferrying his socialite friends around New York's nightclubs on his private bus every evening. Ertegun's former partner on those scouting adventures, Vice President Jerry Wexler, had found himself desk-bound, "supervising staff, hiring and firing."[12]

A product of a poor but liberal Jewish upbringing in the Bronx, Wexler's depth of musical knowledge was matched by a sophisticate's intellect, and a competitive instinct that frequently played out in combative business dealings. It was he who, while working at *Billboard* in 1949, had suggested the name change from "race" to "rhythm and blues." Upon joining Atlantic in 1953, he had become involved with its R&B repertoire, often overseeing and producing the recordings. Yet in 1962, at forty-five years old, he, like Ertegun, seemed now bereft of his former hitmaking mojo and had largely resorted to licensing promising releases from regional independents.

Wexler typically locked these independent labels into long-term deals, one of which was to prove paramount to both Wilson Pickett and Atlantic's future success. In securing a duet between the renowned black radio personality and recording artist Rufus Thomas and his high school daughter Carla ("'Cause I Love You"), Wexler ensured that Atlantic had first option on all future releases by Thomas's label, Satellite. This deal quickly paid dividends in the form of a bigger hit from young Carla, "Gee Whiz," and then in a surprise smash instrumental by Satellite's integrated, precociously young house band, the Mar-Keys, "Last Night." These successes prompted a cease-and-desist from a larger recording company also named Satellite, and the Memphis upstart changed its name, using the initial letters of the founding partners' surnames, Jim Stewart and his sister Estelle Axton. Operating out of an old cinema in Memphis, with a studio on the sloping floor of the theater itself and a record shop in the concession stand on the street, the label Stax would soon become synonymous with soul.

So would the name of Solomon Burke, a prodigal black preacher and proven R&B singer from Philadelphia signed by Jerry Wexler late in 1960. Wexler initially assigned Burke a country-and-western song, following the current trend in popular music, and when that song proved something of a sleeper pop hit, he put Burke in the studio with producer Bert Berns (responsible for the Isley Brothers' momentous "Twist and Shout"). The pair emerged with "Cry to Me," a production dominated by the *baion* rhythm heard in almost every New York-based Atlantic session of the era, but containing just enough in Burke's vocal delivery for it to qualify as "soul," a word that was just starting to eke its way into black music terminology.

When "I Found a Love" landed on the desk of Ertegun and Wexler, therefore, it was both exactly what they were looking for—a regional hit, promotional groundwork accrued, potential popularity proven—and, in terms of its production standards, everything that Atlantic avoided. It was also painfully familiar, for it turned out they had already rejected it. The previous summer, seizing on the Falcons' availability when the group was dropped by United Artists, Atlantic had financed a session for "I Found a Love" and its B-side "Swim" at King Studios in Cincinnati, complete with the Ohio Untouchables. The label had even commissioned another pair of Falcons recordings, in October, and rejected those too.

No one likes admitting to such profound errors of judgment, which is why this particular faux pas was omitted from just about all Atlantic memoirs, interviews, overviews, and documentaries—until Ahmet Ertegun's confession when inducting Pickett into the Rock and Roll Hall of Fame in 1991.[13] In the spring of 1962, however, rather than reject the Falcons a third time, Atlantic sought to make amends by striking a deal with Bob West similar to that it had with Stax and snatching up the single's distribution rights, giving the label first look on upcoming Lu Pine releases, and assigning the Falcons' contract direct to Atlantic. The single was quickly reissued with the Atlantic logo.

Despite Atlantic's renowned distribution and promotional muscle, "I Found a Love" never fully conquered the pop charts: it was too earthy, too raw, too loud, too truly soulful for its period to make any kind of sense on white pop radio. But these exact qualities appealed to the core black audience, and "I Found A Love" spent a solid four months in the R&B Top 40, peaking at number six in the middle of the summer. Pickett finally had himself a hit single.

Yet patience was never his strong point. Watching the Falcons get dropped from United Artists and rejected by Atlantic, he had continued playing solo shows whenever possible.[14] Certainly Pickett thought poorly of Bob West, and he sought separate counsel in the form of Wilbert Golden, a numbers runner in the process of working his way up the hustlers' ladder in what seemed the most obviously lucrative fashion in Detroit at the time: by establishing an independent record label. Golden had been encouraged in his progress by Mickey Stevenson, a veteran of the city's independent record scene, who talked of full partnership with Golden before Berry Gordy made him his own head of A&R; in his place, Stevenson sent over Sonny Sanders and Robert Bateman. Both men had been in the Satintones, Motown's first vocal group, and Bateman had additionally cowritten and coproduced Tamla's first pop number one, the Marvelettes' "Please Mr. Postman." (Bateman fell afoul of Gordy by setting up his own publishing company.) Golden secured Bateman on a profligate $150-a-week salary and set himself up as Pickett's personal manager, arranging a couple of solo shows at the Parizian nightclub at the start of 1962, where Pickett was billed, interestingly, as a "rock 'n' roll singer." In March, Golden brought his team together at the 12th Street studio Stevenson had helped install, and, with various members of the future "Funk Brothers" providing instrumentation and Motown session singers the Adantes providing female backing vocals, they recorded Pickett's debut solo single.[15]

Pickett took sole writing credit on "My Heart Belongs to You," a lyrical ode to yearning and longing, with some inventive chord changes, belying the myth that Pickett needed partners to flesh out his songwriting ideas; he also recorded, and it was considered the more commercial side by his label, "Let Me Be Your Boy," written by its keyboard player Wilbert Harbert. Both recordings fell victim to Bateman and Sanders' ambitious pop instincts, lacking the necessary "nitty gritty," as Pickett frequently described his core soul, devoid of the gospel influence that had rendered "I Found a Love" so transcendent, *too* overtly populist to make sense even alongside Tamla/Motown releases, and yet not quite sophisticated enough to render these various sacrifices worthwhile and compete with the Ben E. Kings of this world. The inaugural single on Correc-tone was briefly picked up by a bigger label, Cub, but it failed to ignite.

In the meantime, "I Found a Love" continued its slow, steady rise, and the other Falcons had to follow it up without Pickett, cutting a single for Atlantic while on the road in New Orleans with the orchestra of Crescent City native Harold Battiste. The conventional accompaniment sounded flat after the wild example set by the Ohio Untouchables, and the results were rendered additionally tame by insipid material. While Floyd, Rice, and Joe Stubbs each embarked on their own solo releases under the official guidance of group manager Robert West at Lu Pine, it became evident that the Falcons were now dependent on Pickett, who was encouraged to return to the King studios in Cincinnati in October 1962 in an attempt to repeat the formula Atlantic had earlier rejected.

Pickett duly stamped his authority over two out-and-out rockers recorded that day. It is, in fact, difficult to decide where lies the stronger evidence of his talents. Is it in the scream that concludes "Let's Kiss and Make Up"? Or in the delightful gospel falsetto that introduces "Take This Love I've Got"? The former has a guitar solo from Ward that defies belief—especially for a label like Atlantic, which rarely allowed for such unscripted performances—but Pickett's delivery is more exuberant on the latter. Loosely based on "Shout," the Isley Brothers's major hit, "Take This Love I've Got" remains the best example of an untrammeled Pickett singing rock 'n' roll. That it failed to make a decent showing even on the R&B charts remains both a mystery and a travesty.

Ultimately the Falcons had too much talent to be contained within one group. Eddie Floyd recalled the end coming over a show that had been booked for the Howard Theatre in Washington, DC. "We all met in the car, we all drove to Wilson Pickett's house. And Pickett comes out, and he goes to the car in front of us, and he says, 'I'm going to do a record hop in Chicago.' That's where we broke up at: in the street! He's going on his own? Well I'm going on *my* own!"

Willie Schofield, having departed shortly before "I Found a Love" and returned somewhere in the interim, recalled the receipt of his draft papers as the final straw. "We had a meeting, and Pickett jumped up and said, 'I'm gonna tell you guys right now, if Schofield leave again, I'm not going to sing with you.' Mack jumped up and said, 'Well we may as well break up then— there goes the group.'"

"When I left the Falcons we all broke up," Pickett confirmed to Michael Lydon. "I thought it was that the guys had gotten so used to me being the lead singer, and the style had changed, that they just didn't want to continue. . . . And they was probably fed up with those six-dollar tires too!" Pickett added of the Falcons' demise that it "was a shame, 'cause they was well loved all over the country." Given their overall run of hits both in the pop and R&B charts, and the group's ongoing popularity in concert, Robert West refused to let their breakup get in the way of their good name. He took Detroit's the Fabulous Playboys, rechristened them the Falcons, and had them out on the concert circuit and in the studio before the audience was much the wiser.[16]

CHAPTER 5

In soul music, there was only a hair difference between the expressions "I need you, Jesus" and "I need you, baby."

Magnificent Montague, R&B/Soul radio broadcaster, *Burn, Baby! BURN!*

Dovie Hall was twenty-six years old the night she went to Phelps Lounge on Detroit's Oakland Avenue in early 1962, and her life changed. Following an early marriage, she was single again. Her young son was living with his father, and she was pulling down a good income working at a pharmacy. "The city was hopping," she said of Detroit at that time. "Everything was moving. Money was being made. There was a lot of entertainers coming out." Phelps featured some of the best of them, but that evening, as Hall tried to focus on the performer on stage, she could not help but notice instead "this handsome guy standing on the wall" who "watched me the whole night. Every time I looked he was looking at me."

This was a very different Wilson Pickett than the one who had joined the Falcons barely eighteen months earlier. No longer the country boy whose initial stiffness on stage had incited hazing by his bandmates, he was the main attraction in one of the city's most established vocal groups, with several solo shows around town to boot—including, on other occasions, at Phelp's. He might have had a wife and two infants at home, he might have had holes in his shoes and no winter coat, but none of that put Dovie Hall, a fine-looking woman who exuded poise and glamor, out of his league. So Pickett watched her that night, but he didn't make his move until someone else did. Only then did he walk over and, after ascertaining that Dovie was not with that man, did he introduce himself by name. Within minutes, Pickett asked if he could take her home.

"I don't know you!" she objected.

"I'm not a fella that's going to harm you," he replied. For the time being, this was true. Pickett had temporary possession of the Falcons' station wagon, and after he drove Hall to her apartment on Boston Boulevard, the two of them sat in the front seat and talked until dawn. At one point in the conversation Hall's age came up, and Pickett lied: "Hey, I'm twenty-six too." When Dovie told him of her marriage and child, Pickett admitted that he had a wife and children of his own. Still, he stressed of Bonnie, "We're not together, we're getting a divorce." It would be decades before Wilson and Bonnie would officially divorce, but his marriage was behind him. That was enough for Dovie. "I didn't question what he did before," she recalled. "It's what you're gonna do with *me*."

The couple connected in a way that neither had with anyone else. "He was a very good looking man, *very* handsome," recalled Hall. "And we had stuff that was in common. And he was very kind." She went to her room alone that night, but, "From that moment, we became close."

In April, Hall read a small item about Pickett in *Jet* magazine that announced his solo single—a considerable PR coup on behalf of Correctone. The item described Wilson Pickett as "a 21-year-old former leader of the Falcons."[1] "My Lord," Hall said to herself upon reading his real age, "I'm going with a baby." By then, it was too late. Wilson Pickett, as he had sung so convincingly before it happened, had found a love. And the feeling was mutual.

Wilson Pickett was determined not to let this moment in the spotlight pass him by. Even as he became entangled with Hall, he maintained an impeccable work ethic. "He would go to the studio every day, and he was truly into his music," Hall said. She accompanied him to the esteemed Graystone Ballroom for a show to promote his solo single, where "he really sung his heart out." Neither of them drank much and Pickett was far too immersed in singing and songwriting to take to a party lifestyle. That impressed her: "I saw he was a person that was going to make it, that this man has talent, and is going places."

Wilson permanently broke free of his wife and children. "They had a love for each other; they just couldn't *be* with each other," his daughter Veda said. She and her older brother Lynderrick were raised to understand their mother Bonnie's sacrifices—"My mother's whole attention was to dedicate her life on raising the kids and supporting my dad," said Veda—but not to criticize their father's absence. "They always spoke good of each other. It was never any bad feelings. She was always happy to hear of his success."

Pickett was living in a "little dinky hotel" when Hall met him, and rather than visit him regularly in such a place, she invited Wilson to stay at her apartment. She invested in his clothing, too. "He had one blue suit, it would go to the cleaners, come out the cleaners, and he wore it over and over. And that's when I went to [local department store] Hughes and Hatcher and bought him a leather coat. I went and bought him shoes. He went to Chicago with the Falcons, and I bought him a watch, and he was showing it to everybody. 'Just look! Just look!' I mean, I didn't have a lot of money, but I had a nice job and I was being paid good. And Wilson told me, 'When I get paid I'm going to be real good to you.'" Before they left Detroit he kept to his word, depositing a cash gift of $500 in her waist belt. Wilson Pickett knew a good thing when he found it.

Over at Correc-tone, Sonny Sanders and Robert Bateman recognized, in hindsight, that Pickett's strengths lay in his gospel roots rather than the pop arrangement of "Let Me Be Your Boy" and "My Heart Belongs to You." The task now was to strike a balance, and it came by reverting to the 6/8 ballad format that had worked for "I Found a Love." When Pickett came up with the core idea for a new song, "If You Need Me," his cowriters and producers fleshed it out.

Bateman drew his inspiration from Sam Cooke's first major hit, "You Send Me," with which "If You Need Me" had in common a simple and predictable melody.[2] Just as Cooke had ended each verse with a wandering "whoa-whoa," Bateman had Pickett stretch the last syllable of his first verse's concluding line, "I'll hurry home," across several different notes—not as a melisma, that ad-lib display of vocal dexterity that was second nature to gospel singers, but as a conscious part of the melody, a means to bring the chords back to the tonic, and an invitation for any and all listeners to sing and swing along.

Recorded with much the same team as Pickett's first Correc-Tone single, adding future Motown "Funk Brother" Eddie Willis on guitar, "If You Need Me" featured an additional calling card—a short, spoken "sermon" after the second verse, in place of the usual middle eight or instrumental section. Pickett addressed his congregation using colloquial grammar—"*Peoples have always said . . .*"—and as he elaborated, both his Alabama accent and his church shout came to the fore, affording the performance authenticity. With the Adantes cooing in the background and the (mostly) Motown rhythm section servicing the song modestly, "If You Need Me" occupied a middle ground between the gospel soul that was Pickett's natural forte and the Motown-style pop that came so easily to his cowriters and producers.

Everyone involved was convinced they had a hit, and equally certain they could not achieve it with Correc-tone, where Golden was burning through his bankroll without the sales to show for it. For "If You Need Me" to reach its potential, it would need promotion and distribution muscle. To that end, a copy was sent to Jerry Wexler. What followed was a classic case of music business hustle, featuring several characters who would become intrinsically involved in Pickett's career.

Jerry Wexler claimed to have received a set of demos of which only "If You Need Me" appealed to him. Unlikely: the song had been recorded with the best musicians Detroit had to offer, musicians who, at Tamla/Motown, were routinely wiping the floor with Atlantic. There was nothing remotely unfinished about the master. Nor was anything lacking in the up-tempo B-side, "Baby Call on Me," penned by Don Juan Mancha. Besides, Wexler recalled that Bert Berns, upon hearing "If You Need Me," "wanted to release Pickett's version," and Berns's production standards were notoriously high. Still, Wexler was equally accurate in observing of Atlantic, "Unlike a lot of other labels, our primary policy was to build the artists already in house." [3] That meant Solomon Burke, for whom Atlantic was actively seeking material, and for whom "If You Need Me" seemed a perfect fit.

Wexler quickly purchased the publishing rights from Golden, assigning the song to Atlantic's Cotillion Music and booking a studio session in March 1963. Despite his admiration of Pickett's original, Bert Berns's production with Solomon Burke confirmed the gulf between Atlantic's mainstream standards and those of the regional independents. Burke's smooth voice sailed effortlessly around the melody where Pickett's had purposefully strained at it, and the spoken sermon was cleaned up, with Burke speaking in "correct" English and evincing no trace of regional roots. A jazzy guitar lick traded off with his voice throughout; the backing vocals were much more pronounced. All of these effects made for a more commercial rendition, which was always at the heart of Atlantic's approach.

The publishing deal Wexler had struck with Golden was in the range of $1,500—enough for Pickett, Bateman, and Sanders to bank a respectable $500 each. The rights, however, were not Golden's to sell, and Bateman, who knew about this stuff from writing "Please Mr. Postman," was not thrilled—especially since he was in Chicago when he heard about it, pushing Correc-tone's recordings and the Pickett single to Vee-Jay Records. As Bateman subsequently noted, he "could have nixed" the Cotillion deal.[4] But there remained, for him, the intriguing prospect of subsequent writers' royalties should Solomon Burke score a hit—and the convenient fact that Correc-tone still owned the Pickett master. Although Vee-Jay bailed on putting out "If You Need Me" as soon as it heard that it would be up against Solomon Burke and Atlantic, Bateman promptly departed for New York, with Pickett's "If You Need Me" in hand. "I went to all the majors first,"

Bateman recalled. "Then I went to the small labels, but nobody wanted to fight with Atlantic."[5] Well, almost nobody.

Born in 1933, raised in the unapologetically racist and segregationist environs of Jim Crow Louisiana, Lloyd Price came on the scene in 1952 with "Lawdy Miss Clawdy," a song he had written at home to learn his way about a broken piano. As recorded by Art Rupe at Specialty Records, "Lawdy Miss Clawdy" featured Fats Domino on piano and Price singing, a combination strong enough to make the song a chart-topper, turning Price, in his own words, into "America's first black teen idol" during a period when black records tended to be sold only in black record stores, when concerts in the South were de facto segregated, and when the riches from any such success rarely trickled down to the performers.

By the time Elvis Presley covered "Lawdy Miss Clawdy" on his first album Price was in Korea, having been drafted just when he hoped to capitalize on his crossover popularity. Upon his return, he took a bold step for a black musician by establishing his own label, Kent Recording Company (KRC), but after a dispute with Rupe that he thought could ruin his small label, he took sanctuary at ABC-Paramount. There he was transformed into "Mr. Personality," from the title of one of his top three singles in 1959. The major hits dried up barely a year later, but by then Price had gone into partnership with promoter Harold Logan, another former numbers runner.

Price said, "When I first came out of Louisiana [Logan] was the first guy I met that I had a lot of respect for, because of the way that he handled himself. In 1959, when I had eleven records in a row, it was just completely crazy, I needed some help—and he gave up his business and came to New York, and was running the office for me. And handled all my booking. Logan was like my shadow. But he was a no-nonsense guy."

ABC-Paramount saw Logan as a "gangster bastard," and according to Price, offered the singer an additional half million dollars on his next contract if he dropped his partner.[6] Price walked. He and Logan instead established Double L Records (named for Lloyd and Logan) as an independent label and began actively looking for artists. Robert Bateman showed up with Pickett's new recording at the perfect moment.

Price, it turned out, was familiar with Pickett already, having seen the singer open for "Honky Tonk" Hammond organ maestro Bill Doggett in Flint, Michigan. "I was impressed," recalled Price. "I had never heard an artist sound like Wilson Pickett. Ray Charles was not using as much of that Jesus soul stuff as he was. He was right there on top of that gospel." When he heard Pickett's "If You Need Me," he was further impressed: "Whoa, this is a monster," he recalled saying to himself. He and Bateman, who didn't mention that the song had already been sold to Atlantic, agreed on terms, and went straight to Bell Sound, where they cut several acetates, one of which they hand-delivered to WWRL disc jockey Nathaniel "Magnificent" Montague.

Montague went back even further than Price. Born in New Jersey in 1928, he was only two generations out of slavery. His parents had migrated from North Carolina, during a time that the KKK would still march through his hometown of Elizabeth. He became a prominent proponent of black history and culture himself later in life, amassing the largest known private collection of African American artifacts with the profits from his high pro-file in radio. While stationed in the United Kingdom during World War II, he observed at the military bases that "wherever you could hear Negro jazz and blues was where you found a handful of hip whites."[7] He reached out to the next generation of these hip whites when he took his self-confessed instinct for hustle onto the airwaves—in Texas, the wrong place, perhaps, for an outspoken advocate of his people. But it was the right time—1954, the year black R&B crossed over. Montague soon gravitated from Galveston to Houston, and then to Texas City, from where his broadcasts reached into the Louisiana home of a white girl with whom he fell in love, sight unseen, when she repeatedly called in to his show. After conducting a rather public, on-air courtship, he and Rose met, eloped, and married.

Montague bounced around radio markets, establishing his reputa-tion as a consummate radio personality and an inveterate expert on R&B, until he came to WWLR in 1962. He introduced himself to the New York masses with a "Down Home Soul Show & Dance" in Harlem, with a lineup that just about defined this new subgenre of R&B. He had Gene Chandler, Dionne Warwick, Little Esther, and the Shirelles; he featured Sam & Dave, a Memphis act signed at the time to Morris Levy's Roulette label; and he included a handful of proven Atlantic stars, among them Ben E. King and the Orioles, indicating the cozy relationship he had already formed with Jerry Wexler and company at New York's preeminent independent. That relationship helped bring him most of the Stax roster, too, includ-ing Booker T. & the M.G.s, the Memphis label's new studio band whose instrumental "Green Onions" was topping just about every chart, and Otis Redding, then just hitting with his powerful debut ballad "These Arms of Mine" and so new to the scene that his name was misspelled on the poster. Getting "If You Need Me" into Montague's hands was clearly important for Double L, given his proven attributes and those of the record in question— and the disc jockey reacted with an instinctive enthusiasm for a record he immediately recognized as special.

"You could hear Pickett," he wrote years later, "and know that he had the kind of voice that brought out in listeners what a great preacher brings out in his congregation—he brought alive the amen corner, those people you see who are high on spirit, alive with emotion, joyously dancing, taking the service to a higher level, responding to the preacher as he speaks . . . Wilson Pickett had that skill that separated an average preacher from a superstar preacher."[8] The night he debuted "If You Need Me" on air, Montague repeatedly backed the record up to its opening, title line, calling on his listeners to phone in and share the love. "This is what it felt like for a record to *burn*," he wrote, "and somewhere during my tenure in New York I started to shout it when I got moved: 'Burn, baby! Burn!'"[9]

The phones lit up. Before his show was over people were at the radio station, asking where they could get a copy. As Price rushed the master to the pressing plant, Jerry Wexler received a call at his home in Great Neck, Long Island. It was his secretary, with Montague on the other end, looking to tip Wexler off to this song called "If You Need Me" that was a "stone smash" if he cared to buy it up from Lloyd Price.[10] Distraught at the news, cursing himself for not securing the Pickett master recording along with the song's publishing, Wexler realized he had been beaten to market.

Wexler invited Price and Logan to Atlantic to try to reach a deal. Price claimed that Wexler offered Double L a substantial three percent royalty to drop Pickett's version; Wexler said that Double L offered to sell him Pickett's master if he canned Burke's recording. It was all just posturing: Double L had already secured distribution with Al Bennett at Liberty Records, which Price had used to lure Bateman down to New York from the overextended Correc-tone in Detroit; Wexler, likewise, had invested too much in Solomon Burke's recording to let it slide.

Wilson Pickett remained back in Detroit, confused by the whole process. He had every reason to be thrilled that Solomon Burke might cover his song, and to be heartbroken if he had to abandon his own single's release. But once his record was assigned to Double L—and knowing that the Magnificent Montague had broken "If You Need Me" across urban New York in a single night—he was ecstatic. He made a career-defining decision. He bought an old green Cadillac with all his savings, and one year into their relationship, he and Dovie hitched their fortunes to "If You Need Me" and drove toward New York City.

CHAPTER 6

Mr. Wexler can promote a rat. But he'd rather, much rather, promote soul music, rhythm and blues, black music. I think that's where the man's heart really is.

Wilson Pickett[1]

Wilson Pickett and Dovie Hall checked into the President Hotel on 42nd Street, in the heart of Times Square, but there was little time for them to settle in. "The game was on," said Jerry Wexler of the battle with Double L over "If You Need Me," and the Atlantic Records VP threw himself into his record's promotion.[2]

Pickett and Burke were both put on the road to endorse their own version of "If You Need Me" over its rival. Burke, however, with the grace that came to define him, refused to play by the script. The two had struck up a friendship on a tour bus during the Falcons days, when Burke was new to Atlantic, and he had told Pickett, "I'm gonna do everything that I can to see that you get a record and get a record deal, because you're a star by yourself." He was about to do the next best thing.

On radio station interviews, Burke would tell the disc jockey, "You need to hear the Wilson Pickett record, which is even better." On a different station, Pickett would be saying, "You need to hear the Solomon Burke record 'cause I wrote it for him." As Pickett recalled, "We ended up being on shows together singing the damn song," and having a blast in the process.

Burke had his own label's marketing muscle: "If [Atlantic] said to a disc jockey, 'This is a hit,' the disc jockey believed it and he put it on.'" But Pickett had an ace up his sleeve: "I got Magnificent Montague saying 'Burn, baby! burn!,' playing the shit out of my record every two minutes on the radio."[3]

Burke came away with the higher chart placing (#2 on R&B, #37 for pop): Atlantic's long-standing cozy relationships with the nation's most influential disc jockeys, along with its ability to prioritize a single 45 over anything else on its schedule, distinguished it from Double L, which was still settling into its partnership with parent company Liberty. Pickett was happy with his own chart placing, though (#30 on R&B, #64 on pop). He had his first solo hit, a semimajor record deal, a growing friendship with Burke, and a new life in New York City.

In the music business, the best way to follow up a near-hit single is to repeat it. Pickett was brought into the esteemed Bell Sound Studios on Manhattan's 54th Street in the summer of 1963, where a significant number of the era's hits were cut, with Robert Bateman again in the production chair and the city's top session musicians, string players, and backing singers on call.[4] All the parts that made "If You Need Me" a success were repeated. Another ballad in 6/8? Check. Chugging guitar and supportive piano and choral female backing? Check. Spoken sermon? Check. Pickett extended his monologue to a full minute this time, to the point that it became the song's primary calling card, earning him the sole composing credit in the process—the only A-side of his entire career for which this would be the case. "I guess most of you are wondering why I always sing a sad song," he began his minisermon, which was disingenuous, not only because he didn't always sing sad songs but also because most listeners wouldn't have been thinking about him in the first place. Now that he mentioned it, however, they might be left wondering what they had missed, in which case the subsequent reference to himself as "Pickett" ensured that they would at least know his name.

Pickett further extemporized with impeccable timing and perfect enunciation, his cadence rising and falling, moving almost imperceptibly from shout to song and back again, finding that sweet spot in between the pulpit and the concert stage, and at one point letting out an ironic laugh at the cruel realities of love. Comfortable in the knowledge that he had delivered, he ended the song with the same ecstatic screams he had introduced in "I Found a Love."

"It's Too Late" was not a greater song than "If You Need Me." But thanks to its predecessor, and with no rival version to edge it off the radio, "It's Too Late" became a late summer sensation, comfortably lodging inside the R&B top 10 and breaking into the pop top 50. Pickett had the solo hit had always dreamed of, and he was still only twenty-two years old.

Wilson and Dovie found a two-room apartment in Hollis, Queens, on the fringes of St. Albans, where many great black entertainers had bought houses. But any attempt at serious homemaking had to wait. The lucrative holiday season was coming, when long-play records were often impulsively purchased. Double L had four proven sides in the can already; just a couple more three-hour recording sessions and they would have a complete album.

The process proved rushed. Bateman's productions, while fully capable and professional, would come to sound dated once the sound of soul music solidified in the coming months and years. And Pickett contributed just one more composition of his own, a slow rocker called "Peace Breaker" on which he roared his heart out. Three other tracks originated from Detroit songwriters, including the up-tempo "I Can't Stop," chosen from among a set of songs entrusted to Pickett by Willie Schofield when he left for the Army; and "Give All Your Lovin' Right Now," by Jackie Wilson songsmith William Weatherspoon, probably the strongest track, with its energetic guitar work and a full-throttled Pickett performance.

But it was a song composed by New Yorkers Dee Irwin and James Willingham, formerly of vocal group the Pastels, that was selected as the next single. "I'm Down to My Last Heartbreak" had fire in its belly, for sure: a ballad in 4/4 time, it allowed Pickett to play off around the lead guitar lines. But that was not enough to distinguish it from the sermons, shouts, and screams of its predecessors, and it had little success as a 45. Any disappointment was tempered by the fact that Pickett's profile was still very much on the rise by the end of 1963, when the LP *It's Too Late* made it to shops.

The cover to his debut album did not include his picture. This was standard practice for black acts new to the pop market—Solomon Burke's LP *If You Need Me* also came without a picture. Two industry assumptions guided this practice. One was that black audiences did not buy LPs in quantity, meaning that labels had to market them to a white pop audience to secure a return on investment. The other was not so much that white pop fans wouldn't buy LPs by black artists, though there was undoubtedly some of that at play, but that white record stores, especially in the South, wouldn't display pictures of black artists in the pop racks. All this reflected the bigger battles over race taking place—many of them, in the year of *It's Too Late*'s release, in Pickett's native Alabama. At the start of the year Governor Wallace had declared "segregation now . . . segregation tomorrow . . . segregation forever" and refused a federal court's ruling to integrate the University of Alabama, leading to President Kennedy's federalization of the Alabama National Guard to enforce the admission of three black students. In Birmingham, nonviolent students campaigning for desegregation were confronted by water hoses and snarling dogs; Martin Luther King Jr. was jailed; and the Ku Klux Klan bombed several churches, killing four young black girls at the city's 16th Street Baptist Church.

A response of sorts came in the Alabamian black migrants' adopted city of Detroit, where the Reverend C. L. Franklin co-organized a Walk to Freedom in June not only to show moral support, but also to raise funds for bail and court cases. The walk attracted some 125,000 people, prominent white civic and union leaders among them. The largest civil rights gathering in US history, it paved the way for (and was quickly overshadowed by) that August's March for Jobs and Freedom in Washington, DC—where King, having delivered a draft in Detroit, gave his "I Have a Dream" speech that was broadcast around the world.

Against such a charged backdrop, soul singers' endless opines to love and heartbreak could have been considered distracting or irrelevant. But their audiences did not see it that way. "When you listen to R&B from 1962 and 1963, it's impossible to separate it from the power of the Civil Rights movement, the awakening of the Negro race, and the gospel influences that were driving everything," wrote Magnificent Montague. "A grand force swept over us, and we called it s-o-u-l music."[5] That term "soul" hadn't yet reached the white mainstream, but it was all over the R&B market, from Montague's "Down Home Soul" concert to Pickett's concert billing: he reopened Harlem's Baby Grand nightclub in the summer of 1963 with the tag "Mr. Soul." Montague was right: this soul music contained a confidence that was more powerful than the popular black music of the previous few years, and song titles were often perceived as metaphors for the larger struggle. Attempts to address subject matter outside of an audience's romantic expectations, however, were considered unnecessary and even unwelcome, both by outside forces and an audience comfortable with convention: when Sam Cooke recorded his ultimately classic civil rights composition "A Change is Gonna Come" at the start of 1964, he was so "scared" of its power that he postponed the song's release in favored of what he saw as more commercial material, and the public only got to hear it posthumously, a year later, after he had been shot dead in a tawdry Los Angeles motel.[6]

In late 1963 Wilson Pickett joined a package tour headlined by two of the year's biggest R&B stars, Little Johnny Taylor and Garnett Mimms & the Enchanters, and additionally featuring hardy Memphis hitmaker Rufus Thomas. Taylor was only twenty years old and had imbued his enormous hit "Part Time Love" with the same gospel sweetness that Mimms, a full decade older, brought to his "Cry Baby," a soaring ballad cowritten and produced by Bert Berns. The two songs chased each other around the R&B number one spot as the tour set off, each becoming enormous pop crossover hits in the process. Still, a wide chasm separated the essentially black

R&B market and the mostly white pop audience, and consequently the tour eschewed the larger northeastern venues for the chitlin' circuit down south, where name recognition and audience reaction could be guaranteed. There was the equal certainty of segregation, as the bands weren't allowed in the white hotels and often had to stay with black households instead.

Pickett followed the tour with his own grueling schedule of predominantly black clubs. As he traveled from Long Island to Manhattan, New Jersey to Connecticut, and all the way upstate to the migrant cities of Rochester and Buffalo, he recognized that he could no longer rely on a different house band every night to do his songs justice. A demanding perfectionist who was also short on cash, Pickett called on the inexperienced and inexpensive Eddie Jacobs, a bass player with whom he had hit it off on the package tour. Jacobs was barely out of his teens.

"I was young, and anxious to go on the road, so I took it," Jacobs recalled, "but that was a very odd situation for a singer to have a bass player as his bandleader. I knew within the first month or two that we really needed a guitar player." Eventually Pickett relented and Jacobs brought in Jimmy Owens, who, less to avoid confusion with the jazz musician of the same name and more because he looked like a certain heavyweight boxer, was soon given the nickname Liston. Between them, Jacobs and Liston could lead and direct a club's house musicians, giving Pickett the makings of a proper live show.

He also had the makings of a reputation. "This cat could not stay out of trouble," said Lloyd Price, constantly engaged in damage control. "Everywhere I sent Wilson, I got the same phone call: 'This guy is nuts.'" Professionally, Price and Pickett had helped each other get their new ventures going. But, Price said, "he and I just didn't kick it. He had the wrong attitude about life. Wonderful artist, very talented, but he was his worst enemy . . . He was an egomaniac, and I don't know how you handle that."

They butted heads particularly hard when Pickett was offered payment from Price in the currency popular with many black artists—a car. Don Juan Mancha (who came to New York with Bateman and Pickett as part of the Double L enterprise) suggested that the car was an incentive for Pickett to sign a management deal with Price. And Wilson Pickett may have taken it—had he approved of Price's choice. Said Price, "I went to Detroit myself and picked out a beautiful blue and white 225 Buick [Electra], drove it back from Detroit to New York and met him one afternoon out in Central Park. And he said, 'I don't want that—I want a Cadillac like you got!'" Price took the car back, feeling unappreciated.[7]

Stuck with his green Cadillac, Pickett decided that he would at least be seen with a driver, and hired his brother James. James had, of his own

admission, developed a drinking problem, exacerbating the longstanding tensions between the brothers. In early 1964 they were heading down
Brooklyn's Atlantic Avenue, with James driving, Wilson and Dovie together
up front, and Jacobs, Owens, and James's girlfriend in the back. Wilson
was in a fierce mood, of the kind that was showing more and more now that
he had become a headlining R&B star.

"Dovie looked back," said Jacobs. "And I don't know whether she was
looking at me or at Liston but suddenly I saw a side of [Wilson] I never saw
before."

"What the fuck are you looking at?" the singer snarled at his girlfriend.
"Keep your head straight, there's nothing back there for you to look at."
James came to her defense. Wilson argued with James in turn: Who was
the star? Who was paying everybody? Whose car was this? James tried to
pull the rank of big brother. Wilson went into his briefcase for his pistol
and, said Dovie, grabbed James around the neck with one hand, keeping
the gun in the other, insisting James pull over.

"Get the fuck out of my car," commanded Wilson.

Though he wasn't talking to them, the three passengers in the back
immediately jumped out. James calmly got out of the front seat, and took
their place in the back seat. "Drive your own car," he said. "I'm not going
anywhere."

Wilson pointed the gun at his brother.

The ex-Marine just sat there, cool as ice. "Hey man, you got the fucking
gun. Shoot."

Wilson shot.

The bullets missed. On purpose. "I didn't shoot to hurt him," he told
his de facto stepmother, Helen, once word got back to Detroit. "I shot to
scare him."

It was a thin line that required a sure hand. Yet the truth is that for all
the violence Wilson Pickett would inflict on people, for all the times he
waved his gun around, and for the occasions where he fired his gun, he
never actually put a bullet in anyone. For the time being, though, gunfire
on a prominent street was guaranteed to bring the cops. Jacobs and Liston
grabbed their possessions and walked to the former's home on Cumberland
Place. When the police came, they confiscated the car and locked Pickett up
overnight. But, said Dovie, "James, being his brother, didn't press charges.
We went to court the next day and he dropped it."

This incident, for Wilson, was a victory, and it gave him further confidence to play tough. The way he saw it, he had "brought" Double L three hit
singles and an LP.[8] A personal manager might have informed him how long
it took a record company to get paid by its parent label, that royalties were

distributed twice a year, and that a hit record would not generate royalty income for at least a year. But Pickett had walked away from Golden's representation, and if Price was now acting as his manager, that was clearly a conflict of interest. Pickett went to his label's offices in the Music Building and called in his debt.

"They told me, 'The company don't pay royalties,'" he recalled to Michael Lydon. "I said, 'What kind of company don't pay no royalties, man? You crazy.' So I said 'Well I'm not recording any more, I'm leaving,' and they threatened me real good. But I was a kid then, I didn't know what a threat was. Didn't know nothing 'bout no gangsters."[9] He was presumably referring to Logan, who'd had Price's back when it had been Price's turn to ask for his money. "Logan was no joke," confirmed Price. "Logan would have hurt him—and that's really not necessary. Because Wilson's an artist— and if we can't deal with him, we will go to the next page." In other words, Double L had less demanding singers on its books than Pickett, with whom they could prioritize instead.

In years to come Pickett would frequently assert that he never "got one dime" from Double L, adding them to a long list against whom he would claim malfeasance and yet with whom he would continue working.[10] In the early 1980s Pickett and Price sat for a lengthy television interview with Dick Boggs, and the two appeared to enjoy a perfectly cordial relationship—even as Pickett said that Price had never paid him. "He told that lie right in front of me, on TV," said Price. "I didn't follow through with it; I figured, 'I know Wilson, I know his rep, I know how he is.' I brought him to New York, so I didn't let that get to me. But Wilson did not tell the truth, and he knew it."

There may be no simple "truth." As Pickett became more successful, the "lost" debut album It's Too Late showed up on any number of temporary independents, making it almost impossible to follow the trail of money. Double L folded in 1966, Liberty was sold, and eventually the catalog - and Pickett - found their way to Atlantic Records.

The way that Wilson Pickett later told the story, it was upon leaving Double L's offices after the royalties showdown that he first met Jimmy Evans, who would soon become his manager. "I met him on the elevator. He told me to come by his office; he could see I had a problem, and he had heard about me and knew who I was."[11] Evans was a well-known agent ensconced in the Music Building, and already booking shows for Pickett and other Double L artists; the only real surprise was that they had apparently yet to meet.

Evans was Italian. Like many of his fellow countrymen, and like Jewish, Greek, and other immigrants too, he had changed his name partly to avoid negative racial and national associations. In his case, it only worked so well.

"Jimmy Evans was 1,000 percent about the business," said Maxwell Pickett. "He didn't want Wilson doing nothing unless he got paid. And it didn't hurt either, that he was Italian and tied in with the mob. The mafia, they do no-nonsense management. When something needs taking care of, they just take care of it."

Evans would remain Pickett's manager for the rest of his life, appearing to enjoy a productive and trusting relationship with his client throughout. As late as 1977, when the singer's career was in the doldrums, Pickett still referred to Evans as "a great man," and Dovie Hall concurred: "Jimmy Evans was a good manager," she said. "He would argue and get Wilson Pickett where he needed to be. He was a good man."

Other than to inform Lloyd and Logan that Pickett was no longer their client—a decision they appeared to accept readily—Evans's first act as Pickett's manager was to secure a meeting with Jerry Wexler. Wexler was more than happy to take it.[12] Having twice turned down the opportunity to sign Pickett, giving up a hit record on each occasion, Wexler was not about to let the singer get away a third time. Besides, he was a committed fan and would remain so almost until the end of their relationship. "Pickett is, to me, the greatest Rhythm & Blues singer of today," he insisted, as late as 1971.[13] For now, Wexler had only one question. He wanted to know if the singer was still sore about the situation over "If You Need Me." "Fuck that," he recalled Pickett responding. "I need the bread." And that was it. Wilson Pickett was an Atlantic artist, at last.

Signing with Evans and Wexler proved to be smart commercial decisions, not unrelated to the color of their skin. Pickett's musical world had existed until now within a self-enclosed black community, from the gospel churches of his Alabama childhood through to his touring and recording experiences with the Violinaires, the Falcons, and what would become known as the "Funk Brothers" in Detroit. And his management, producers, and label heads had all been black: Joe Von Battle, Robert West, Wilbert Golden, Robert Bateman, Lloyd Price, and Harold Logan. Yet Pickett had remained somewhat marginalized, an R&B star outside of the pop charts. To cross over musically he needed to cross the color line professionally, working directly with white people every day—a stark contradiction to his vows in the cotton fields of Prattville. For Pickett, as for many black Americans at the time, the long-term promise of integration involved short-term sacrifice in self-determination.

Pickett would have no problems returning to the South to work with white musicians, whom he saw as kindred spirits. But his association with Wexler brought out another brand of prejudice. In his estimation, every white person of power in the music business was, like Wexler, a Jew—and therefore both shrewd and greedy in matters of finance. This centuries-old stereotype overshadowed for Pickett (and for many others) the fact that progressive American Jews had a history of being the most prominent champions of black American music outside of the black community itself. Pickett exposed his bias almost naively when he said, "How could this Jew man, you know, that coulda been somewhere eating bagels and saying the rosary. . . . How could he understand what's inside of black people? And Jerry Wexler did."[14] It was probably intended as a compliment.

Almost immediately upon signing Wilson Pickett, Wexler brought the singer into the Atlantic offices on 61st Street and Broadway to introduce him to a prospective songwriting partner, Don Covay.

"Hey, motherfucker, how are you doing?" said Pickett by way of greeting, and with that, a lifelong friendship was born, one that would engender a number of superb shared compositions as well as a fair share of wild times, as exemplified by their party slogan: "Give me some juice, turn me loose, let me hang out like a wild mad goose."[15]

Covay had three years' age on Pickett, and an accordingly longer resumé. Born in South Carolina, the son of a Baptist preacher, he migrated to Washington, DC, where his teenage gospel group gave way to a secular vocal group, the Rainbows, whose membership included at various points Marvin Gaye and Billy Stewart. Covay became Little Richard's chauffeur, opening act, and protégé, recording under the nickname Little Richard had given him: Pretty Boy. After Chubby Checker took his song "Pony Time" on top of the charts in 1961, Covay moved to New York, settling in at the Brill Building, from where he was soon delivering hits for, among others, Solomon Burke at Atlantic. He simultaneously persisted with his group the Goodtimers, adding a young guitarist by the name of Jimi Hendrix, and was officially signed to Atlantic as a staff songwriter and the marquee act for Magnificent Montague's boutique label Rosemart (named for Montague's wife and son), housed within Atlantic's offices as insurance against a future "If You Need Me" type of battle.

Pickett and Covay wasted no time getting down to work. In May 1964, for Pickett's Atlantic debut, they took their cocomposition "I'm Gonna Cry (Cry Baby)" into the studio, alongside a fiercely soulful composition from Don Juan Mancha, "For Better or Worse." The results represented a shift from Pickett's Double L recordings. "I'm Gonna Cry" was jazzed up with a prominent brass section, and the female singers dominated the recording. "For Better or Worse" found Pickett in more commanding form, the addition of what sounded like a Hammond organ over the brass section establishing a blueprint for future recordings.

A week later it was Covay's turn in the studio, and he leaned toward the twelve-bar blues on his cocomposition, with Harold Ott, for the Goodtimers "Mercy, Mercy," the first occasion that Jimi Hendrix was heard on vinyl. When Atlantic released Pickett and Covay's singles simultaneously but on different imprints, "Mercy, Mercy" exploded on radio and was soon topping the R&B charts. "I'm Gonna Cry," by comparison, performed miserably.[16]

It would be six whole months before Pickett made another record, by which point Wexler had decided to double down on the singer's crossover potential by bringing Pickett, alongside new signing Tami Lynn, to producer Bert Berns, who had worked wonders for the Isley Brothers, Solomon Burke, and Garnett Mimms.

Pickett was assigned material by white writers: "Come Home Baby" by Barry Mann and Cynthia Weil. It was meant to be an honor, given that Mann and Weil's partnership had already resulted in such classics as "On Broadway," "Only in America," "Uptown," and "You've Lost That Lovin' Feeling." But Mann and Weill's talents were as wasted on Pickett as his voice was on their composition. The singer had to dig deep into his range just to find his opening notes, only to sound more like crossover master Ben E. King than the powerful preacher of "If You Need Me" and "It's Too Late." As the orchestra of the great Teacho Wiltshire—with Cornell Dupree on guitar and Jimmy Lewis on bass—danced nervously around him, Pickett sought fruitlessly for a groove; by the time a ceremonial trombone-to-trumpet solo took over, Pickett had all but left the building.

If anyone enjoyed the experience that day, it was Tami Lynn. "I was crazy about 'Come Home Baby,'" she recalled, "'cause it just allowed me freedom to sing it in a way that I wanted to sing it." She stole Pickett's thunder, rising from the initial moans that she interjected into his verses to pronounce the chorus in a more-than-passable imitation of Ronnie Spector on the similarly titled "Be My Baby." In the other duet recorded that day, "Teardrops Will Fall," Lynn bossed Pickett all over the song. For those who had not heard the original version, it could have passed for R&B, which was testament to their delivery; it was atually a cover of an appallingly saccharine five-year-old doo-wop hit by an all-white group named Dickie Doo and the Don'ts.

Lynn's vocal confidence notwithstanding, she was in awe of Pickett, a man of such energy that he had already earned the nickname "Kick It Pickett" around Atlantic. "Pickett was something else," she said. "Pickett would get to singing and by that time he didn't give a shit who was looking and didn't care who didn't give a shit." For his part, he compared Lynn to Aretha Franklin, laboring at the time under even more misguided A&R direction at the Columbia label than he was at Atlantic.[17]

"Come Home Baby" was released at the start of 1965, just as "You've Lost That Lovin' Feeling" soared to the top of the charts. Spector had taken several months to complete his Mann-Weil epic, whereas Berns cut "Come Home Baby" in three union-clocked hours. "Come Home Baby" proved an elaborately expensive and perhaps mercifully unheralded failure. Under the circumstances, Pickett's subsequent assessment of Berns, that "he produced one of the weirdest sessions on me I ever heard in my life" and that the single "didn't sell two records," seems entirely appropriate.

CHAPTER 7

To have Wilson Pickett in the studio with you was magic; he brings something with him that is indefinable. He opens his mouth and the indefinable becomes Wilson.

Wayne Jackson, trumpet player, Mar-Keys/Memphis Horns/Stax

Pickett's recording career may have been floundering; his live reputation was not. A couple of songs on *Saturday Night at the Uptown*, one of two live revue LPs that Atlantic released at the end of 1964 in imitation of the successful Motown packages, confirmed not just his vocal gymnastics, but his appeal to the young ladies in the audience—judging by the screaming that accompanied him on the record. And his performance at the Apollo Theater in New York in March 1965, billed beneath the Marvelettes, Kim Weston, and the Ad-Libs, must have impressed the venue's notoriously demanding manager Frank Schiffman. At the beginning of May, a Freedom Week revue, whose proceeds went to various civil rights organizations, had a hitch after its star performer Clyde McPhatter's sister died right before opening night; Pickett was hired as a replacement.[1]

Joining Pickett on the bill was his old Falcons buddy Mack Rice, who had prefixed his name with an honorary knighthood and was now busy promoting his first solo single since leaving Bob West and Lu Pine. "Mustang Sally" was a straightforward blues-based song, composed by Rice, about a guy who lost his girl to the new Ford he now regrets buying for her, impressively produced at Detroit's United Sound by former Fortune mainstay Andre Williams, and it was faring well on the R&B charts. Without national distribution and a stronger singer, however, it wouldn't go any further.[2]

Pickett and Rice had an unexpected visit during this residency from Willie Schofield, who had landed in New York at the end of his stint in the service. Schofield figured on the Apollo as one of the few places he knew he would feel at home. He was greeted, appropriately, like a returning war hero—Pickett, he said, "almost broke his neck getting down (the stairs), picked me up, kissed me."

After the Apollo closed that night they went to a Harlem club, where Pickett implored Schofield to work for him as road manager. "I'll make us rich," he insisted. Schofield figured the offer was partly because "he wanted someone to run interference for him 'cos he's always going to instigate some stuff." Sure enough, when a hanger-on came by to cadge a drink, Pickett confronted him, making the visitor pay for the singer's entire entourage. Schofield turned Pickett down. After returning to Detroit, he landed a job at Ford. "That road thing," he said, "had wore off on me."

There was another surprise visitor during those Apollo engagements: Pickett's baby by a white woman. The child, Michael, was born in early December 1964, and the mother's parents made it clear that they wanted nothing to do with a mixed-race child. She brought Michael to the Apollo and handed him off to his father.

Wilson called Dovie at home, sounding uncommonly sheepish. "He said, 'I have a baby out here,'" she recalled. "He said, 'The mama has bought the baby and left the baby at the Apollo. Would you please help me with this baby?' I said, 'Yes. I love you. Bring him on here.'" When Dovie saw the child, she saw he had been terribly neglected. "He was so hungry and starving, I cried," she recalled. "I really cried. He was *so* hungry. He ate and ate and ate."

Michael's arrival confirmed what Dovie had always suspected, that a man who plied his sensuality for a living could not help but take free advantage of its effects, and that he was not prejudiced in doing so. "You kinda know this is gonna happen," she said of the infidelity, "'Cause women are pulling after him. It bothered me, but I loved him, so I stayed with him." As with other wives and partners of the era's R&B and pop stars, Dovie took a philosophical attitude toward their relationship. "I don't worry about what's going on on the road, 'cos I know he's a man, he's going to do those things, okay? I worry about when you come home. Don't bring me any disease home, cos that I *don't* want. Whatever you doing out there, I'm not trying to find out. But I know you are doing *something*." Dovie went on to raise Michael as her own child, and Michael regarded Dovie as his birth mother. The fact that Dovie was herself light-skinned provided cover, and it would be many years before even their closest friends would know the truth.

Wilson, however, had problems with the boy. He and Dovie had talked about children early in their relationship and agreed that the three they already had between them were enough. Wilson therefore looked upon Michael as the child he didn't ask for, the child he didn't need—especially at this critical stage of his career. In Michael, he saw his own infidelities and weaknesses reflected, and he didn't like it.

Down in Memphis, in the converted cinema on E. McLemore that Stax called home, soul music was thriving. Not everything that came out of the studio there was a hit, but all of it carried a distinct groove, the mark of a house band whose players knew each other well enough that they didn't need written arrangements. They could show up in the morning with new musical ideas for their own acts (the Mar-Keys, Booker T. & the M.G.s) or ready to work on the songs of the in-house writers and contracted singers. With just a little practice and improvisation, they'd be ready to roll the tape.

This process was working wonders for Otis Redding, who scored with a trio of tightly wound, wonderfully emotive pleas—"Security," "Chained and Bound," and "Mr. Pitiful"—in 1964. For Pickett though, awareness of Otis went all the way back to the song "Pain in My Heart," which he had first heard in late 1963, while out on that package tour, on Nashville station WLAC, via black-sounding white disc jockey John "R" Richbourg. Pickett had fallen instantly in love with the timbre and tone of Redding's delivery and the sound of the Memphis musicians around him. He recalled, "I was like, 'Shit! I want to go down there and record.'"[3] After the debacle with Bert Berns, he was now determined to get his way.

Jerry Wexler recalled, "His manager finally said 'Listen, do it or else.'"[4] All implications of mob intimidation aside, the "or else" essentially meant "or let Wilson Pickett out of contract," which would have spelled unwelcome defeat for all concerned. Fortunately, there was recent precedent: upon signing former Roulette artists Sam & Dave, Wexler had suggested to Stax President Jim Stewart the notion of "loaning" them to Stax, figuring that the pair's natural dynamics would stand a better chance of being captured on tape in Memphis than in New York. Now Wexler asked to send down Wilson Pickett to capture some of the Memphis magic that all the money in the Atlantic bank accounts couldn't buy on its home Manhattan turf—but unlike Sam & Dave, this venture would not carry the Stax logo. Stewart insisted on a cut of the proceeds, and the two label heads agreed that Pickett would meet with Steve Cropper to firm up the songs, with the credits split evenly between the pair of writers. Wexler additionally suggested he fly down in person, so that the Atlantic-Stax deal, which had operated on little more than a handshake these past four years, could be formalized, especially in the wake of the Sam & Dave loan.[5]

The way Cropper understood it, Atlantic's attitude was, "We've got this great singer, we just cannot come up with a hit record for him." Meanwhile, at Stax, said Cropper, "We were in the business of making hit singles, that's what we did. They [Atlantic] were coming from the days of Lavern Baker, that crossover from jazz church. It's still swing music, it's still kind of jazzy, it wasn't really R&B." He had a point: Wilson Pickett on Atlantic was not really R&B. Nor was Solomon Burke, for that matter. The music was too smooth, too sophisticated, too meticulously arranged, and at times (as in Pickett's "I'm Gonna Cry"), too jazzy. Otis Redding or Carla Thomas, on the other hand . . . now, that was R&B.

On May 11 1965, just a few days after Pickett's unexpected Apollo head-line billing concluded, and with the surprise baby newly ensconced at home, he and Wexler flew down from New York and checked in at the Holiday Inn on Union Street, where Cropper met him.[6] "He was a guy off the street that treated me like another guy off the street," Cropper said, "I didn't look at him as a black guy. And he also didn't look at me as a white guy. It was just two musicians writing songs and having fun." Such assertions of color-blindness at Stax were commonplace; they tended to emanate mostly from the label's white owners and musicians who, having been raised in one of the most intransigently segregated cities in the United States, perhaps felt the need to display their bona fides publicly.

Wilson Pickett, after his experience with a white producer on a song written by whites, was happy just to be back in the South with true R&B musicians of any color. He and Cropper quickly settled in at the Holiday Inn with their guitars—Cropper with his Telecaster electric, unplugged, Pickett with his acoustic. "He could play guitar," said Cropper of Pickett. "He had a good musical ear, he could groove." Wexler's claim that the pair were slipped a bottle of bourbon to lubricate proceedings is false: Jim Stewart ran a tight, dry ship and Cropper followed suit. "We'd never have got the songs written" otherwise, he insisted. And write them they did. When Stewart and Wexler came back from a business dinner, "We played them a couple of the songs and [Wexler] said, 'Whoa man! I'm getting out of the way.'"

It was a smart move. Four songs were recorded the next day, coinciden-tally the anniversary of Pickett's first session for Atlantic. Each was far bet-ter than anything else he had cut for the label, but one in particular stood out: "In the Midnight Hour," fairly summarized, in the words of one music historian, as "perhaps the song most emblematic of the whole southern soul era."[7]

Indeed, more than fifty years later, "In the Midnight Hour" remains impervious to the thought of improvement. It was recorded in mono; the pianist is all but inaudible; there are no hidden complexities. There is, in fact, almost nothing to it. Every chord required of the song is announced in the opening two bars and one beat, a descending pattern that, like a guitar beginner's tutorial, follows the dotted marks of the fret-board from a high D major down to an open E major. Yet behind this simplicity lies every possible layer of masterful musicianship. It's there in the power of Al Jackson's opening roll, on a single tom. It's there in the way trumpet players Wayne Jackson, Andrew Love, and Packy Axton blaze those initial descending chords, on the last of which one of them breaks off to play the root note an octave higher, emphasizing the incoming E major. It's there in the way that they then vacate the space and let the rhythm section assume responsibility, Donald "Duck" Dunn establishing the groove with a lightly loping bass line, as baritone sax player Floyd Newman pokes in with exquisitely timed interjections at the deep end. It's there in the core of the rhythm itself, driven by Jackson and Cropper, who hammer home the second and fourth beats in tandem with an almost imperceptible mutual delay, the former with a snare sound so bright that it defies the mono recording, the latter with a sharp, consistent downstroke.

The song thus anchored, Pickett starts singing, reintroducing that refrain he's been throwing into his recordings and performances all along, that reference to the time of night when his love "comes tumbling down" (as Clyde McPhatter had sung on the Dominoes' "You Do Something For Me" over a decade earlier). He continues with further lustful promises and assurances, familiar to anyone courted on the dance floor of the era. He sings and shouts, growls and rasps through the song but never screams; toward the conclusion of the second verse, when he proclaims "you're the only girl I know," his voice ascends to a thrilling falsetto instead.

At the end of each verse, Cropper and Dunn throw unexpectedly to the major seventh chord before resolving on the fifth, the guitarist reverberating his Telecaster through the measure before locking back into the two and the four. When the trumpets join Pickett on the second verse, they do so almost as an afterthought, in languid but harmonious contrast to the precision of the rhythm. Those trumpets then restructure their melody for an instrumental interlude that sounds as effortless to perform as it is easy to hum—but again, there's a sudden push to the major seventh chord again just when the listener least expects it. The song is so locked in its groove by this point that the third verse just alternates between the I and the IV chords, inviting a vocal vamp that Pickett readily assumes before the song fades out at two and a half minutes *precisely*, his final words being those of the song title.

Officially, Stewart and Cropper produced the momentous session, but Wexler could not help but play the backseat driver. Crucially, he suggested to Cropper that the guitarist change his original guitar riff—a move that required chutzpah, considering Stax's hits under Cropper's production.

Cropper duly abandoned his original, busy part, and fell in line with Jackson's snare instead. He was glad to have done so. "That backbeat thing was just magic. It doesn't get any simpler than that, but it actually had a function as well." The function was to emphasize the jerk, a dance craze that R&B vocal group the Larks had celebrated in a chart-topping song a few months earlier—and which Wexler promptly came down from the control room to demonstrate. It must have been quite the sight for the young studio band to behold a forty-eight-year-old executive from New York "just dancing around the studio, shadowboxing," in the words of Cropper, an accurate description of the jerk's emphatic arm movements in tandem with the downbeat.[8]

Steve Cropper and Al Jackson largely had that rhythm down already. Recording without head phones, Cropper preferred to watch Jackson's left hand rather than just listen for it, to hit his guitar chord the absolute moment the drummer came down on the snare (with the thick end of his stick, a practice Jackson had picked up in the nightclubs), emphasizing that downbeat and ensuring there was no "slap." If Wexler wanted anything more from them once Cropper had abandoned his syncopated riff, it was merely to give it an extra emphasis. Either way, the result was ideal for the song in hand. While there was enough of a contemporary jerk to the beat of "In the Midnight Hour" to render it popular on the 1965 dance floor, there was never too much to date it. If anything, that emphasis on the downbeat rendered it subtly familiar with the same young white audience that was otherwise buying the Beatles, the Rolling Stones (who had recorded Pickett's "If You Need Me" on their first visit to Chicago's Chess studios in early 1964), and the other British Invasion bands, given how that rhythm was to become a staple of rock music. "In the Midnight Hour" was probably the first southern soul recording to have such an effect on such a young white audience, yet it was every bit an authentic rhythm and blues record too, the rare kind of single that appealed to everyone without compromising.

The final stroke of musical genius surrounding "Midnight Hour" was the decision to leave it well alone. There were no female backing vocals, no additional sweetening. "In The Midnight Hour" was released, unadorned, while the tape was still warm. It was backed by "I'm Not Tired," another song from the session that was similarly kept free of female vocals, allowing Joe Hall, the pianist barely audible on "Midnight Hour," to flex his blues chops. "I'm Not Tired," said Cropper, was "a gospel shuffle, it's [Pickett's] thing, it's where he came from. It was easy to do, and the band learned it in five minutes." The process of making music (and magic) at Stax really could be that simple.

Reflecting on this session later in life, Wexler wrote, "My understanding was broadened and deepened so much by watching records being made from scratch rather than deductively from written arrangements." The experience, he continued, "changed my life!" and with it, Atlantic's approach to recording and production.[9]

In August, Wilson Pickett was invited to participate in a Stax package visit to Los Angeles, alongside Booker T. & the M.G.s, Rufus and Carla Thomas, and the Mar-Keys. Awaiting them was Magnificent Montague, who had left New York behind and was now hosting the morning shift on a small but significant black Los Angeles station. Montague had jumped on "In the Midnight Hour" as soon as he had heard it, and he wasn't the only one: the week that the Stax Revue came to town to play the 5/4 Ballroom in Watts, the single topped the R&B charts. It was the first recording from the Stax studios to do so since "Green Onions" four years earlier, and it made Pickett, the only non-Stax performer on the bill, by far its biggest attraction in Los Angeles, helping guarantee Montague two sellout shows at the 5/4 Ballroom in the black neighborhood of Watts.

The migration of blacks to Los Angeles may have occurred later than to northern cities, but it had been met with equal discrimination. Restricted housing covenants had crammed the emigrants into what became known as Negro L.A.—parts of south and central Los Angeles, with Watts at its heart. A Fair Housing Act to end the discrimination that was passed by the California legislature in 1963 was promptly overturned by voters in November 1964. By the time the Stax revue showed up the black community of Los Angeles was tired and angry, but in the middle of a long, hot summer, it was thrilled just to come out and party.

The two concerts, on August 7 and 8, represented the sole occasion that Wilson Pickett performed live with Booker T. & the M.G.s, and the recording of "In the Midnight Hour" from the second night is truly electrifying. Pickett and Montague engage in a comfortable back-and-forth as they build up audience anticipation for the song, with Pickett offering thanks to the disc jockey for his support and Montague accepting with uncustomary modesty. "You made it *possible* for me to sing it," Pickett half-sings, half-shouts, in finest preacher fashion, "You told the soul sisters . . . You told the soul brothers." At the point that he eventually references the song title itself, he manages to evoke its gospel antecedents even as he is clearly rallying a young crowd for the introductory refrain of a popular hit record

Finally, he brings in the band—two white guys and two black guys representing the power of music to bring people together when institutionalized society refuses to do so. Al Jackson breaks into a drum roll, the audience erupts in a collective scream of appreciation, and the M.G.s launch into as hard and heavy a version of "In the Midnight Hour" as Pickett ever captured on tape. It's all the stronger considering that the horn section, which had also played on the record, is standing off stage, mere onlookers to the musical proceedings, but Booker T. Jones makes his presence known on the Hammond, while Cropper chops away at his guitar in a syncopated groove closer to that which he originally intended for the record.

After the final verse, several screams, and exhortations of "Lord have mercy," Pickett commands the band to bring it down. He invites a female audience member onstage to respond to his call, to echo his shouts and screams. He sets her dancing on stage, while he vamps with the band about the feeling down in his soul. He screams some more and commands Montague to rejoin him.

The MC rises to the challenge: to every Pickett utterance of the word "feel," Montague responds with a "burn." "Feel . . ." "Burn . . ." "Feel . . ." "*Burn . . .*" Back and forth they go, either side of a single microphone, the two men lock into the phrasing together. "Feel it *down in my soul* . . ." The audience joins in the chant, until eventually, Montague directs the concert to its conclusion.

Three nights later, on August 11, with many Stax team members still in the city recording an instrumental album under a pseudonym for Montague's latest label, a supposedly routine traffic stop in the heart of Watts built into an altercation between the white policeman and the black driver. The mother of the driver came on the scene, and a crowd gathered, restless and volatile in the summer heat. Tempers frayed, people pushed and shoved, the police drew guns, the driver and his mother were arrested, rumors spread, the crowd grew bigger, the police sent for reinforcements, the crowd hurled objects at them . . . and before anyone could quite figure it out, Watts was aflame, the black community setting fire to white businesses in several consecutive midnight hour outpourings of pent-up anger and frustration. As they did so, they could be heard chanting Montague's on-air catchphrase, the one that had followed him all the way from New York: "Burn, baby! *Burn!*"

It would be several days before the National Guard, 14,000 of them in all, could restore order. By the time they did so, thirty-four people had died (most of them shot by the police or National Guard), over a thousand had been injured, three and a half thousand arrested, and, with almost three hundred buildings destroyed, damage was put at around $40,000,000. It was the largest and most costly riot—or rebellion, depending on one's perspective—of the civil rights era.[10] And it gave "Burn, baby! Burn!"—Montague's expression intended purely to emphasize musical heat—an entirely new meaning.[11]

CHAPTER 8

There were a lot of stories about him, man. But they were good stories. A lot of the times musicians liked some musicians better than others: we *loved* Wilson.

Floyd Newman, saxophone, Mar-Keys/Memphis Horns/Stax

"In the Midnight Hour" followed up its brief stay on top of the R&B charts by landing just one place outside the pop top twenty; in Britain, where classic singles came and went on a weekly basis, it went further still, threatening to break into the top ten. Atlantic rushed out an album of the same name to capitalize on its popularity, and it made Pickett's Double L debut look like a grand design by comparison. The four recordings from the May 12 Stax session, which indicated Pickett's path forward, were joined by the five previous Atlantic recordings, which most certainly did not. Rounding out the LP were tracks dating back even further, Pickett's three lead vocals from the Falcons days: "I Found a Love," "Let's Kiss and Make Up," and "Take This Love I've Got," now credited in the singer's name alone. What the other Falcons thought of this was not entirely clear.

At least this LP sleeve featured Pickett's picture, a black-and-white shot of the singer at the microphone, sharply dressed in the tight suit that was the uniform of every honest-to-goodness nightclub singer. Still, it might be considered proof of the lingering segregation in the record racks that the *In the Midnight Hour* LP nearly topped the R&B charts but stayed outside the pop 100.

In the Midnight Hour was promoted with a second single from the original Stax session, "Don't Fight It." An exhortation to a wallflower to come out on the dance floor, the song used the same winning rhythmic formula as "In the Midnight Hour," and benefited enormously from Joe Hall's bluesy piano playing. But Hall was absent when Atlantic flew Pickett back to Stax for another session in September. He had apparently nodded off at the keys one morning, exhausted from his previous night's gig—Jim Stewart took it as drunkenness and Hall was never used again. In his place was Stax staff writer Isaac Hayes, who played to perfection on the ballad "It's All Over," selected as the "Don't Fight It" B-side. Both songs were embellished by Atlantic artists the Bluebelles—Patti LaBelle, Sarah Dash, Cindy Birdsong, and Nona Hendryx—in the label's New York studio. "Don't Fight It" quickly became Pickett's second top-five R&B single.

The singer made the most of his heightened profile and increased earnings. Having let go Eddie Jacobs and "Liston" Owens before "In the Midnight Hour," he rehired them, building a proper band around them this time: drummer Tyrone Green, whom he nicknamed "Crusher" for his emphatic playing style; trumpet player Louis Risbrook; sax player Jack Philpot; and another sax man, Claston Higgins, who acquired the sobriquet "Patience," a necessary virtue around Pickett.

Pickett's international success brought with it a first overseas trip: in November, he flew to England to perform "Don't Fight It" on the country's leading television music show, *Ready Steady Go!* Backed by a British rhythm section, he also played at one of Swinging London's elite nightclubs, the Scotch of St. James. He was photographed for publicity, incongruously wearing a British policeman's helmet and wielding a truncheon, and enjoyed being paraded as not just a new star, but as something of a phenomenon. "In the Midnight Hour" had almost instantly become a soul standard, covered by any number of the British R&B groups that were then invading America, and "Don't Fight It" was enjoying considerable success on its own.

He was back at Stax five days before Christmas, where he was reunited with Eddie Floyd, newly engaged in his own songwriting partnership with Cropper. Floyd's path to Stax had been circuitous. After the Falcons breakup he had moved to Washington, DC, where he teamed up with prominent disc jockey and former civil rights activist Al Bell. Along with a former Moonglow, Bell and Floyd formed a label, cutting solo singles on Floyd, but faring better by supplying Carla Thomas with "Stop! Look What You're Doin'." Invited to her recording session at Stax, Floyd was welcomed into what he called its "family thing," as songwriter *and* artist. Bell was likewise lured to Memphis, as promotions director, the label's most critical hire since Cropper.

The song that Floyd and Cropper had been working on for Pickett was "634-5789," a blatant rip-off of the Marvelettes' hit from back in 1962, "Beechwood 4-5789." It was the closest Pickett would ever come to sounding like part of Motown, which may explain why someone added the parenthetical title "Soulsville, U.S.A." to rival Motown's claim on "Hitsville."

In the recording, Pickett comes across as a little too comfortable and self-conscious. Al Jackson's drumming, however, is relentless. "I don't think Motown has as much accent on the drums as Stax," Pickett said. "There's a big difference in the R&B beat and the Motown beat."[1]

Pickett, Cropper, and Floyd then wrote together for the first and last time, creating one of Pickett's most distinctive singles. It stole whole-sale from the long-standing Holiness Church gospel standard, "Lord I'm Running, Trying to Make 100, Because 99 and a Half Won't Do." Floyd and Pickett transformed that dedication to God into lust for a partner, but lingering close to the surface was a hint of a higher calling. Soul singers were still scared of speaking truth to power; the posthumous success of Sam Cooke's "A Change Is Gonna Come" was the exception that proved the rule. As such, at the end of a year that saw the historical civil rights march from Selma to Montgomery, the Watts riots, and the passage of the Voting Rights Act, Pickett's exhortation during the fade-out, "Ain't no use in fooling ourselves, we ain't gonna get by with ninety-nine," was taken by some listeners as a demand for full equality.

Cropper's contribution to the song they titled "Ninety-Nine and a Half (Won't Do)" proved pivotal; in contrast to the simplicity of the earlier hits with Pickett, he came up with a riff that alternated between G major and a G diminished chords, inviting a melodic bass line from Donald "Duck" Dunn and jazz inflections from Hayes. At the end of each verse the other instruments dropped out, leaving Cropper to alternate between a fifth and a suspended fourth for a brief interlude that Al Jackson interjected with tightly syncopated kick drum. The horns swept in and out, and Pickett was in his element: he ascended into a shrill falsetto of sheer delight as the song entered its vamping coda, only to raise the notes even higher and longer.

Wilson Pickett's three sessions at the Memphis studio had resulted in nine finished masters, of which four were hits, two of those going on to become recognized classics. Yet Jerry Wexler was abruptly informed after the last of the recording dates that Atlantic acts were no longer welcome at the studio. The official reason came primarily from Jim Stewart. "Pickett got to be an asshole," he told Stax biographer Rob Bowman. "The guys didn't want to work with him, and I wouldn't ask them to do it."[2]

The guys in question flatly deny Stewart's statement, however. "I never knew anything but greatness," said Cropper, who spent more professional time with Pickett than anyone else in Memphis and who would have been the go-to person for complaints from other musicians. None of them came to him. The sessions in Memphis, said trumpet player Wayne Jackson, who accompanied Pickett to the Memphis clubs at night, "were strictly a ski ride. They were fast and fun."

If there was antagonism at Stax, then, it was behind the scenes. "Jim was vague," admitted Wexler. "I knew that Pickett had irritated him."[3] But possibly so had Wexler, who had taken full advantage of Stax's hospitality. On the heels of the initial session that produced "In the Midnight Hour" and "Don't Fight It," and in the wake of successful recordings for Sam & Dave too, he had additionally sent Don Covay to Stax; the four songs recorded there resulted in two soul mainstays, "See Saw" and "Sookie Sookie." Pickett apparently attended that session alongside his friend: double the fun for them, double the trouble for Stewart. "Jim didn't get along with Don," said Cropper. "Just didn't understand Don." Covay never came back.

Stewart supported and promoted an integrated work environment at Stax, and did so in the midst of an overtly racist climate in Memphis. The city had recently shut down its public swimming pools rather than allow blacks to use them, and the predominantly black sanitation workers had to petition the city to have access to showers.[4] Yet despite his efforts toward integration, Stewart still may have expected deferential behavior from black artists—like Otis Redding, who got his start carrying another musician's equipment and politely asking for an audition. But having turned their backs on the old southern ways and moved to New York City, Pickett and Covay were of a different sort, more than willing to treat white people as equals—but never as betters. And Stewart was certainly not their better, or even equal, with the music. Much though he tried, he had not shaken his own background as a country fiddle player and small-town banker. "Jim wanted to be a part of it," said Wayne Jackson, referring to the rhythm and the harmony on the studio floor. "But he was too white. He didn't have a black leg in him."

There was also the question of whether Stax needed the outside sessions. Once Al Bell arrived at Stax in the second half of 1965, and the company's promotions were no longer in the hands of Atlantic staffers serving multiple masters, the label went on a roll. Redding recorded a trio of hits in the summer of 1965 that formed the backbone of *Otis Blue*, one of the great soul albums.[5] Sam & Dave, whom Stewart considered a Stax act, were finding their feet in the studio, and just about everyone who traveled to Los Angeles for the Magnificent Montague show launched singles into both the pop and R&B charts. With the benefit of his prior vantage point in Washington, DC, Bell knew that Stax could challenge Motown—no small aspiration given that the Detroit independent, somewhat astonishingly, sold more singles than any other American record company in 1965. To do so, however, meant acting with as much self-interest as Motown, by protecting its trademark: the band, the studio, and the sound that combination produced.

There is another explanation for the split, one that has been implied in many ways over the years by a number of people—among them the studio sax player, Floyd Newman, who recalled that Pickett had told him: "I had my songs together when I came here, but every time I come here I don't leave with 100 percent of the song I came here with, they've given it to someone here. I'll never be back here, you'll never see me again." In short, Pickett accused Stax of muscling in on his compositions. He did so frequently, and consistently. "I shared all of my songs with Steve Cropper, in order for him to play," he said in 1969.[6] "This Steve Cropper come in, he was a producer, and writer, he said, 'You got to give me half of the songs if I'm going to play for you in the band,'" in 1977.[7] "One thing I had to do was share the song [writing credit] with Steve Cropper, because he had the band," in 1999.[8]

"I'm saddened he thought that," said Cropper. "Because if that was true, how come I didn't cowrite everything with Otis? And I didn't cowrite everything with Wilson either, but I did that [first] night with those songs because they were unfinished." Actually, Cropper ended up with an equal share on eight of the nine songs Pickett cut at Stax, as well as on the four songs cut with Covay; the only exception was "I'm Drifting," cocredited to Pickett and Stax writers David Porter and Homer Banks. Stax assigned all these songs to the label's publishing arm, East Music (it did the same with part of Otis Redding's publishing, regardless of whether Cropper wrote with Redding or not). Floyd Newman, who had played on the original Stax hit "Last Night," for which he did not receive a cocredit or an invitation to join the touring Mar-Keys, offered the following explanation:

> Every artist that came in here, they'd have their songs all together, but when they leave they had to give up a piece of it, to a certain person. But this person, you couldn't be mad at him, because he didn't own Stax, Jim Stewart owned Stax. And this guy was doing what Jim Stewart told him to do, so you can't be mad at him. Hey, somebody offer you some money, you get it.[9]

Such was the way the music business often worked, especially in regard to copyrights, which had a long, unruly history of being assigned, traded, sold, and gifted. When Atlantic sent Pickett to Stax, what better way might there have been for Jim Stewart to share in any potential profits than to insist on half the publishing? And what better way to incentivize Cropper than for Stewart to offer him a cut of the songs? In Pickett's defense, the singer likely did not fly down empty-handed on the eve of that first session; he must *surely* have had concepts for several songs, or Wexler would never have authorized the session. But certainly *something* creative must have happened between Pickett and Cropper, because the material Pickett laid down in Memphis was far superior to the songs he had previously claimed as his own.

At the heart of the dispute was "In the Midnight Hour," for which a coauthorship credit proved the equivalent of a gilded, life-long pension. Pickett insisted that he went to Stax with the idea for the song in hand. Cropper has always said that upon hearing of Pickett's arrival at Stax, he went to the Satellite store to see what they had on the singer; whether it was "I Found a Love" by the Falcons or the live version of "I'm Gonna Cry" recorded at the Uptown, on which Pickett had extemporized in a gospel style during its coda, he heard Pickett intoning "In the midnight hour."[10] At the Holiday Inn, said Cropper, "I reminded him about 'midnight hour' and we wrote it." And in his more generous moments, Pickett admitted that he received help: "He worked with me quite a bit on that one," he said in an interview used for a major TV documentary in the late 1980s.[11]

Would Wilson Pickett have preferred total ownership of an incomplete and possibly insignificant "In the Midnight Hour"? Or was he better off with his half-share of an evergreen that would become one of the most broadcast, recorded, and performed songs of all time?[12] He likely did not understand that having the basic idea of a song did not mean owning a collaborative finished product, something Willie Schofield had explained in claiming his own share of "I Found a Love." "Pickett didn't have any chord pattern. He had a couple of lyrics. I'm working with him, giving him the chord change, the feel of it. Then we're going in the studio and I've gotta show the band how to play it because we didn't have arrangers. That's part of the songwriting. But he didn't understand. He felt he wrote the lyrics so that's it." A person like Pickett who had brought himself up from nothing probably didn't like the notion that he required other people's help to get further—and liked even less the idea that he had to pay for it. If he kicked up a storm at Stax about the cost of making hit records, who could blame Jim Stewart if it provided the perfect excuse to say goodbye to all Atlantic outside artists?

None of which alters the fact that Pickett's three sessions at Stax are the stuff of legend, all of it captured on a mono tape machine.[13] Nor that, as "634-5789" took up a seven-week residency at the top of the R&B charts, becoming a worldwide hit single in the process, Pickett and Wexler were jettisoned from the very environment that had produced such magic, suddenly left to find another location to continue their musical journey.

CHAPTER 9

He reminded me of a black leopard, you know, look but don't touch, he might bite your hand.

Rick Hall, proprietor/producer/engineer, Fame Studios[1]

In early May 1966 Wilson Pickett flew down to Muscle Shoals, Alabama. He had returned to his home state several times in the decade since he had left, on tour and once to introduce Dovie to his family, but in general he avoided the place. He was a superstar now. "634-5789" had nearly grazed the top ten in the pop charts, and held fast at number one in R&B charts. He was making money, appearing on television, playing to huge audiences for high fees. He had just bought a home, on Laurelton Parkway in Queens, and treated himself to a new Cadillac El Dorado. And now here he was, back in Alabama, supposedly to record an LP—and none too happy about the prospect.

Rick Hall, proprietor of the Fame studio into which Pickett had been booked for the next few days, was waiting for him when he stepped off the plane. Hall carried himself with the commanding presence of a sheriff. Pickett took one look at him and concluded: redneck. Hall took one look at Pickett in turn, wearing "black pegged pants, black wing-tipped shoes, and a white satin shirt with a black hounds tooth coat slung over the shoulder," and figured him for "a dangerous man."[2] The short drive to the studio was tense. "I'd look at him and he'd look at me," recalled Hall, "and I could see in his eyes he was thinking, 'Now what am I doing with this cracker down here in Alabama?'"[3]

That's *exactly* what Pickett was thinking, and as they approached the studio, the singer's worst fears were confirmed. Across the road from the box-like building with the word FAME spelled out in incongruous capital letters were cotton patches filled with black workers. "So . . . they're still slaves here," he recalled thinking to himself. "I said, 'Oh I'm gonna be ruined. I *know* I'm gonna be ruined.'"[4]

He was anything but. Over the next three or four days, Pickett cut ten songs at Fame, one of which would become his biggest American crossover hit. He returned twice more to Fame over the next nine months to put down another two albums' worth of classic material, including several major hits; he came back again a year after that, recording, among others, a soul-rock anthem that unveiled one of the greatest guitarists of his generation. In the process Pickett firmly put Muscle Shoals—and Fame in particular—on the international music map. He afforded it a reputation that attracted not only his fellow soul greats Otis Redding, Aretha Franklin, and Etta James, but just about every white artist looking to absorb a little southern soul for themselves, from the Rolling Stones to Bob Dylan, Paul Simon to the Osmonds. It was Pickett's favorite place, his happiest of studio times. In the late 1970s, when disco was up and Pickett was down, he'd team up once more with Rick Hall in the hopes that they might be able to revive the good old days.

"Pickett and I were soul brothers, we really were," said Hall, and the singer spoke of the producer and studio proprietor in equally glowing terms.[5] "Rick is a beautiful person," he pronounced.[6] Several years after that, his estimation had only increased. "I love Rick Hall," he stated, a verb he didn't use lightly. "I named him Rick Homes. Because you're at home with Rick Hall."[7]

The notion of Muscle Shoals as a cornerstone of southern soul appears as mystifying to anyone who hasn't studied, let alone visited the region, as it did to Wilson Pickett back in May of 1966. Why here? Why, as a BBC documentary on southern soul labeled it, this "God-fearing rural backwater?"

But the "Shoals"—the towns of Sheffield, Florence, Tuscumbia, and Muscle Shoals itself, spread either side of the sprawling Tennessee River in the northwestern corner of Alabama—was never a backwater. W. C. Handy, the "father of the blues," had been born there, as had Sam Phillips, a key founder of rock 'n' roll, and Buddy Killen, a powerhouse in country music. The Shoals was home to the Wilson Dam, a flood-prevention project that created a significant number of jobs at the peak of the Great Depression; it had subsequently been chosen as the location for the Tennessee Valley Authority, the first (and to this day, largest) Federal regional planning authority, bringing not just more employment, but introducing electricity to vast swathes of the South and with it, facilitating the boom in radio. Sure, the Shoals was Alabama, with everything that stood for (and against) during the civil rights era, but it was northwestern Alabama, removed

1. The cinderblock house on Route 29, in rural Prattville, Alabama, where Wilson Pickett grew up. Courtesy of Tony Fletcher.

2. The Falcons, "the World's First Soul Group." Although Wilson Pickett sung lead on their 1961 hit "I Found A Love," no official photograph was ever taken of him with the group. L–R: Eddie Floyd, Joe Stubbs, Lance Finney, Mack Rice, Willie Schofield. Gilles Petard/Getty.

3. The historical marker for Wilson Pickett Jr. in downtown Prattville, dedicated in 2009. Courtesy of Tony Fletcher.

4. Wilson Pickett Sr., the singer's father, in an undated photograph. Courtesy of the Wilson Pickett Jr. Legacy LLC.

5. The earliest known photograph of Wilson Pickett Jr., shown with son Lynderrick (born 1959) and daughter Veda (1961). Courtesy of the Wilson Pickett Jr. Legacy LLC.

6. An early promo photograph of Wilson Pickett, solo singer. Pictorial Press Ltd/Alamy.

7. At the 110th Street Harlem Armory, June 12, 1964, farewell concert for disc jockey Magnificent Montague, who helped break Wilson Pickett's first solo hit, "If You Need Me." The pair would perform together again in Watts, Los Angeles, the following summer. Michael Ochs Archives/Getty.

8. Pickett shown performing to a mixed-race audience in an unidentified location circa 1966. In the American South, audiences were still mostly segregated at this point. ZUMA Press, Inc./Alamy.

9. At Fame studios October 1966, the sessions that resulted in "Mustang Sally." Top: Rick Hall. Middle row: Chips Moman, Charlie Chalmers, Spooner Oldham, Roger Hawkins. Middle of photo: Jerry Wexler, Wilson Pickett. Bottom row: Ed Logan, Tommy Cogbill, Jimmy Johnson. Courtesy of Fame Studios.

10. With Esther Phillips and Percy Sledge at the Prelude Club in Manhattan, May 5, 1966, at an Atlantic Records party celebrating Sledge's number one single "When a Man Loves a Woman." Cornell Dupree and Jimi Hendrix, then playing with bandleader King Curtis and his Kingpins, are on guitar. Popsie Randolph, courtesy of Michael Randolph.

11. The eternally suave Wilson Pickett in an undated photograph from the mid 1960s. Courtesy of the Wilson Pickett Jr. Legacy LLC.

12. Wilson Pickett and long-term partner Dovie Hall in the early 1960s, shortly after they met. Courtesy of the Wilson Pickett Jr. Legacy LLC.

13. With partner Dovie Hall. The pair met in Detroit in early 1962, and stayed together for fifteen years, until Hall left after extensive physical abuse. "To the day he died, I loved him," she said. Courtesy of the Wilson Pickett Jr. Legacy LLC.

14. Outside the Howard Theater in Washington, DC, circa 1967. L–R:Pickett, Vincent Pitts (trumpet), Bob Perkins (piano), Baby James (driver), Jack Philpot (sax), Gus Hawkins (sax), Billy (trumpet, last name not known), Carlton McWilliams (guitar). Buddy Miles, in the group at the time on drums, is out of the shot. Courtesy of the Wilson Pickett Jr. Legacy LLC.

15. With guitarists Jimmy Johnson and Bobby Womack at Fame Studios, circa 1968. Womack wrote or cowrote several of Pickett's hits. "Whatever Pickett said, he stuck by it," said Womack, who credited the singer with giving him "my first break." Courtesy of Fame Studios.

16. With backing band the Midnight Movers in Pisa, Italy, early 1969. L–R: Chris Lowe (trumpet), George Patterson (sax), George Chillus, Leon Lovejoy (drums), Jack Philpot (sax), Wilson Pickett, Danny White (valet/vocals). Photographer: Curtis Pope (trumpet). Courtesy of Curtis Pope.

17. Pickett in Pisa. Courtesy of Curtis Pope.

18. At Fame Studios with Duane Allman, November/December 1968. "He stood right in front of me, as though he was playing every note I was singing," said Pickett of Allman's groundbreaking solo on "Hey Jude." Michael Ochs Archives/Getty.

19. Pickett in fur, late 1960s. The singer had a fondness for expensive clothing. Courtesy of the Wilson Pickett Jr. Legacy LLC.

from the battlegrounds of Birmingham and Selma; true, it was dry, but the towns on the Tennessee side of the border were packed with boozed-up juke joints and nightclubs, the better for young Alabama musicians. By the late 1950s, it was only a matter of time before someone like Rick Hall set up shop there.

Like Jim Stewart at Stax, Rick Hall had been born in the early 1930s; like Stewart, he had been raised on country music and considered himself an accomplished fiddle player. How he and Pickett could become "soul brothers" when the same was most certainly not true of Pickett and Stewart surely lies in their equally ornery nature. There was nothing Pickett could teach Hall about childhood poverty that Hall didn't already know, having been raised among poor white folk of the Freedom Hills, a largely lawless, unsurveyed region of rolling timberland that overlapped the northern Mississippi–Alabama borders, where communities had names like Gravel Hill and Rock Creek, and "bad news was all people talked about."[8]

Hall certainly endured his share: his brother died after falling into the family's boiling laundry pot; his mother left for a life of prostitution; his first wife died at seventeen after the car Hall was driving careened off the highway; his father died just two weeks after that—under the tractor Hall bought him, no less. Such calamities drove Hall toward a hard-drinking lifestyle among the country music players who entertained the Hills' moonshine-making bootleggers; it was not until his late twenties that he and fellow musician Bobby Sherrill decided to try their hand at songwriting in the Shoals. There they recorded demos at the tiny studio belonging to James Joiner, hobbyist proprietor of the pioneering Tune label (the first in Alabama), where they had just enough success for another Shoals music entrepreneur, Tom Stafford, to invite them in as partners in a publishing company. Hall formed a rock 'n' roll band, the Fairlanes, now that his musical tastes had expanded, which brought him a regular vocalist in the teenage Dan Penn.

Penn was not so much a mere student of R&B as a product of it: "I wouldn't even listen to you if you weren't black," he later said.[9] All the same, Penn's first successful composition was for Conway Twitty, and with country music the obvious path to success for white musicians in Alabama, Hall frequently drove three hours to Nashville to shop demos—so frequently, in fact, that Stafford and Sherrill fired him for being a workaholic. Hall was left with the name of their company, Florence Alabama Music Enterprises, and not much else.

Hall turned bitterness into further ambition, building a small studio out by the Wilson Dam where he learned to overdub using two mono recorders, and he earned a steady income producing radio jingles. He got his break into the recording industry when a repentant Stafford called to ask for help with a singer he had found, Arthur Alexander, and a country-tinged R&B song Alexander had written, "You Better Move On." At Fame, Hall cut it to perfection but initially had a hard time shopping it: Alexander was black, and the racial delineations between country and R&B laid down by the record industry were immutable. The song was eventually picked up by the upstart southern independent Dot and became a massive hit. Hall took his check from Dot and built a new studio on East Avalon Avenue in Muscle Shoals itself, its dimensions copied from the CBS studio in Nashville. Long and narrow, with a tall ceiling and no exterior windows, it included what one of his regular assistants considered "the best vocal microphone in the world," along with an echo chamber built purposely without corners, and a control room at the far end, imposingly set up on top of several steps. There, Hall fed multiple microphones and live echo into a mono mix: what went into the tape machine was essentially what came out of it.

So equipped, and with Arthur Alexander's hit to its name, the Fame studio became the obvious port of call for other regional black artists looking to cross over, among them Jimmy Hughes, Bobby Moore & the Rhythm Aces, and Joe Tex, whose ten-gallon hat announced his country leanings but who had struggled to record anything of merit in Nashville, where his race was viewed as an obstacle. At Fame, as produced by Hall, he immediately hit pay dirt with "Hold What You've Got."

Hall clearly had a magic touch, and his next move, understandably, was to start a Fame record label (he already had a publishing company), which brought him into the orbit of Joe Galkin, Atlantic's man down South. On a visit to Galkin's office in Atlanta, Hall was briefly put on the phone with Jerry Wexler, who said to call him next time Hall thought he had a hit record.

That opportunity came through the back door. While Hall continued to record pop and country, anything that would pay the bills, a white share-cropper's son called Quin Ivy opened a second Shoals studio, Norala, specializing in R&B and using the Fame rhythm section with Hall's blessing. Ivy's A&R man had introduced him to Percy Sledge, a local hospital orderly with a powerful if reedy voice and an incomplete song that was knocked into shape at Norala, with Fame's house guitarist Jimmy Johnson as engineer, Dan Penn's songwriting partner Spooner Oldham on keyboard, and Fame's regular drummer Roger Hawkins holding the gentle beat. Ivy brought it to Hall for a second opinion. Hall took one listen and dialed Jerry Wexler.

Wexler was initially brusque; he was hosting a weekend pool party at his house for record executives at the time. "You said to call you if I heard a hit," Hall reminded him, "and this is a number one." Wexler listened down the phone line, asked Hall if he was certain, and then snapped up the song for Atlantic. "When a Man Loves a Woman" duly became the first southern soul song to top the pop charts, and a relationship formed between Hall and Wexler at the perfect moment for an Atlantic label whose soul singers were no longer welcome at Stax.

On May 5, 1966, Atlantic threw a swanky party at the midtown Manhattan Prelude Club to celebrate Sledge's success. Joining Sledge as the evening's star performers were Atlantic's soul veteran Esther Phillips, shilling her response single, "When a Woman Loves a Man," and the label's reigning soul star, Wilson Pickett. Photographs show the house band for the night, King Curtis and the Kingpins, widely considered the best R&B act in town as led by its coolest and nicest musician, dressed to the nines—with current guitarists Jimi Hendrix, fresh from a stint with the Isley Brothers, and Cornell Dupree, both in bow-ties and tuxedos, looking delighted with proceedings as they back Pickett on "In the Midnight Hour." It was the only time Hendrix and Pickett were known to perform together. Within a couple of weeks, Hendrix had set sail for Greenwich Village and a career under his own name. Within forty-eight hours, Pickett was on that plane to Muscle Shoals.

Wilson Pickett was in for a surprise upon arriving at Fame and being introduced to the rhythm section. Johnson, Hawkins, Oldham, and bass player Albert "Junior" Lowe were all white. So were the two additional guitarists who had driven down from Memphis: "Chips" Moman and Tommy Cogbill. If not for a couple of the Memphis horn players, Pickett would have been the only black person there. Recording with an integrated rhythm section at Stax had been a new thing for Pickett; recording with an all-white rhythm section was something else entirely. He was not alone in later expressing the opinion, "It's amazing how these guys could play black stuff, you know."[10]

Still, the Fame rhythm section of the mid-1960s were already steeped in the music they became so adept at playing. Johnson's backstory was emblematic. "My dad was into Country and Western. All my early age he was encouraging me to play guitar like him. I wasn't interested, I didn't like the music. As soon as I heard 'Johnny B. Goode' on our AM radio station, I said 'Hold it, I want to learn how to do that.'" Johnson and Hawkins formed a band, the Del-Rays, among the few white acts hired by the white southern college fraternities that loved authentic black R&B even as they maintained rigid segregation.

These members of the Fame rhythm section may have been born at just the right time to be part of the change they wished to see in the world.

Johnson recalled how "when Kennedy was elected President, the South was almost a block against him: he was a Catholic. But after the assassination, I got angry about it. Before then, I guess I was going along with what I was being told. But then I had a total shift of thinking." The climate at Fame, as it became increasingly in demand among R&B and soul artists, played its own role. "You make your living with black people, you *will* change."

All the same, it was not Stax. The Fame rhythm section had no Steve Cropper figure as bandleader; Rick Hall commanded sole authority as the studio's producer and proprietor, though on this occasion of Wilson Pickett and Atlantic's first session, he was relegated to the role of engineer by the presence of Wexler. Also, the musicians didn't read music; they went by the "Nashville number system," substituting digits for chords, making it easier to change keys. Third, they didn't rehearse much. Typically, they'd listen to a demo (unless the writer was present to play the song), agree on the tempo, run it through once and then record, an approach so casual as to give pause to Wexler's new enthusiasm for the "southern" way of recording.

Further, as specific to this inaugural Wilson Pickett session, a number of the players had yet to meet each other, let alone the singer. Only the brass players from Stax—Wayne Jackson, Andrew Love, and Floyd Newman—were familiar with Pickett. Charlie Chalmers, a twenty-two-year-old white saxophonist who had toured with Jerry Lee Lewis, recorded with Bill Black and Charlie Rich, and was now regularly engaged as Willie Mitchell's go-to player and arranger at Mitchell's Memphis-based Hi Studio and label, was new to the singer. Tommy Cogbill, a naturally gifted jazz guitarist, came at the invitation of "Chips" Moman; both were recording with the Fame rhythm section for the first time. Moman had started out his career in the Cropper role at Stax, producing the label's breakout hit "Last Night," before falling out with Stewart and Axton over his share of the proceeds; he had then opened his own Memphis studio, American, while hiring himself out as a guitarist. He had visited Fame just once, for the session with Joe Tex that had otherwise featured external musicians.

And few of those present at Fame that day had met Wexler. "Jerry was intimidating," said Jimmy Johnson of first impressions. "He wasn't designed to be that way, but the language . . . he had this unbelievable vocabulary, that would immediately disarm anybody. He was so smart. He really, immediately got our attention and respect to the highest degree." As a result, "We were scared that if we couldn't play a lick that Wexler wanted us to play, that might be our last session."

This underlying tension would become apparent in the first song they recorded that day, as played by Jerry Wexler on a portable record player set out in the middle of the studio floor: "Land of 1000 Dances" by Cannibal & the Headhunters.

The song was something of a standard, having been released many times since its composer, Louisiana native Chris Kenner, took his one-riff recitation of contemporary dance crazes, produced by New Orleans great Allen Toussaint, into the charts in 1963. Kenner had passed the song on to Fats Domino; Rufus Thomas had picked it up for his Stax LP *Walking the Dog*; along the way, it had been lyrically updated and adopted as an easy-to-play floor-filler and crowd-pleaser by seemingly every white garage band that had popped up across the United States in the wake of the British invasion.

But only when the singer in one such band, East L.A.'s the Headhunters, adopted a "na-na-na-na-na" chant on stage one night after forgetting the words, was the song awarded a chorus. So infectious did it prove to be in concert that the Headhunters stuck their chant at the front of the song and released it as a "live" single, making the top 30 in the spring of 1965. The audience's overdubbed screams were blatantly copied by other acts who hoped to emulate such success, among them both the Walker Brothers *and* Bill Haley and the Comets. Shortly after Wilson Pickett shared Murray the K's Christmas 1965 revue at the Brooklyn Fox theater alongside Cannibal and the Headhunters, he introduced the song into his own set; road saxophonist Jack Philpot recalled the group working up an arrangement in Buffalo prior to the recording session at Fame, even though the touring band was not invited to participate in the studio.

"Land of 1000 Dances" was essentially just a repetitive two-chord groove. But its simplicity was challenging, and the assembled musicians at Fame couldn't quite pull it off. "Being the first song, we were all scattered," said Johnson. "We didn't know what it was going to be." Moman came up with a suggestion: a simple repetitive chinking riff, placing it front and center where guitars had been absent from the garage band hits, allowing Johnson to fall in with "some pretty fast Chuck Berry licks" alongside him, and establishing in the process an especially fruitful and mutually respectful working relationship between the two Fame guitarists. Wexler stepped in next, recommending a descending sixteenth-note bass line that would bring the band straight into the first verse, the Headhunters' call-and-response be damned. But the part was demanding, revealing the bass player, Junior Lowe, as the least capable link in the chain.

Less out of inspiration than impatience, Pickett assumed authority. "Come on!" he shouted, and then he screamed a count-in. "One-two-THREE . . ."

"Everyone just knew," recalled Charlie Chalmers. "We were *there*." He and the other horns came together and blared out a resounding opening chord. "One-two-THREE!" Pickett screamed again. They blared the other chord, setting up the bass for its descending intro.[11] That was it. They rehearsed the intro once more, and then, assuming they had already wasted far too much of Atlantic's budget, they went for a take. The following one hundred and fifty seconds were furious and frenetic, all but anarchic, as evidenced when the musicians eschewed the second verse for an instrumental section and Chalmers, in his own words, "jumped in there before anybody." His solo was all over the place, almost impossible to replicate, and all the better for it. During the subsequent vocal verse, all the brass players but one forgot to come in at the end of the first line. Typically a producer would have gone back and rerecorded it, but this was a straight-to-tape single-track recording, and nobody was going to call human error so late in the game.

Pickett's delivery, meanwhile, was riotous, raucous, damn-near Pentecostal. He name-checked his sister Louella, Lucy Coot—"my little Lucy"—who had attempted to teach him how to dance some of these moves. And when not reciting the dances by name, he grunted, shouted, screamed, exhorted, did whatever it took to keep the song moving. "Once he started singing, he captured us," said Jimmy Johnson. "Because of what a talent he was. He had the magic." So did Roger Hawkins, whose relentlessly perfect pounding simply made "Land of 1000 Dances," and never more so than when the instruments dropped away before the chorus chant and Hawkins hammered the crisp bass-to-snare rhythm like a metronome, holding steady at a preposterous 175 beats per minute: the Chris Kenner version had been 134 bpm by comparison.

At the end of the take—there was only one—Wexler descended the stairs from the control room and onto the studio floor. "He said, 'Roger,'" recalled Hawkins. "I said, 'Yes, sir.' He said 'Roger, you are a great drummer,' and all of a sudden, I just kind of . . . relaxed—and became a great drummer, just like he said I was."[12] Wexler's compliment served as a vote of confidence for the nervous core rhythm section and helped instigate a career long friendship.

The rest of the session was a breeze by comparison, albeit notable for the fact that like the one that followed it in October, it was completely devoid of Pickett compositions. The reasons for this were never made clear, but the outcome was without dispute: whereas Pickett until now had been an originator, he was about to become known primarily an interpreter—and arguably the very best in his field. With "Mercy, Mercy," for example, he did both its composer (Don Covay) and its publisher (Wexler) a financial favor while also appealing to the white fans of the Rolling Stones (who had covered it in 1965) who may not have known the original version. In two songs by Spooner Oldham and Dan Penn (the ballad "She Ain't Gonna Do Right" and the mid-tempo "I Need a Lot of Loving Every Day"), he did the composers and their publisher (Rick Hall) a similar favor and took credit for the first recorded interpretation. In each case he did so with consummate ease, the joy of the occasion captured in a memorable photograph of himself surrounded by a gleeful core rhythm section. "That [first] session was a mind-altering experience," said Charlie Chalmers.

The feeling was mutual. "After my first night in that studio," Pickett said of his Fame debut, "I was convinced that (Muscle Shoals) could be a recording home for me from now on."[13]

Released as a single in July, Pickett's "Land of 1,000 Dances" could barely be contained. By September, it had become his third number one R&B hit, had risen to number six in the pop charts, and had become his fourth British hit single in under a year. Atlantic took six of the songs from the Fame session, added them to six more from those at Stax, and released an LP titled *The Exciting Wilson Pickett*, the cover portraying the singer leaping halfway in the air in a finely tailored red suit and tie. The presence of five solid hits (Atlantic included "In the Midnight Hour" a second time) paid off when the LP went one place short of the top twenty and spent six months in the R&B charts, peaking at number three; it would prove to be Pickett's most successful long-playing release, at least by chart positions. His stature as America's leading soul man became apparent when Otis Redding, the one singer Pickett truly looked up to, went to England later in 1966 to record a TV special, closing with Pickett's version of "Land of 1000 Dances," right down to the shouted count-in.

Pickett and Wexler returned to Muscle Shoals in October 1966, this time with recording engineer and producer Tom Dowd. Dowd had spent much of World War II working on the Manhattan Project; the technical expertise he brought to the music industry was credited with helping develop its multitrack system of recording and for replacing rotary studio knobs with sliders that facilitated the manipulation of those multiple channels. At studios like Stax and Fame, whose studio owners stubbornly resisted even the notion of stereo, Dowd served as Atlantic's troubleshooting go-between.[14] At the Atlantic studio on Broadway and 60th, Dowd took these studio mono tapes and, in the case of Pickett, added any necessary background vocals, brass, or lead vocal rerecording. He often received a producer credit, even if he had not been at the original session.

There were small changes of personnel at Fame, too. Junior Lowe had been replaced by Tommy Cogbill, and the Stax brass section had been reigned in from their moonlighting: Charlie Chalmers was joined this time instead by fellow sax players Eddie Logan and Gilbert Caple, the teenaged Ben Cauley, and thirty-something trumpeter Gene "Bowlegs" Miller, an old-time Beale Street player. "Bowlegs was outstanding," said Chalmers, who would appear on more Pickett records than any other sax player. "He was killer. He had these big eyes and he'd be looking around . . . He had a lot of fire."[15]

The amended team proved every bit as outstanding as its predecessors. Pickett cut the first rendition of Dan Penn and Rick Hall's future classic "You Left the Water Running" and also of Penn and Spooner Oldham's "Up Tight Good Woman," delivering a spoken sermon of incredible intensity. And he introduced Covay's intensely soulful "Three Time Loser," which also served as a showcase for Cogbill's bass playing. Mere album cuts for Pickett, all three songs would become significant singles for other artists.

He followed up his earlier cover of "Mercy, Mercy" with two more songs known to some in his increasingly white audience only via the Rolling Stones: the 1964 Irma Thomas classic "Time Is On My Side," and Solomon Burke's "Everybody Needs Somebody to Love," on which he name-checked Burke in his spoken introduction. He covered Bobby Hebb's current hit "Sunny," and he also dared cover Eddie Floyd's brand-new Stax single "Knock on Wood," a cocomposition with Steve Cropper that inverted the descending chords of "In the Midnight Hour" for its opening riff. Pickett let the Fame musicians respond to the challenge of distinguishing themselves from their Memphis counterparts by speeding the song up considerably, Cogbill somehow improving upon Donald "Duck" Dunn's bass line in the process. Powerful though their rendition may have been, it was wisely reserved to LP status; no point competing with a record that already had its own momentum.

When it came to another former Falcons singer, Mack Rice, and "Mustang Sally," it was a different matter. Rice's own version had never hit the big time, although the Young Rascals—the first all-white group ever signed to Atlantic, albeit one genuinely steeped in R&B—had slowed it down to a moaning blues tempo for the B-side of their number one hit, "Good Lovin'," meaning it was already present in over a million homes and fully familiar to Wexler and Dowd. Pickett's "Mustang Sally" returned to the source for its inspiration. Roger Hawkins enlivened the core rhythm by opening up his hi-hat just before the last beat of each measure; Chips Moman and Jimmy Johnson interacted with consummate ease, the former playing the simple, dominant two-note riff, the latter quietly strutting a single-string line in the background. Ultimately, though, "Mustang Sally" belonged to Spooner Oldham, who opted to use the Fame studio's Hammond M100 Spinet (essentially, a B3 with a built-in speaker) for the occasion. After Pickett sang "You've been running all over town now," Oldham held a high note, then offered what he called "my representation of what it would sound like if I drove a Harley Davidson motorcycle through the studio." Up in the control room, Hall and Tom Dowd added echo via the studio's in-built chamber, mixing it in live. Rick Hall observed that the result "sounded like a dog barking in a cave," although many a listener would presume it to be a female backing chorus letting out a collective "whoop-whoop."

Oldham's idea, and Hall and Dowd's execution of it, was sublime. So was the rest of Oldham's organ playing, which he would modestly claim to be "just sort of noodling one-note frills." Provided with such a solid foundation Pickett could hardly fail, and he sounded like a man in musical clover throughout. At the end of almost every vocal line, he threw in one of his increasingly familiar personal asides: "What I said now," "Oh Lord," "a loo-kee here," "Let me say it one more time now," and so on, ascending into both a celebratory falsetto and his inimitable scream as the song reached the three-minute mark.

Everyone in the studio was having a blast. "It was one of those days where those magical components all came together, working for the same cause, making a good record," said Oldham of the performance. "If you're on a session and you're a player, you know when it's right. You stand up and leave your instrument and without any announcement, you want to go hear the thing. You go up the stairs to get in the control room." But on that occasion, when they got there, someone inadvertently hit the recorder at either the wrong speed or before the spool was locked down. The reel promptly spun off the machine, and the tape spun out of control, breaking into dozens of tiny pieces.

There was a moment of stunned silence as everyone looked at the fruits of their perfect take, cast across the studio like so much aural confetti, before Pickett apparently unleashed a serious flash of the temper that he generally kept under control in the recording studio. As Oldham described, "Everyone knew that was the one, the magic one, and we could never improve upon it."

Tom Dowd calmly told the musicians to leave the studio, get some food, and come back in an hour. When they returned, he and Rick Hall had spliced the tape back together. Splicing, of itself, was nothing new: engineers and producers did it when they needed to edit out a section to reduce a track to a radio-friendly length. Doing it required precision with a razor and peace of mind. Doing so as many as forty times over, without advance knowledge of which piece went in which order, required nothing less than total serenity and no small degree of genius. Tom Dowd possessed both, and "Mustang Sally" was saved. Fans were none the wiser; as with "Land of 1000 Dances," Pickett's rendition became the template that launched hundreds—if not thousands—of covers over the years. There is one rhythmic hiccup in the final verse of the song, at the 2:23 mark; this may be a moment of bravado on the part of Roger Hawkins—or the sole evidence of the respliced master recording.

Along with a couple of holdovers from May, the October session was packaged as an LP, the first by Wilson Pickett to have been recorded in one studio with essentially the same group of musicians. It was a record of considerable importance, a further building block in his career. It also introduced the moniker that he would eventually come to endorse and embrace. In the late 1980s, Pickett recalled how he came by it: "Noreen Woods from Atlantic Records, she called me that one day because back in that time, the secretaries were wearing these miniskirts. One of these girls was leaning over the desk. On a clear day, you could see the San Francisco Bay. So I went and pinched her. Noreen saw it: she said, 'My, my, you are *so* Wicked.' Jerry Wexler ran out of his office. 'That's it baby, that's it, that's the name of his next album, baby. *The Wicked Pickett*, that's it, put it down.' "[16]

CHAPTER 10

We all have a light aside and a dark side. He would gravitate at the wrong time to the dark side.

Eddie Jacobs, bass player and bandleader

In early 1967 Wilson Pickett's manager and agent, James Evans, put together a brochure promoting soul music on the burgeoning concert circuit. "Over the past ten years there have been a score of new auditoriums and arenas built on the outskirts of major cities, especially in the South and Southwest," it announced. "These arenas need attractions, and super R&B packages have helped fill that need." He gave numbers: "Today a giant R and B package can cost a promoter $4,000 to $7,500 in salaries, transportation, and rentals. But the average gross runs between $10,000 and $15,000 per night and in a large auditorium can reach up to $40,000."

The brochure did not state that Pickett was its prime beneficiary; Evans had a large enough roster that he could mix and match artists to help fill any package. But the accompanying pictures were almost exclusively of his main client, and the message was clear: there's money to be made in these new venues, and Pickett is your man. Still, there was a caveat: that only one singer on the scene could carry a venue on his own: "James Brown is such a powerful box-office attraction that he doesn't need any supporting acts on his show," Evans stated.

Pickett knew he was a better screamer than Brown. "James, he'll scream between the notes," he said in 1969. "He screams but nobody never know what key he's in!"[1] Wexler agreed. "When James Brown used to scream, it was a scream," he once observed. "When Pickett screamed, it was a musical note."[2] But Pickett couldn't compete on many other levels, especially Brown's theatrical live show with its elaborate dance moves, which had been transformed into a self-financed, genre-bending, million-selling LP, *Live at the Apollo!*, before Pickett had even established himself at Double L.

Pickett never aspired to Brown's title as the Hardest Working Man in Show Business. He wasn't interested in a flotilla of male backing vocalists and pantomime gestures, the act with the cape—and doing the splits was beyond his skill set. What Pickett did aspire toward was being the best, most honest, direct, real damn soul singer in the game, and to that end Brown had certainly demonstrated one thing: you needed to keep your live band in shape. "He modeled his management style on things he picked up from James Brown," said Wilson's brother Maxwell, who moved to New York upon graduating high school in 1966, working as an assistant to Wilson on the road until the Army called him in 1968. "James Brown ruled his organization with an iron first."

"Pickett was really serious about his craft," said Ernest Smith, a bass player who came up through the Howard Theater in Washington, DC and did several stints with Pickett. "If you hit a wrong note, he'd go off. He'd say, 'This is how I get paid, this is my living.' He wanted to be the best at what he did." Danny White, first a valet and later an opening singer for Pickett, confirmed, "He was a perfectionist. He wouldn't hesitate to go shut your instrument off in front of you. He's done it at the Apollo: the guitar player was hitting the wrong chords, he walked right over and pulled the plug out of the amplifier."

When Pickett returned to the United Kingdom to solidify his early success with a string of dates at core venues like London's Marquee and Flamingo Clubs, he was teamed up with a local band of primarily West Indian immigrants, the Maroons. "From the very first meeting, he was abrasive," recalled Paddy Corea, their sax player, "a real slave driver—but he didn't ask you to do anything that he didn't do himself on stage. James Brown is considered the hardest working man in show business. The Wicked Wilson Pickett was right behind." Danny O'Donovan, a British promoter who brought many of the American R&B stars of the 1960s over to Europe for their first tours, confirmed that "his musicians were very tight, by necessity, because he wouldn't accept anything less." O'Donovan recalled having to intervene when Pickett drew a gun on a band member in Germany. "He was one of the toughest artists I ever worked with. The only other one in that league that really gave me a hard time was James Brown."

"A lot of musicians were afraid of Wilson because they knew that he would physically challenge you," said Eddie Jacobs. "Crusher [Green, drummer] told me that Wilson grabbed Patience [Higgins, sax player] by his shirt and was shaking him and when he was finished with him, his shirt was still standing there and he was petrified," said Jacobs. "Wilson went through some rages, man."

The ability to roll with the physical harassment depended on the person's character and upbringing. "I came out the backwoods," said sax player Jack Philpot. "I understood why he was like that, 'cos he was so afraid. He didn't trust anybody, and the money he got he didn't want to lose it."

Touring in the mid-1960s was a cash business, and one of the greatest responsibilities Pickett could charge an employee with was to either collect or look after that cash. He did so with Danny White. "It was nothing for me to have $40–$50,000 in my room," said White, who soon learned that Pickett was something of a savant when it came to numbers. "I've never seen anybody count money as good and as fast as him." When it came to percentages—the "overage" on a good gig—Pickett could calculate the sum in his head, to the amazement of promoters, who quickly learned not to cheat him.

"If it sounded like he was getting crossed, he would go through the roof," said Philpot, who confirmed Pickett's way with numbers. "If you didn't explain it the way he could understand it, you were a crook. James (Brown) was the same way." Philpot, likewise afforded financial responsibility, recalled occasions on stage that he'd have $10,000 in one pocket and a .38 Derringer in the other. In holding the cash, he said, he was essentially a courier: "If nobody knows where the money is, there's nothing really to be worried of." As for the gun, "We didn't hurt anybody, but we had to get some money one time. It was just a general culture of being ripped off by promoters—didn't matter if they were black or white, they'd get ya."

Then again, said Carlton McWilliams, a bass player Pickett acquired, literally overnight, in Wichita, Kansas, in the middle of a tour, "Everyone carried a pistol, man, everybody!" Indeed, one of the first questions Pickett asked Bobby Womack when his friend joined the group in 1966 was, "Bobby, have you got a gun?"[3] On tour in the summer of 1967, in Kingston, South Carolina, "everyone bought a pistol," said McWilliams. When they came back up for a headlining engagement at the Apollo in New York, where possession was illegal, he hid his between the pillows in his hotel. The maid discovered it, and he was arrested. "Spent ten days in the tombs, when I came out Wilson had already hired someone else." McWilliams was at least given his fare home.

Loyalty, evidently, was hard won and easily lost on the road with Pickett, and touring lineups were never stable. For Pickett and many of his peers, the stage group was more like that of a sports team, drawn from a large rotation of available talent. When you had a winning lineup you'd try and keep it stable; when that team stopped firing on all cylinders, you changed it. Sometimes that meant bringing back a veteran who knew the songs, sometimes it meant hiring someone new with fresh ideas. Regular musicians, rarely afforded a retaining salary, might prove unavailable at short notice, having secured another gig. Players could pass through through the ranks on their way to individual success (original sax player Louis Risbrook went on to form B. T. Express with his brother; brass and bass player Leon Pendarvis became musical director of the *Saturday Night Live* band) or obscurity. Occasionally, the lineup was expanded for a major concert or TV show: Pickett built up his brass section to outrageous proportions through 1967, perhaps to prove a point, then pared it back down again because of cost. Arguments might mean a wholesale clear-out.

Those arguments were almost always about pay. Eddie Jacobs grew frustrated at being crammed into a station wagon with a U-Haul on the back and splitting $1,000 a night between all the players (who were also responsible for their own hotels), while Pickett rode ahead in his new El Dorado, chauffeur J. W. Valentine at his wheel, the bulk of the tour's cash with him. "I said, 'When you retire and you have your home with a swimming pool and a Rolls in the front, I want to retire and have a house with a Mercedes in the front.' He said, 'Well Eddie Jacobs, you know what you need? You need a motherfucking hit record! If I go on stage and I got a guitar and a harmonica around my neck they gonna pay me $10,000—what they gonna pay Eddie Jacobs and his band?'"

Jacobs quit. (He'd be back.) "Pickett's thing," said Jacobs, "was to show that he didn't need anybody: he was Wilson Pickett and you couldn't dictate to him what you wanted. And all this stems from his upbringing, because he came up poor, didn't have a lot to eat, maybe lived in a one-room shack, and everything he had to do he had to fight for it. So his mentality was to keep musicians hungry—just enough to have food to eat and clean your clothes and be on the road with him. But as far as having a future, there *was* no future—and that was the same mentality as James Brown."

Jacobs was bandleader during one of Pickett's first Apollo headlines; the musicians were celebrating Jerry Wexler's compliment that they had the Memphis and Muscle Shoals players down "verbatim," when, in Jacobs's recollection, "Someone banged at the door. I went to see who it was, and it was James Brown, Bobby Byrd, and Danny Ray, the guy that would hold the cape over him. James Brown has his coat over him, and Wilson's rack is over here with his clothes. So, as James Brown came in, he said, 'Wilson Pickett, the star of the motherfucking show,' and Wilson went to shake his hand . . . and JB passed him and started pulling his clothes to see what costumes he had, and then turned around and walked out. I said to myself,

'I heard a lot about James Brown, but I see for myself—he's an arrogant, ignorant man.'"

Outwardly, Pickett rarely wasted an opportunity to put his rival down. "James Brown, to me, is strictly small-time," he told the *New Musical Express's* Nick Kent in 1979. "Just some Georgian kid workin' in some cramped sweaty bar where the stage is so damn small there's only room for him and the drummer. Guitar player's workin' his lips in the bathroom, sweat drippin' off the walls, ha! Yup, that's how James Brown started and that's how I always think of him."[4]

Pickett had a point somewhere in the midst of his insult: James Brown records of the mid-to-late 1960s were thin, reedy, and emblematic of the fact that they were recorded in haste, on the road, often around a single microphone. By comparison, Pickett's craft was built around his voice and his studio performances, where time and money were never an issue for Atlantic; his recordings were among the most accomplished and polished of the era. Brown's loose funk offered a direct connection to Africa; Pickett's tight jerk became a cornerstone of American rock. In the process, Brown won the loyalty of the black audience; Pickett crossed over to the whites. Brown might have owned the Apollo, but Pickett could go straight from a headlining stint there to a weekend gig at the mainly white Manhattan midtown Cheetah Club, or an appearance at the equally pale Action House on Long Island.

When living in Queens, Wilson and Dovie were invited to visit Brown's mansion in nearby St. Alban's. Dovie recalled that the occasion was essentially an opportunity for Brown to grandstand. "He always liked to give you lectures," Pickett noted, recalling one occasion when Brown "came by to see me" at an unnamed club.

"Ah, Pickett, you know you're a good singer, can't nobody out-sing you," he recalled Brown saying. "But you know there's one thing wrong with you."

"What's that, James?"

"You ain't black enough."[5]

Not black enough? You couldn't get any blacker than Wilson Pickett. But Brown wasn't talking just skin color. In the summer of 1966, Brown had issued "Don't Be a Drop Out," a single directed to the black youth of America. He followed it up the next year with "Get It Together." Brown saw it as a musician's responsibility to lead by example, to supply encouragement, offer judgment if need be, and he was not alone: Stax issued a promotional LP to black radio stations in 1967, *Stay in School, Don't Be a Dropout,* with announcements to that effect by most of its leading artists, including Otis Redding.

Pickett was never interested in taking such a direct approach to politics. He preferred to set his example in the way he went about his everyday business. In late 1966 or early 1967, after one of those periodic clear-outs, he was in search of multiple musicians, and he found them in Montreal's Esquire Show Bar on Stanley Street, which had long attracted the greatest names in rhythm and blues. Among them was drummer Buddy Miles, a native of Omaha, Nebraska, who had been on the road since the age of twelve, touring alongside his jazz-playing father. Miles recommended two Montreal locals: Bob Parkins on keys and Walter Rossini on guitar. Both were white.

Rossini, a committed student of soul music, passed his audition by proving he could play Steve Cropper's subtly complex introduction to "Ninety-Nine and a Half (Won't Do)." Joining the band was a whirlwind for the teenager—and an eye-opening experience about deeply entrenched racism he hadn't before seen. "I witnessed the KKK bullshit," he recalled in a 2005 interview. "We were often refused gasoline; two out of three gas stations would not permit us to use the washrooms, and when the boys in the band would get the munchies or need cigarettes, I would go into the restaurant and order, and as I would walk out with the goods I was called a nigger lover." He noted, "I experienced quite a few close calls. The hard core rednecks were the dangerous ones." On more than one occasion, one of them would sidle up after him to the cash register and buy a gun. "There were no questions asked, only, 'Will you need ammunition, sir?'" At such times, Rossini feared for his life.

So did his employer. "Pickett was very worried for me and so was Jack Philpot," he said. "I often use to ride with Pickett in his limo; he always wanted me close to him. They both were very supportive and loving."

Pickett was all too familiar with the segregation of the Deep South, and so were countless others among the musicians who had passed through his ranks and experienced the same abuses and often racist police aggression. In the recording studios of Tennessee and Alabama, Pickett had encountered integration, however, and he knew that was the way of the future. Rossini recalled Pickett choosing to make an unprompted statement during a show in what was effectively the singer's home-town, Montgomery:

> Imagine a packed arena with white people to the right and black people to the
> left, 20,000 fans split down the middle. There was so much tension. Imagine
> how I felt up there on stage? During "Land of 1000 Dances" he brought the band
> down to a very low volume and started preaching to the sold out segregated
> audience about racism, he went on and on about what it means to have soul,

then says, "Why do black people think that white people have no soul? Soul is from within no matter what color you are." He calls me to the front of the stage and introduces me and says, "As you can all see, Walter is white, and he'll prove to you all that white people also have soul, Walter show the people how much soul you got." I cranked up my volume full blast and took a screaming guitar solo, and as I was playing Wilson danced all around me, and the people stood up and went wild. The tension in the audience calmed, it was amazing to see 20,000 people getting along, dancing and having a good time. What a beautiful experience.[6]

Pickett was among the first of the soul stars to play with an integrated live band, and he would later say, "I don't think Martin Luther King can take all the credit for kind of scraping shit out down there [in the South], 'cos I think the black entertainers of America had a lot to do with it. I tell you man, we opened the doors, 'cos we were traveling down through there all the time. We stopped going to the back doors, and all that shit. We fought our way out the place, we've been shot at, all kinds of shit, had glass put in our food, oh yeah."[7]

For Easter 1967, white disc jockey and consummate self-promoter Murray the K bowed out of the Revue business with an elaborate swansong. He moved his traditional Brooklyn Fox extravaganza to the RKO Theater on 58th Street in Manhattan, calling it, with typical hyperbole, Music in the Fifth Dimension. Smokey Robinson & the Miracles were listed performers, but on opening day Robinson walked out after a heated argument with Murray about money.[8] Mitch Ryder, the new hero of blue-eyed soul with two top 10 hits in recent months, became the headliner, with Wilson Pickett second. It might seem to be the same old story—black artists doing all the hard work to establish a new music, white imitators following in their wake and cleaning up—but Ryder and Pickett, who had shared roots in Detroit, hit upon a strong working relationship that resulted in further tours together. At the RKO the Blues Project were also on the bill, and on certain nights they were all joined by the Young Rascals, Simon & Garfunkel, the Blues Magoos, or Phil Ochs. The major media focus, however, was on two British rock acts, each on their debut American visits: Cream and the Who.

It was a lineup for the ages: the Who, Cream, Wilson Pickett, Mitch Ryder, the Blues Project, and the Young Rascals all on the same stage. Better yet, the nature of such revue shows meant that a committed music fan could buy a ticket first thing on a weekend morning, and over the course of the next eight or ten hours, sit through several sets each by some of the very best rock and soul acts of the entire decade. Many did just that and were awestruck—especially when the Who ended each song set by smashing their equipment, something American audiences had never witnessed.

Pickett followed this destructive act and didn't take kindly to it. The Who's Pete Townshend recalled, "Wilson Pickett called a meeting because we were using smoke bombs, and he felt that we were very unprofessional, and that the smoke was affecting everybody else's act."[9] The group's singer Roger Daltrey attempted to mollify Pickett by assuring him that they all were great fans. (Many years later, Daltrey narrated a Pickett documentary for BBC Radio.) Ultimately Pickett decided that if he couldn't beat them, he'd join them. At the end of the run, after an Easter Sunday show where the Who destroyed their equipment for good, he treated everyone with a generous tip, reportedly giving the promoter, the various acts, and even the stagehands a bottle of Scotch each. "[10]

For Buddy Miles and Walter Rossini, as for so many others either on stage or in the audience, the RKO Easter extravaganza served as an epiphany. The R&B circuit—the long drives between shows in a beat-up station wagon, the enduring segregation in the South, the poor pay, the equally poor PA systems, the short sets—lost its allure to the emerging rock scene, and they each quit. In the case of Miles, Pickett may not have cared; trumpeter Chris Lowe, who'd joined the band overnight the previous year when it swung through Augusta, recalled the drummer being given "a kick up the rear end" for playing "too much drums." While Rossini abbreviated his name to Rossi and formed a progressive rock group called the Influence, Miles joined white blues man Mike Bloomfield in the Electric Flag, which made its debut at the Monterey Pop Festival that June; he would later become part of the Band of Gypsys with Jimi Hendrix, who returned that summer of 1967 from the United Kingdom having transformed from journeyman R&B guitarist into psychedelic rock star. Unveiled to American audiences at Monterey, Hendrix outdid the Who by setting fire to his guitar before he destroyed it.[11]

As Music in the Fifth Dimension ushered out the theater revue package, Monterey Pop introduced the outdoor festival, with longer stage sets and, briefly, the integration of different musical styles. The bill at Monterey included Lou Rawls, a former member of the Pilgrim Travelers and a Sam Cooke backup singer who had finally made his presence known as a solo act a full decade later by calling his latest album *Soulin'*. Rawls was outshone at Monterey, however, by a mesmerizing performance from Otis Redding, with Booker T. & the M.G.s behind him, wearing tight-fitting suits that contrasted sharply with the free-flowing hippie attire of the audience and most other musicians. Those who witnessed it spoke of Redding's show in religious terms, as if he had taken them to church. Still, it probably didn't harm Redding that he included his cover of the Rolling Stones' "Satisfaction" in his set.

Pickett would surely have held his own had he performed at Monterey, given the evidence of his sole performance with the M.G.s in Watts. Indeed, the description by Redding's manager Phil Walden of the Big O at Monterey could as easily have applied to Pickett and his singing: "Otis didn't have to burn a guitar. He didn't have to tear up an amplifier. He didn't even have to get down on his knees. He just got up there and performed his music." Monterey elevated Redding to superstar crossover status, and if that left Pickett to wonder why he hadn't been invited along for the ride, he could certainly argue that he had done his part to bring the music to this point.

CHAPTER 11

Whatever Pickett said, he stuck by it. No matter. He was tough, but also a lovable guy, a sweetheart, would do anything for you. He didn't trust a lot of people, however and—mostly—I don't think he trusted himself.

Bobby Womack, singer, songwriter, guitarist (*My Story*)[1]

Wilson Pickett was a solo artist, in every sense. Considered a loner as a child, he maintained that aura of self-imposed isolation throughout his career. He didn't like partners, didn't trust them; even when invited into the Falcons, he maintained his solo status. He always wanted to be in control, so he sought to divide and conquer: he didn't bring his live band into the studio, didn't take his studio band on the road. There was only one person with whom he struck up a productive and faithful musical relationship that straddled all aspects of his music: Bobby Womack.

Born in 1944, Womack was the middle of five boys who came up dirt poor in Cleveland; some days, their steelworker father would tell them that they were "fasting"—which the boys readily understood meant that there was, in fact, no money to put food on the table. That father, named Friendly, a part-time gospel singer back in his native Charleston, was a religious man, beating the boys for the slightest transgression. When he discovered that Bobby had been fooling around on his one personal luxury, an acoustic guitar, he was set to give the boy the whuppin' of his life—until Bobby, barely nine at the time, demonstrated that he could actually play. His style was utterly unique: Bobby was left-handed, and he had learned his way around his father's guitar upside-down. As a result, it was noted by those who played with him, even his rhythm chords always sounded different.

The Womack boys soon became the Womack Brothers, singing and playing gospel in the local churches, with their father as their manager. He talked them onstage in 1953 with a visiting Sam Cooke and the Soul Stirrers, after which they spent every weekend and holiday on the Gospel Highway. Sam left gospel behind and became a crossover teen idol, and Friendly Womack eventually reached back out to Cooke, who brought the brothers onto his SAR label for an effort at recording gospel. When the single flopped Cooke had them change their name to the Valentinos, rewrite a sacred tune in the secular vein, and after the result, "Looking' for a Love," hit big in 1962, he sent them money to come join him in California. Even though several of the brothers were still of school age, Friendly Womack didn't try to stop them; in fact, he threw them out for singing the Devil's music.

The Valentinos struggled for a follow-up, but Bobby's star continued to rise: he wrote, arranged, and sang just about as well as he could play guitar, and Cooke brought him into the studio and on the road as his teenage protégé. In 1964 Womack wrote the Valentinos' only other (minor) hit, "It's All Over Now"; the Rolling Stones covered it for their first UK number one, and Womack learned the value of a songwriting copyright.

The good times with Sam Cooke came to a halt when the singer was murdered in December 1964; they worsened when Bobby wed Sam's widow, Barbara, just three months after the funeral. Bobby claimed he was looking out for Sam's legacy, protecting the family; he later said Barbara forced him into it. Either way, Bobby was viciously beaten by Sam's brothers for doing so and socially ostracized by just about everyone. When he attempted to resume his musical career with "Nothing You Can Do," which took the ubiquitous guitar riff from the Rolling Stones "Satisfaction" as its bass line and blended British Invasion vocal motifs with soul, he was effectively boycotted; he recalled that disc jockeys would throw the record into the garbage can in front of him.

Not Wilson Pickett, though. He and Bobby went back to their days on the Gospel Highway. Pickett knew Bobby's talent, and in recording "Nothing You Can Do" and the Valentinos' 1962 single "She's So Good to Me" at his first Fame session, set out to rehabilitate his friend's reputation. "He was my first break," Womack later admitted of Pickett, lamenting that he never credited the singer as such while Wilson was alive.[2]

"He was going round worrying about how people felt about him marrying Sam Cooke's wife," Wilson Pickett told Rick Whitesell. "I said, 'Well, you can tell them to go fuck themselves and you go fill Sam Cooke's shoes. How do you do that? You go out and make a career on your own.'"[3]

But it wasn't easy, and when a period as a Ray Charles sideman ended acrimoniously in 1966, Pickett invited Womack to join his own live group. Pickett had another quality guitarist at the time, Freddie Tyrrell; adding Womack to the mix raised the live show's standard considerably. Womack's arrival also affected the younger players. "Bobby was just a different person," said Chris Lowe, nineteen at the time. "I was just mesmerized. I can remember the first time we checked in the hotel, and I just walked by the room and he had his door open, he was just sitting in there playing. I just stopped in front of the door, like a little awestruck kid." Womack, three years Lowe's senior but with a lifetime's more experience, invited him in. Lowe was amazed. "We were only going to be there one night, but Bobby unpacked everything. He had all his suits arranged in the closet, he had all his shoes lined up, I'd never seen anything like it." Jack Philpot often shared a hotel room with Womack; his major regret in life was turning down Womack's invitation to write songs one evening to go pursue girls. "He was a star in himself," Philpot said.

Womack's presence had a settling instinct on Pickett. "I noticed a drastic change in his attitude towards his bandleader when he hired Bobby Womack," said Maxwell Pickett. "He had such high respect for Bobby Womack that the way he talked to him was different from the other guys, the way he paid him."

"Once I got to know him, he was a nice guy, but moody," wrote Womack of Wilson. "He wasn't a man that you could mess with. You could joke with him about something one minute and in the next he'd be on you and trying to kill you. Everybody called him Wicked because Pickett wasn't the kind of guy who thought about what he did. Self-destructive. He kept a lot of stuff secret."[4]

Pickett, meantime, sang Womack's talent from the rooftops, taking him to Atlantic and insisting on an audition. "After I was finished, they said, 'We're afraid to sign him, there's too much negative talk on him from marrying Sam's wife.'"[5] Undeterred, Pickett offered to record Womack's songs for himself. "Every time they see Wilson Pickett on a label," the singer explained to his friend, "they're going to see Bobby Womack underneath."

The first fruits of this arrangement were hand-picked for Pickett's third session at Fame, for which the singer flew down to Muscle Shoals at the end of January 1967, a monumental month for the studio, and by extension, for popular music. Otis Redding had only recently brought by his protégé Arthur Conley to cut "Sweet Soul Music," a cover of Sam Cooke's "Yeah Man," that took the opening line—"Do you like good music?"—and then diverted Cooke's lyrics away from its rewrite of "Land of 1000 Dances" into a celebration of contemporary soul artists.[6] Backed by the same Fame musicians who had worked on Pickett's recordings through 1966, Conley threw the spotlight on Lou Rawls, Sam & Dave, Otis (but of course), and "that wicked Pickett ... singing 'Mustang Sally,'" further ensuring that the Prattville boy would be forever remembered by his rhyming nickname.

Concluding with the affirmation that James Brown was "the king of them all, y'all," "Sweet Soul Music" packed such a joyous punch that it would become one of the bestselling singles of the year—across *all* genres—and a pop hit all over the world.[7]

Redding seized the opportunity of his first visit to Fame to record a vibrant personal demo of "You Left the Water Running," as had just been unveiled on *The Wicked Pickett* that same week. Only a few days later, Aretha Franklin came down to record—as a brand-new Atlantic artist, Columbia having finally given up on her. Aretha did not need much encouragement from her new patron, Jerry Wexler, to follow in her friend Wilson Pickett's footsteps and head down to Alabama—to Fame and, hopefully, good fortune.

Franklin's session on January 24, 1967 has become the stuff of legend, not only because it resulted in "I Never Loved a Man (the Way I Love You)" and launched her career as an authentic soul singer, but because it fell apart after Rick Hall went to Aretha's hotel to make amends for comments made earlier in the day by a (white) trumpet player from Memphis, and ended up in a fistfight with Franklin's husband and manager, Ted White. Franklin flew home the next morning and never returned to Fame. The incident marked the end of the professional honeymoon between Wexler and Hall, and the beginning of an incredibly productive period of side work for the Fame rhythm section, whom Wexler later flew, under false pretenses, to New York to finish Franklin's debut album on Atlantic's home turf.[8]

On February 1, just a few days before the first of those New York sessions took place, Pickett, the man who had done so much to put Fame on the soul music map in the first place, was back there to pick up where he had left off. He brought with him three Bobby Womack compositions –all ballads, a significant change in approach for a man previously known as a party artist. Presented as a trilogy, on side two of the subsequent LP, the strongest, "I Found The One," came first. Complete with firmly stated piano triplets from Spooner Oldham and the purity of the Blue Belles' choral support, it was followed by "Something Within Me," a secular update of the sacred song of the same name. "I'm Sorry About That," came last, again benefiting from the musical empathy provided by Oldham on organ and the Blue Belles.

None were obvious hits, but they afforded the album an authenticity that the singer was keen to demonstrate—given not just its straightforward title, *The Sound of Wilson Pickett*, but his views about the commercial cover versions that were fast becoming an expectation:

> Wexler used to come down there with a whole suitcase full of other records that
> he wanted me to do. As a matter of fact me and him had, almost a falling out one

time about that. Because I felt he was bringing too many, like Rascals records down, Rolling Stones, Beatles, all this kind of thing.[9]

The Beatles was yet come, but Wexler did indeed bring a Young Rascals song for Pickett in early 1967 ("Love is a Beautiful Thing"), and Pickett had a right to chafe at the notion that a soul artist of his proven reputation was being asked to cover songs by white artists who were only imitating the very style he had helped create in the first place. He'd also recorded three "Rolling Stones" songs in his first two Fame sessions (even though they were all R&B hits first). As publishing checks from "In the Midnight Hour" and his other Atlantic hits began coming in, he must have come to realize anew the financial value of the songwriting he had abandoned after Stax, as well as the artistic importance of being known as a composer.

"I was mostly trying to create, like an original career of Wilson Pickett," he said. "My songs, original songs like 'In the Midnight Hour.'" He then did a perfect impersonation of Wexler's response to his protestations.

"Hey baby, you got to record these things. You seem to do well with them."
"Yeah, but they're not original, Jerry."
"Hey baby, they're making you money . . ."[10]

They were, to some extent. But they were making Atlantic an awful lot more. As the number of soul singers proliferated faster than the amount of available material, it mattered not to Wexler whether Solomon Burke or the Young Rascals covered Wilson Pickett, or whether Pickett covered Burke, the Young Rascals, Don Covay, or Percy Sledge, as long as the records sold and the copyrights belonged to Atlantic's publishing arm.

Pickett went ahead and sang "Love Is a Beautiful Thing," but hippie lyrics like "life could be so nice" did not roll off his tongue easily, and the finished version, with the backup singers featured prominently in the mix, was ultimately tucked away as the LP's finale. Pickett and Wexler appeared to find a healthy compromise and a creative share in the subsequent spoils when they cowrote "Soul Dance Number Three," a suitably dirty stomping groove that name-checked the boogaloo, the skate, and the shing-a-ling, threw in a reference to girls in their miniskirts, and added several screams and "Lord Have Mercy"s, plus a blinding sax solo. "Soul Dance Number Three" provided Pickett with a top ten R&B hit early in the summer, backed by the exuberant "You Can't Stand Alone," delivered direct to Pickett from the pen of Rudy Clark ("Good Lovin'," "The Shoop Shoop Song"). Recorded at a pulsating tempo, featuring some astonishingly dexterous bass from Tommy

Cogbill and the rare sound of a Spooner Oldham solo on the Wurlitzer, "You Can't Stand Alone" subsequently enjoyed an R&B chart run of its own.

Pickett additionally had a writing credit on the song that had made his name in the first place, "I Found a Love," covered at Fame less than two years after the Falcons' version had been included on his debut Atlantic LP. The group recorded one version that went unreleased, and then a longer version at a more stately pace than the original, and with Robert Ward's crazed guitar licks replaced by Spooner Oldham's hymn-like Hammond accompaniment and the Blue Belles at their most church choir-like, it was arguably more sacred than the original, too. Indeed, it opened up into a prolonged preaching section on which Pickett appeared genuinely ecstatic, even breaking into laughter at one point, ultimately concluding with a euphoric scream that took him back to 1962. "I Found a Love" would be released in the spring, ahead of the album, as a two-part single, a format that was becoming increasingly popular in black music now that it was starting to stretch beyond the confines of the typical three-minute single— and it performed impressively in the charts for such an authentic gospel rendition.

The album's biggest hit nonetheless came from one of Pickett's contemporary interpretations. As "soul" had become the familiar by-word for modern, commercial rhythm and blues, used in all manner of song titles and co-opted by "blue-eyed soul" white acts, another musical genre would inevitably take its place in the black cultural underground. It arrived in the form of "funk." In use as far back as early jazz, by the mid-1960s the word signified a syncopated rhythmic alternative to the conventional melodies and chord changes of soul, and stood for the more endearingly earthy aspects of black culture as a whole. The first single known to use the word in its title was recorded in 1966—a five-and-a-half minute, one-chord workout in the emerging James Brown style by Dyke & the Blazers, a group that had relocated from Buffalo to Phoenix, Arizona.

That single, "Funky Broadway," had just started a slow climb up the R&B charts when Pickett decided to cover it. The Blazers' recording quality was mediocre at best, and when it came to vocal delivery, front man Arlester "Dyke" Christian was no match for Pickett. The Fame musicians also rose to the occasion, thriving on the simple groove. Chips Moman flexed his guitar at the start of the song, Tommy Cogbill bent into a bass line that seemed to slide up and down the entire instrument every two measures; Roger Hawkins largely avoided the syncopation of the original recording and instead maintained a conventional backbeat, ensuring the song crossover appeal. Charlie Chalmers took a typically bright sax solo, with his fellow Memphis horn players (Floyd Newman, "Bowlegs" Miller, and Jimmy

Mitchell, the younger sibling of Hi Studio owner Willie Mitchell) sweeping into a bright refrain on the coda that allowed for plenty on-stage vamping over the years to come. After just two and a half minutes, they had not only nailed what would turn out to be Pickett's fourth R&B number 1 in barely two years, but also his second top ten pop hit. Along the way, they were the first to take the word "funk" into the charts—several years, as Pickett would be keen to observe of his major rival, before James Brown.

CHAPTER 12

He was one of a kind in the sense that most good artists are one of a kind. With Wilson Pickett, you hear the voice, you know who it is, no matter what song it is. Why? God made him that way.

Spooner Oldham, keyboard player, Fame and American Studios

A t the top of his game and acutely aware of it, Pickett was back in the studio before *The Sound of Wilson Pickett* had even been released. Chips Moman had recently upgraded his American Studios in Memphis with an eight-track console, leaping over Fame and Stax's limited technology. Moman cut his first seminal soul recording there, James & Bobby Purify's "Shake a Tail Feather," in the midst of its installation, giving him the confidence to hawk the place to Atlantic. The timing was perfect: the fallout over the aborted Aretha session at Fame had created hostility between Wexler and Hall, and while Wexler continued to bring the studio's players to New York for sessions, it made sense to keep Pickett recording down south where he was in his element. In early July 1967 the singer was booked into American, discreetly situated in a strip mall on the north side of Memphis. He was the first Atlantic act to record there.

Wexler did not attend, which may have reflected his allegiance to Aretha's skyrocketing career, or a need for him and Pickett to take a break from each other. Tom Dowd flew down to assume coproduction duties alongside bass player Tommy Cogbill, who joined Moman as a permanent part of the American team. (So did Spooner Oldham and Dan Penn, defecting from Rick Hall, though neither was directly involved with Pickett's session.)

Cogbill, Dowd, and the Memphis horn section were familiar faces for Pickett. But he hadn't yet been acquainted with most of the new rhythm section. As at Fame, they were white. Unlike the musicians in Muscle Shoals, however, who had been raised on black rhythm and blues as it transitioned into soul, the team at America was slightly older—and it showed in both their pedigree and their performances. Guitarist Reggie Young, from Arkansas, had worked extensively with the Bill Black Combo, opening for the Beatles in both America and Britain. Keyboard players Bobby Wood and Bobby Emmons, both from Mississippi, had toyed with solo careers. And drummer Gene Chrisman, the only Memphis native, had toured with Jerry Lee Lewis alongside Charlie Chalmers. To this considerable pool of talent was added two black musicians, King Curtis and Bobby Womack. Curtis was there to start work on an album of his own as soon as Pickett's was completed, and he garnered immediate respect. "Friendly and sensitive," said Emmons; "the best musician I had ever worked with at the time I met him," said Young. On this session Pickett would actually call him out by name, shouting "Blow your horn, King" at the start of a solo on Sam Cooke's "Bring It on Home to Me."

Womack was there to play on his own compositions and, hopefully, to secure work as a session guitarist. His presence invigorated the rhythm section. Bobby Emmons noted that Womack could afford to be cocky: "Very talented guy: I learned a lot from him about what was hip and what wasn't in his style of music."[1] Reggie Young welcomed Womack's presence. "We almost swapped styles," said Young. "I learned a lot from Bobby Womack, and there's a lot of things that I would play—thirds, for example—that he then started playing." The pair of them formed a mirror image as they sat opposite each other, each with a right-handed hollow-bodied guitar, Womack as always playing his upside down.

The two guitarists' ability to communicate was never more acutely heard than on the title track of the subsequent Long Player, "I'm in Love." A searing mid-tempo ballad on which Young took both the high introductory riff and the mid-song solo, with Womack weaving around him, it would have been difficult to tell where one guitar finished and the other started if not for the stereo separation. "One of the prettiest songs I ever made," observed Womack, "I'm in Love" was supposedly his riposte to the critics who claimed he had married Barbara Cooke for her money.[2] But Pickett infused the song with his own interpretation, producing one of the most truly soulful vocal performances of his life. "He beat me singing that song," admitted Womack, who would later record it under his own name. "He just made you really believe he's in love."[3]

Tom Dowd was equally taken with the subtle intricacies of the performance. "It was the most unusual record for meter and for time," he recalled. "Womack looked at Pickett, and said, 'Wherever you are, I won't be on the same thing.' Pickett said, 'You just tell me where to sing, I'll sing.' It was completely off the wall, and when Jerry heard it, he said 'How did you get him to do that?' and I said 'I don't know.'" Pickett, concluded Dowd, was just "intuitive."[4]

Dowd commanded his own accolades from the studio musicians both for his easy-going nature and his ability to "organize" the instruments, as manifested in a particularly sublime final mix of "I'm in Love." Barely more than two minutes long and yet fully complete, "I'm in Love" was a markedly different sound for Pickett, and it was hard to believe that it had been recorded just fourteen months after "Land of 1000 Dances." Released as a single at the end of the year, it fared considerably better on the R&B charts as a top five hit than it did at pop, where Pickett was still pegged as primarily a party man. Probably the most revered of all Wilson Pickett singles among his musical peers, "I'm in Love" was surely the most underrated by his audience.

Bobby Womack brought three other songs to the studio. The fiery ballad "I've Come a Long Way" dated back to the Valentinos but was completely revamped at American. Womack supplied the majestic introductory lead guitar line, and Reggie Young responded in kind. "We've Got To Have Love," cowritten with Pickett, was resolutely upbeat, with Floyd Newman contributing his delightful honking baritone sax from the second verse, the rest of the horns dominating a middle-eight section, the assembled chorus of female singers joining Pickett on a sing-a-long chorus, Cogbill delivering a series of constantly free-flowing half-notes, and Bobby Emmons making himself prominent for once with a flexibly pulsating organ part.

Given that Pickett was recording so many of Womack's songs, Bobby tipped off Wilson to the merits of owning one's own publishing. Pickett promptly took a meeting at Atlantic with Womack in tow, telling them he was done assigning his songs to Cotillion. They were presented with no objections, and when "We've Got to Have Love" was released, the label listed a new publisher: Veda Music, named for Pickett's oldest daughter— even though he hardly ever saw the girl.

The fourth of Womack's songs for Pickett, "Jealous Love," written with King Curtis, was a grand statement that opened the album, and was the first Pickett song to feature a string section since he had started recording down south. The general theme of the song, "Why can't you trust me some time?" appeared almost comically inappropriate, given Pickett's own distrust of his partner Dovie Hall.

"He was extremely possessive of Dovie," said Jack Philpot. "She was a very attractive woman. But you can't watch her twenty-four hours a day." Philpot said if Pickett called her from the road and she didn't answer the phone, "He'd get raging mad, extremely angry, and he would get on a plane and go home." Hall acknowledged, "He was always accusing me of someone . . . I would be accused of someone I didn't even know! I knew I wasn't doing it, and he knew I wasn't doing it. But he was going to accuse me anyway." At the same time, Pickett was out playing the field nightly. "I could see women were just lined up," Dovie said. She knew she wasn't like those one-night stands: "These women thinking, 'He's got money, I'm going to get him' . . . how they gonna get him when there's five or six of them? I know he was coming home. Whatever he's doing, he's coming home."

Not that Hall was incapable of standing up for herself. At one point when she suspected Jimmy Evans's secretary of having intentions on her man, she spent the entire day at the office, sitting in reception, staring at the woman in question, who squirmed at her desk knowing that the only way out of the office meant walking right by Dovie. "I just looked," said Hall. "And looked. Wilson told me afterwards, 'You know that girl quit? You made her leave her job!' I said, 'That was my intention. Because she's guilty. Only a guilty person would do that.' So I got rid of that situation."

Dovie didn't have close friendships beyond those with wives of Wilson's most trusted companions like Don Covay and Jack Philpott. "It was my choice," she insisted, "because I knew how jealous he was"—which means, in effect, it was no real choice at all. Associating with the band members themselves was strictly forbidden: "I can't tell you half the band members' names 'cos I wasn't around them. I didn't say much to them, 'cos I'd get in trouble if I did." When she attended the Apollo, Pickett would eject his musicians from the dressing room rather than risk them hearing her use the bathroom. In his memoir, Womack recalled that Pickett might start out asking, in a friendly way, "You like my old lady?" and within moments would have twisted the affirmation: "You trying to *fuck* my old lady?" To be safe, just about all of his friends and musicians, Womack eventually included, kept an emotional distance from Wilson and a physical distance from Dovie.

For all the original compositions unfurled at American, the subsequent album's biggest hits came from elsewhere. One of them dated back to December 1895, where at the Bill Curtis Saloon in St. Louis, Missouri, two black men, "Stag" Lee Sheldon and Billy Lyons, friends and drinking partners fatefully organizing for competing political parties, got into an argument. At some point during an increasingly drunken debate, Lyons seized Sheldon's Stetson hat; when he refused to return it, Sheldon took out his revolver, shot Lyons in the stomach, picked up his hat and calmly walked out. Lyons later died from his injuries.

As one of five murders reported in St. Louis that day, Lyons's death might not have made much more than the local headlines—but for the fact that ragtime had recently arrived on the musical scene as a new means by which to tell such a story. A song about the subsequent court case was first reported in a Kansas City newspaper less than two years after the original killing, after which the song went on a journey: in 1910, a version made it to the musicologist John Lomax via a correspondent in Texas.

By then, "Stagger Lee" had already become part of folklore, ripe for constant retelling and revamping. The advent of recording only accelerated this process, and in 1950, a euphoric "Stack-A-Lee" by New Orleans pianist Archibald proved so popular that it made its way to military bases in Korea. There Lloyd Price adapted it for a play he put on while in the military, added an introduction, and upon return to America and his career, recorded it for release.

By this point, little remained of the original incident: rather than debating politics, the two men were playing dice outdoors after dark, Billy falsely calling seven on a roll of eight and taking Stagger Lee's money, the latter going home to get his .44, finding Billy in a barroom, and then shooting "that poor boy so bad" that the bullet went through Billy and broke "the bartender's glass." Placed on the back of a single more conventionally titled "You Need Love," Price's "Stagger Lee" was so rhythmically addictive that disc jockeys couldn't help but flip it, and although Dick Clark cited the song as too violent for *American Bandstand*, it spent February 1959 at number one. As typical with folk songs that date back beyond copyright protection, Price and his partner Harold Logan were able to claim the songwriting credits.

By 1967, plenty of people saw Wilson Pickett as embodying certain attributes of the folkloric Stagger Lee. Rick Hall liked to tell this story about him:

> He had shot his way out of his last recording contract before he came to Atlantic Records. I asked him, "Pickett, how did that happen?" He said, "It was simple. I just got on an elevator and went up to the twentieth floor where the boss was. I walked up behind and put my arm around his neck and took a .45 pistol and stuck it in his ear and told him that I came to get my contract. He quite willingly gave me my contract back."[5]

Hardly. Anyone dared put a gun to Harold Logan's head needed to be sure it was the very last thing that man knew.[6] And that was never Pickett. "He'd be like, 'I'll blow your brains out,'" said Philpot. "But he wouldn't. He would hit you! But I think he was aware of the consequences of murder. I think he was very aware that he would do some time if he killed someone. He knew he couldn't buy his way out of *that*."

At the same time, Pickett was an especially compulsive dice player in an R&B music community that was full of them. In his dressing room at the Apollo it wasn't uncommon for him and his entourage to engage in a $20,000 freeze-out, which meant that if you bet such a sum and lost it, you were done, no going back to the bank. Then again, depending how many were in the game, you could be in to win $100,000 on one roll of the dice. Not surprisingly, such stakes would attract the accredited high-rollers and notorious hustlers alike. Pickett's own band members could only stand back and watch.[7] Pickett threw out people who accused *him* of cheating at dice, and his former bandleader Eddie Jacobs offered the following justification for why Pickett and crew (including himself) packed heat on the road: "Guys shooting dice . . . a lot of them carry a gun. And sometimes you get guys who are sore losers and want to retaliate and you wanted a fair chance."

All in all, it was hardly surprising that Pickett felt encouraged to claim "Stagger Lee" for himself, recording the song during that first session at American. Gene Chrisman played a rapid-fire snare drum intro, Tommy Cogbill employed a machine-gun bass line throughout, and the brass section offered enough musical ricochets as to render the listener exceedingly nervous. Pickett's lyrics were not a straight copy of the Lloyd Price version—he swapped out Stagger Lee's "Stetson hat" for a Cadillac, and added a recitation at the start of an extensive coda warning that Billy's example ought to "teach the rest of you gamblers a lesson," directed perhaps at those looking to roll their crooked dice on him. Yet the bitter irony was that by including Lloyd Price's original introduction, he had effectively "covered" that version and therefore sacrificed all songwriting claims to Logan and Price.

Pickett's version was released on the flip of the "I'm in Love" single. While both tracks performed well at R&B, pop DJs uniformly preferred "Stagger Lee," and it became a substantial hit in late 1967. The singer dodged a bullet of his own when a rendition by James Brown, curiously recorded at much the same moment, was released first, but only on the *Cold Sweat* LP and not as a single. The two versions, heard side by side, confirmed the substantial differences in rhythmic approach and audio standards between two of the era's leading soul men.

Yet "Stagger Lee" was not the biggest hit from *I'm in Love*. Pickett's cover of a more contemporary R&B song, "She's Looking Good" by Oakland's Rodger Collins, took that honor. Like "Funky Broadway," Collins's original was built upon a simple groove. Unlike Dyke and the Blazers, Collins and his recording group had put in a first-rate recording, and there was little for Pickett and his band to improve upon—other than, as always, to make it harder and heavier, relegating the original (an excellent recording in its own right) into the footnotes of history.

The completed ten-song *I'm in Love* was the most advanced and mature of Pickett's albums to date. Perhaps due to the experience of the musicians around him, *I'm in Love* felt more all-around southern, never shying away from a certain country underpinning, the kind of white gospel Rhythm & Blues that Elvis would shortly re-embrace. Much less of a party record than those recorded at Muscle Shoals, and with considerably more original content, it had a cohesion and coherence that the Fame sessions had lacked.

Atlantic appeared to recognize as much, and commissioned a lengthy essay by the *Rolling Stone* and *Crawdaddy* journalist Jon Landau for the back cover, in place of the usual poor copy written by whatever DJ needed ingratiating that month. But the front cover picture of a debonair Pickett in houndstooth three-piece suit, complete with flashing handkerchief and leather gloves, stood at odds with the psychedelic fashions of the era—Pickett coming across as an old-time dandy, Stagger Lee as Sherlock Holmes. More frustratingly, rather than release *I'm In Love* on the heels of "Funky Broadway" and *The Sound of Wilson Pickett*, Atlantic held the record back, instead milking their star's popularity over Christmas 1967 with *The Best of Wilson Pickett*. *I'm in Love* wasn't released until February 1968, nine months after it was recorded.

Pickett was back at American at the beginning of the following month, March 1968. The studio had just celebrated its first number one hit, recorded by a young white Memphis group, the Box Tops, whose "The Letter," produced by Dan Penn, was an overnight sensation. The Box Tops confirmed Pickett's influence on young southern whites—singer Alex Chilton's first gig had consisted of two songs, "In the Midnight Hour" and "Sunny," and he had subsequently auditioned for the Box Tops with "Mustang Sally." The Box Tops were therefore delighted when, in the wake of their sudden success, they were invited on to an otherwise all-black arena tour that swung through Virginia, the Carolinas, and Tennessee at the end of 1967, headlined by Pickett. The teenagers, who had to stay in separate hotels and eat in separate restaurants from the black artists, were nonetheless amazed by the lifestyle. "They were smoking so much pot (in the men's' room) I could hardly see," recalled guitarist Gary Talley of Pickett's band. "It's really amazing that those redneck cops didn't catch them and put them in jail."[8]

The rhythm section at American, which now included Bobby Womack, played most of the instruments on the Box Tops' debut LP (not that the fact was advertised). They were eager now to pick back up with Pickett, for whom their contributions would be credited. There was only one apparent problem. Pickett didn't have the songs. The way Bobby Womack later told it, "I was supposed to go down there and sing and play these songs for *me* and record. But Pickett was there with no ideas. He said, 'What you got in that bag?' I said 'Songs, I'm full of them, I'm fresh.' He said, 'Why don't you pull out some and let me sing?'"[9] All six songs cut by Pickett at American subsequently included Womack's name as a composer.

Womack, having established himself as a session guitarist both at American and on sessions for Aretha in New York, finally had a solo deal with the Minet label, and had come off the road with Pickett to focus on his studio work. Regarding Womack's claim, it's possible that Pickett gate-crashed Womack's solo LP session, showing up to offer moral support and then commandeering the studio. But that wouldn't explain Tom Dowd's presence as producer and arranger, nor the absence of corroboration from other participants. It's also worth observing that of the six songs in question Womack had already recorded and released two of them, and that Pickett claimed a cowriting credit on two more. That left only two of which it might be said that Pickett talked Womack out of keeping for himself.[10] The likelihood is that Pickett had his own session booked all along, and that Womack's involvement as prime songwriter was voluntary, the continuation of a proven good thing.

Key among the pair's shared writing credits was "I'm a Midnight Mover," which would open the Pickett LP, become its lead single, and give the record its title. (It appeared on Womack's ensuing solo LP as well.) Musically, it played off Reggie Young's memorable opening descent, Womack's response, and the interaction between Bobby Emmons's pulsating organ parts and Tommy Cogbill's fluid bass. Vocally Pickett was always in control, the Memphis brass section punching in with their own confidence and swagger, the backing singers adding suitable reinforcement to the title character's boasts. Lyrically, the definition seemed simple enough: as the session's engineer (and occasional cosongwriter) Darryl Carter put it, "the midnight mover moves around in the midnight hour, doing what the midnight mover does!"[11] That was Bobby, and that was Wilson.

Certainly, Womack could be generous with his compositions. On "I Found a True Love," released under his own name back in 1965, he now gave part of the copyright to guitarist Reggie Young for coming up with a new, majestic opening guitar lick.[12] Listening back to this second Pickett album from American almost a half-century later, Young would observe wistfully of his parts, "Now I'm playing like Bobby Womack," and that when he eventually moved to Nashville to work country music sessions, "I didn't change a thing. I was playing that Womack style on country records, instead of the hillbilly stuff—it changed the whole bed of country music."

The two guitarists were at their most distinctive on "Let's Get an Understanding." Written by Womack, Pickett, and Carter, the lyrical plea for romantic compassion could easily be heard as a metaphor for racial and social respect ("Some of us has got to be wrong, getting together shouldn't take so long"). Midway, Pickett suggested he "step back and let the band cook a little bit," allowing Reggie Young to break into the briefest of psychedelic jams before the singer called on Womack to "bring it back on down to that soul groove."

The ballads were exquisite in their own right. On "Trust Me," which Womack had already released as his debut solo single the previous year, the subtle guitar interplay was only rivaled by a gorgeous trumpet solo; "It's a Groove," for which Womack gave a half-share to his then fourteen-year-old step-daughter Linda, threw right back to the traditional R&B ballad.[13] The mid-tempo "Remember, I Been Good to You" had a rare male backing chorus in the form of the Masqueraders, newly signed to Moman's burgeoning in-house label.

Why the album wasn't completed there and then with additional material—perhaps the cover versions that typically supplied Pickett with his leading singles?—remains uncertain. If it was a matter of time constraints, Atlantic could have easily booked another session to complete the record. Certainly there should have been no rush, given that *I'm in Love* had only just been released. Yet in July, only five months after *I'm in Love*, along came *The Midnight Mover*, which took the six superb songs from Memphis, threw in an incongruous pair that Pickett had recorded in New York, and rounded out the set with the singer's initial Atlantic single from back in 1964, "I'm Gonna Cry" and "For Better or Worse." In short, Atlantic took its top male soul star, someone finally building a reputation as an albums artist at the very moment that medium was becoming ever more experimental and important, and turned his latest body of work into a half-baked compilation record. Barely clocking in at twenty-five minutes despite the additional songs, *The Midnight Mover* suffered in sales, even as its lead single joined Pickett's impressive track record of top thirty pop hits. As a final mark of the label's inattention to the final detail, the back cover erroneously backdated the LP to 1966.

CHAPTER 13

He was a game changer. Anybody that worked with him and could really play his music, Pickett was a game changer.

Curtis Pope, trumpet player, the Midnight Movers

On December 10, 1967, the private plane carrying Otis Redding, his pilot, and six members of his touring band, new Stax signings the Bar-Kays, crashed into Lake Monona on the approach into Madison, Wisconsin. Everyone on board—with the exception of trumpet player Ben Cauley—perished.[1]

It was the second time in just three years that a leading light of soul music had a shocking and premature demise, and as with Sam Cooke before him, conspiracy theories briefly abounded before the risk-ridden reality of the touring routine sank in. Just as it was potentially perilous to indulge in illicit, adulterous relations, such as brought Cooke to a violent end, so it was gravely hazardous to fly small planes from gig to gig during Great Lakes winter storms—especially when the pilot had reported a low battery.

Though remembered as one of the greats, Redding was not the biggest solo male star in soul music when he died. On the basis of hit singles that title belonged to Wilson Pickett, who had placed five songs in the American top 40 in 1967, and seven in the R&B charts, four of which were top ten hits.[2] But Redding had made his impact during that crucial period of soul music's birth, in 1963 to 1964, attracting Pickett and others to Stax in the process; he conquered Europe ahead of Pickett, securing TV specials and headlining a groundbreaking Stax/Volt tour of the continent just before his spellbinding performance at Monterey crossed him over to the psychedelic/hippie audience. Additionally, Redding had an unblemished personal reputation, unlike Pickett and James Brown. "Man's head was on straight," said Joe Tex, a pallbearer at Redding's funeral, alongside Johnnie

Taylor and Joe Simon. "Didn't nobody fight with Otis Redding."[3] Pickett, like James Brown and almost every other American soul singer, attended that funeral, at which Jerry Wexler delivered the eulogy. "Otis was a natural prince," said Wexler. "When you were with him he communicated love and a tremendous faith in human possibilities, a promise that great and happy events were coming."[4] It provided scant comfort down the years to friends and fans alike that Otis Redding's musical reputation would also remain untarnished—preserved at its peak by his early death.

His loss shocked the R&B community. To the black male musicians who wore the tag "soul singer" as a badge of pride, theirs was a brotherhood. Pickett often partied in Queens with Don Covay and Joe Tex; he went way back with Solomon Burke and Ben E. King; and like all of them, he idolized Otis Redding. As these singers crisscrossed stages and television screens, they celebrated their collective rise with a sly dig at the KKK that would have kept them subjugated, calling themselves the Soul Clan.

The Clan was built, first and foremost, on friendship: "the kind of love we had was an everlasting situation," Don Covay said.[5] Covay saw in this camaraderie the prospect of a musical collective that would serve both his talent and his need. Burke, the Clan's elder statesman, had more lofty designs: the Soul Clan was "to benefit our people and to benefit our own selves and our own families, to incorporate our own publishing companies, to establish our own writing pool, to agree to do each other's songs, and to keep each other's names alive in the records, and the songs and the shows, to pool our money together to buy property and land, to build homes and different things that we wanted to do."

In short, recalled Ben E. King, "Soul power would be the thing." King, as an ex-Drifter, had been on the periphery of the southern soul boom until he charged himself with answering the question "What is Soul?" on a rollicking 45 at the start of 1967. He now joined Joe Tex alongside Covay and Burke in formalizing the Soul Clan as a musical project. So did Pickett and Redding, the two biggest solo artists in the genre. "There's never been a time in history when you've had six artists like this on record," Covay reflected.[6] (At this juncture, all-star collaborations were largely unknown outside of jazz.) Getting the six of them in the studio together, however, was another matter entirely, complicated by the members' insistence, according to King, that to maintain it as an entirely black enterprise meant eliminating their white managers and agents. The result was endless procrastination. "We were too busy to make it happen," said King. Burke later conceded that perhaps asking Atlantic for "a million dollars" for the Soul Clan might have been "a little premature."[7]

It was also poorly timed. As the sixties progressed, Jerry Wexler had watched other independent labels fall by the wayside in a market increasingly given to the expensive production and marketing of Long Players; more interested in making records than distributing them, he urged his partners to stay in the game by cashing out. Ahmet Ertegun, courting the new wave of rock artists, remained unsure; his brother Nesuhi, the label's jazzman, sided with Wexler, however, and in October 1967 Atlantic was sold to Warner Bros.-Seven Arts for $17.5 million. Those new corporate owners were hardly likely to cough up the seven figures demanded by the Soul Clan.

Regardless, the Clan made plans to record, waiting for Otis Redding to recuperate from throat surgery and then complete his own studio commitments, those that yielded the number one single "Dock of the Bay." Redding then died before the Soul Clan session could commence, and shortly thereafter, Pickett reneged. "He got talking crazy," Joe Tex recalled, "talking he don't want to be no part of this, he don't want to be no part of that, he had hit records and he didn't need nothing like this, all that kind of shit."[8] The Soul Clan nonetheless went ahead in early 1968 with Don Covay and Bobby Womack cutting backing tracks for two compositions that featured five lead voices: Burke, Tex, King, Covay, and, in Redding's place, that singer's protégé, Arthur Conley. The A-side, "Soul Meeting," was a disappointment. But the ballad on the flip, "That's How It Feels," more than made up for it, the trading off between the vocalists all the more impressive for the fact that they were apparently never all in the studio together. Years later, in the notes for a massive soul music compilation, David Gorman described it as "a barely secular sermon that addresses all of the hurt and injustice facing a man growing up poor and black in the South," and that only makes it more disappointing that Pickett did not participate.[9]

Pickett shared Burke's frustration with Jerry Wexler. "We was like his childrens," he said down the line. "He wanted to claim us as his children and he was the guardian over us and our money. The little we got."[10] Wexler's loyalty, just like Pickett's, could prove mercurial. "He had a street mentality, he would walk over you if he could," said Jerry's son Paul.[11] Jim Stewart learned this when he discovered that the deal he had signed in 1965, back when Wilson Pickett first came to Memphis alongside Wexler, gave Atlantic complete ownership of all Stax masters. This included the increasingly lucrative Stax back catalog, the contract to Stax's second biggest artist, Sam & Dave, and the treasure trove of unreleased Otis Redding recordings, which would yield four bestselling albums over the next two years. Wexler forever denied inside knowledge of this clause. Atlantic's new owners, meanwhile, could care less about the morality of the deal, only the goldmine it produced.[12]

As the men of the Soul Clan vied for Redding's crown, a woman ascended to the throne instead. Working with the undivided attention of Jerry Wexler and with the same Memphis/Muscle Shoals musical axis Pickett had pioneered for Atlantic, Aretha Franklin recorded three bestselling LPs in just ten months. The third, the legendary *Lady Soul*, was released just a week after Pickett's delayed *I'm in Love*—and left Pickett's album in the dust.

Pickett's excuse for blowing off the Soul Clan session was not without some justification. At the point he would have been required in the studio, he was furthering his own career instead, onstage, on camera, in bowtie and dinner jacket in the Italian Riviera, competing in the prestigious and popular Sanremo Music Festival.[13] It was a risky move for a man who had lived exclusively in the world of authentic soul these past three years. Yet he pulled it off. The song he brought to Sanremo, "Deborah," released in Italy to coincide with the contest, had been recorded a few weeks earlier in 1968, in New York City. Signifying the distinction of the session from his usual southern recordings, Nesuhi Ertegun took the producer's chair, with Arif Mardin handling arrangements for a crack studio team that included King Curtis and the emerging rhythm section of bassist Gerald (Jerry) Jemmott and drummer Bernard Purdie. Singing "Deborah" partly in Italian, Pickett articulated each foreign syllable of the opening verse perfectly, with an emphatic vibrato that called to mind the dramatic delivery of Welsh soul singer Tom Jones. He then suddenly switched both language and time signature for a chorus about "good times walking down Broadway" with a pronounced swagger—the transition largely fed by a bass run improvised on the spot by Jemmott. The result was infectious.

Pickett performed "Deborah" in Sanremo in February, joining a number of other American artists at the Music Festival, including Dionne Warwick, Bobbie Gentry, Paul Anka, Shirley Bassey, and Eartha Kitt. Aside from Warwick, known for her pop-soul sound, Pickett was the only soul singer among the group—representing a style not often heard on that competition stage. And yet he not only made it to the final but finished fourth overall, placing higher than any other non-Italian singer. The judges appeared to have rewarded him, in particular, for performing with his own group rather than using the resident Italian orchestra.

And what a group it was. The members had been imported wholesale from Gene Chandler after Pickett's previous band had largely moved on in the aftermath of Monterey and the Murray the K extravaganza. Back on bass was Ernest Smith, who provided the introduction between Pickett and his new group. On drums was twenty-six-year old Elbert "Woody" Woodson, a highly regarded player who had toured with Jackie Wilson, Marvin Gaye (and the rest of a Motown revue tour in the process), and Otis Redding, and was featured on Redding's *Live at the Whiskey a Go-Go* concert from 1966 that Atlantic released as a posthumous LP. On second guitar was Charles "Skip" Pitts, all of twenty years old and so precociously talented that once guitarist Freddie Tyrrell dropped out, Pickett didn't bother to replace him. On tenor sax was twenty-four-year old George Patterson, the group's arranger and bandleader, who had been part of the Jazz Interpreters in Chicago, and who brought the twenty-two-year old trumpeter Curtis Pope along. Other than Patterson, they all hailed from Washington, DC. Teaming up with Pickett, Jack Philpot, and trumpeter Chris Lowe, the group became known as the Midnight Movers.

The quintet departed from Chandler with experience and enthusiasm, a working knowledge of each other's musical skills and personal foibles—there was "a lot of love" between them, as Ernest Smith put it—and a desire to move it all up a notch. Coming over to Pickett provided not just more money, but a promotion to the pinnacle of soul. "Wilson was a hitmaker," said Woodson, the most experienced of Chandler's defectors. "Everything he touched turned to gold. He was dynamite on stage. Wilson had them all jumping off the rafters, didn't matter who was in the audience. I loved working with Wilson. He was the best." Pope concurred, "Pickett was joyous. He was always smiling and he gave us the impression that we were going to have some fun. And all the music that he had was a joy to play. He put his heart and soul into that. When we got with Pickett our whole perspective changed." Jack Philpot noted, "Out of all the people I've played with, Pickett was probably the funkiest. Every time we went onstage, you'd get goose bumps when it was really rocking. When Pickett was in the zone, you couldn't beat it." And Chris Lowe put it most clearly: "I worked with Sam & Dave, Otis Redding, Clarence Carter, Percy Sledge, Etta James, but Pickett was . . . It! He was a pure singer, dangerous screamer, he was an entertainer, he was a performer, he had the full package."

Suitably invigorated, a strong work ethic kicked in. "The rhythm section would practice by themselves," said Philpot, "and the horn section would be practicing horn lines and dance steps on the other side of town, just to perfect it. It was intense. We rehearsed more often than we played sometimes." Their dedication and expertise was evident in Sanremo, where Patterson conducted the two lone Italian musicians while playing his own sax, bringing their volume up and down to allow Pickett full expression of his almost operatic voice. After their Italian triumph, the Midnight Movers moved on to gigs around Europe, where the group really let loose. Smith and Pitts took lead vocals in a Stax-based warm-up set of Otis Redding and Sam & Dave hits, and the whole group performed outrageous steps and routines during instrumentals like "Soul Finger" before Pickett emerged for his own electrifying performance. One such concert was captured on a German television special, filmed by a cameraman who appeared to be dancing around the stage himself—the final edit was rendered additionally chaotic (but no less riveting) by multiple zoom effects and constant stage invasions from black and white kids alike. This rare, preserved performance of the Midnight Movers makes for a harder-hitting comparison to that of the M.G.s at Monterey or on the Stax/Volt Revue tour. Pickett, of course, matches his band every beat of the way, his foot-stomping, sweat-inducing delivery amplified by his natural on-stage charisma; while the quality of the surviving footage is no match for Otis at Monterey, it remains the best audio-visual example of Pickett's onstage magnetism at that time.

For the musicians, most of whom had never before been outside the United States, the reaction in Europe was a cultural epiphany—especially their treatment at Sanremo, where they had people running after them, embracing them, stopping them for autographs. In England, plenty of people knew their music and could converse about it in detail with them. And the fact that as black men, they were seen as exotic—kids reaching out to touch their unfamiliarly textured hair—rather than threatening or inferior was a welcome change from their home country.

"Those was probably the best times for Wilson," his brother Maxwell said. "He had a great band backing him up, he was working as much as any artist would want to work, he was playing all of the big houses. He had no problem getting booked. We just stayed busy. We was constantly on the road, state to state, gig after gig after gig."

There were still arguments to be had over money. Pickett was meticulous about paying his taxes; he routinely deducted his member's contributions "at source." Those who had toured extensively with other artists tried to convince him to make less money available to the IRS in the first place. Pay your band members' hotels, write it off as an expense, then we all make out better. Get a tour bus rather than have the backing band crammed into a unreliable converted Checker cab - but be sure to lease it, so that if it breaks down, it's not your famous name on the side of the bus when the repair truck comes along and can hold you ransom.

Bobby Womack cited the poor conditions for the musicians as one of the reasons he came off the road with Pickett, even though he rode in comfort, alongside the singer in a chauffeur-driven Cadillac. He was specifically unhappy at the singer's refusal to bail Carlton McWilliams out of the New York jail in the summer of 1967, despite the fact that McWilliams himself carried no grudge: "Of all the artists I ever worked with, I most enjoyed working with Wilson Pickett," said the abandoned bass player.

Truth was that Womack was no innocent party to Pickett's personality issues; specifically, he turned the singer on to cocaine. Womack claimed that he had been taking the drug as a means to block out, or at least compensate for, the musical and social ostracism he had experienced because of his marriage to Barbara Cooke. It would become a major addiction for him but, oddly, not a creative obstacle: he was one of the few that had the stamina, the constitution for it. Pickett, initially, may have felt the same way. The first time he asked Womack how he managed to stay up and alert all night, Womack shared his supply. The guitarist recalled the result: "Man, he was dancing like James Brown, all over the place: 'Whoo, that shit is good.'" But Womack also admitted, "I made Pickett worse."[14] And Dovie Hall insisted, "Bobby Womack was the one who hooked him."

Fame, fortune, drugs, women: a familiar and addictive cocktail. On a subsequent visit to Italy—memories have it as Milan, after a rare day off—Pickett offered to treat the band to a night out on the town. Some of them took him up on it, but Woodson, a year older and with more touring experience than Pickett, could see how it was going to play out: there were beautiful white girls in tow, the singer was keen to impress them, it was going to cost a fortune, Pickett was bound to get drunk, and then it was likely to get ugly. Sure enough, several hours later, Pickett and various band members brought the girls back, who were then expected to sign in as guests. Several of them did not want to leave any such paper trail, and Pickett, after a loud argument with the hotel manager, decided to take it out on the drummer who'd declined to attend—the logic being that he had brought back enough girls for *everyone*, that the meal had cost him $500, and that nobody in his band was grateful for shit.

"He had this bottle of wine and he kept coming towards me," said Woodson, "and when I saw him turn around and grab the bottle at the top I thought, 'you crazy,' so I got up off the bed and got the bottle out of his hands." The drummer disarmed the singer—"I didn't hit him but I bounced him around"—and threw him out of the room.

In the fray, Pickett left his mink coat, his watch, and his wallet—with tens of thousands of dollars inside—in Woodson's room. "He came back the next morning," said Woodson. "Sat there counting his money, he knew how much money he had, he *always* knew.' He said 'Woody, all my money is here,' I said, 'What do you think I was gonna do? If I was gonna take your money I'd be gone already!' So right there something connected. He said, 'I'm sorry, I don't know what got into me.' I said 'I know what got into you—you think you crazy. And you are!'"

"After he sobered up he realized he had messed up," said Lowe. That evening—it was show day—he called doctors to his dressing room, claiming to have been poisoned rather than admitting to a hangover, and insisting that the band go on stage without him. "So we played one of the best shows we had ever played," said Lowe. "We kicked him dead in his rear end." Philpot opined, "Pickett didn't like his opening band to kick his butt. But I think he appreciated *us* kicking like we did, because he could say that was *his* band."

In the meantime, the younger members of the Midnight Movers learned to avoid confrontation. "He'd be talking down fellow musicians," said Chris Lowe. "I'd say, 'Yeah, uh huh, I know what you mean.' That was the extent of my therapy session. Even if I'm saying in my mind, 'Oh, you crazy,' I did not say that to him. Why argue with him? He's the boss. And he's paying you."

Curtis Pope, for whom a fat bankroll was still a novelty, said, "I knew that he was the boss and I enjoyed making that money. I wanted to stay out of his way; I wouldn't cause no trouble."

Pickett was quite capable of causing trouble for himself. One of the more memorable—and potentially fatal—incidents occurred in Charlotte, North Carolina, after a concert. "We went back to the hotel," recalled Danny White. "He went upstairs with two girls. So we [White and Higgins] are standing outside, there was a main door of the hotel and then there was a side door, the side door had about three little steps. We're hanging in the lobby of the hotel and we saw these two girls came down. One was real angry. I said, 'What happened babe?' She said, 'That black motherfucker slapped my friend.' He had disrespected her. The two of them start trying to call the Black Panthers on the phone. Didn't get a hold of them. So I just left, went out through the side door, and went across the street, myself and Claston Higgins . . . Pickett comes out and stands right across the street on one of those little steps. The girls that came out went down to their car. I'm standing talking to Claston, I saw a car coming up real slow, real slow, and my instinct—I looked and I saw the driver leaning over the passenger side, and instantly I just said 'Pickett, LOOK OUT!' and he heard me and saw the car—and as soon as he hit the floor and went down, Pow! Pow! Pow! Three shots ring out and hit exactly where he was standing. I went over and looked: *exactly* where he was standing."

CHAPTER 14

He was a cyclone. Everybody else was low-key, waiting for the energy to hit them, whereas he came in on fire. He would come in full tilt and we would just go on from there.

Jerry Jemmott, bass player, Atlantic Records/Fame Studios

The assassination of Martin Luther King Jr. on April 4, 1968, by a white gunman at the Lorraine Motel in Memphis, unleashed a torrent of revolt among black communities across the United States. From Chicago to Baltimore, Kansas City to Louisville—and especially in Washington, DC, where angry crowds reached within two blocks of the White House before a force of 15,000 Federal troops turned them back—American inner cities erupted in outright fury. Many would never recover.

In Boston, James Brown went ahead with his scheduled concert at the Garden the night of April 4; the city televised the concert live, Boston remained largely peaceful, and Brown's reputation as a positive black leader was duly enhanced. It was then almost immediately reduced, at least among blacks, by his decision to take his group on a USO tour of bases in Vietnam (interpreted as support for the war itself because of many of his own comments), and to release a cover of "America Is My Home."[1] The newly emergent Black Panthers demanded a sit-down with Brown. Exactly what was said is not known, but soon after the singer replaced his familiar process hairdo with an Afro and released "Say It Loud, I'm Black and I'm Proud," a song that could quickly be heard reverberating from every inner-city street corner.

As the daughter of a prominent Baptist Minister and civil rights activist herself, Aretha Franklin had known King personally; he had presented her with a special award at a Detroit concert celebrating Aretha Franklin Day just six weeks before his death. She sang "Precious Lord" at his memorial service, but was so griefstricken she later could not remember the occasion.

Her public and political appearances, including one at the historically tur-
bulent Democratic National Convention in Chicago that year, ensured that
she remained immune to the type of criticism that Brown invited, and her
prolific musical mastery and the sales it continued to generate led to a new
deal with Atlantic Records only eighteen months after she first signed with
the label. At a celebratory luncheon at the Hotel St. Regis in New York, Jerry
Wexler told the invited audience that her new contract was "the greatest
that any single recording artist has signed in the history of the recording
industry."[2] The men of the Soul Clan listened to the hyperbole and took a
careful look at the meager percentage points on their own contracts.

The repercussions of King's assassination were felt across black radio,
where many disc jockeys had stayed on air the night of April 4, often past
their FCC curfew, attempting to calm their angry listeners. The National
Association of Television and Radio Announcers (NATRA), once "an old-
boy network of black dee jays" infamous for "leaving an enduring impression on hotel managers" after the parties at its conventions, but which
had undergone a change in leadership in 1965, now demanded sit-downs
with initially reluctant white radio station owners.[3] (Of the several hundred black-oriented stations across the country, whose playlists consisted
of over 90 percent soul music by 1968, less than ten of them were actually black-owned.[4]) The new NATRA leadership had plans to announce—at
the forthcoming convention it hoped would display the organization in
an improved light—a school of broadcast science in Delaware, funded by
donations already pledged by major record companies. But in the post-King
environment, militants talked of "reparations" from white labels, threatening black jockeys who would get in their way. In Miami, where the conference took place, one (white) old-time record executive from New Orleans
was viciously pistol-whipped, Otis Redding's (white) manager Phil Walden
was threatened, and Jerry Wexler, in attendance to accept an award on
behalf of Aretha Franklin, was whisked from the opening event in the main
ballroom under the protection of King Curtis, who insisted that Wexler had
been "marked." The new NATRA leadership abandoned the organization
not long after.

This ominous mood proved particularly strong in Memphis itself. The
Stax community had always considered the Lorraine Motel a home away
from home; it was a place where artists mingled freely, unimpeded by
the racial discrimination that had brought King to Memphis to campaign
on behalf of the city's black sanitation workers. Already reeling from the
calamitous run of bad news that had threatened to bring the label down at
the end of 1967, Stax now had to justify itself as a white-owned business
in the midst of a black community. The Stax employees were aggressively

hustled, primarily by local gangs masquerading as something more powerful. The employees took to carrying weapons for self-defense, and Al Bell was forced to hire protection, an enforcer by the name of Johnnie Baylor. The gangs were soon scared away, but Baylor was there to stay, with Bell's blessing: if Stax was going to survive, let alone prosper in this newly militant climate, it would do so by any means necessary.

Wilson Pickett refused to get involved. He was never one for campaigning to begin with: "I don't sing nothing about civil rights," he had stated early in the King era. "Everybody needs rights, but they don't have to be civil."[5] Pickett had always displayed ample cynicism toward the white establishment, from the plantation owners in Prattville to the record companies in New York, and on to the banks in which he refused to keep his money: that's "the white man figuring a way to steal back what he gave me," he said when revealing a closet full of cash to Bobby Womack one day.[6] Yet he had no interest in joining the black militants of the post-King era. Before King was assassinated, Pickett had stated, "I'd go along with Martin before I'd go along with people like Malcolm X."[7] A year later, he was largely dismissive of the emerging movement. "Too many leaders out there," he said. "Too many people out there sayin' the wrong thing. You know what I do? I support 'em all. And I just live my life. I don't get involved in that stuff."[8] Pickett saw in all the uncertainty and confusion that there was an ongoing need for someone who could reflect the black struggle through success. For Wilson Pickett, the soul purist, it was always about the music.

In September, Pickett returned to the studio at Fame for the first time in nineteen months—concluding the cooling-off period between Jerry Wexler and Rick Hall that had followed the Aretha Franklin debacle. Wexler stayed away, and that was fine by Hall, who was eager to prove that he could produce classic Pickett records on his own and who, as a businessman building a significant publishing catalog with his own team of writers, could also supply the necessary material.

Key among his in-house composers was George Jackson, who would have a hand in over a hundred songs during his Fame heyday, singing many of the demo recordings better than the artists who eventually cut the masters. Born in Mississippi, discovered by Ike Turner, rejected by Stax, and taken in across Memphis at the Goldwax label where he wrote for the mighty but troubled soul singer James Carr, Jackson came to Fame upon recommendation of Billy Sherrill. He had barely arrived in Muscle Shoals before he learned that Pickett was on his way. Jackson, who liked to tailor his songs to a specific singer, immediately sat down with a trio of other writers and set about providing Pickett with a ready-made anthem, "A Man and a Half."

The song so perfectly defines its singer that ironically, Pickett could never have composed it for himself. The apparent egotism of the lyrics— much of it sexual but not exclusively so—was delightfully over-the-top, especially when Pickett assured listeners, "no brags, just facts." As a logical sequel and musical partner to "I'm a Midnight Mover," it was only appropriate that Bobby Womack was on hand at Fame to supply the song with its lead guitar lines. These he played with emphatic self-assurance, alongside Jimmy Johnson, who noted that everyone at Fame was just "blown away" by Womack's musicianship and personality. Womack, newly turned on to the Fender Telecaster by Reggie Young, soon convinced Johnson to switch out his Gretsch for the same instrument.

With Tommy Cogbill and Spooner Oldham having moved up to work with Chips Moman at American, Johnson and drummer Roger Hawkins were the only hold-overs among the rhythm section from the last time Pickett had recorded at Fame. Over the coming weeks of his extended sessions, the role of bass was shared between David Hood, who had started out on trombone at Sheffield High School, Johnson's alma mater right down the road from the studio, and Jerry Jemmott, the jazz-trained Bronx bassist who had played on "Deborah." Similarly, the keyboard parts were shared or doubled between Barry Beckett, an Alabama native, and Marvell Thomas, son of Rufus, sister of Carla, and veteran of the Stax studios from its inception, having played on many of the label's recordings that didn't feature Booker T. Jones or Isaac Hayes. Charlie Chalmers was missing from the brass section for the first time since Pickett had left Stax. "Bowlegs" Miller now had the leadership role, joined by Jimmy Mitchell, Jack Peck, Aaron Varnell, and Joe Arnold.

Some of these musicians' recollections of working with Pickett for the first time are telling. For all that his aggressive antics, especially on the road, were starting to precede him, his attitude in the studio continued to be one of absolute dedication and commitment. If anything, the sessions at Fame in late 1968 suggested an *increased* focus on the task at hand, reflective perhaps of the fact that he had finally freed himself from the oversight of Wexler and Dowd.

"He was like an actor in a movie," observed Marvell Thomas. "He would listen carefully to the tapes of that day, and he would fix, change, make modifications and things, that we did, that he did, in arrangements and approaches. We were all staying in the same hotel and he'd come beat on the door at 6:30 the next morning, ready and energized to go back to the studio and do what he needed to do to." Barry Beckett, who would work with Pickett far into the 1970s, took a more nuanced view: "I think he lived to cause tension ... but that's the way he sung, too. He was a very soulful guy."[9] David Hood, ditto, likened Pickett to "a coiled spring, ready to ... *Boing!*" Quite. Pickett's delivery on "A Man and a Half" and four other songs recorded in September 1968 had a vitality and ferocity that showed considerable maturity in both the sheer power and also the careful control of his voice.

Bobby Womack, as ever, earned his session fee in part with songwriting royalties. His "People Make the World" had been recorded twice at American over the previous year, once in a four-four format by the Box Tops, and again, just recently, by Roosevelt Grier with the same studio backing band. Grier, a former pro football player, had been working as a bodyguard for Democratic Presidential hopeful Robert Kennedy's wife Ethel when, on June 5, 1968, the candidate was shot dead in front of him at a hotel in Los Angeles following a victory speech; with a modestly successful R&B singing career that dated back to the start of the decade, Grier went into the American studios almost immediately to update the song as a personal and pronounced tribute to his employer and friend. At Fame, Pickett and Womack abjured the saccharine string accompaniment of Grier's rendition, bringing the song down to a funerary six-eight tempo, rendering it a true soul ballad, with glistening lead guitar, mournful brass, gospel backing vocals from the Sweet Inspirations in New York, and a searing delivery by Pickett that brought him right back to church.

Like "Jealous Love" a year before it, Don Covay's "Night Owl," a warning to a female partner about the cost of all-night carousing, seemed somewhat hypocritical for Pickett to sing, but his delivery was no less devastating for it. George Jackson presented a sweet song of romantic endorsement "Woman Likes to Hear That," and Pickett and Womack wrote the fiery "Sit Down and Talk This Over" together.

That his return to Fame had been an unqualified success was confirmed by Atlantic's decision to release "A Man and a Half" and "People Make the World (What It Is)" as a single before Pickett came back to Muscle Shoals to complete the album. When he did it was without the increasingly in-demand Bobby Womack, in whose place at Fame he found a guitarist that would reshape his musical trajectory and, with it, the way people thought about southern music.

Duane Allman and younger brother Gregg had been raised by their mother in Daytona Beach, Florida, after their father, a World War II veteran, was shot dead in a Christmas 1949 hold-up. The boys had come of age at the ideal time to fall for white rock 'n' roll, but were intuitive enough to study black rhythm and (especially) blues, and had played in bands together, both on guitar, since junior high. They recorded a single for Buddy Killen's Dial label and then, as the paisley-clad Hour Glass, went to California, where they jammed with the likes of Paul Butterfield and Pickett's former drummer Buddy Miles. Duane experienced a musical epiphany watching Taj Mahal's slide guitarist Jesse Ed Davis, and he subsequently took an empty Coricidin pill bottle and practiced the technique until he was the best young slide player of his generation.

The Hour Glass secured a deal with Liberty in California, but after two disappointing albums they returned south in April 1968 to self-produce some demos at Fame, where a former bandmate Eddie Hinton was now working. The tapes, engineered by Jimmy Johnson, were rejected by Liberty, and after a handful of southern gigs—at which the group's self-composed rock songs were interrupted by demands for "Midnight Hour" and "Mustang Sally"—they broke up. Duane Allman followed Hinton in seeking session work at Fame—and Rick Hall put him off. The official (and plausible) reason was that Hall had plenty other guitarists already on the books; the unofficial (and equally plausible) explanation was to do with Duane's appearance. Allman had scraggly long blonde hair parted in the middle, and sideburns that led to distinctly incongruous moustache. He wore denim jeans, cowboy boots with a dog collar around one ankle, and a leather waist-coast with tassles. "Looked like he hadn't slept in a week, and was high, and was dirty, and looked like hadn't had a bath in a week either," was Marvell Thomas's first impression.

Jimmy Johnson, however, was not about to let Allman slip out of sight. "He was the most natural talent, the kind of guy had the guitar in his hands eight hours a day. None of us was *that* dedicated." Slowly but surely, and not least due to his irrepressibly positive personality, Allman worked his way onto sessions, but his initial contributions at Fame, for Clarence Carter and Laura Lee in September 1968, were relatively minor, as if showing off the full range of his talents would be a dangerous move too early in his employ.

Pickett's first encounter with Allman was typical of time and type, mistaking him for a "gorgeous blond" upon seeing him in the back of a car.[10] But once they got to working in the studio together, they bonded instantly. Pickett saw and heard in Duane an equally dedicated student of his chosen musical genre, another perfectionist carving his own distinct path, another iconoclast who couldn't easily be towed into line, and a gregarious, outgoing person who could not be cowed or awed. They shared in common a reputation for being inherently crazy, the types that would fill a room with their presence, and they were able to complement, rather than conflict with, each other.

"I called him Sky Man," Pickett said, "because he stayed so fucking high all the time." (Already answering to the name Dog, Allman would combine the two monikers as Skydog.) Pickett recalled one evening in the studio when "everybody (was) acting strange, engineer was all fucked up. I said, 'We ought to cancel the session tonight.' Sky Man came in and said, 'You know what I done, man! I put two pills (of mescaline) in the water tank, baby!' I said, 'Wow, you dumb ass, you fucked my session up, man!' But I loved him, he made it up for it the next day. I mean, he could *play*!"[11]

Rick Hall ensured that they had plenty of songs to work on, and George Jackson supplied several of them. "Search Your Heart" and "Back In Your Arms" were southern soul ballads of the purest kind, Pickett pleading, preaching, and screaming, backed by sublimely simple accompaniment in each case, from the effortlessly harmonious brass section to the instinctive interplay between Beckett and Thomas. Allman held back on both. Jackson's "Save Me" picked up the mood considerably, Allman playing off of Johnson much like Womack and Moman had before him, coming back at the end to throw in a few lead overdubs. There was also "Mini-Skirt Minnie," which had first shown up on a Stax subsidiary under a different title before being rewritten by Steve Cropper and sung by Sir Mack Rice (newly signed to the Memphis label). Jackson had now added to the song, and recorded a demo version for Pickett in which his own impressive voice fought tooth and nail for dominance with Allman's piercing solos. On Pickett's rendition the rhythm section hit on a yet more relentless boogie—but although Allman can be heard playing the main riff while Johnson chugs along beneath him, the solos are curiously absent. Those who never heard the Jackson demo were ultimately none the wiser, and when "Mini-Skirt Minnie" was justifiably released as a single the following spring it duly scored high at R&B, one of the best (and most underrated) of all Pickett soul singles.

Pickett returned to Muscle Shoals for a final session at the end of November. Allman had gained credibility in the interim with a blistering slide guitar solo on Clarence Carter's rerecording of "The End of the Road"—to which Carter had exclaimed, on tape, "I *like* what I'm listening to!" The solo was additionally notable for its volume, and Allman went out of his way to explain to Hall how modern amplifiers offered greater resonance, how the harmonic convergences created richer textures and phantom notes.

On November 27, while the others broke for lunch, Wilson Pickett, Duane Allman, and Rick Hall were left alone in the studio.[12] Allman hung back with the excuse that he wanted to spare the other musicians the "looks" he invited wherever he went, and let them eat in peace without him. Most likely, having hit it off so well with Pickett, he just wanted his new buddy's ear to push an idea he had—that Pickett cover the Beatles' "Hey Jude."

Allman's suggestion was not necessarily out of left field. Among R&B acts, both Otis Redding and the Vontastics had covered the Beatles' "Day Tripper" to considerable success; Little Willie Walker had tackled "Ticket to Ride"; the reconstituted Bar-Kays had recently released an instrumental of "A Hard Day's Night." In fact, Allman had played, albeit without distinction, on Arthur Conley's tepid cover of "Ob-La-Di, Ob-La-Da," from the Beatles' recently released eponymous *White Album*, just a few days earlier. Nascent rock bands were covering soul songs, too: Atlantic's Vanilla Fudge had just scored with a ponderously slow cover of the Supremes' "You Keep Me Hanging On." It was all part of the post-Monterey cross-cultural mood of the times.

Still, Pickett initially recoiled at the thought. It was one thing to sing distinctively in Italian for a European song festival, but it was something else entirely for this particular soul man to cover what Pickett still considered a white pop band.[13] Additionally, "Hey Jude" was a multimillion seller getting relentless airplay, having only just vacated the number one spot after nine consecutive weeks. Pickett and Hall—who objected to Allman's idea far more stridently—knew that you simply didn't cover a million-selling single while it was this hot unless you could do it better and bigger. And in the case of the Beatles this was likely impossible.

There was also the matter of its length. "Hey Jude" had famously crammed over seven minutes of music onto one side of a seven-inch single. Much of that time was given over to a repetitive four-bar coda, its sing-along chorus anchored by drums, piano, acoustic guitars, and a brass instrument or two, with Paul McCartney ad-libbing over the top.

The Beatles knew what they were doing with this. The coda began at precisely the three-minute barrier, if pop radio disk jockeys wanted to bring the fader down at that point. But over at the "freeform radio" that had begun operating on the American FM dial, the new breed of air hosts didn't care about three-minute limitations. They preferred the extended and ambitious musical statements of the now dominant Long Player (LP) format. "Hey Jude" worked perfectly in both formats, the first single deliberately designed to do so.

Allman also knew what he was doing. He listened to the arrangement, the coda, the chorus, those brass lines and the ad-libs—and he heard a song suited both for Pickett's vocal ad-libs and for his own desire to extemporize on guitar.

By the time the others returned from lunch, Pickett had somehow been convinced, Hall had gone along with it, and the singer was halfway through memorizing the number. The rest of the musicians were used to being told what to play upon arrival, and were quite familiar with picking up a song in a matter of minutes. "Hey Jude," typically sly Beatles chord structures aside, was no great shakes. The tape was soon rolling.

McCartney had led the Beatles' recording with his own voice and piano, delaying the entry of the others until the second verse; at Fame, the keys, bass, and drums of Thomas, Jemmott, and Hawkins opened proceedings in simple unison. "There was no reason for flash in that song, none," said Thomas. "Just because you have Bachian technique doesn't mean you have to use it every five minutes." This unfussy foundation gave Allman the breathing space to introduce Pickett's voice with a bluesy emulation of McCartney's piano phrasing, and to then respond to the singer's every line with a soulful lick. As in the original, the Fame arrangement then picked up energy as the song progressed, until they reached that three-minute mark.[14]

Allman was unusual among contemporary session guitarists in that he played his instrument, a Fender Stratocaster, standing up, as if on stage. Pickett would have it no other way for his own part—and the moment they hit the coda, Pickett unleashed a primal scream that led into a high-pitched holler and the two locked into a musical communication that took on a life-force of its own.

"He stood right in front of me, as though he was playing every note I was singing," Pickett recalled with enthusiasm just four months later. "And he was watching me as I sang, and as I screamed, he was screaming with his guitar."[15] Almost a half-century later, Jimmy Johnson seemed no less astounded than he was at the time. "You know what happened there?" he asked. "*We* don't know! *Something* happened. We only did that vamp one time, and we couldn't stop. We just let it go, and kept going and going and going."

Quite how long they kept it going is uncertain; the final mix faded out just after four minutes. But for as long as Pickett and Allman traded off each other, it was Rick Hall's unenviable task to keep the volume unit meters from peaking. His job was rendered none the easier by the fact that everyone was playing live, brass section included. Though a perfection-ist readily given to multiple takes, Hall knew he couldn't possibly call for another run-through on this occasion: what was taking place in the studio was a moment of musical transcendence.

Pickett recalled an instantaneous reaction. "People were going crazy. There's this one secretary ain't spoke to me since I been coming down there. All of a sudden she got her arms around my neck."[16] Jimmy Johnson said, "We realized then that Duane had created southern rock, in that vamp." It was, indeed, both the lighting of a musical touchstone—and the passing of a musical torch. For if southern rock was born that day at Fame, then southern soul, it could safely be said, would never be quite the same.

At the studio the next morning, with everyone assembled, Rick Hall played a rough mix of "Hey Jude" down the phone line, and in New York Wexler listened along in astonished reverence, asking upon conclusion, "Who's the guitar player?" (Hall had Allman signed, sealed, and contractually delivered to Fame within days.)[17] Then Wexler pulled his promotions team off of "A Man and a Half," even though it was just about to enter the R&B Top 40, where it would reside throughout December regardless. The tape of "Hey Jude" (with "Search Your Heart" as the B-side) was expressed up to New York, where Tom Dowd brought in the Sweet Inspirations to add backing vocals. But given the frenetic interplay between Pickett and Allman on the coda, and allowing for the additional heady presence of the brass section, Dowd had trouble shoe-horning them in, and the "na-na-na-nas" that were the bedrock of the Beatles' coda were only to be heard, low in the mix, for the final few seconds. Pickett's "Hey Jude" was then quickly handed off to radio, where it took up residency on the rock radio airwaves just as the Beatles' version was waning; crucially, it proved no less popular at black stations. The single was in the shops by Christmas and entered the charts the week after.[18]

In the States, "Hey Jude" was *not* the monster hit one might expect of such a momentous studio performance; in terms of chart positions, it performed almost identically to "Stagger Lee" from a year earlier. But a song's influence and longevity can rarely be measured by instant sales, and Pickett's "Hey Jude" became a musical benchmark, a song often referenced as the highlight of his career subsequent to, and sometimes even including, the early trifecta of "In the Midnight Hour," "Land of 1000 Dances," and "Mustang Sally." In Europe, it was massive—his biggest hit of all in the United Kingdom—and further opened up his already extensive young rock audience. More importantly, Pickett effectively cemented the trend of black soul artists covering white rock songs, standing once again at the vanguard of the shifting musical tides. Barely a month after Wexler heard "Hey Jude," the Fame rhythm section was back in New York, accompanying Aretha Franklin on a version of "The Weight" by the Band—with Duane Allman on slide guitar.

Before Franklin's New York session could take place, however, Pickett and that rhythm section had an album to finish in Muscle Shoals. A break in Pickett's recording schedule might have given the singer and his collaborators both at Fame and Atlantic a chance to think through how a full album could be built around this monumental single. But in the euphoric aftermath of "Hey Jude," they focused instead on hastily trying to duplicate it. A decision was made to cover "Hey Joe," the folk-rock song that had become a psychedelic rock anthem in the hands of Jimi Hendrix; the choice of title, and the arrangement, was each far too close to "Hey Jude" and it was wisely left off the forthcoming LP. There appeared to be less concern with "Born to be Wild," a recent number two hit for Steppenwolf, who had performed it as a rock anthem for the outlaw biker generation, but it proved a leap too far. Pickett's singing about "heavy metal thunder" was profoundly unconvincing, and black audiences, in particular, recoiled: upon release, "Born to be Wild" became his first single since "Come Home Baby" not to crack the R&B top 40.

Away from the interpretations of rock songs, George Jackson and team came through with "My Own Style of Loving," with its free-flowing funk pushing into the realm soon to be labeled southern boogie. And there may be no finer example of Pickett burying someone else's song than his cover of Johnnie Taylor's "Toe Hold," a Hayes-Porter composition confined to a lukewarm Stax B-side in 1966 but ecstatically brought to life at Fame, with Pickett straining to his limits and Allman delivering intensely pitched licks that exploded like musical firecrackers. The performance left the conventional "soul" format far behind.

The debatable miscalculation of "Born to Be Wild" aside, *Hey Jude* was the perfect Wilson Pickett album for early 1969. It was his most powerful, varied, and consistent, and with five A-sides spread across four separate 7-inch releases, potentially his most commercial. Yet *Hey Jude* ultimately underperformed. Atlantic's packaging and marketing kept Pickett confined to the R&B and soul section of the record stores at the very moment he should have crossed over into rock. The album cover itself seems uninspired—a slightly fuzzy photo of the singer (although dressed characteristically to the nines) is framed dead-center on an otherwise solid, forest green front cover. And on the back, the poorly written disc jockey sleeve notes contrasted notably with the creative graphics and imagery of Atlantic's (white) rock stable. The careless inattention to detail was evident in the fact that in yet another blatant error on a Pickett album sleeve, Atlantic credited the lead guitarist—the future legend they would soon have under contract—as *David* Allman.

CHAPTER 15

If you were to ask me who the greatest entertainer was, certainly within the R&B/soul world, I would say Pickett hands down. I had never seen an artist who could do the things he did.

John Abbey, editor, *Blues and Soul*, and Wilson Pickett
concert promoter, Europe

Pickett was living large now. His publishing and record royalties had worked their way through the system, and his live fees were constantly increasing. He bought a Thunderbird boat with twin engines and had "the Wicked Pickett" emblazoned on its rear; he owned a Ferrari that opened up its V12 engine only once it hit a hundred miles an hour, and he gifted Dovie a Lincoln.

He also brought his family out of Alabama. His grandfather Shepherd Jackson had passed away in 1964, unable to afford the medical care to ease or prevent a long, painful demise from kidney failure. Pickett could have hardly have helped back at that point. But now—though he could not forget the physical abuse and was not given to public statements of forgiveness—he offered to relocate his mother. She suggested Louisville, Kentucky, where her two eldest daughters had settled. Wilson bought her a duplex for $22,500 in cash, carried from New York in a suitcase, and those of his younger sisters still in Prattville joined her. The family had now officially left the cotton fields of Alabama behind.

One of those sisters, Jeannie, Wilson's childhood singing partner in the Jericho church choir, had always hoped for a singing career of her own, and seemed to resent that her successful brother was unwilling to finance or otherwise mentor her aspirations. Instead Wilson began grooming Alder Ray, a former member of girl group the Buttons, who already had a couple of independent singles out under her own name. Ray, singing Aretha and Etta James hits, joined Danny White as an opening act. The idea was to launch a recording career for both, and he now had Wilson Pickett Enterprises, Inc. with which to do so. But come the following spring, when White was allotted his own set on the bill along with the Midnight Movers at Pickett's Apollo residency, Alder was gone. "Her patience got short," Pickett explained.[1]

He was hardly one to preach on that score, given his own short fuse and the many investment opportunities he spurned. Maxwell Pickett told of how, at a party at Smalls Paradise on 135th Street after one of his brother's many headlining stints at the Apollo, "Wilson loved the sound" of the house band, a young Kool and the Gang. "At some point during the course of the night, a couple of the guys came over and said they would like to discuss some business with him and could they come by his office and see him. They hadn't gone on the road yet, hadn't hit it big, had all these songs in the can, they wanted someone to put some money behind them so they could get their careers going." Wilson held the meeting but balked at the potential sum: $30,000. Maxwell noted that this was not the only time his brother passed up such investment opportunities.

Nor did he show an inclination to promote the Midnight Movers. According to Curtis Pope, they recorded a commercial for Texas-based Pearl Beer together, but that was as close as they got to a full session: "We were strictly a road band," acknowledged Jack Philpot. So, when presented with the opportunity to record with the Isley Brothers, exiting a troubled Motown contract and looking to revamp as they relaunched their T-Neck label, most of the Midnight Movers—Patterson, Philpot, Pitts, Pope, and Woodson—jumped.[2] The session promptly yielded "It's Your Thing." A signatory funk anthem, propelled by Pitts's effortlessly fluid guitar work and punctuated by Patterson's sassy brass arrangement, it sold a million copies upon release in February 1969, rising to number two on the pop charts in the process, far beyond anything Pickett had achieved, a game-changing, benchmark recording.

Naturally, Pickett was furious once he learned of it. Fortuitously perhaps, he and the Midnight Movers first completed another visit to Europe, including a return visit to the Sanremo Music Festival. Pickett's entry for 1969, "Un'Avventura," was none so strong a song as 1968's "Deborah," but that didn't stop him delivering a typically full-throttled performance, this time with imported soul brothers *and* full Italian orchestra (the only time he was televised with such backing); nor did it stop him from again placing the highest among American finalists, beating out Stevie Wonder along the way. Pickett's superstar status in Italy was further confirmed when he became godfather to the newborn baby of a family in Turin, perhaps as a favor to his manager. Photographs show him at the service, complete with pastoral collar—the sole black face in sight. As they moved on through Europe, a concert in Stockholm on February 10 was recorded for radio broadcast and subsequently bootlegged. Though this performance didn't quite live up to the German TV show of a year earlier, it still leaves open the question why neither Pickett nor Atlantic ever committed to an official live album—especially at a time when Pickett's major rivals in the soul market were successfully releasing them, and he had an excellent band well worthy of the effort.

He wouldn't have that band for much longer. In Paris, the new drummer, Leon Lovejoy, got in a scrap with Pitts. Pope stepped in to protect his longtime friend, Lovejoy (as Pope recalled) introduced a razor, and the singer had to jump in to defuse the situation. After returning to the States, Pickett used the in-fighting to justify firing the band, saying, "I didn't want my image to be that"—a curious statement, given his own behavior.[3] He held onto several of those who had not played with the Isley Brothers, however, which suggests what his real reasons may have been for the firing.

The Midnight Movers were not looking to leave. What they were looking for, after "It's Your Thing," was proper recompense, to which end they put themselves out for hire as a self-contained unit. Pickett quickly denounced their price as too high for people he thought were morally indebted to him. "George (Patterson) told Wilson that the Isley Brothers had more money than him," recalled Curtis Pope. "Pickett said 'You gave them my songs . . .' We didn't write the songs, we just played the music." Pickett's sudden accusations of disloyalty and musical theft did not compute. "Maybe he would have got something out of us akin to that" in the studio, said Pope. "But he wouldn't use us."

The core Midnight Movers (minus Woodson) were later heard on most of the Isley Brothers' recordings of 1969 and 1970, a phenomenal run that included the funk classics "I Turned You On," "Get Into Something," "Freedom," and "The Blacker the Berrie." They also took to the road with the Isleys, spending the 1969 summer solstice at Yankee Stadium—as large a venue as anyone in rock *or* soul could have contemplated at this point—an event filmed and recorded for a souvenir movie and double album. Patterson, Philpot, Pitts, Pope, and Ernest Smith, as the Midnight Movers, then signed direct to T-Neck's parent company, Buddah, and released their own album, *Do It in the Road*, which led to lawyers' letters over their use of a band name that Pickett felt was his. Most of the defecting musicians would return to Pickett's fold at various points over the next thirty years (some of them several times over), but the unfortunate truth was that the singer would never again have a backing band to match the Midnight Movers of 1968.

He wasn't the only one to lose his group. In Muscle Shoals, on March 20, 1969, Rick Hall received a formal visit from the Fame rhythm section. Disappointed by what they saw as a broken promise to cut them in on Fame's profits, Jimmy Johnson, Roger Hawkins, Barry Beckett, and David Hood announced that they had purchased an old studio in a former casket factory at 3614 Jackson Highway, to be renamed Muscle Shoals Sound Studio. Hall proclaimed himself utterly and totally betrayed, all the more so when Jerry Wexler then gave the group an interest-free loan to upgrade their new premises from four- to eight-track, and sent (white) Atlantic artists Cher and Boz Scaggs to record their albums as the studio's first clients. While the indefatigable Hall wasted no time putting together a new rhythm section (and for the first time with what came to be called the Fame Gang, a multiracial one), he stopped working with Atlantic on anyone but his own production client, Clarence Carter.

Before the fallout, Wexler had bought Duane Allman's contract from Hall for a pittance. He then financed and distributed a new rock record label, Capricorn, to be run by Otis Redding's former manager Phil Walden and his brother Alan. The Waldens, like Wexler, felt embittered by their treatment at the troubled NATRA conference of 1968 and the cold shoulder they'd then received on visits to black radio stations, and they were disinclined to continue mining the formerly rich "black belt" of musical artistry that ran through the Deep South. Duane got back with brother Gregg, the pair formed the Allman Brothers, signed to Capricorn, and the rest, as they say, is musical history.

Wexler had largely relocated to Miami by this point, conducting many of these deals from the luxury of his yacht. Into his fifties now, he was tired of jumping on a plane every time he had to attend a session and, in the hope of creating his own, on-hand American/Fame/Stax scenario, imported two rhythm sections into Miami's Criteria Studios.

In August 1969, Pickett came to Miami and Criteria to work with one of them. Atlantic had recently released "Hey Joe," suitably buffered from its name-sake "Hey Jude" by interim singles, but it was patently lacking two of the key ingredients that had rendered the Beatles cover a classic: Wilson Pickett's screams and Duane Allman's licks. "Hey Joe" helped reestablish Pickett's authority with the soul crowd after the cool reaction to "Born to be Wild," but it fared even worse than its predecessor on the pop charts.

Pickett was assigned to record with Cold Grits, a quartet of white R&B enthusiasts from Louisiana who had played on John Fred and his Playboy Band's 1968 one-hit wonder "Judy in Disguise (with Glasses)" before coming up to Alabama, where they had impressed Wexler enough to relocate them in Miami. For producer, Pickett was handed over to the rising Atlantic staffer Dave Crawford, the first black man the singer had worked with in that capacity since coming to Atlantic—and someone who, like Pickett, had been raised in the music of the southern Baptist church. A gifted gospel pianist, Crawford wasted no time propelling Pickett's church influence to the fore.

Earlier that year, in April, as the Edwin Hawkins Singers' gospel anthem "Oh Happy Day" tore up the pop charts, Pickett had been asked about recording a gospel album. His response was equal parts anguish and enthusiasm:

> The company won't let me. They don't think there would be enough sales in it. When you're with a big company like Atlantic Records, they out there to sell records, that's the only thing they're interested in, they're not interested in your feelings or what you want to do. 'Cause I think I could cut me a good Gospel album. I got some gospel tunes I wrote ain't never been heard, man; they've got dust on 'em man. If the Gospel thing come in right now, I'm going to pull them out.[4]

This, then, was his chance. Sadly, Atlantic (mostly) shut him down. Among the cuts unearthed in a 2009 box set was a riveting Pickett composition, "Believe I'll Shout." The singer can be heard instructing and then counting in the group, Crawford quickly picking up his directive on piano, Cold Grits falling in enthusiastically behind the pair of them, their resident keyboard player Billy Carter especially empathetic on organ as the singer actively lives up to the church context of the title.

At Criteria, with Crawford, he did secure the release of one authentic gospel cover version, the only one of his Atlantic career. "Steal Away"— which "I first used to sing when I realized that God had given me a talent as a singer," as he declared in its introduction—was a slow burner on which Dave Crawford accompanied him every step of the way on piano. The addition of vocal backing from Cissy Houston, Judy Clay, Jackie Verdell— and the male voice of John Utley—then lifted the song into the musical heavens. Cold Grits stayed very much in the background. Perhaps because it jarred so much with his "wicked" image, "Steal Away" was held back to become the album's final statement.

The gospel influence was nonetheless emphatically present on "Cole, Cooke & Redding," an update of the recent Dion hit "Abraham, Martin and John" on which Pickett paid tribute to the three deceased black singers in his spoken introduction and some ad hoc sermonizing regarding his own mortality. Released as a single, "Cole, Cooke & Redding" would soon graze the R&B top ten. Gospel was apparent, too, in the country church of "Sweet

Inspiration," written the previous year at American by Spooner Oldham and Dan Penn as a showcase for the Atlantic backing singers of that name, finally being brought into the spotlight as artists in their own right. And gospel was evident in the sweet ballad "She Said Yes," a powerhouse writing collaboration between Pickett, Don Covay, southern soul singer turned reggae pioneer Johnny Nash, and the former Motown A&R chief Mickey Stevenson.

During a break from playing all this church music, Cold Grits "doodle(d) around" with "You Keep Me Hanging On"—the Vanilla Fudge rock cover version, not the Supremes' original. According to bass player Harold Cowart, Pickett came running back in to the room upon hearing them, screaming "Let me sing that!" at which the tapes were quickly set rolling. The Grits' enthusiasm is evident in the recording, which slightly speeds up the notoriously slow Fudge "sludge," and features their strongest collective performance of the Pickett session. Released as a 45, Pickett's "You Keep Me Hanging On" appeared to be one interpretation too many, and too similar in its arrangement to that of Vanilla Fudge, for success at pop; it fared far better in the chart that *Billboard* had just renamed for the first time in forty years (since Wexler's terminology "rhythm and blues" had been introduced, in fact). "Soul," wrote *Billboard*'s executive editors in explaining the change at the header of the black music charts, better reflected the "broad range of song and instrumental material which derives from the musical genius of the black American."[5] The new header also reflected the impact that pioneers like Wilson Pickett and his soul brothers and sisters had had on rhythm and blues over the past decade.

With half an album in the bag, there was then a sudden change in studio personnel. Earlier in October, Wexler had convinced the Muscle Shoals Sound rhythm section to vacate their new studio to spend a few days with Aretha Franklin in Miami. She didn't show for the session, and Pickett was encouraged to fly down to Florida at short notice to make use of both the studio and the band. This would explain why the LP was completed with Wexler at the helm, Pickett's former Fame gang on hand, and a shortage of good quality material.

The best of the bunch was a soaring, gospel-tinged ballad, "Lord Pity Us All," gifted to Pickett by Mac Rebenack, newly signed with Wexler under the stage name Dr. John. The strangest pick, without doubt, was the decision to cover "Sugar Sugar." Fresh off a month on top of the pop charts, it was primarily the compositional work of Jeff Barry, whose cowriting career included such phonetic epics as "Da Doo Ron Ron," "Hanky Panky," and "Do Wah Diddy Diddy." "Sugar Sugar" was the apotheosis of this style, written for the Archies, a cartoon group who existed only as a TV show and whose songs were recorded by session musicians. Pickett's task in tackling such a commercial, simple, even vapid song might have appeared hopeless. But he slowed the pace, giving everyone room to breathe and, greatly aided by the brass section imported again from Memphis, he emerged with something authentically and impressively soulful. In the spring of 1970, "Sugar Sugar" reversed Pickett's sudden downward singles spiral with a highly respectable top 30 placing at pop and a massive top five showing in R&B—where the Archies' version had, unsurprisingly, not charted. Sometimes you simply couldn't predict these things.

The finished Pickett album, *Right On*, wasn't a bad record, per se; every song was satisfactory. But few of them were great, and with its multiple producers, rhythm sections, and musical moods, *Right On* lacked direction and cohesion, as well as a sense of *place*. As David Hood put it, "Muscle Shoals and Memphis are a long way from Miami, culturally," and even more so given that Pickett was not working with native musicians. "Hey Jude," it was now apparent, had been both a blessing and a curse. At the time, it had appeared to put Wilson Pickett on a road to the lucrative rock market; in the long run, it led him into a commercial and creative cul-de-sac. The man who had started the decade by almost single-handedly creating a template for authentic black soul had ended it by covering synthetic white pop. It was a journey that sorely needed redirecting, if it was to continue at all.

CHAPTER 16

That was the highlight of my career, to be able to play with him.

Earl Young, drummer, Sigma Sound Studios, Philadelphia International
Records, MFSB and the Trammps

Soul music at the dawn of the 1970s remained as lucrative and popular as ever, but its sounds were becoming increasingly diversified. Soul was now Sly & the Family Stone, out of Oakland, California, confounding expectations by including black females and white males alike, alternating between dreams of racial harmony ("Everyday People") and reality checks ("Don't Call Me Nigger, Whitey"). Soul was Chicago's Curtis Mayfield and his Impressions addressing contemporary dynamics in "Choice of Colors." Soul was Motown's Temptations updating their sound, style, and lyrical substance on "Psychedelic Shack." Soul was Detroit's Chairmen of the Board, produced by ex-Motown powerhouse trio Holland-Dozier-Holland, reinvigorating the music of the Motor City streets with the urgent "Give Me Just a Little More Time." Soul was James Brown screaming, "Get On Up (I Feel Like Being a Sex Machine)," the Jackson 5 harmonizing "I Want You Back," Aretha Franklin begging "Call Me."

Soul was now emphatically Isaac Hayes, emerging from behind his songwriting and production desks at Stax as the surprise runaway success of the label's ambitious relaunch, with *Hot Buttered Soul*, which turned its back on all presumed confines of the R&B market, featuring just four long songs, two of which (both covers of white pop songs) nonetheless became massive crossover hits on the LP's way to a million sales—success on a scale that even Otis Redding had never enjoyed, let alone Wilson Pickett.

And, for those paying attention to the changing times, soul was increasingly the sound coming out of Philadelphia. There, in an American city steeped in a rich R&B tradition, from Chubby Checker to Barbara Mason, from the Uptown Theater to the Mashed Potato, a new team of musicians, songwriters, and arrangers was coalescing around twenty-six-year-old Kenny Gamble. Originally schooled at Philadelphia's Cameo-Parkway, fronting the vocal group the Romeos, he went on to establish his own Gamble label, from where he took the Intruders to the top of the R&B charts in 1968 with "Cowboys to Girls," written in partnership with Leon Huff, a recent arrival from New York. While Gamble's former Romeos singing partner Thom Bell enjoyed his own success writing and producing for Philadelphia's the Delfonics ("La-La Means I Love You," "Didn't I Blow Your Mind"), Gamble and Huff contracted themselves out as independent producers and writers, overseeing hits for white crossover group the Soul Survivors ("Expressway to Your Heart") and Jerry Butler ("Only the Strong Survive"), as well as for Atlantic's new signings from Houston, Archie Bell and the Drells ("There's Gonna Be a Showdown"). When Cameo-Parkway's former engineer Joe Tarsia opened the eight-track Sigma Sound Studios in August 1968, on North 12th Street in the heart of Philadelphia, Gamble and Huff, employing Thom Bell, a rhythm section that included former Romeo Roland Chambers, and a "staff" (as they subsequently referred to them) of songwriters, more or less moved in. Philly Soul had found its headquarters.

"The Sound of Philadelphia, to me," said Gamble years later, "is a little bit of jazz, a little bit of gospel, a little bit of blues . . . and classical."[1] At the start of the 1970s, that frequently meant male leads singing in high falsetto—a holdover from the city's influential doo-wop era—as accompanied by sophisticated orchestral arrangements. This high-voiced, hybrid style did not exactly coalesce with the deep southern soul of a macho shouter like Pickett, and when Jerry Wexler decided to commission Gamble and Huff on Atlantic acts other than Archie Bell and the Drells, he did so first for Dusty Springfield and the Sweet Inspirations. The results were impressive, and all-inclusive: Gamble and Huff not only supervised the studio, the rhythm section, and the recording; they supplied the sweetening, the final production, and, crucially, the songs themselves.

Sending Pickett to Philadelphia in the wake of Springfield and the Sweet Inspirations presented an intriguing proposition for Wexler. It would eliminate the time-consuming search for material and the inevitable debates over cover versions; in fact, for the first time since Pickett's debut Atlantic LP five years earlier, it would mean a complete *absence* of covers. Sending Pickett to Philadelphia would also mean Atlantic no longer having the responsibility of importing a brass section from Memphis, or hiring backing singers in New York; it would mean cutting Tom Dowd and Jerry Wexler out of the production process and Pickett out of the publishing proceeds. All this represented a complete break with tradition, an enormous act of trust, a full-throttled risk. But in a world where the super smooth sound of Isaac Hayes represented the new personification of cool, it was a risk worth taking.

Jerry Wexler later stated that he made the decision out of "desperation." This might have been the case artistically, if he was as disappointed with the soon-to-be released *Right On* as the public would prove to be.[2] But it hardly indicated a lack of long-term faith, given that at the start of 1970, just before the Philadelphia sessions commenced (and before the release of "Sugar Sugar" reaffirmed the singer's hitmaking status), he signed Pickett to a new contract with Atlantic—one that would "guarantee (Pickett) as much as $150,000 a year in royalty payments" and which, echoing the hyperbole surrounding Aretha Franklin's deal of eighteen months earlier, Wexler termed "one of the best" that a recording artist had ever signed.[3]

Then again, Pickett was not your average soul star. In 1969 alone, he had headlined London's prestigious Royal Albert Hall; sung in Italian with an orchestra at the Sanremo Music Festival; performed on the *Tonight Show* alongside Joe Tex and Jimi Hendrix, when Flip Wilson covered for Johnny Carson; played at Harvard stadium with the Rascals and Sly & the Family Stone; toured with Jeannie Riley (of "Harper Valley PTA" Fame); and appeared alongside the host of *This Is Tom Jones*, one of the finest soul singers ever to come out of the United Kingdom, on a memorable duet of "Hey Jude." And as usual, he also headlined the Apollo. His appeal, provided he and Atlantic could keep making hits, seemed almost universal.

Pickett spent his advance lavishly. He showed up for the sessions in Philadelphia, a couple of hours down the New Jersey Turnpike from New York, in a $40,000 Rolls Royce that had only one previous owner: Rose Kennedy. Pickett later offered some plausible reasons for the purchase: that it maintained its value, that other drivers preferred to avoid it rather than run into it, and that, given the problems in stripping it for parts, let alone offloading them, it was less likely to be stolen than his other fancy cars. "Every time I look around, my Cadillac was *gone* out of my driveway," he later recalled.[4] Further, showing up in Philly in such style demanded respect from the producers and musicians alike, a reminder of who was truly the star of the show.

"Those guys were very curious about how they would get along with me in the studio," Pickett said years later. "Back at that time, a lot of talk was going around—a lot of lies actually—that Wilson Pickett is hard to get along with, and all of this ... Gamble and Huff, especially Huff, he would stand back beside the wall and just stare at me. I wondered why he was doing that and finally the engineer said that he was waiting for me to go off or do something. I said, 'Well, that's a hell of a thing to do. I'm here to make records, you know?'"[5]

His reputation had an effect on drummer Earl Young. Born the same year as Pickett, Young had come up equally poor, learning to play on phone books and coffee cans, working his way up the chitlin' circuit in what he called the "backwoods hills." Bandleader Sam Reed (whose horn section would grace the Pickett album) brought him into the house orchestra at the Uptown Theater in the early 1960s, from where he subsequently worked his way into the city's studios, playing behind Barbara Mason, the Ambassadors—and the Fantastic Johnny C on the 1967 smash "Boogaloo Down Broadway." Along with bassist Ronnie Baker and guitarist Norman Harris, Young was one-third of a self-contained rhythm section that was constantly busy in Philadelphia, albeit only at session rates, eschewing potential royalties for the reliability of an hourly wage. Yet for all his experience, Young confessed to being daunted by the impending arrival of a man whose records he had been purchasing for five years now. "You always get a little nervous when you meet a superstar, 'cos some of them is assholes and some of them is pretty cool. And from what they said about him, I thought he was going to come in there with an attitude."

To some extent that's what Pickett did, but the encounter was to prove entirely positive. "First thing he did was come over to me. I thought, 'Oh shit what I do wrong now? This ain't gonna be a good day.' He said, 'Put that music down, I want you to put it right *here*,'" at which Pickett started stomping the floor. Young was happy to oblige. "I was never a fancy drummer, I just laid the four on the floor. And that's what he grooved by." Pickett was impressed by Young in turn. "That drummer they had was fantastic," he said when asked about the session years on. "He could play different stuff, you know what I mean? He was a funky drummer but he wasn't wearing himself out all over the place. He was just *there*. And he's grinning and laughing all the while he's playing . . . He really amazed me."[6]

Down the line, there would be some bitter irony to this initial harmony. More than anyone else in Philadelphia, perhaps in all of popular music, Earl Young would prove responsible for the disco groove. His gradual switch to a hi-hat shuffle, as heard on countless Philly records through the 1970s and eventually in his own act the Trammps, would soften soul to the point that it could no longer contain a giant vocal presence like that of Wilson Pickett, and would in fact put Pickett (and others) out of business.

For now, however, the musicians met him more than halfway. It perhaps aided proceedings that the Sigma team was integrated in a manner that additionally reflected the changing times and scenes. At the helm were those two self-made black men, Gamble and Huff; lead guitarist Bobby Eli was Jewish; vibes player Vince Montana was Latino; organist Lenny Pakula was a long-haired white guy; Jamaican-born Thom Bell had been raised as a middle-class classical music prodigy. This was a musical melting pot as could not easily be found back down south, and for the *Wilson Pickett in Philadelphia* album, it came together to create a sound that exceeded anything any of them had collaborated on before.

For proof, just listen to the opening measures of "Run Joey Run"—the first song on the LP, and the first to be recorded. It's an instant fanfare, the organ, bass, and drums competing against Eli's tightly wound lead guitar and Sam Reed's resplendent horn section through an introductory four bars of melody that ascends menacingly, all instruments then suddenly dropping out but for a lead guitar until Larry Washington joins in on the congas with a buoyant Latin rhythm never heard before on a Pickett record. The full band then kicks in on the third refrain with a patently jazzy melody, redirecting the song over again. All this has occurred in just fifteen seconds. Yet when Pickett joins the party, he sounds completely at ease—in part, perhaps, because underneath it all, the lyrics and melody conform to expectations: it's still a soul song.

That was not often to prove the case in Philadelphia. A couple of ballads, both arranged by Bobby Martin, were to clearly demonstrate the inherent sophistication of his new musical surroundings. The epic "Days Go By" opens with grand piano gestures rejoined by gesticulating brass and soothed by soaring strings, this pseudo-symphonic refrain repeating after each verse, a constant wave of unexpected shifts in rhythm, timbre, and tone. Pickett's voice has a rasp by now, but if anything, it only humanizes his trademark screams. "Wilson *killed* that song," said Sigler, its cocomposer, who had shared an Apollo bill with Pickett when he had a solo hit in late 1967. "He could sing anything."[7] Bobby Eli wrote "Help the Needy" with his friend Carl Fischer upon hearing that Pickett would be in need of material. The singer's final rendition would be marked by Don Renaldo's hefty string section once more but also by jazz chords on guitar and electric piano and Larry Washington's syncopated cowbells as anchored by Young's tightly controlled snare, stopping and starting at the end of each verse for dramatic effect.

"International Playboy" stood out as the only old-fashioned soul composition and arrangement alike, an obvious choice for single under normal circumstances. Cowritten by Sigler, it was very much in the vein of "I'm a Midnight Mover" and "A Man and a Half," the singer claiming a girl in every port, and of being a "legend in my own time." ("He always told me, 'Man, I ain't no playboy,'" recalled Sigler. "I didn't care what he said as long as he cut the song.")

Holding back "International Playboy" from the 45s market proved to be a wise move—the singles initially selected from the album yielded two of the biggest hits of Pickett's career. On "Don't Let the Green Grass Fool You," composed by the members of a minor Philly vocal group called the Corner Boys, the infectious introduction pitches a softly toned bass riff against an equally fine-tuned jazz guitar. Pickett quickly comes in to remind his girl of all they've been through together, why she shouldn't give it up now just because a rival has come along promising riches on the other side, and before thirty seconds has passed, he's at the chorus. The Sweethearts of Sigma (as the studio's backing singers came to be known) join Pickett through the title refrain as additional guitars flex and funk, a church organ pulsates, and the cowbell offers a single knock just ahead of the fourth measure to keep the rhythm fluid. It's impeccable in composition, arrangement, and performance, one of those rare recordings assured of classic status before it's even been released.

"Get Me Back on Time Engine Number 9," however, is a different story, and was perhaps the most ambitious Pickett recording to date. One can hear the band finding its way into the groove on a couple of early takes released on a box set almost thirty years later; they'd clearly been rehearsing it before putting one down on tape, and once they do so, it's immediately evident that they're onto something.

Pickett took personal responsibility for shepherding the group to this productive point. "They kept experimenting with it too much. You know how you do something so much and then you lose it? So I said, 'Let's break and go to lunch. Come back and I want you to do this with me. Go back to the original same song we started with, because that's the hit record.'"[8] Bobby Eli said, "Pickett liked to record live as much as he could. 'Engine Number 9' was recorded live with the band; he was on one side of the room, we were in our little place. I think he was used to doing it that way."

Of these eventual takes, the first is quickly aborted, but the second is a good one, concluding somewhere close to four minutes. Cleaned up, sweetened, given a fresh lead vocal, it would likely have been a hit—but the musicians are still feeling their way into their individual contributions, and they know they can do better. On the take that finally nails it, they are utterly faultless, Ronnie Baker laying out a four-bar bass line that would have made James Jamerson envious, Larry Washington accompanying him with a clave rhythm on the cowbell and shaker, this pair then handing off the next four bars, first to Bobby Eli's wicked fuzz guitar, then to Norman Harris's response on bass and finally Larry Washington's echo on cowbell.

Round and round it goes, an infection of Philly-style funk, the most adventurous and ambitious Pickett rhythm track to date.

And yet it's the simplest of songs—half sung, half recited, an easy chord change from I to IV and back, barely a couple of verses punctuated by Eli's dirty lead guitar work. It's all in the groove, and Pickett knows as much: he's quickly ad-libbing, inviting the "boys to cook a little bit," to extend beyond the length of the earlier takes. They seize the opportunity, and all of a sudden an electric piano is vying for attention with Eli's guitar, before both instruments drop out to bring us back to the core rhythmic axis of Harris, Washington, and Young, the latter's snare suddenly draped by echo from the mixing desk, Eli then pinching and punching his way back in from the top end of his guitar, Baker doubling up behind him on bass, the entire group somehow sensing and landing upon a return to the core groove at the very moment one imagines they might fall over their own ambition. No wonder Pickett lets out a profound "Lord have mercy!" as the track moves beyond the three and a half minute mark and into its distinct, instrumental part two.

Gamble and Huff would take the songwriting credit, and Bobby Martin that for arrangement, but the profound success of "Get Me Back on Time, Engine Number 9" is largely down to the studio musicians. "That's about the only song we ever recorded like that," said Young, "passing off to each other. It was really interesting, 'cos we never did that before." Yet when comparing *In Philadelphia* to other records made at Sigma Sound during those years, it's clear that Pickett has raised the energy level in the studio, brought the best out of the assembled musicians, just as he had previously at Stax, Fame, and American, and for that reason, he too deserves all due credit.

After several weeks of postproduction, *Wilson Pickett in Philadelphia* was released in September 1970, just six months after *Right On*—so soon, in fact, that Atlantic used the same photo session for its back cover images. "Engine Number 9," a potentially risky first single given its lack of recognizable structure, promptly became Pickett's biggest hit at both pop (#14) and R&B (#3) since "Funky Broadway," with which it shared the honor of a Grammy nomination.[9] At the start of 1971, "Don't Let the Grass Fool You" fared even better. A certified million seller (Pickett's first, somewhat surprisingly, although that might be down to the haphazard nature of sales accounting in the rough-and-tumble mid-sixties era), it was held off the top spot at R&B only by the Temptations' masterpiece "Just My Imagination." *In Philadelphia* reversed the singer's recent downward trend on the albums charts too, spending a solid seven months in the R&B top twenty.

The success of *In Philadelphia* heralded the launch of a potentially prosperous new phase for Pickett. Just months after his label's predilection for commercial cover versions had threatened to derail his career, he was again to be found at the vanguard of popular black music, helping set the standards by which others would follow. At the start of the 1970s, just as had been the case back in 1965, Wilson Pickett defined the current direction of soul.

CHAPTER 17

Pickett is, to me, the greatest Rhythm & Blues singer of today.

Jerry Wexler, 1971[1]

Early in the new decade, Wilson Pickett swapped out the functional house in Queens for a lavish one in Englewood, on the New Jersey side of the Hudson River. Though he was officially now in the suburbs, in actuality he was closer to Manhattan than when he had lived in the borough of New York City itself—barely ten minutes from the George Washington Bridge, and twenty from the Apollo on a fast drive home. The Isley Brothers were up the road in Teaneck, Ben E. King was down the road a ways, Dizzy Gillespie lived nearby. Pickett was in a place where black musicians born into prejudice and poverty could—and did—demonstrate that they had made it. Still, it was not exactly the mansion on the hill. The property on 75 Brayton Street was barely a half-acre, and from the exterior it was nothing as lavish as his taste in clothing and cars might suggest. He paid the $74,000 purchase price in cash and then sank tens of thousands more into fixing it up, adding a Japanese tea room in the basement, alongside a wet bar, a pool table, and an indoor barbeque pit within vast walls of heavy duty stone.

Now that he had a house in which he could entertain properly, he finally invited his children from Detroit to come visit. For Veda, it was the start of a close relationship that would lead to fishing trips and holidays in the Bahamas; but for Lynderrick, the attempt at reconciliation came too late. For son Michael, meanwhile, who turned seven late in 1971, the visits from his half-siblings came as a mixed blessing: "They'd come for a couple of months in the summertime," he said, "and when [Wilson] got tired of them and got ready, he'd send them home. Then I'm taking the repercussions."[2]

Philadelphia was now the epicenter of American soul, thanks in part to Pickett's album, and Kenny Gamble and Leon Huff sought to seize their moment by establishing a new record label named for their home city. Atlantic, despite the patronage that had helped bring the pair's reputation to this point, was quickly priced out of the bidding war. Instead, Philadelphia International Records was financed in 1971 by Clive Davis at CBS; it would go on to dominate early 1970s American black music culture, much like Motown a decade earlier.

A repeat visit by Pickett was unlikely. The singer fixated not on the success of *In Philadelphia* but on the cost. By all accounts, the invoice was substantial: Pickett quoted a figure of over $100,000, but even the officially stated $60,000 represented a fortune in 1970 studio bills.[3] And as was the case for musicians, it was due to come out of his royalties. Pickett, in his own words, "raised a little hell about that," at which he recalled that Jerry Wexler offered to kick in $20,000. Such a nonrecoupable contribution, especially after the fact, was rare in the industry, but it wasn't enough to assuage the singer: "I could see myself making an album but not getting a cent, you know, in the final analysis." One would hope that with his new contract and the album's substantial sales that this was not true. Regardless, there was a value to *In Philadelphia* that could not be measured in dollars: the importance of the record in reestablishing his credibility and visibility (and, in all likelihood, his appearance fees). Pickett was back on top, and he had Philadelphia to thank.

Still, he didn't return. "Gamble and Huff, that's two black Jews, man," he later said. "They was good. But I was good too, you know, man. So if they're gonna make some money, I'm gonna make some money too. Right? Okay?"[4]

Pickett went back to Muscle Shoals, instead, to the former Fame rhythm section at their new studio on Jackson Highway. There he was additionally reunited with Dave Crawford, now working alongside Brad Shapiro, a Miami native whose résumé included many of that city's major players (a band alongside Steve Alaimo in the 1950s, writing songs with Henry Stone in the 1960s), a process by which, like Crawford before him, he came to Jerry Wexler's attention and onto the Atlantic payroll.

The assembled team had already engaged in a trial run of sorts, at Muscle Shoals Sound in the late spring and early summer of 1970, when they rerecorded "She Said Yes," the powerhouse composition from *Right On* that had been mysteriously buried toward the back of that LP's second side. Slowed down from its original rendition, its gospel tendencies emphasized by a team of backing singers, afforded a string accompaniment, and emboldened by the performance of a rhythm section that knew the singer better than had Cold Grits, "She Said Yes" was but a modest commercial success upon release as a single in the fall, yet satisfying enough from a creative perspective that it appeared to help justify the commissioning of a full album session at the start of 1971.

Shapiro and Crawford had just come off producing the J. Geils Band's debut album, and they worked well together. Pickett, said Shapiro, who would go on to produce more albums for the singer than anyone else, "had a great instinct about the songs. Pickett knew when it was right. He was an authentic talent." They had met for the first time at the office of Pickett's long-time manager, Jimmy Evans, whose creative input with his client remained minimal. "A pure gangster," Shapiro recalled of him. "Proper mafia. But he was a nice fellow, really, really was. You don't think things like that happen but they really do. He wanted to get involved with the songs. We said, 'Thank you, we'll take it from here.'"

By the time recording started, In Philadelphia had just been released, "Engine Number 9" was roaring up the charts and taking over dance floors, and Shapiro and Crawford set to recreate its winning formula, right down to the Latin percussion. Pickett had successfully worked with all of the rhythm section except for rhythm guitarist Tippy Armstrong, another of Duane Allman's former bandmates. (Jimmy Johnson, who had previously occupied that role at Fame and Muscle Shoals for Pickett, had shifted to the engineer's chair.) The Memphis Horns—reduced now to Andrew Love and Wayne Jackson—were also familiar. To emulate the funky lead guitar work of Bobby Eli, the producers turned to Dennis Coffey, who had provided the distinct wah-wah guitar that helped modernize the Temptations' sound on "Cloud Nine," "Psychedelic Shack," "Ball of Confusion," and, most recently, "Just My Imagination." His distinct playing could also be heard on the Supremes "I'm Livin' in Shame" and Chairman of the Board's "Give Me Just a Little More Time."

Coffey had a similar initial impression of Pickett as most everyone else. "He was just the authentic funk singer, man, that's all there is to it," he recalled, using the term that was replacing that of "soul" among musicians and aficionados alike. "He got down. He was the man when it came to that. I don't think there's ever anybody could sing funkier than Wilson."

The most overt duplication of Pickett's Philly success, beyond that of the studio lineup, came with the production techniques employed on the album's title track and major hit single, "Don't Knock My Love." "Pickett had the hook—'If you don't like it, don't knock it, somebody else might wanna rock it'—but not the verse," said Brad Shapiro, for whom this would be the first of many cowrites. "And I picked up a yellow pad and I started writing the verses down, and Pickett said 'That's it!' and within twenty minutes the track was cut. It was over. That fast."

Roger Hawkins concurred, "As soon as we heard that song, we knew we could jump on it and make it happen," and Wayne Jackson confirmed, "I remember just being carried away by the thing."[5] "Don't Knock My Love" represented something new for the Muscle Shoals players with Pickett, something smoother and, indeed, *funkier* than they were used to, and it was to their credit that they recognized as much and immediately responded to the challenge, elevating their reputations and improving their repertoire in the process.

For the album's overdubs, Shapiro and Crawford brought in two more players from Motown, the percussionists Eddie "Bongo" Brown and Jack Ashford. Brown's congas and Ashford's tambourine were placed at the front of "Don't Knock My Love," affording the song a sense of continuity from "Engine Number 9," as did an instrumental part two. Anchored by David Hood's fluid bass in tandem with Brown's (overdubbed) percussion, it showcased Coffey's psychedelic funk guitar as run through his newly acquired Condor unit, an early guitar synthesizer attached to the guitar's pickup that allowed each string to trigger harmonics and the sound of other instruments. On "Don't Knock My Love" Coffey used the Condor to double up on the bass and emulate the sound of a harpsichord; around him rhythm guitar, brass, and a frequently dissonant string section all contributed to a pulsating four-minute instrumental that rivaled the best of Motown's turn-of-the-decade recordings.

Shapiro recalled the reaction to the track at Atlantic. "Everyone was excited. Jerry Greenberg [Atlantic's General Manager at the time] said, 'Let's get it out on the street,' and Jerry Wexler said, 'Can we have half the publishing?' Pickett looks at me and says. 'Over my dead body.'" (The publishing was duly assigned to Pickett's own company, now called Erva.) Two years later, Motown would assign "Don't Knock My Love" to Diana Ross and Marvin Gaye for a cover version. According to Pickett's managerial assistant at the time, Lee Wade, Erva earned $60,000 from that rendition in just a few months.

Unlike the Philadelphia album, however, there was no Gamble and Huff-style songwriting factory on hand. Inevitably, talk turned to cover versions of existing rock songs, despite mixed results for Pickett since the "Hey Jude" breakthrough. Fortunately, the producers made an inspired choice with "Fire and Water," the title track of the recent debut album (but significantly, *not* a hit single) by English rock band Free. As covered at Muscle Shoals, the rhythm groove was solid, Dennis Coffey provided a rotating solo in the middle on his Gibson Firebird such as would have rendered any hard rock guitarist instantly jealous, and Pickett's delivery was emphatic. It was a mark of its successful adaptation from its original format that Pickett would eventually perform "Fire and Water" on America's black dance music show *Soul Train*. Pickett and company also covered Randy Newman's "Mama Told Me Not to Come" as had recently topped the charts in a version by rock band Badfinger, though with significantly less originality.

Of the inevitable under-the-radar soul covers, two hailed from Detroit. The fiery "Not Enough Love To Satisfy" had been undersold as a B-side by 100 Proof Aged in Soul, the latest vocal group to feature Pickett's former Falcons' rival Joe Stubbs who, after such a promising start, had spent the past decade as a second-string vocal group journeyman; "You Can't Judge a Book By its Cover" had appeared on Stevie Wonder's most recent LP. "(Your Love has Brought Me) a Mighty Long Way" had been cowritten by Pickett's former stage bassist Carlton McWilliams for Arthur Conley a year earlier. On a version sped up considerably at Muscle Shoals, Pickett finally got to play harmonica in the studio, proving himself perfectly adept, begging the question as to why this talent wasn't more greatly utilized in the studio. A George Jackson ballad, "Covering the Same Old Ground," brought Pickett back to the soul of the Deep South, and a Brad Shapiro cowrite with Miami's Clarence Reid, "Hot Love," afforded the opportunity to wax sensual.

Rounding out a stellar set of material, Shapiro and Crawford's composition "Call My Name, I'll Be There" served as a straight-down-the-line early 1970s soul-stomper; and Pickett cowrote "Woman Let Me Be Down Home" with Clyde Otis, who, as the first black A&R man with a major label, had brought the Falcons to Mercury Records. The producers then segued the songs into each other, using existing backing vocals, percussion, and Coffey's guitar effects to provide a seamless transition through each side. In doing so, Shapiro and Crawford took the concept of *In Philadelphia* a step further, lifting Pickett's latest LP out of the haphazard R&B format to which Atlantic had frequently consigned the singer. Judged by multiple standards—consistency of material, commercial success, contemporary production standards—*Don't Knock My Love*, released at the end of 1971, was surely Wilson Pickett's finest Atlantic LP. It was also to be his last.

CHAPTER 18

As a performer and a peer, there was no one better than Pickett. Maybe as good, but not better.

Sam Moore, singer, Sam & Dave

At the end of February 1971, Wilson Pickett boarded a plane bound for West Africa. He was making the journey not as a tourist (although there would be several cultural excursions over the following week), but as an international superstar—the headlining act for the first modern black American musical package ever to visit Africa.

The event in which he was to participate, Soul To Soul, had come about at short notice. In the fall of the previous year, James Brown had become the first American soul singer known to have performed in Africa. Traveling with a twenty-two-piece band, Brown's tour took him to Zambia and Nigeria, eight shows in all. In the former he played for the President, Kenneth Kaunda; in the latter, he played for Fela Ransome Anikulapo Kuti—which, when it came to African music, was more or less the same thing. Prior to his stadium show in Lagos, the Nigerian capital at the time, Brown's people were approached by Tom Mosk, a twenty-four-year-old graduate student whose parents, entertainment lawyer Ed and writer Fern, were in the midst of producing a feature film of the postcolonial Nigerian novel *Things Fall Apart* by Chinua Achebe. The younger Mosk suggested that considering he had the crew and the equipment on hand, and given the historical importance of Brown's journey, it might make sense to film the concert. His offer was declined. Mosk went to the show anyway. Brown, he observed, was treated "like a God."[1]

Tom Mosk immediately recommended to his parents that they arrange a concert of their own in Africa. But not just a concert, a festival—and not just a festival but a truly African American festival, one that would bring a wide range of top black American musicians to play alongside equally prominent African musicians in a cross-cultural event that could ride the tide of American black pride, and harness the strength of its back-to-Africa movement, while tapping into the continent's own politics of pan-Africanism. The Mosks were not of African descent, nor was the partner they recruited back in America, Pacific Jazz label founder Richard Bock. Nor were most of the others who came to work on the movie. But it was only because of Bock's considerable contacts and production experience, the senior Mosks' experience in international travel and entertainment law, and their son Tom's indefatigable determination that the event actually took place— although not, as originally intended, in Nigeria.

The event landed, instead, on the former British Gold Coast. Even before it became the first sub-Saharan colony to gain independence, in 1956 the country had welcomed Louis Armstrong for a highly celebrated performance, funded by the US State Department. (This provided an important precedent for the Mosks' proposal once they concluded that Nigeria was too politically unsettled and dangerous.) Following Independence, in March 1957, the nation newly known as Ghana put out the welcome mat for African Americans. The novelist Maya Angelou came to live there in the 1960s, and routinely invited fellow American artists of West African descent to appear at Ghana's annual independence celebrations. When a violent military coup overthrew the nation's visionary leader, President Kwame Nkrumah, in 1966, Ghana entered an unsteady period of transition and turnovers in the ruling parties, leaving little room for peaceable artistic efforts such as Angelou's. In 1969 the military government transitioned into civilian rule, Prime Minister Kofi Abrefa Busia of the Progress Party was elected, and as one of his first acts in power, hundreds of thousands of noncitizens, especially Nigerians, who had flocked to Ghana during its early days of independence were expelled. Yet soon after this upheaval, there was a calm in the political storm that allowed Ghana to reposition itself as a figurative homeland for those of African descent. The nation was, for now, relatively peaceful, relatively prosperous, and a good prospect for an African American festival—it even had a long-standing Arts Council that could help coordinate such an event. The government accepted the Mosks' proposal, suggesting that the event be held on March 6, 1971—the fourteenth anniversary of the nation's independence—and agreed to allow use of Black Star Square in the nation's capital of Accra, with its dramatic backdrop of the Atlantic Ocean. Originally constructed as a celebration of independence, the square had been used only for military and political affairs up to this point.[2] Soul To Soul would be the first event to break that pattern.

Warner Bros. Films soon backed out of its original investment, convinced, after a number of broken assurances, that the Ghanaian government would not honor its side of any bargain. But by then, the wheels were already in motion and Atlantic Records was on board, having committed $100,000 for the rights to the soundtrack—which would feature several of the label's own acts. Joining Wilson Pickett on the chartered plane to Ghana were Ike and Tina Turner, the Staple Singers, Roberta Flack, the former Pacific Jazz artists Les McCann and Eddie Harris, the all-female, all-teenage Voices of East Harlem along with their twelve-year-old male mascot Kevin Griffin, and Santana—the only band with any white musicians, and the only group, thanks in part to guest percussionist Willie Bobo, to actively include Afro-Cuban rhythms in their sound. In the States, where they had dazzled at Woodstock and where "Black Magic Woman" was in the top five at the time, Santana might well have headlined this package. In Ghana, however, there was only one contender. "Wilson Pickett was the ticket that everyone wanted to see," said Tom Mosk. "Once we were set that Wilson was going to be part of the concert, we were pretty sure that it was going to be knock-out."[3]

But why Pickett? It was James Brown's loose-limbed, syncopated, follow-it-till-it-almost-falls-over-then-get-back-on-the-beat funk that provided the more obvious connection to the polyrhythmic, percussive music of Africa. Pickett would instead lay hold of a song like "Funky Broadway," iron out the kinks that gave it that funk, and take it to the mainstream—sounding positively western by comparison. But that was an intrinsic part of Pickett's popularity. He was a soul purist, but he was also a committed populist, and his hits were a part of the international lexicon played regularly on transistor radios worldwide.

The chartered plane landed in view of nearly a thousand onlookers, crowding the terminal rooftops to greet the man who disembarked in a finely tailored, garish mauve suit (along with the rest of the famous entourage, of course).[4] Pickett was immediately mobbed by well-wishers, and was treated with reverence and affection throughout the week-long build-up to the main event. His name dominated the posters, the advertising, and the printed program, and his picture appeared on the front of the *Weekly Spectator* with his last name spelled out in block type across the page: "Here Is—Great Soul Brother PICKETT".[5]

Pickett welcomed the adulation, but did not immediately grasp his hosts' visceral connection. "They kept saying 'Back home Willie P,'" he recalled in an interview years later. "I didn't know what they were talking about, I ain't from over here!"[6] Like many descendants of slaves, Pickett's family had not been able to trace their roots all the way back to Africa, but as an editorial in black newspaper *The Pittsburgh Courier* noted at the time of the Gold Coast's Independence, "the ancient empire of Ghana was the land of the forefathers of most American Negroes."[7] For many black Americans who visited Ghana, this connection proved visceral. Louis Armstrong noticed on his tour how an Ewe woman "danced and sang like my mother, and when I went over to talk to her she even held her head like Mama."[8] Fifteen years later, several of the Soul To Soul performers recognized their own commonalities. While on an excursion with the traveling group, Mavis Staples spotted mannerisms in an older lady remarkably similar to those of her grandmother back in Mississippi. On another excursion, Tina Turner jumped up to join in a village tribal dance that included many of the same moves as her floor show. But for Pickett, that recognition moved in the opposite direction. In the days leading up to the concert, wearing ceremonial kente cloth for the occasion, Pickett was presented to King Nana Osae Djan II—who informed the singer upon examining him that he was an Ashanti, the dominant ethnic group of Ghana descended from the historic rulers of the Ancient Ghanaian empire. To this king, at least, the wayward singer had returned to his ancestral home.

In the film, Pickett's limited commentary about the trip does not reveal whether he appreciated any social or cultural significance in what some of the musicians cited as a "return" to Africa.[9] But several of the African American musicians were brought to tears when visiting Fort James, a slave fort just outside of the area. (Pickett was part of the entourage; his reaction went unrecorded.) Elsewhere in the film, Les McCann engaged in an energetic discussion about African complicity in the slave trade with a local professor, one who talked of his own travels to America and his ability to identify the original native nation of many African Americans he met on his trip. Mavis Staples, who had been raised by her guitar-playing bandleader Pops to understand her place in history as a powerful black woman of the civil rights era, appeared determined not to waste a single moment of the trip. And Tina Turner, who wrote a theme song for the event, respectfully chose to sing the title "Soul To Soul" in Swahili. Wilson was arguably more engaged throughout the film than Tina's husband Ike, whose stony-faced veneer softened only occasionally to reveal a fascination with his surroundings, and who confessed almost four decades later: "I didn't know nothing about Africa, period. Still don't."[10] By comparison, upon return from Ghana Pickett immediately expressed his delight at the native rhythms he encountered on the cultural visits, especially the Fontomfrom talking drum: "Those African drums, man, they're fantastic, they really speak."[11]

The day before the concert Ed Mosk finally, and under duress, signed a contract. The document had been so extensively rewritten by the Ghanaian government that by doing so, Mosk was breaking the terms of the deals he'd already made with the movie's financier and new distributor. That night, a torrential thunderstorm blew down the PA system, ripped off part of the grandstand roof, and filled electrical equipment with several inches of water. It took all of the next day to dry out, and the fourteen-hour concert started several hours behind schedule. By that time, the streets of Accra were full of people heading to Black Star Square. "People walked for a week to get there, carrying their own chairs on their heads," said Pickett.[12] And those with the income paid accordingly for VIP seating in front of the stage.

The show built slowly, at least until nightfall. The Ghana Arts Council had provided stellar local entertainment in the form of high life pioneer Kwa Mensah, part-time American resident Guy Warren and, especially, local psychedelic rock act the Aliens (an intentionally provocative name given the government's ongoing repatriation program). Les McCann brought on stage a shamanistic *kalabash* player and medicine man, Amoah Azangeo. Santana was captivating, credited by one local journalist in attendance with having a significant influence on the nation's musical community from that evening's performance alone.[13] And as the penultimate act, Ike and Tina Turner all but stole the show, a resplendent Tina in a see-through blouse performing mock oral sex to Ike Turner's guitar moans on a mesmerizing cover of Bobby Bland's "I Smell Trouble," the Ikettes delivering added sex appeal and synchronized dance steps—a spectacle that would have demolished almost any performer to follow before they even stepped on stage.

After that set, Ike and Wilson got into it backstage. Pickett was perturbed to find Turner in his dressing room. He didn't realize that only one room had been provided, and that the incoming act had to share the space with the outgoing one. According to Pickett's managerial assistant, Lee Wade, Turner tried to placate Pickett with cocaine—but on one condition. "He wanted to feed him," said Wade. In other words, the singer would have to sniff the powder off the guitarist's knuckle, in an insulting position of subservience. "Pickett said 'You don't feed *me*,' so Ike Turner took it to the window and threw it out. Pickett was fit to be tied."

Fired up by this encounter, the singer took to the stage. It was around four in the morning, and he was wearing what *Ebony's* Phyl Garland, one of three journalists flown in for the event, described as a "skin-tight, rhinestone-studded jumpsuit that displayed every inch of his masculinity."[14] (Pickett's stage costumes, like those he wore for his album covers, were evolving elaborately with the times.) By this late hour the audience had overrun the VIP section up front, and were extending backward and sideways as far as anyone could see. Conservative estimates put attendance at 100,000, but no one would ever really know for sure.[15] "I've never seen so many black and beautiful people in one place—250,000 of them," said Pickett himself.[16]

Pickett's band had been hastily assembled for the event. Some of his regular musicians, unaware of the magnitude of the occasion, had chosen to stay in the States as the time away seemed too long for just a single paying gig, though Pickett still had alongside him veterans Jimmy Owens, Ernest Smith, and Claston Higgins, who were joined by, among others, relative newcomers Bobby Banks on sax, and Wesley "Wally Gator" Watson on drums. It didn't make for his tightest of bands, but the moment they broke into the descending chords of "In the Midnight Hour," the crowd's reaction was electric. The young African men who had commandeered the front rows fell into the pogoing mosh-pit of a punk rock movement still several years and a continent away—jumping, leaping, dancing, and excitedly shoving those around them. And the police broke from their official baton-wielding crowd control duties to join in with the joy of the moment. Still others in the frenzied crowd—to throw back to Tom Mosk's observation of James Brown in Lagos—stared upward at Wilson Pickett as if in the presence of a deity.

Sensing the immensity of the occasion and the enormity of his popularity—he could hardly ignore the multiple cameras around him, after all—Pickett was eager to deliver on all fronts. As "In the Midnight Hour" boiled over he bent note after note, screamed at a high pitch, and when the four-man brass section vamped the coda, he leaned down to pull a young boy—surely no more than twelve years old—up onstage to dance with him. Soul to soul, indeed.

A genuinely funky "Funky Broadway" followed, and when the set moved on to "Land of 1000 Dances," Pickett pulled the familiar call-and-response party trick he'd been playing for years. In every performance he called out a different roster of characters during the extended introduction, and that night in Accra he summoned the spirit of Ringo Starr to ask the eternal question, "What is soul?" Anyone who knew Pickett's rap already knew the answer, knew what Pickett would say almost down to the last word. But most out in this audience had never seen him perform in the flesh, and they were delighted by the whole call-and-response build-up—raising their hands aloft at his request to prove they got soul. And they were just as ecstatic to leap all over the square again as soon as the band broke out of its opening vamp, through the initial brass blasts, and into that one-chord riff. Wally Gator held his own on the tight Roger Hawkins backbeat as they broke it down, and several thousand Africans chanted the famous "na, na-na-na-na" chorus back at the American singer.

Pickett descended from the main stage to a lower platform, allowing the front rows to reach out and, as Mavis Staples later put it, "touch the hem of his garment."[17] Another boy, older than the first and in a fancy dark suit with red lining, clambered onstage to dance alongside his idol—before stage-diving back into the throng. He was replaced by other young Pickett imitators who flanked the singer as he turned sideways, mirroring his dance steps. Pickett left them to it as the festivities closed out, his band bringing it on home, and a few more young Ghanaian men taking to the stage to dance what looked—to Mavis Staples among others—suspiciously like the funky chicken.

As the star of Soul To Soul left the stage, there was no doubt about it: Wilson Pickett was on top of the world. And he was not yet thirty years old.

CHAPTER 19

There is the sense that Pickett is the embodiment of that peculiar aggressiveness one has seen in black boys that ended up in the man's jail before they reached manhood, and the further sense that he is the ideal expression of how all that energy, if not harnessed, can blow this world.

David Llorens, *Ebony* magazine, October 1968

Wilson Pickett returned from Ghana understandably exuberant at the reception he had enjoyed there, and ever more convinced as to his worth, materially as well as musically. He had reason to think of it, at the time, as another step on a ladder ascending ever higher; he had no inclination that Ghana would prove to be the peak celebration of his international popularity.

Certainly, in the weeks and months immediately following his return, business continued in what he had come to perceive as its usual lucrative self. In May, Pickett headlined the Apollo above Eddie Kendricks, and Atlantic released "Don't Knock My Love" alongside a second *Best of Wilson Pickett*. The new single wasn't actually included on the compilation, but "Don't Knock My Love" shot up the charts anyway, becoming Pickett's third top 20 pop hit in barely six months and his fourth R&B number one; as with "Don't Let the Green Grass Fool You," it would be certified gold for a million sales. The sterling second collection of singles, for all that it gravitated toward white pop and rock cover versions, performed on par with *In Philadelphia*.

Pickett returned to Muscle Shoals in the late spring of 1971, where Dave Crawford played piano alongside Barry Beckett's Hammond on the gospel standard "Rock of Ages." Pickett rendered the old hymn from the perspective of a man who admitted he had strayed from the path ("I can remember a time when I didn't have no God on my side, when it seemed like everything

I did was wrong. But I'm so glad now I'm a child of God"). Sadly, "Rock of Ages" would not be released in his lifetime. Nor would "Many Roads to Travel," a six-and-a-half-minute parable/morality tale set to a novel funky country rhythm that ascends to an ecstatic gospel sing-along finale. "Call My Name, I'll Be There" was released as a 45 instead, and though it stalled at pop, it made the soul top ten at the end of the summer. As autumn beckoned Pickett returned to Europe, where he headlined major theaters, including London's prestigious Hammersmith Odeon.

The *Soul To Soul* movie hit theaters in October, marketed as being of significant cultural importance to African Americans. It was received accordingly, playing at major black theaters like the Apollo, where it had such success that it was held over for a second week. It also played at mainstream urban cinemas and in art houses across the country. It played, too, across Africa, in Europe, Japan, even Russia. Everywhere it went, the film received excellent reviews. The final edit struck a fine balance between thrilling concert souvenir and cultural documentary, but a balance nearly tipped as the African musicians' performances were mostly eschewed for footage of the visiting Americans' excursions into more traditional locales. If, in the process, *Soul To Soul* inadvertently played up certain primitivist stereotypes of Africans, it also depicted the 100,000-strong audience who represented somewhat westernized Ghanaian middle and upper classes, and displayed an exuberance and vitality among the entire audience that was far from always evident at American festivals.

James Brown had been silent upon his own return from Africa in 1970. The *Soul To Soul* performers proved anything but. Only two years after Pickett had squirmed at an interview's question about the phrase "black is beautiful," saying, "I don't even like to go into this kind of things," he allowed himself to be quoted extensively on the topic as part of the movie's official press kit, and his comments reflected a sense that perhaps the event had served to influence, inform, and even inspire him in a way that domestic politics had not.[1] "There's a lot of talk at home in the States about developing a sense of black pride," he said, "but you'll never really know it until you've gone back to your roots and seen what a beautiful country Ghana is and how beautiful your African brothers and sisters are."[2]

At the start of 1972 the *Don't Knock My Love* album was finally released, trailed by its opening cut, "Fire and Water," which rose to number two on the soul charts and just a few places outside the pop top twenty. By this measure, it was the most successful of all his white pop and rock covers, "Hey Jude" included. It was also to be his last major hit.

The cover of the new album depicted Pickett in a lavish cream-colored suit with frilly attached cravat, leaning on the hood of his Rolls Royce in front of what appeared to be some form of mansion, all of it a statement of success—and excess—that played into the popular Isaac Hayes mold of the soulful lover man who would ply you with champagne and caviar and a chauffeur-driven ride home. This was all part of a coordinated new approach, a conscious marketing exercise. When Lee Wade had joined Pickett's management just before the singer went to Africa in 1971, she came from publicist Billy Rowe, and immediately applied her experience to an image that she saw as in need of an update. "Any time you saw Pickett's face in the papers he had on one of those shiny suits and greasy hair," she observed. "I went into Atlantic and X'd out all of those pictures and put in new pictures, and then he had a bigger offering to the people. More class . . . Although he *had* class to the people on the chitlin' circuit."

Wade felt that Pickett's live career was coasting. Jimmy Evans, she said, "had good connections and back then the connections were, who owned the clubs in your circuit. And the boys owned the clubs, and you're one of the boys." Evans, she felt, had it easy. "His acts were all hot acts. So therefore they were self-selling. All he had to do was funnel it. You want Wilson Pickett, then you go to Jimmy Evans. The telephone rings . . . 'We want him in Indianapolis.' 'I ain't going to let you have him for that, motherfucker!' He had an act. It was abrasive, something that Wilson Pickett could relate to. And Jimmy was connected in Boston, who was then connected to the Florida mob."

Wade was an African American who lived on the bohemian Lower East Side, and of a markedly different type than most who had worked alongside the singer until now. "I was a hippie," she said. "We were into astrology, mind and body. They taught you how to meditate." These were potentially useful tools in dealing with Pickett's mercurial nature, but the singer remained immersed in his own world. Not for him a performance on Bill Graham's Fillmore circuit, let alone the festival scene. Nor did he engage in the contemporary commentary of acts like Sly and the Family Stone, for whom his friend Bobby Womack had recently supplied guitar on the acclaimed LP *There's a Riot Goin' On*. Rather, Pickett now thought it time to get away from the one-nighters completely, and the Apollo as well—*anything* that didn't present him as living in the lap of luxury he felt that he had deserved and the audience now expected of him. It was time to cash in.

On February 24, 1972, Wilson Pickett opened at the Copacabana in Manhattan, on East 60th Street. The preeminent supper club in New York City, if not all of America, the Copacabana was the place where black artists went for confirmation from white America that they had made it. Sam

Cooke had made a grand statement by playing there all the way back in 1958—and made a point of coming back in 1964, recording a successful live LP in the process. Berry Gordy placed the Supremes there the following year, and the Temptations and Marvin Gaye after that, all of whom also released live albums intended to appeal to that part of middle America that preferred its soul delivered politely, at the dinner table, rather than in ecstasy on the dance floor.

Opening night at the Copa had the aura of a special occasion. The famous black comedian Bill Cosby introduced him. Aretha, known among her friends for producing down-home gifts from her kitchen, brought Pickett some freshly cooked collard greens before joining Dionne Warwick and Melba Moore in the audience, all three of them, according to *Jet*, accompanying the singer during the second set.[3] From the stage, Pickett got Peter Zage, his Rolls Royce dealer, to buy all his friends champagne. Jackie Moore, whose hit single "Precious, Precious" had been written and produced by her cousin, Dave Crawford, served as opening act. During rehearsals Pickett had realized that the house band was incapable of providing the kick that his soul required, and invested in a strong team of his own hand-picked musicians, including guitarist Cornell Dupree, while Wade Marcus, who had arranged the strings for *Don't Knock My Love*, conducted the group on stage.

Bill Cosby, a good connection for a black entertainer to have at the time, was one of the few celebrities to attend on a regular basis; a respected jazz drummer, he frequently joined in on tambourine. According to Eddie Jacobs, Pickett felt that Cosby was basking in the singer's glory, "and when Bill Cosby heard this he pulled away from Wilson because he was a star in his own right." Danny White recalled Cosby attempting to play the role of mediator during a dispute over pay. "Bill talked to the band: 'Hey man, let's be civilized. It's hard to get in here, now we're here.'" The result was much the same. "When Bill went up there and started talking to Wilson, he cussed Bill out so bad, you never saw Bill Cosby again." Pickett would alienate and insult more important connections yet.

There was an inherent risk in credibility for any black artist of substance in performing at the Copa, as evidenced by a review in *Billboard* from opening night, which noted that Pickett seemed "not terribly wicked next to a filet mignon."[4] Perhaps inevitably, then, the novelty of this soul man on the Copa stage quickly wore off. A review by John Abbey in *Blues and Soul*, from later in Pickett's run, lamented that the audience "rarely showed interest in what he was doing and frequently rudely just continued talking," that "a good proportion of the older folks were long gone from the club before Pickett's show was complete," and that "Hey Jude" was "sadly the only song that audience gave any reaction to."[5]

The Copacabana booking ran its course after two weeks, and Pickett did not return prior to the venue's closure in 1973. His career intent was nonetheless evident in the fact that he followed it up almost immediately with an engagement at the Hilton International Casino in Las Vegas. As with the Copa, Vegas signified success. It paid, extremely well; the artist could live in luxury for the duration of his appearance, usually two weeks at a time for Pickett, who would play as many as four engagements a year for the next four years. He had reason to presume he was in good company, given that he was performing at the same hotel as Elvis Presley, Carl Perkins, and Tony Bennett. But they were all in the main room, the Internationale. Pickett was in the Casino Lounge, alongside the likes of B. B. King and Chuck Berry, remnants of an older R&B generation. And Pickett's new status as a family-friendly entertainer was exemplified by a promotional color postcard that showed his name, on one of three Hilton marquees, alongside those of Perry Como and Ann-Margret.

Moving up to the Copa and Vegas was one thing; when it came to recording—Pickett was always recording—he preferred familiar, tried and trusted locations. He returned to Muscle Shoals Sound Studios, to Dave Crawford and Brad Shapiro, where his producers brought Coffey, Ashford, and Brown back from Detroit to rejoin the familiar former Fame rhythm section. Crawford and Shapiro collaborated with R&B legend Luther Dixon in writing "Funk Factory." The session also included the George Soule composition "You Can't Stop a Man in Love," and, with the Memphis Horns and Bongo Brown's congas to the fore, "Don't Forget the Bridge," another morality tale in the manner of "Many Roads To Travel," complete with joyous extended musical workout. Pickett covered the ballad "One Step Away" from a recent Gladys Knight album, and alongside his producers, cowrote the string-soaked "I Can't Let My True Love Slip Away." Strings were applied with similar effect on a remake of "If You Need Me," which further amplified the gospel spirit at the root of the song by extending it and allowing Pickett complete vocal freedom.

In May he appeared on *Soul Train*, wearing a dazzling sequined suit which ensured that viewers' attentions were focused not on the show's renowned elastic-limbed dancers but the soul man in front of his nine-piece band ("Crusher" Green now back on drums, "Liston" Owens still on guitar). Host Don Cornelius afforded him all due respect: "If the soul music business was ruled by a system of government that was structured along the same lines as the US government, the man I am about to introduce would stand an excellent chance of being elected president, for there is no one who has contributed more to making soul music what it is today and certainly there cannot be found anywhere in the world a more exciting performer."

There is only so much praise a man can take before it affects him. In the summer of 1972, Wilson Pickett demanded a new contract from Atlantic. As far as he was concerned, he was releasing back-to-back gold records and wasn't being paid accordingly. "Here I was in a record company, being robbed blind," he told Sue C. Clark in a rambunctious, rambling and revealing interview only a few months into the following year. "I didn't know which way to go. My manager and all of them, kept saying to me, 'Pickett, this is going to hurt you, this is going to hurt you.' 'Well, I couldn't be more hurt than I am now.'"[6]

Pickett, who had helped carry Atlantic through its last ten years, to the point that Wexler and the Erteguns were able to sell it for millions, likely felt left out of the payday. It didn't help that in April 1972, the label celebrated its twenty-fifth anniversary with an all-expenses paid, first class trip to Paris—but only for employees and not for the artists. "We had really built that company," Pickett said in 1977. "R&B built that company. Then every rock group would come through there and get millions of dollars. And we couldn't even get a new deal, a better contract."[7]

Actually, Pickett had re-signed at the start of 1970, in the deal that Wexler had touted for its generosity. Still, Pickett noted that just after he made that new deal, "they turn around and give the Rolling Stones ten million dollars."[8] There was an obvious reason that the Stones could secure millions of dollars up front: they sold millions of albums. Pickett had always been a singles artist, and though he had made some fantastic LPs over the years, Atlantic had historically marketed them to the R&B market. *Don't Knock My Love* was the first Pickett LP that sounded like a true long-player.

Wexler responded to Pickett's latest demands by playing hard to get. "They would just ignore the situation," Pickett told Michael Lydon. And on those occasions that Pickett or Jimmy Evans *did* get to talk to Wexler, "His excuse was that he didn't own the company . . . Warner Brothers had bought out the company. But Warner Brothers didn't give a shit about no black artists. Warner Brothers ignored our values. [And] Jerry Wexler could have done something about it because he was still running the company at that particular time."[9]

Or, as he paraphrased himself talking to Wexler, "Hey man, my deal is with you, Mr. Jerry Wexler, my deal is not with Kinney Music, Warner Brothers, they don't know nothing 'bout me. Let me sit down and talk to *you*, because when I signed my name, this is who I signed with."[10] That was the "key man" aspect that Jim Stewart at Stax had insisted upon in print when signing with Atlantic—not that it had done his own label much good at the end of the day, considering what else went into that contract. "He was asking for a fair increase," said Mario Medious, an Atlantic promo man who had been raised poor in Mississippi and worked his way up from Atlantic's accounts department. "The increase is one thing, but you just didn't know what he might do, because of his temper and stuff."

The apocryphal story of how he had gotten out of his previous contract, perhaps through retelling, now became self-fulfilling in a way. "He'd come in and talk of killing people," said Medious. "He'd go round the place with a gun."

Ahmet Ertegun had his own story to tell. "Jerry Wexler never liked Crosby, Stills & Nash because they wanted so much freaking artistic autonomy," he recounted. "While we were arguing about this, Wilson Pickett walks in the room and comes up to Jerry and says, 'Jerry,' and he goes, 'Wham!' And he puts a pistol on the table. He says, 'If that motherfucker Tom Dowd walks into where I'm recording, I'm going to shoot him. And if you walk in, I'm going to shoot you. 'Oh,' Jerry said. 'That's okay, Wilson.' Then he walked out. So I said, 'You want to argue about artistic autonomy?'"[11]

It was becoming increasingly difficult for Jerry Wexler to meet Pickett's demands. "As far as the music, Jerry loved producing him because he was a hell of a singer," said Medious. "And he wasn't that difficult in the studio. He was difficult out of the studio about his business. It always came down to money with him."

Pickett complained years later that he had tried to gain access to the books. It was always a risky demand at Atlantic: when Leiber and Stoller had requested an audit and found that they were owed $18,000, Wexler offered to pay up—and cut all ties. Pickett found himself "something like $286,000 in debt to the company," he recalled, entirely possible given the additional advances of his new contract, the steady increase in recording costs, the limited LP sales, and the usual record label tendency to charge anything it could to an artist's account.[12]

If so, those figures were only going to get worse. In May, Atlantic released the newly recorded "Funk Factory" as a single; it underperformed. In October, it went back to the superlative *Don't Knock My Love* LP, almost a year after release and almost two years since it had been recorded, hawking "Mama Told Me Not to Come" as a 45. The single barely made the Top 100, Pickett's worst showing since 1964.[13]

For the time being, Atlantic continued financing sessions with Crawford and Shapiro in Muscle Shoals. The provocative "Sin Was the Blame," cowritten by Pickett and his producers, reviewed American constitutional history, dared spell out the word n-i-g-g-e-r (and suggest that it had led to the definition of cops as p-i-g), and stated that "If Martin Luther King had been Jesse James, we'd have a better solution." "Sin Was the Blame," said Shapiro, "was written right on the spot, in the studio, on the floor." Still, much of the material seemed to lack focus. Ultimately, said Pickett, "I just stalled," and Wexler lost interest.[14] Unable to hear hit singles, unwilling to impose a change of artistic direction (although his earlier dismissal of Pickett's gospel urges seemed somewhat short-sighted now that he was championing Aretha Franklin's famed return to church, *Amazing Grace*), unprepared to give the singer a new contract, and unable to live with the fear of what might happen any time Pickett walked in the office, he decided to cut his losses.

In his memoir, Wexler relegated Pickett's departure to a footnote about a short-lived blue-eyed soul duo, Delaney and Bonnie. At the same time as Pickett was following up *Don't Knock My Love*, the pair had just spent a small fortune recording an album in the coke-filled studio den Ike Turner had built for himself in Los Angeles. Wexler considered the results to be "dog meat," but "as far as the world knew, they were still hot." He sold Delaney and Bonnie's contract to Columbia, along with the record he refused to release himself. "We threw in the dog-meat album. I had to do it; a business obligation, it had nothing to do with my attachment to the artists. I'd done the same with Solomon Burke and Wilson Pickett after their sales had peaked."[15] And that was it. A decade of making hit records together had come to an end. Loyalty for Wexler, as for Pickett: hard won, easily lost.

Pickett's sales had in fact peaked, just as he would never play to a bigger crowd than in Ghana, but nobody could be certain of that at the time. Perhaps Wexler foresaw Pickett's decline, but in the last three years the artist had enjoyed eleven consecutive top twenty soul hits; in the last two years he'd had three top twenty pop hits, two of them million-sellers. He was the headlining act of a major cultural movie. He had a contract in Vegas; he could stir it up on *Soul Train*. He was increasingly popular overseas. And according to Lee Wade, Hollywood was interested. The modest sales of his most recent singles aside, that was more than enough criteria to guarantee serious offers from major labels—even at the price listed by *Billboard*, in a news item at the start of 1973 confirming his availability and stating that he was looking for "a million dollars in front from a new label."[16]

He got it, from RCA. It seemed a strange pairing at first; the week of *Billboard*'s news announcement, the label had but one act in the top fifty soul singles and soul LPs charts. But RCA was the home of Elvis Presley, which gave it some of the deepest pockets in the world—and before that it had been the home of Sam Cooke, which perhaps gave it special relevance to Wilson Pickett. And, in Winston "Buzz" Willis, it had an A&R director who had been encouraged to set up his own R&B division and had

20. With producers Dave Crawford and Jerry Wexler, Criteria Studios in Miami, November 24, 1969. Michael Ochs Archives/Getty.

21. With Atlantic Records artist Jackie Moore, Criteria Studios photo session, November 24, 1969. In 1981 the pair collaborated on a remake of Moore's 1971 hit "Precious, Precious." It went unreleased. Michael Ochs Archive/Getty.

22. Outside the house in Englewood, New Jersey, with the Rolls Royce Pickett bought for himself after signing a new deal with Atlantic Records in 1970. Wilson's son Michael is off to the right; Dovie Hall, shown with Wilson, raised him as her own. Courtesy of the Wilson Pickett Jr. Legacy LLC.

23. A rare early 1970s shot of Wilson with his wife and three children. L–R: Lynderrick Pickett, Wilson Pickett, Bonnie Pickett, Kenneth Felder (Bonnie's brother), Veda Pickett. In front: Michael Pickett, Wilson's son by an unnamed white woman. Wilson and Bonnie had separated in 1962; they finally divorced in 1986. Courtesy of Veda Pickett Neal.

24. In Ghana, 1971. L–R: Nat Grant (keyboards), Jimmy "Liston" Owens (guitar), Wilson Pickett, Jerry "Conseaula" (organ), Claston "Patience" Higgins (sax). Courtesy of the Wilson Pickett Jr. Legacy LLC.

25. The postmidnight hours of March 6, 1971: Wilson Pickett headlining the Soul To Soul festival in Accra, Ghana, arguably the zenith of his career. "I've never seen so many black and beautiful people in one place—250,000 of them," said Pickett. ZUMA Press, Inc./Alamy.

26. At his thirtieth birthday party in Lousville, KY, cutting the cake alongside, from left to right: Solomon Burke, Don Covay, Mrs Covay, Hezekiah Pickett, Dovie Hall, Lena Pickett, Maxwell Pickett, and Brenda Pickett. Courtesy of the Wilson Pickett, Jr. Legacy LLC.

27. At his thirtieth birthday party, March 1971, Louisville, Kentucky, singing with sister Emily Jean. Behind them are Solomon Burke and Don Covay. Courtesy of the Wilson Pickett Jr. Legacy LLC.

28. At the house Wilson bought for his mother in Louisville, Kentucky. L–R: Wilbert Harbison, Lena Pickett, Hezekiah Pickett, Dovie Hall, Wilson Pickett, Albert Jackson, Bertha Harbison (née Pickett). The girl in front is Cynthia Harbison. Courtesy of the Wilson Pickett Jr. Legacy LLC.

29. With personal assistant and sometimes lover Lee Wade, 1977, on the occasion of an interview for the *New York Times*, at his home in Englewood, New Jersey. Photo by Ellen Mandel © 1977.

30. Onstage in Japan, 1974. A double live LP from his first Asian tour went unreleased in the States. Courtesy of the Wilson Pickett, Jr. Legacy LLC.

31. The four Pickett brothers: William James, Hezekiah, Wilson, Jr. and Maxwell. Date unknown. Courtesy of the Wilson Pickett, Jr. Legacy LLC.

32. With daughter Saphan Pickett, born in 1982. Courtesy of the Wilson Pickett Jr. Legacy LLC.

33. Wilson Pickett and trumpet player Curtis Pope in Japan, 1988. "Pickett had to nurse me back from the ghetto," said Pope of rejoining the Midnight Movers, which he then led for fifteen years. Courtesy of Curtis Pope.

34. At the recording sessions for the LP *I Want You*, Le Studio, Marin Heights, Quebec, 1981. L–R: producer Andre Perry, Pickett, and songwriters and musicians Marty Simon and Jean Roussel. Photograph by Yaël Brandeis Perry.

35. The Soul Clan at their press conference on the eve of their reunion show of July 24, 1981. L–R: Ben E. King, Joe Tex, Don Covay, Wilson Pickett, Solomon Burke. Photo by Ebet Roberts.

36. With Dan Aykroyd at the Atlantic Records 40th Anniversary Concert, May 18, 1988, Madison Square Garden. The concert was the first time Pickett had performed with former Stax musicians bassist Donald "Duck" Dunn (on right), and guitarist Steve Cropper, since 1965. Preston/Corbis.

37. At the recording session for the Blues Brothers 2000 remake of "634-5789," with producer Paul Schaffer (standing) and Steve Cropper (sitting at right). Photo by Ebet Roberts.

38. Pickett performing in New Orleans, 1995, in between his two prison sentences. "The potential for his career, even in the mid- nineties onward," said booking agent Chris Tuthill, "was still huge, if he had been able to pull himself together." Photo by Ebet Roberts.

39. Pickett with Roger Friedman and Sam Moore at the DVD release party for Friedman's movie *Only The Strong Survive*, January 28, 2004. Moore would lead the all-star rendition of "In the Midnight Hour" at the Grammys shortly after Pickett's death in 2006. ZUMA Press, Inc./Alamy.

signed the talent to fill it, with Main Ingredient, Friends of Distinction, and Jimmy Castor all scoring crossover hits over the last couple of years. Willis had attended De Witt Clinton High School in Harlem, one of the training grounds of New York's vocal group era. He had worked for Maurice Levy's Roulette Records, and, after college, MGM/Verve. He was prominent within NARAS (National Academy of Recording Arts and Sciences, the governing body of the Grammys), the Harlem Professional League, the Black Congressional Caucus, and Jesse Jackson's Operation PUSH (People United to Save Humanity). Political clout, commercial success, and access to a major corporation's label's coffers: Willis appeared to offer everything that Pickett might have wanted from a new deal—along with the signing bonus and an equally lavish per-album advance that included artistic freedom and the right for the singer to record and publish his own songs. Wilson Pickett signed on the dotted line—and he would regret his decision for the rest of his life.

PART II

Fall 1973–1996

CHAPTER 20

Those years with Atlantic were really special when I look back.
Wilson Pickett, 1976

To review Wilson Pickett's career with RCA Records is to endure an abject study in artistic decline. He went in as one of the biggest names in soul music. He came out a has-been. In the three years he was with the label he made four studio albums, each of which fared worse than the last, until he was off the charts entirely; his singles also fell off the commercial cliff. It became the textbook example of how a career, an entire *life*, can revolve on one single decision.

It all started so promisingly. RCA trumpeted his signing with a full-page ad in *Billboard*, and to some of the finished tracks from Muscle Shoals added four more from a return visit to Sigma Sound Studios. Gamble and Huff's Philadelphia International label was celebrating its first number one single at the end of 1972 (Billy Paul's monumental "Me and Mrs. Jones"), alongside a couple of close challengers ("Backstabbers" by the O'Jays and "If You Don't Know Me By Now" by Harold Melvin & The Bluenotes), so it seemed appropriate to bring Pickett back to a studio that he had helped put on the map. But his return to Philadelphia bypassed Gamble and Huff themselves, confined by their label deal with Columbia. Brad Shapiro and David Crawford stepped up to produce the proven rhythm section of Eli, Harris, Baker, Young, and Washington, all of whom had played on *Wilson Pickett in Philadelphia*.

Eli and Carl Fischer, the same duo behind *In Philadelphia*'s "Help the Needy," supplied Pickett with one of the new songs, "Mr. Magic Man." It featured electric organ played by Crawford, chimes, female backing vocals, and, perhaps most prominently, a svelte string section courtesy of Dave Van De Pitte, the man behind some of Motown's most memorable orchestral arrangements. These were the right components for the era, but arguably not for Pickett, whose voice was ultimately buried by the arrangement. RCA released "Mr. Magic Man" as a 45 anyway, and it performed almost identically to its predecessor at Atlantic, "Mama Told Me Not to Come," passably at soul (#16), and poorly at pop (#98), suggesting that Pickett's appeal to the white, rock-based crossover audience had faded but that his sweeter sound still appealed to a core black audience. Regardless, RCA felt suitably enthused as to change the title of the impending LP, which had been trailed on the single's labels as *Tonight I'm My Biggest Audience*; it was released instead as *Mr. Magic Man*.

On the front cover of that album Pickett, with billowing afro and moustache, seated on a stool, is wearing a red crushed velvet suit accessorized by frilly white cravat and cuffs, smiling vacantly off to the camera's right. On the front of *Don't Knock My Love* he had also worn an outrageous suit, but the cream-tinged imagery of that shot had softened its tone—and leaning on his Rolls in front of the big house, he at least looked like a high roller, a man who had made it. On *Mr. Magic Man*, he didn't look like a man at all; he looked like a ventriloquist's dummy.

The record's prospects were hardly helped by Atlantic's destructive tactics. The label had already packaged up a third *Greatest Hits* of their now-former artist—this one a double LP with gatefold sleeve—and put it out before RCA could claim the shelf space.[1] Now Atlantic took "International Playboy," always the most commercial of remaining tracks from *Wilson Pickett in Philadelphia*, and, reflecting the changing musical mood of the last three years, flattened the emphasis on Earl Young's tight drums, upped the slick guitar, added female backing vocals—and released it on top of "Mr. Magic Man." The two competing singles canceled each other out commercially.

A sense of mild panic was evident in Pickett's interview with Sue C. Clark on the eve of his new album's release. To the question "What's happening with your new record?" he hinted that maybe he had let the green grass of RCA fool him: "This is my first release on RCA which has yet to reach the black market like they should . . . and be played on black radio. I'm on the phone every day to RCA, saying 'Hey, I'm over here and I don't hear the record man!' The cat say 'Take it easy Pickett, we'll get the record on.' Then Atlantic's throwing out stuff on top of it. You know it's hard to get two records of an artist on, when your thing is programmed. I told Buzzy Willis and them, you all better go try and find out why Atlantic has this!"

By August, Willis had departed RCA.[2] Pickett became a textbook victim to music biz musical chairs: a marquee signing, orphaned by the departure of his A&R man, and not yet having had the hits he'd been paid big bucks for. By the time of Willis's departure Dave Crawford had also gone, to a staff job at ABC/Dunhill where he was immediately allowed to indulge his gospel tendencies with Mighty Clouds of Joy, and with considerable success. Brad Shapiro remained, bringing Pickett down to Nashville for the first time. It may not have seemed such a major departure from Memphis and Muscle Shoals, as Nashville now formed a recognized southern recording triangle with these two cities—all the more so given that many of the musicians he'd worked with in those previous locales had moved there in the interim, including Reggie Young and Tommy Cogbill. Dennis Coffey—who, like much of the Motown Corporation, had relocated from Detroit to Los Angeles—joined them at RCA's Nashville studios in March, and again in May 1973, and at the midway point Pickett sounded ecstatic about the results: "I'm not doing country sound. I'm doing funk. Funk. You'll be surprised when you hear the session! You won't think it was cut in Nashville."[3]

That depended on your definition of funk. The finished LP, *Miz Lena's Boy*, with a back cover soft-focus shot that reimagined Pickett's childhood as one of a comfortable slatted house complete with porch pillars, far from the poverty of his real upbringing, was somewhat harder-hitting than *Mr. Magic Man*, but a Nashville country influence was clearly audible. Still, the album scored two top twenty hits on the soul charts: the opening Pickett-Shapiro composition, "Take a Look at the Woman You're With," peppered with a requisite "Lord have mercy" or two and some typically unearthly bass from Cogbill, and "Soft Soul Boogie Woogie," a Troy Seals, Don Goodman, and Will Jennings collaboration supplied especially for Pickett, the one song to find the sweet spot where country, funk, rock, and soul met and mated.

A relatively saccharine cover of Chuck Berry's "Memphis, Tennessee" was placed between the two singles; it was the first time Pickett had ever covered a song from the classic rock 'n' roll canon. A version of Kris Kristofferson's "Help Me Make it Through the Night," recorded in recent years by Elvis Presley as well as by Gladys Knight, revealed the influence (and arrangements) of his fellow Vegas performers. Several Shapiro-Pickett compositions were relegated to side two, meanwhile. The LP clearly lacked hands-on A&R direction, and it was released just five months after *Mr. Magic Man*. The rush backfired; *Miz Lena's Boy* was the singer's first LP since he had signed to Atlantic not to make the American top 200.

RCA nonetheless continued down the same well-trodden paths in hopes of recouping its investment. Pickett returned south once more, Brad Shapiro still alongside him as coproducer, back to the proven stomping ground of Muscle Shoals Sound, to the "Swampers," as the old rhythm section were now unofficially known, and the Memphis Horns, with Charlie Chalmers in a new guise as a backing singer alongside his wife Sandra Rhodes and her sister Donna. The new LP's title, *Pickett in the Pocket*, was uncommonly inspired; however, the record itself lacked the rhythmic precision of the old days. Its two strongest moments both featured Pickett stepping onto the pulpit. On a remake of the Clyde Otis song "Take a Look," originally recorded by Aretha Franklin in her Columbia days, Pickett added a reference to writer Nikki Giovanni, famed in part for her "Poem for Aretha" and at whose thirtieth birthday celebration he had just performed in New York City. On "You're The One," composed by one of Aretha's favorite gospel singers, Jackie Verdell, who had supplied backing vocals on *Right On*, Pickett morphed at the three-minute mark into a spoken-word finale that turned love of God into love of woman. "I Was Too Nice," a cowrite with Barry Beckett, and a reworking of the originally vibrant Ben E. King hit "Young Boy Blues," saw the band descend into a slow, ponderous blues boogie. "I Was Too Nice" was released as a single, but it withered and died, as did the entire album.

It was evidently time for a change of scenery, to which end one could only *wish* that a news item trumpeting Bobby Womack as potential producer had come true: Womack was finally a highly successful soul man in his own right, with critically acclaimed and commercially popular movie soundtracks (*Across 110th Street*), albums (*Facts of Life*), and single anthems ("Woman's Got to Have It") all to his name. Alas, it didn't pan out, and Pickett made a record of such little consequence that few people even knew it existed. Fewer still claimed involvement, including the singer, who is not known to have ever mentioned it. The sleeve of *Join Me and Let's Be Free* set the scene for the calamity: a pastoral portrait of the singer in a psychedelic pseudo-African robe, surrounded by autumnal trees and presumably representative orbs, the kind of painting a singer might have been gifted backstage by an overobsessive fan and conveniently have left there. The record was recorded in Los Angeles, Pickett's first time in a West Coast studio—or studios, given that no less than three of them were credited. It was produced and largely cowritten by Yusuf Rahman, a member of Los Angeles's 103rd Street Watts Band with limited additional credits to his name. Extensive synthesizers were programmed and played by Robert Margouleff, who, in the same guise for Stevie Wonder, had revolutionized that singer's career. But there was little oversight: Rahman's composition "Higher Consciousness," in which Pickett sang about doing "yoga on your head," was followed by the singer's self-penned country song "Bailin' Hay on a Rainy Day," the title of which was absolutely metaphorical. A scathing review in Britain's *New Musical Express* honed in on all the album's weaknesses, suggesting, "Perhaps. . . he needs a decoke."[4]

True. But Pickett wasn't the only one off form on these records (and likely not the only one doing cocaine, either). Musicians who could so clearly remember their involvement in the Pickett hits from the 1960s, down to the finest detail, seemed unable to recollect anything about their involvement in his 1970s flops. Robert Margouleff, who would later produce an entire Wilson Pickett LP, could not remember even being involved with *Join Me and Let's Be Free*. There is a sense amidst the mess of overplaying that cluttered up this period, the lack of stand-out musical moments that conspired toward a gap in the musicians' memories, that nobody's heart was really in it any more. Shapiro was perhaps only the most honest of them when he admitted that he stayed in the game with Pickett "because I was getting paid, if you want to know the truth."

Pickett, for all his concerns about the label's marketing capabilities, stayed in it for the same reason. "He knew there was a big check at the end of it," said Shapiro. "Whereas that was never the case at Atlantic Records. He could have got anything he wanted [at Atlantic], and he did at times, but not like at RCA." Pickett was often the first to admit this. "I couldn't have been treated any nicer than those people treated me," he said of RCA's accounting department. "They paid on time, they didn't give me no problems." Or, to put it another way, "RCA gave me millions of dollars and didn't sell one fucking record."[5]

Over the years, including those when he was actually on the label, he would speak openly about his failures with RCA. In late 1975, just after his contract had expired, he offered: "I went into material that was so personal for me. And I had forgotten about the outside world that really wasn't that deep into this kind of thing, that seriousness. They want to hear a fuckin' beat, man, and 'sock it to me' with the *Soul Train*."[6] He nonetheless remained proud of *Mr. Magic Man*. "I liked it very much," he told John Abbey in 1976, "because it wasn't a screaming album and I was sick of screaming. I wanted to sing. I guess it was too close to me, too personal for me to be constructive." Pickett surmised that Atlantic would have made more of the material from *Mr. Magic Man*: "Jerry [Wexler] never liked it at all because he felt it wasn't the Wilson Pickett that the world wanted. So he let me buy it and take it with me. Time, of course, proved him right—but I'll never believe that if that album had been released on Atlantic it would have sold badly."[7]

He surely had a point. RCA released a grand total of five singles from across Pickett's first three studio LPs, and none from *Join Me and Let's Be Free*. The label apparently lacked confidence both in Pickett's music and its ability to get the records played. "They had all the money in the world and they were willing to spend it," Pickett told Abbey in 1976. "But I tell you where I think it all went sour. The company would not under any circumstances get involved in backhanded payments—payola, as it is known. They had a reputation of bypassing black jocks and so the black jocks would retaliate by not playing the product. I used to bang my head against the wall by calling them (the radio stations) and saying that they were ruining my career and didn't a brother's career matter to them? They would just answer that they'd play me—anytime I left the company!"[8]

"RCA didn't understand what to do with Wilson, just like Columbia didn't know what to do with Aretha," said Dennis Coffey. "Berry Gordy knew how to do what he did; Columbia and RCA never got it. They never knew how to work with funk and soul and stuff." "They weren't really listening" to the albums at RCA, said Shapiro. "Unlike Atlantic, there wasn't any Ahmet Ertegun, Jerry Wexler, Tom Dowd figure there. They had the largest record distribution in the world—but they couldn't get the airplay Atlantic Records could get. They tried, but they just couldn't."

Clearly, RCA *could* get its records played on radio: in the summer of 1974 it had a number one crossover hit with Hues Corporation's "Rock Your Boat," one of three iconic dance floor chart toppers that year, along with George McRae's "Rock Your Baby" and the PIR/Sigma Studios house band MFSB with the Three Degrees' "TSOP"—shorthand for "The Sound of Philadelphia," or the theme from *Soul Train*. Although Pickett had his live band open shows with the disco-tinged "TSOP," for now he stayed away from the new disco style in the studio; he had learned from *Mr. Magic Man* that it was not what people wanted from him. But he had yet to find a viable commercial alternative. Without direction, without a firm helping hand—without a Jerry Wexler, however tempestuous their relationship might have been—he was just another 60s soul man fading into the background.

The disaster of the RCA years, from which Pickett's public profile would never recover, inspired in him a retroactive review of his relationship with his former label. In 1974, in only his second year at RCA, he was asked by John Abbey whether he regretted leaving Atlantic, and he replied:

"Sure, I regretted leaving. They brought me a long way, we came a long way together. I'll always be grateful and appreciative of the fact that Atlantic put me where I was. It was they who opened the door to all of the success I enjoyed and money I earned."[9]

Trying to save face, Pickett would not come out and admit that RCA eventually dropped him. "I wasted enough time on them, I was just taking their money," he said. "I don't like that. I'd rather sell records than have millions of fucking dollars, so I asked them. One day I just went in there and told them, the relationship was no good. They could have the rest of the money, just let me go."[10] He'd already told journalists, back at the start of the deal, that the deal was for three years with an option for two more. Come 1975, that period was up, RCA was ready to see the back of him, and no other major was in any sort of a hurry to acquire him. The million-dollar deal for Wilson Pickett was a thing of the past.

CHAPTER 21

Pickett was a good person until he got on drugs. He was a loving person, a caring person . . . and I think he still cared but it was something else controlling him.

Dovie Hall

In the summer of 1972 Wilson Pickett had agreed to play a benefit concert, alongside Johnny Nash and Lou Rawls, for Cleveland's struggling Forest City Hospital, in the city's main arena, at which Muhammad Ali, the recently deposed Heavyweight Champion of the World, was to participate in a number of opening bouts to warm up a triple-card ticket of professional fights. The conduit for Ali's involvement was none other than Lloyd Price, who had befriended the boxer in Ali's Louisville, KY hometown during his performing days, as he had the owner of Cleveland's leading club on the chitlin' circuit, Don King. King had recently served four years in jail for larceny and was looking for a way to bounce back into promotions; the benefit in Cleveland, thanks to Price, would serve as King's first foray into boxing.

When Pickett's plane landed, there was nobody there to meet him. He called his assistant Lee Wade, who had arrived ahead of him, and fired her on the spot. He then told her to sort out his transport anyway—no limo, no benefit. Wade, for whom being fired by Pickett was such a regular occurrence she bore it little heed, called Don King, and, as she recalled, "Ali had a motorcycle police escort take him out to the airport. Just as they got there, Pickett was getting ready to board a plane coming back to New York. Ali stopped him, got him out, and later on that evening when Ali met me, he said 'I've got to help you because this nigger's crazy!' Cos Pickett had taken him through it. . . ."

The benefit went ahead. Ali boxed ten rounds against five different opponents, the concert ran overtime, and the entire event grossed $81,000, breaking a thirty-year record for an exhibition match. The hospital saw just $15,000 of it, and Don King was up and running as a boxing promoter.[1]

The Cleveland incident says a lot about Pickett's ego: if it had grown too big even for Muhammad Ali to rein in, it had grown too big, period. Yet it was only to get bigger. Early in his Vegas residency at the Hilton International, Pickett took issue with his billing. "Wilson said something onstage," recalled Dovie Hall, "'cos Elvis Presley was in the big room and he was in the small room. And Wilson said something about Elvis Presley. The 'Memphis mafia' kicked our door in. The whole door came down, and if I'd been sitting there it would have killed me. And they told Wilson, 'If you *ever* say something about Elvis Presley . . .'" Dovie also recalled the time she got a call from Jimmy Evans; Pickett had upset some "Mafia goons" to the point that they were "fixing to drop him in the desert," and she was needed to calm him down.[2]

There was a likely explanation for his increasingly confrontational behavior. As Carlton McWilliams, who had recently rejoined Pickett's band on guitar, put it: "I know that out in Vegas, Wilson was doing a lot of coke." Dovie Hall noted, "After RCA, the drugs got heavy," and that "it was the disappointment of the records not selling." Hall couldn't understand why Pickett had left Atlantic in the first place: "RCA was his downfall," she said. "He was spending $3,000 a week on drugs, and I used to say, 'Wilson, this is not going to work out, you're going to spend all your money on this.' . . . He said it was something he wanted, and it was his money. So I left him alone." But Wilson could not then leave Dovie alone. "It made him violent," she said. "He became a very violent man. . . . After he started with the drugs, that's when it got bad. Now he's *really* hurting me."

"He would beat her, beat me, beat me, beat her," Michael Pickett said in *Don't Let the Green Grass Fool You*. "It didn't matter who was around. Basically, she had it worse than I did. What she went through, she didn't deserve."[3] Danny White recalled a visit to Englewood with his wife: "Dovie comes down, she had shades on. She dropped the shades, said 'Look what Pick did to me . . .' Back then, there was no such thing as domestic violence, it was unheard of." By this White was not denying its existence, but rather that it was rarely prosecuted. "You would beat up your wife or your girlfriend, cops come to your house, they're like, 'This is this man's wife, I don't get involved in this,' and that's how it used to be." In her book, Louella Pickett-New recalled that Wilson had been beating Michael since he was a couple of years old. When, on occasions she served as witness, she pleaded "Please don't beat him like that," he'd reply, "Mama beat me!"

Increasingly isolated in the Englewood house, scared to spend evenings out for fear of Wilson's jealousy and frightened to spend too much time at home with him, Dovie went back to school, "trying to better myself." Her goal was to get a job and gain some independence, but Wilson wouldn't let her. He built her an office within the Brayton Street house, on the pretense that she would be working for him. "So he built me this nice office with this big white desk and this big white chair that I could wheel around in. And he paid me a hundred and fifty dollars a week for my own office. You know how many phone calls I got? Two."

In the meantime, she suspected that Wilson was having an affair. She was right. "We had a little thing going on," admitted Lee Wade. "You had to love him to be with him. You end up loving him. He was a sweetie pie, and gorgeous as a man. He had thirty-two perfect teeth, the one percent of the universe who doesn't have to go to the dentist." Dovie decided to take action. "I said, 'Tell your secretary not to speak to me again. I really don't like her. She's doing quite a few things I don't like.' I went in the dressing room, and I'm not an evil person, but she was in there, and I took this fifth of vodka and cracked it straight across [her] head. I was tired of her."

The catalog of incidents escalated. Pickett had always been renowned for his professionalism in the studio; during the sessions for *Miz Lena's Boy*, in Nashville, however, "Wilson got into this huge argument with the drummer, and I thought they were going to come to blows," recalled Dennis Coffey. "I said to Wilson, 'Your chances of finding another drummer in Nashville at two a.m. are slim to none, so maybe if you guys tone it down a little we can get this done.'" Coffey stopped in to see Pickett in Vegas at one point during those years and was recruited to play the entire gig, but like many people, became wary about hanging out much with the singer. "He was wired a lot," said the guitarist.

At the start of 1974, the *New Amsterdam News* reported that Pickett had been issued a summons after he "allowed a bar-room 'broad' to bait him into a brawl."[4] Then, in November of that year Pickett went on a hunting trip to the Catskills with his friends Rudolph and O'Kelley Isley, and the stakes were raised considerably. "He got to the hotel," said Maxwell Pickett, who was not present but whose version of events correlated closely with the official police reports. "And they started shooting the bull and have some drinks. And he had some words with Rudolph, who's a big guy. He's a quiet guy but he ain't gonna take anything from nobody, not Wilson. So for some reason when that kind of thing happen, Wilson he just got to mess with it . . . He challenged Rudolph to go outside. They go outside, lock horns and they're out tussling and wrestling in the snow. Well, the way I heard it, Rudolph turned him every which way but loose and when Wilson saw he was not going to be able to get the best of Rudolph, he got mad and he went back inside, and he got this two-shot Derringer. The Isley Brothers went on back in the room, and the next thing they know, Wilson was shooting the door, and he kicks the door open and when they hear the shots, they all run for cover and hide."

"People like Wilson," concluded Maxwell, "if they're determined to get the best of something and they can't, they're going to reach for whatever is going to help them achieve their goals. And for Wilson, guns was it."

Pickett was charged with "first-degree reckless endangerment" and "criminal possession of a dangerous weapon," the gun named as a .38 caliber two-shot Derringer. The charge carried a maximum prison sentence of seven years. The singer was released on $500 bail, and Jimmy Evans pulled every string to ensure that his client got away with merely a fine.[5]

Money, after all, was not the issue. Pickett, according to *Jet*, was earning $17,000 a week in Las Vegas (while he stayed in a Hilton-provided suite, his band remained off-Strip, paying for their own hotel). He still had regular television appearances (including one on *The Midnight Special* in June 1973 that had him duetting with the Bee Gees on "Hey Jude"). He did a television commercial for Schlitz Malt Liquor ("When it comes to drinking, I only have to look out for Wilson Pickett"). In 1974 he celebrated his thirty-third birthday by buying his mother a bigger house in Louisville, enjoying a family reunion, and then taking his children on a fishing trip to the Bahamas. ("That was my most memorable time," said his daughter Veda.) And he replaced the Rolls Royce with a Stutz Blackhawk.

The car came with a 7.5 liter, V8 engine capable of 425 horsepower, weighed five thousand pounds, and was decked out in floor coverings of Australian lamb's wool or mink, leather seats, twenty-four-carat moldings, a liquor cabinet in the back, and an eight-track tape player in the front. In purchasing one of the just eight Blackhawks shipped to America from Italy in 1974, Pickett joined a select group of elite entertainers who owned such a vehicle: Elvis, Sammy Davis Jr., Lucille Ball, and Dean Martin. The Stutz cost him close to a hundred thousand dollars—precisely how much it was reported in *Jet* that he brought home from his tour of Japan in 1973.[6]

Thus was revealed the dichotomy of his career by the mid-1970s. The successful Atlantic years had not met with the money Pickett thought he was due, but money was free-flowing during the commercially floundering RCA years. By the time Ben Fong-Torres caught up with him in Las Vegas late in 1975 for a brief feature in *Rolling Stone*, those lucrative bookings were drawing to a close.

"He had an incident out there," recalled Carlton McWilliams. "He was doing his show, he was fucked up. The way we did his show, after we finished a tune, Doc Smith on the organ would play an interlude between the songs, almost a gospel type of thing. Wilson got out there and got into that interlude and got caught up in it and started moaning, 'Turn around, turn around,' and then said, 'Y'all motherfuckas don't know what I'm talking about,' threw the microphone down and stormed off stage. For the next couple of days out in Vegas we did no show, we didn't know if we were going to get home." McWilliams said that Jimmy Evans intervened to make sure that they saw out the contract. "But it didn't get renewed."[7]

Pickett spun it as best he could. "It's the type of gig (where) you can neglect the rest of the music world," he told Fong-Torres of his Vegas lounge residency. "I don't think it's the place an artist of my caliber should just stay. I had a four-year contract; I honored my contract, and I'm finished. You see, I have to get back out there now."

Pickett may have been ambivalent about playing Vegas, but he loved to make records. As soon as he knew he was off RCA he reached out to Brad Shapiro, who was currently enjoying considerable success producing Millie Jackson.[8] Shapiro called on his old Miami songwriting partner and long-term Florida R&B kingpin, Henry Stone. Stone's new venture T. K. Records, a collaboration with Shapiro's former Miami bandmate Steve Alaimo, had hit the ground running the previous year with George McRae's number one proto-disco hit "Rock Your Baby." That song had been written and produced by the leader of a group formed out of Stone's distribution warehouse: Harry Wayne Casey of KC & the Sunshine Band. T. K. seemed like a perfect home for Pickett. The label knew black music, it was rolling in hits, it wasn't so big that it couldn't focus on every act and every record, and its key man, Henry Stone, owned the company and was therefore unlikely to be leaving any time soon. Pickett was even given his own label, Wicked. Claiming independence for the first time since he originally started hustling back in Detroit, Pickett had finished recording his new album before he even left Vegas.

Chocolate Mountain was not disco, despite the fact that Pickett and Shapiro wrote three songs with future Bee Gees producer and writer Albhy Galuten, and hired Mike Lewis for the sweet string arrangements that Lewis also applied to the Bee Gees and KC & the Sunshine Band. Nor was it more of the same old country funk, even though Shapiro had brought Pickett back to Nashville to record most tracks (at the Sound Shop, owned by Buddy Killen) with an all-star, all-white group that included guitarists Reggie Young and Pete Carr, pianist Bobby Wood, drummer Larry Londin, and percussionist Tom Roady.[9] Rather, it found an ideal niche in between these two sounds, with Pickett sounding energized just by the prospect of it.

A renewed sense of focus was apparent from the title of the opening cut, "I'm Gonna Do It All Over." Pickett, with help from Shapiro and Galuten, sang of his background in the church and where it had taken him: "Had to be something inside me, kept on leading and guiding me, must have been good for my soul."

A reinvigorated Pickett was equally evident on "The Best Part of a Man" by Clarence Reid, who had just recorded it as lead track for his next LP on Henry Stone's long-standing soul label, Alston. Reid's version of his song was classic southern soul, to the extent that it could almost have been dated to the sixties. Pickett's rendition, which actually came out first, was more overtly contemporary, swapping out Reid's firmly stated piano chords on the introduction for a glittering glissando down the keys instead, switching the brass punctuation for a lead guitar melody, accentuating the string arrangement, and emphasizing the choral hook. The Nashville musicians locked into the groove, inspired perhaps by Tom Roady's congas, which supplied a rhythmic lubricity lacking at Pickett's previous Nashville sessions. "The Best Part of a Man" was selected as *Chocolate Mountain*'s lead single, where it immediately garnered airplay at black radio.

Pickett also took on Captain and Tennille's "Love Will Keep Us Together," a recent number one hit. Unlike his soulful rearrangements of "Hey Jude" and "Sugar Sugar," however, Pickett brought little to the musical table; although there was nothing wrong with his version of the song, composed by old-time Brooklyn writers Neil Sedaka and Howard Greenfield, he paid the price when it performed poorly as a single. And by Pickett's own admission, there were "a couple of disco things in there . . . to get across to a new market." He was apparently uncertain about this move, adding "But then I've made some disco records in the past, right? Only they . . . were just good dance records in those days!"[10] Elsewhere, Pickett leaned on his good friend Mack Rice, whose songwriting credibility had soared with his half-share of the Staple Singers' anthem "Respect Yourself," for the slower funk of "Let Me Know," and on former Falcons songwriter and producer Sax Kari, now ensconced in Miami with Henry Stone, for the swamp-ridden "Sweetwater Jail," complete with uncredited slide guitar that harkened back to Duane Allman, who had died in a motorcycle accident in 1971, aged just twenty-four. And Pickett returned to the subject of the church on the ecstatic choral gospel song "Are You Ready," by Phillip Mitchell from the Muscle Shoals Sound Studios' growing stable of writers, complete with a coda, on which he rapped lyrical about the glories of Jesus.

It was a strong performance. But listening to Pickett's shouted count-in on "I'm Gonna Do It All Over" next to "Land of 1000 Dances," or his rough-voiced screams on "I'm Changed" against his full-throated "Hey Jude," shows clearly that something had been lost over the years. "The drugs had taken their toll on his voice," said Shapiro. "And those guys can only sing like that for so long. He wasn't the same Wilson Pickett any more. His voice had changed." Shapiro was also frustrated with Pickett, the person. "I realized we were in trouble," he said when, at Criteria, "the Bee Gees wanted to meet him, and Pickett got high. I was embarrassed. Normally he'd have been thrilled. And he said 'I fucked around and got high.'" Then again, Shapiro might also have been part of the problem. "Whether Pickett was right or wrong, seemed like Brad wouldn't stand up to him," observed Reggie Young. "And Pickett could get sideways with the producer."

He got sideways with Henry Stone, as well. It had started so promisingly, "The Best Part of a Man" taking Pickett back into the soul top 30 for the first time in two full years (and for the last time ever) at the end of 1975; he returned to *Soul Train* early the following year to lip-synch the song. But it didn't cross over, nor did the album make a dent on any chart anywhere. Pickett had been thrilled about having his own label, with the opportunity to release other artists, but other than a single from Carl Gardner of the Coasters, nothing else emerged. Pickett then discovered that he didn't actually own Wicked Records, that it was merely a subsidiary of T. K., and this provoked a bust-up. Henry Stone had been though these situations plenty of times before, and with KC & the Sunshine Band taking up residence on top of the pop charts and hits coming out of other subsidiaries (for Gwen McRae, Dorothy Moore, and others) quicker than he could launch them, the aggravation was more than Stone wanted to deal with. Pickett later proclaimed, "The lawyers fucked my contract up," but at heart he knew he only had his own distractions to blame. Next time, he insisted, "I won't be in Las Vegas, playing lounges at 4 a.m., when the contracts are being done in New York."[11]

CHAPTER 22

Pickett loved kicking ass, I mean physically. That would just come out of him. And then at the same time, he was the most humblest person you could ever meet.

Bobby Womack[1]

In the spring of 1976 Wilson Pickett returned to Africa, traveling to South Africa this time, whose apartheid regime had been declared a "crime against humanity" by the United Nations in 1973. Despite government censorship of music, Pickett had become something of a legend there. A radio show titled *In the Midnight Hour*, broadcast from neighboring Mozambique as of the mid-1960s, had helped propagate soul as music of protest and freedom, leading to a thriving soul scene in the townships where indigenous black populations had been officially ghettoized. But by the time Pickett visited, other soul musicians had surpassed his popularity—most notably Dobie Gray, the first to insist on mixed audiences as a condition of touring the country—and Pickett's reputation was nothing like what it had been in Ghana at the start of the decade. He came back complaining to the black American press of travel and payment problems and expressing bewilderment at apartheid. "South Africa is a concentration camp," he told *Jet*. To other artists, he said, "Don't go, whatever is offered."[2]

His promoter in Cape Town, Paul Zamek, a young white man deeply committed to the anti-apartheid movement, had as difficult an experience with Pickett as Pickett had with South Africa. The singer arrived late into town, took to the stage clearly the worse for the wear, incited the crowd to break police cordons to come closer to him, played less than the contracted time, and ended the night by picking a fight with a traveling salesman in his hotel bar.

And Zamek was amazed that Pickett seemed uninterested in the nation's politics. "He was saying 'I don't give a fuck about my brothers, just give me the diamonds and gold,'" he recalled. "That stung me, because I thought, 'Here's a black guy supposed to be part of the movement, and I'm a white guy trying to help the black guys,' and I was looking for some kind of support from a black American for our black brothers in South Africa. And I must tell you, from my side I never got that at all. I don't know if he was apolitical or just didn't care. He seemed to be more interested in the material cause of why he was in South Africa." Yet while Pickett's brief tour served to highlight differences in perception between the races, especially on foreign continents, and the limitations of white liberalism in the face of black self-empowerment, Zamek, like so many others, was ultimately forgiving. "It was worth it because he was such a great singer."

Back in the States, the soul scene was going through wholesale changes. Jerry Wexler had returned to New York from Miami, only to find himself a stranger in his own company—losing his hitmaking touch in the process and the allegiance of Ahmet Ertegun as a consequence. In 1975, two years after Atlantic had been forced to move in to Warner Brothers' midtown Manhattan corporate headquarters, Wexler cashed out.

In Memphis, Booker T. and the M.G.s had gone their separate ways. Any hope of a reunion was permanently rent asunder when, on September 30, 1975, drummer Al Jackson Jr. was shot dead in his house. No one was ever prosecuted for the crime. Then, during the week before Christmas that year, Stax was declared involuntarily bankrupt and padlocked. Al Bell was prosecuted on charges of conspiring to defraud the Memphis bank that loaned Stax more money than ever made sense, and, crucially for those who saw him as a (black) scapegoat, was found not guilty. Jim Stewart, who had single-mindedly plowed his proceeds from a lucrative deal Stax signed with Columbia in 1972 back into the company as it struggled to maintain cash flow, lost everything, including his house. Pickett's former Falcons at Stax, Eddie Floyd and Sir Mack Rice, became free agents by the bankruptcy, but with no record deal, no control over their back catalog, and still beholden as songwriters to East/Memphis Music, which was now owned by the bank in question, Union Planters.[3]

The famed black theaters at which the Falcons, collectively and individually, had cemented their popularity in the first place, had fallen on their own hard times, as America's inner cities declined under an onslaught of drugs and attendant crime, and the more successful black acts such as Pickett gave them up for lucrative engagements in Vegas and elsewhere. The Howard in Washington, DC, first shuttered in 1970, only opened periodically through the subsequent decade; the Uptown in Philadelphia ceased regular revues in 1972; the Royal in Baltimore was demolished in 1971, the

Regal in Chicago in 1973; the Detroit Fox hung on only by programming Blaxploitation and martial arts movies; and New York's legendary Apollo closed in 1976, after an eight-year-old child was shot dead on the premises.

And all around, the increasing dominance of disco. In its original incarnation, as programmed by innovative new turntable disc jockeys for (primarily) gay people of color congregating at semilegal loft parties and transient dance clubs, the music that would come to be termed disco ran a global gamut of styles. Among its more prominent acts were Cymande, from the West Indies; Osibisa, Ghanaian and West Indian percussionists living in London; and Manu Dibango, a Cameroonian saxophonist whose "Soul Makossa," originally released on a French independent, embodied the African adaptation of a previously all-American music. Such artists shared the dance floor with Americans like Eddie Kendricks, the former Temptations' lead; instrumental party bands out of the New York City area such as B. T. Express and Crown Heights Affair; and the continuous run of classics out of Philadelphia. The single "Love is the Message" by Philadelphia International Records' house band MFSB, featuring most of those who had played on *Wilson Pickett In Philadelphia*, became *the* unofficial anthem of the music's true believers.

As the movement gathered chart momentum, however, the popularity of the more commercial discotheques and the equally mainstream music the venues favored saw a transition in public awareness. "Disco" became represented in large part by the sound of Miami—that same sound Pickett had tapped into before falling out with Henry Stone and company. And this was not just the phenomenon that was KC & the Sunshine Band, but the Bee Gees too, with "Jive Talkin'" and "You Should Be Dancing." As the floodgates opened, the very people Wilson Pickett had grown up with in gospel and soul began cashing in on the disco craze: the Miracles with their "Love Machine," the Ohio Players (the former Ohio Untouchables whose Robert Ward, long departed, had so enlivened those monumental Falcons singles) with "Love Rollercoaster," and Johnnie Taylor, who jumped straight from the Stax collapse into a deal with CBS, and right on board the disco train with it. Taylor's easy-going "Disco Lady" was not only the first single to take the word "disco" to the top of the charts, in the summer of 1976, but the first single ever to earn a platinum certification for two million sales. It was recorded at Muscle Shoals Sound Studio.

Pickett's ambivalence about disco was reflected in a song he wrote with Sir Mack Rice, recorded at his own return to Muscle Shoals Sound in early 1977, on his own dime, for the launch of his own Erva label. On "Time to Let the Sun Shine On Me" the two veterans reviewed their illustrious pasts ("I did alright out there in the soul field"), considered the need to address their current prospects ("time for me to make a change"), and called for a rosy future, per the song's title. The song's lyrics also referenced the rise of the disco as part of that future, though whether out of choice or career obligation appeared uncertain. What was not open to dispute was the emphatic and successively repeated line, "I changed my clothes, I didn't change my soul." Anchored by especially taut rhythm from drummer Roger Hawkins and bassist David Hood, augmented by Pete Carr's wah-wah guitar and Barry Beckett's brisk electric piano, with the backing vocalists engaging in a vibrant call-and-response, and the Muscle Shoals Horns employing a wonderfully muted trumpet riff, "Time to Let the Sun Shine On Me" is perhaps Pickett's finest piece of mid-seventies soul. Unfortunately, it ended up on the B-side of the one-off single that resulted from this disco adventure; the A-side went to a passable if unspectacular George Jackson composition, "Love Dagger."

The relationship with the team at Muscle Shoals came to an abrupt end around that single. "I was mixing what we produced on him," said Jimmy Johnson, who noted that Pickett was drinking and "doing a lot of stuff in the studio." "He called me one day and said I was taking a little longer than he thought I should. I was just trying to get it better." That wasn't good enough for Pickett, who had taken on the responsibility for running his own record label, without any staff members to buffer his increasingly acrid personality. "He said, 'If you don't have that in my hands by tomorrow, I'm a gonna kill you.'" Johnson took Pickett at his word and ensured the master tape went "counter to counter" the following day—from an airline desk at Muscle Shoals airport to one at Newark. Pickett duly released "Love Dagger"/"Time to Let the Sun Shine on Me" on Erva, but without the necessary promotional tools in the summer of disco's takeover, the single died a quick death. As for Jimmy Johnson and the other Swampers, "We didn't work with him for twenty-five years."

Reflecting on the sad end to a productive partnership that dated back to the legendary "Land of 1000 Dances" session of 1966, Johnson was magnanimous. "I realized it wasn't the Wilson I knew. He wasn't that way when we first started. Life had gotten tougher for him. He'd lost Atlantic, the kind of company you could retire with. Alcohol and drugs were taking a toll. I don't think he'd ever have said what he said to me if he hadn't been that way. We'd been too close, from the go. He was mean. He got meaner. And not just wicked, but mean."

Back in New Jersey, Pickett's behavior finally pushed Dovie Hall over the edge. "He was at that point where for breakfast, he was having a drink," she remembered. The drink would lead to drugs, and the drugs would lead to violence, with Dovie on the receiving end. "I tried to reason with him and see if he was going to make a change," but she ultimately had to admit to herself that "things are only going to get worse. And you're going to only get abused more."

The final straw came, she said, when "he jumped on me, and he hit me with a folding chair and knocked me to the floor. And then he hit me three or four more times, and Michael was looking. He beat me so bad . . . I said, 'This is the end of it. This child don't need to see this, I have to go.'" Hall concluded that if she stayed, "he's going to kill me," and decided to make a change of her own. "I told Michael, 'I'm taking you to your grandmother's in Kentucky.' I packed his clothes." The following morning, Wilson started the day as he had ended the night before, "with a drink in his hand." Hall called a taxi. "And I told him, 'I'm gone. I'm taking Michael to your mama's. And I'm going.' He didn't try to stop me. Wasn't nothing he could do. I just went and got in the taxi with Michael. And he was sitting there with a drink."

Dovie Hall had been Wilson Pickett's partner for fifteen years. She had seen the good, the bad, and the ugly. She would always focus on the good: "I loved him very much and I really think he loved me a lot; I know he did. Because he did too much for me. To the day he died, I loved him. It bothers me that things went down like it did, but what can I say?"

Hall and Pickett talked a couple of times on the phone after she left, but other than her attendance at the funeral of Wilson's grandmother at his request, they never saw each other again.

CHAPTER 23

It's a wretched, puny form of music but it's the contemporary sound, dig.
Wilson Pickett to Nick Kent, *New Musical Express*, 1979

There is, in the entire Wilson Pickett catalog, no more excruciating a recording than "Dance With Me," a career calamity highlighted by the fact that it was chosen to open his 1978 LP, *A Funky Situation*. Generic disco of the blandest kind, it featured all the genre's requisite trademarks: hi-hat shuffle, constantly ascending bass line, clipped guitar riffs, jazzy electric piano chords, and backing singers intoning the song's title over and over again before the putative lead could even sing his first line: "Going down to the disco, where all the lovely people go." To hear the most forceful soul singer of the 1960s reduced to such a feeble attempt at relevance represented an especially dark moment in the annals of disco overkill.

It would, therefore, be mildly reassuring to find that Pickett had little to do with *A Funky Situation*'s choice of material. The facts unfortunately indicate otherwise. After falling out with his former friends from Fame, Pickett promptly reached across the Shoals to Rick Hall, whom he had not worked with since the *Hey Jude* LP almost a decade earlier. Hall immediately made himself, his still-thriving studio, his latest rhythm section, and his songwriters all available; he even proposed to shop the results to record labels. All he asked of Pickett was a guarantee to cover the initial recording costs.

The four songs initially recorded revealed the conflict of artistic interests that Pickett and other genre-switching musicians faced at the time. "Who Turned You On" and "Funky Situation," both from the pen of Curtis Wilkins, headed into the dirty, sensual groove of Parliament/Funkadelic, while "Dance You Down," composed partly by one of the studio backing singers, hinted ominously at Pickett's impending resignation to the disco craze. His own "Lay Me Like You Hate Me," meanwhile, by nature of its raunchy title and aggressive arrangement, suggested that now and then he could firmly turn his back on mainstream appeal.

Hall shopped the four completed songs to record labels, and despite Pickett's recent commercial disappointments, secured a couple of serious offers. The singer ultimately spurned Epic for an opportunity to come "home" to Atlantic, via the quasi-independent Big Tree, whose roster included Johnny Rivers, Demis Roussos, and Hot Chocolate. With Big Tree's cofounder Dick Morris serving now as President of Atco and "custom" labels, and with Motown's former hit songwriter-producer Eddie Holland an Atlantic VP, Pickett may have expected the kind of priority attention he had lacked at RCA.

Atlantic, though, was a very different place than it had been in the 1970s, from its physical location to its corporate structure, and the label was now following the trends in black music more than it was leading them. In the spring of 1978, that meant disco. The *Saturday Night Fever* movie, released at the end of 1977, had immediately broken box office records. The accompanying double album would become the bestselling soundtrack of all time, eventually claiming seven American number one hits. Five of these were by the Bee Gees, which meant that the most popular act in what had initially been an American dance music of color was now dominated by a white group hailing from Australia. At the time Pickett signed with Atlantic, he had just finished up filming as part of the all-star cast finale in the Bee Gees' vainglorious vehicle *Sgt. Pepper's Lonely Hearts Club Band*. In this attempted follow-up to *Saturday Night Fever*, Pickett appeared alongside everyone from Bobby Womack and Nona Hendryx to Dr. John and Donovan. The cinematic train-wreck would turn out to be one of the most widely reviled musical movies of all time, though this would not become apparent until its late summer release.

With his small part in the can and a new record deal in his hand, Pickett returned to Fame to complete what would become *A Funky Situation*. To "Dance You Down," he added "Dance With Me," and a couple more obligatory nods to disco—a horrendous remake of Tony Joe White's "Hold On to Your Hiney" that was laid down alongside an equally egregious "She's So Tight." Thankfully, Pickett repented for these disco-esque atrocities with the enduring ballad "The Night We Called It a Day," made famous by Frank Sinatra, and an endearing, updated arrangement of the Young Rascals' 1967 number one, "Groovin'."

A Funky Situation was unveiled in September 1978, bookended by singles of two of the more respectable cuts: "Who Turned You On" and "Groovin'." Still, with the disco songs placed right up front on the full album, none could doubt that in direct contradiction to the lyrics of "Time to Let The

Sun Shine On Me," which was included toward the end of side two, Pickett had not only changed his clothes—his fulsome beard on the cover also went with the fashion of the times—but that he had changed his very soul. And while Pickett frequently railed against disco in public, he and Hall sought on this album to professionally profit from it through their respective publishing companies: "Dance With Me," from the pen of the studio's horn arranger Harrison Calloway, was assigned to Pickett's Erva Music, while "She's So Tight" came through Fame Publishing. But the royalties would hardly prove worth the effort. Pickett watched almost helplessly as the singles made the smallest of noises on the soul charts while *A Funky Situation*, despite a considerable push, failed miserably.

Disco was clearly not Wilson Pickett's strong suit. But record labels can prove slow on the uptake. Not only did Big Tree commission another record from Pickett; they specifically asked for more of the same. As producer André Perry recalled of receiving the assignment, "They wanted a disco album."

Perry, a Canadian native, came with considerable pedigree. In 1969 he had engineered John Lennon/Plastic Ono Band's "Give Peace a Chance" in a Montreal hotel room, and the following year, he opened a studio within a downtown Montreal church. In 1974 he created one of the North American continent's first state-of-the-art, residential recording destinations, named simply Le Studio, on 250 acres in Morin Heights, a small ski town of barely 2,000 people an hour northwest of Montreal. He had worked with the Bee Gees at Le Studio for five months, recording the 1976 LP that first featured "You Should Be Dancing," which may have been what convinced Big Tree of Perry's suitability. Still, the producer had only walked into the record company's offices in the first place to pitch a demo he had recorded with a black New York act; "it was around the beginning of rap," he recalled. Despite doubts about the disco directive, Perry accepted the label's surprise offer. "I didn't want to turn down doing a Wilson Pickett album," he said, the standard refrain in years to come of all those who felt that they might be the one to turn the legendary singer's career around.

Back in Montreal, Perry reached out to partners Jean Roussel, a classically trained pianist who had recorded with Cat Stevens, 10cc, and Robert Palmer; and Marty Simon, a local drummer and disco enthusiast. Roussel and Simon went to New York for writing sessions with Pickett, returning with disco compositions only marginally better than those that had appeared on *A Funky Situation*—and the singer was, again, complicit in the most painful of them all, taking a cowrite on the awkwardly titled "Granny."

Aware of these shortcomings, the Montreal production team then decided to deviate from the script. "We said, 'Well, maybe we can deliver one side disco and one side more of a crossover record,'" recalled Perry. Without notifying Big Tree of their intent, they went ahead and recorded an album of seven long songs, with three overt disco productions held back to the end, and three attempts at something more innovative and hopefully enduring placed up front. "Live With Me," emanating from the proven partnership of Pickett and Don Covay, served as a buffer in between. Titled *I Want You* after its lead track, the album had a forward-looking, 1980s sound, with electronic textures, synthesizers and syn-drums, and keyboard-sounding bass lines. The project, Perry insisted, "was treated with class," and the result, he admitted, was a "slick sound."

All of this music was at odds with the Wilson Pickett of convention, as the singer noted in an interview with British journalist Nick Kent. "You just can't get that sound no more," he lamented of his good old days. "It's all to do with this new equipment they've got in the studios. It cleans up the sound, makes it real, uh . . ."

"Bland?" suggested Kent.

"Yeah, I guess that's the word," confirmed Pickett. "'Cos you sure can't get that ole gritty sound, that dirty, raunchy, punchy kind of sound that we got on those old sides."[1]

Walter Rossi, Pickett's former live guitarist and Montreal native who was recruited as part of the studio band, recalled that the singer actively disliked the songs on *I Want You*, just as Rossi struggled to find a place for his rock guitar amidst the multiple layers of keyboards. Perry agreed that Pickett found himself "embedded into an environment and a way of working that he wasn't accustomed to," but that he "went for the ride. He felt fine because of the mix of the other people that were there. There was enough for him to lean on to."

Perhaps. But Pickett was also unaccustomed to recording in Canada in the midst of winter, and he didn't take well to the imposed isolation, in which the artist's guesthouse was a considerable drive across the grounds from the studio itself. One evening after Perry deposited him at his accommodation, the producer went to shut the screen door. It was frozen; he had to slam it to do so. "And he took it for granted that I was pissing him off," said Perry of Pickett. "He looks at me, and then he comes to me, and then he hits me with everything he's got, right on the side of my face." Perry should have been floored, "but for some strange reason, I didn't move. It must have been where he hit me. I never felt a thing."

The standoff was embarrassing for the singer, once he realized why Perry had slammed the door. "Had I been hurt," said the producer, "I'd have sent him home the following day." Instead, "He came in the next morning like a little boy to apologize, and from that moment on he was an angel." Perry felt that such a confrontation was ultimately forgivable because of the singer's undisputed merits. "He was from the school of Sinatra. He sang the song from beginning to end; it was always a performance; if you could get to him to do three or four takes, it would never be the same. He was really giving it his all."

Yet while the three Roussel/Simon songs intended as crossover material—"I Want You," "Love of My Life," and "Shameless"—succeeded in taking Pickett into new territory, and while the three disco songs would prove ultimately embarrassing, Atlantic stood its ground. "They were disappointed that we didn't do a full disco record," said Perry. The album was rejected. Unwilling to see the project abandoned, Perry reached out to a management friend, and the album was picked up by EMI America, which effectively bought out Pickett's contract from Atlantic in the process. *I Want You* was released at the end of 1979, whereupon it spent three months in the lower reaches of various LP charts, without quite threatening the sections that mattered. There was an attempt to shake further life into the record with a second single, "Groove City," the most respectable of the three disco cuts, and one that, with its rigid 137 beats per minute rhythm dictated by synth-bass sixteenth notes, served as a precursor to the 1980s form of (largely gay) disco known as Hi-NRG. But to no avail.

Perry refused to see *I Want You* as an artistic failure. "The bottom line is that this particular record is different. He sounds different, his voice is much cleaner. For me, that was the goal, [that] at least there should be a possibility for him to move on with his career. I was so saddened by the fact that it was half an album. But I'm still very happy with those [first] four tracks." Thirty-three years later, superstar rapper Rick Ross would sample the most innovative of those songs, "Shameless," for the core of "Ashamed," a track on his number one album *God Forgives, I Don't*, perhaps confirming that those elements of *I Want You* that didn't sound completely dated within months were, if anything, ahead of their time. That record also marked, sadly, the one occasion on which Wilson Pickett—and only posthumously—could claim his presence on a number one album.

Disappointing though sales may have been, *I Want You* fared considerably better than its predecessor, and like Atlantic's Big Tree, EMI America opted to commission another album in entirety. The label duly deposited Pickett in a New York City studio with Jeff Lane. The king of New York's predisco soul-funk heyday, Lane had discovered Brass Construction and had produced classics by B. T. Express and Mandrill, among others. In more recent years, those successes had brought him major label commissions for Eddie Kendricks and Garnett Mimms, respectable sales that made him a logical choice for Wilson Pickett.

Lane did his best to place Pickett back in the singer's comfort zone, assembling a team of primarily black and largely unknown studio musicians for the recording sessions. Certainly, the album's lead song and title track, "Back on the Right Track," was a buoyant declaration of intent. "I'd been fooling around, until I lost my way," Pickett announced, while the musicians backed him with funky flair. Unfortunately, only a couple more of *Right Track*'s seven songs were particularly strong: "If You Can't Beat 'Em, Join 'Em," a cover of a Mark Radice hit that Lane had produced three years earlier, and "Don't Underestimate the Power of Love," featuring a delicious guitar groove that would have been at home on one of Michael Jackson's albums of the era. The only single that made it to the shops, however, was the urbane, sophisticated ballad "Ain't Gonna Give You No More," credited to Lane and Pickett as composers, which offered no suggestion that Pickett might have regained his energetic sixties soul mojo.

The album cover offered little by way of further encouragement. *Right Track*'s front sleeve featured a colored portrait pencil of Pickett in profile that looked amateurish; the back had—yet again—typographical errors. *Right Track* proved a commercial disaster, and EMI America cut him loose. After five albums released on four different labels, Wilson Pickett found himself once more without a recording contract—and with no indication that his situation was about to improve.

CHAPTER 24

Baby, I am a mean motherfucker. Don't be writing nothing nice 'cause you be jivin' people.
    Wilson Pickett to Gerri Hirshey, *Nowhere to Run: The Story of Soul Music*, 1981

Dovie Hall had been more than Wilson Pickett's domestic partner; she had raised Wilson's son Michael Pickett as her own. In both respects, however, she had no legal claim, and shortly after she dropped Michael with Wilson's mother Lena Pickett in Kentucky upon leaving her partner, en route to her own family in Michigan, Wilson demanded that his son return to live in Englewood. It was to prove a terrifying existence for the boy. At the age of fourteen, in 1979, Wilson sat him down for a "birds-and-the-bees" talk, placed a saucer of cocaine on the table, and insisted that Michael indulge. "And I'm not gon' say no to him," Michael recalled in *Don't Let the Green Grass Fool You*, "because if I did, by him being under the influence, I might get thrown through the window."[1] Not surprisingly, Michael Pickett would go on to endure his own drug addictions.

He was left similarly scarred, in one case permanently, from Wilson's physical abuse—by "baseball bat ... cable wire," whatever was at hand.[2] As he got older, he was accused of having eyes for his father's younger girlfriends or one-night stands. When Michael would show up at his (private) school with black eyes and bruises, and his teachers pressed for the truth, he would beg them not to report Wilson to the authorities.

Lee Wade was also badly beaten and did not call the police, either. "I was so protective of his name. I was in love and I knew his character was always being demeaned because he was a black man and a mean one and always causing arguments and fights and stuff. So I wanted to keep it on another level."

Wade stuck around into the early 1980s, by which point she had concluded of Pickett that "He was sick, he was bi-polar." Although others would

come to their own conclusions that Pickett was suffering from an identifi-
able medical condition, Pickett refused professional help and never had a
formal diagnosis.[3] "I tried to get him to go to a psychiatrist," said Wade, but
"he didn't want to be telling no woman his dirty linen, and no man either,
because he and the man are equals."

As Wade had discovered, Pickett needed women in his life for compan-
ionship as well as for sex. Additionally, he needed people to keep his books,
write his checks, and handle his correspondence. Given his lack of trust, he
generally only employed people he could control, like his romantic partners.
The women often served as secretary, bedroom partner, and punching bag.

Several of them nonetheless stuck around. There was Evelyn Roberts,
introduced to Pickett in 1976; she wrote about their long-term, on-off
relationship for an unpublished book subsequently turned into a published screenplay. There was Karine Zein, who claimed that her daughter,
Soumaya, born in 1968, was his. (According to the Pickett family, eventual
DNA testing proved otherwise.[4]) In the 1980s Pickett resumed their relationship, which ended abruptly with a violent attack on Soumaya, seventeen and pregnant at the time.

There was Stephanie Harper, from whom came a daughter, Saphan—
Pickett's fourth and last acknowledged child. The couple met in 1980, when
Stephanie's brother Bruce, a running back with the New York Jets, dated a
policewoman providing security at a local Wilson Pickett show. Stephanie,
said Saphan of what she subsequently learned from her mother, a local
middle school teacher, "wasn't into the limelight," but accompanied her
brother and went backstage anyway—"and the thing that impressed her
the most was his intelligence. She was totally thrown aback by how smart
the man was. And from that moment on they were an item." Saphan came
along in February 1982, and a month after she was born, Stephanie packed
her bags. "She told me they were fighting," said Saphan. "And he was heavily into the drugs and alcohol. And there was a baby in the room . . . so she
moved out."

Then there was Jean Marie Cusseaux, a semipermanent fixture alongside Wilson at the Englewood home and on the road throughout the ensuing decade, his most consistent companion since Dovie Hall. Like those
that preceded it, the relationship involved an alarming degree of physical
abuse; this one, however, would end in court.

Come 1981 not one of the Soul Clan, those pioneering Atlantic Records
vocal giants of the mid-sixties, had charted anywhere for at least three
years: disco had seen to that. But now, as a direct result of market satura-
tion, disco was finally on the way out. At the same time, the 1980 movie

The Blues Brothers helped bring soul music back to the fore. The film had white comedians/actors Dan Aykroyd and John Belushi playing a couple of degenerate adult orphans (as first introduced on *Saturday Night Live* and then turned into a 1978 number one live album) "getting the band back together" to raise last-ditch rent money for the convent in which they had been raised. That band included Steve Cropper and Donald "Duck" Dunn; the movie saw musical cameos from Aretha Franklin and James Brown, and a final concert scene included a stirring rendition of the Solomon Burke composition and Wilson Pickett hit "Everybody Needs Somebody to Love." What better moment, then, than to revive the all-star lineup of the Soul Clan—and this time, with Pickett?

Pickett, Burke, Don Covay, Joe Tex, and Ben E. King (original member Arthur Conley had moved to the Netherlands) announced a one-off Soul Clan concert at the Savoy Theater in Manhattan, on July 24, 1981. On its eve they held a press conference, where Pickett demonstrated his capacity to attract attention by wearing black leather pants and yellow silk shirt, and telling the assembled media: "I think you all realize we all have our own personalities and our way of expressing ourselves. Me? I'm mad as shit."[5]

The comment appeared to reflected the singer's anger at feeling forsaken these last few years. "R&B was just cast aside during the disco age," he continued. "Cast aside by radio-program directors and record companies. We were thrown to the dogs! But you can't cry. The thing to do is to team up."[6]

As the press conference ended, Solomon Burke was seen arranging for some of the Clan to visit one of those "radio-program directors," the disco kingpin Frankie Crocker at WBLS. Pickett would certainly not be joining them: in an interview with Rick Whitesell six months earlier, he had decried of disco's dominance: "You had a fool programming five radio stations across the country, and that's Frankie Crocker. A freak like him ruined the music industry." Those words went unpublished at the time, but they surely came *after* Pickett reportedly punched Crocker, and most certainly alienated him, at one of his many Englewood house parties, thereby throwing *himself* to the dogs.

The Soul Clan concert proved a fiasco. "Don had so much to drink that he fell over backwards into the drum set," Ben E. King recalled of Covay's set, which was duly described in a *Billboard* review as "an exercise in chaos."[7] "Joe Tex was out there doing 'Skinny Legs,' and he had girls with skimpy outfits on, and Wilson came onstage with his robe on and pulled one of the girls off. And she was raving and yelling, 'I'm going to call my husband, and he's going to come and punch you out.'"

The finale saw the five singers come together without even performing the Clan anthem "Soul Meeting" from 1968. "The whole thing was comic," said King. "We just didn't have anyone to hold our hands and keep us out of trouble. I think we were overwhelmed with the success of what we had achieved that day, with the crowds that were there, the entertainers that had come to see us. Not taking away from our talent, but we partied too soon for the party, if you know what I mean. It was like watching the three Stooges. I had more fun that one night than I ever had in my life."

For King, it was just one more adventure with Pickett in a long line of them. "Like everyone else, I've had my chip with Wilson," King recalled in late 2014, a few months before he passed away. "He'd call me at home, curse at my wife. I'd have to say, 'OK, let me go up to Englewood and talk to Wilson.' I'd go and bang on the door. 'Who is it?' 'It's Ben, Wil.' 'What's up man?' 'Look, don't call my house and abuse my wife if you don't mind. I'd appreciate it.' But that's Wilson; a ticking time bomb, that guy."

The bomb duly exploded the following spring all across Europe, on a package tour featuring Pickett, Carla Thomas, Sam Moore, and Eddie Floyd. Moore was touring for the first time without his former partner Dave Prater, undergoing detoxification from heroin at the time, his partner and manager Joyce McRae traveling with methadone and appropriate doctor's papers. Joining them was McRae's fifteen-year-old daughter, Michelle.

Pickett traveled with both personal tour manager Ernie Baxter and a valet. His band, meanwhile, which also backed Carla Thomas, was the usual combination of veterans ("Patience" Higgins, "Crusher" Green), current mainstays (keyboard player Sky "King" Williams), and newcomers. Among the latter was Marc Ribot, a young white guitarist who had come to New York City from neighboring Jersey in 1979, joining a punk-oriented R&B group called the Realtones, which brought him into the playing orbit of musicians who had originated such music, including Carla Thomas and Chuck Berry. Upon being hired by Green, he was given what were fast becoming standard instructions for incoming musicians regarding Wilson Pickett: Don't look at him, stay out of his face, don't have anything to do with him.

"The cat was kind of a gangster," Ribot said of Pickett. "Musically, it was a great vibe. But you never knew when you got off stage: you could play a great night and Wilson would be in a bad mood and he would dress the band down like a drill sergeant. Get in the face of some new recruits. It wasn't pleasant, it wasn't nice. And he was accompanied by a bodyguard at all times, who was reported to be armed."

The tour was being copromoted and managed by John Abbey, the *Blues and Soul* editor who had interviewed Pickett multiple times and promoted a brief tour of American military bases in Germany for the singer a decade earlier, when he was still at Atlantic. "In terms of talent, his showmanship was second to nobody," said Abbey, who recalled a London Hammersmith Odeon concert in the early 1970s where Pickett clambered over the PA stacks. Offstage was a different story. "He was a very insecure man. He was a very complex personality—and you could run the gamut where in the space of three hours, he could go from the nicest guy on the planet to an absolute demon."

The latter character showed up most on this tour once Pickett became convinced that his tour manager was short-changing him. At the hotel in Rome, Pickett decided to take drastic action, holding Ernie Baxter over the railing of his suite's balcony, several floors above ground level, until the tour manager "would admit to cheating or stealing Pickett out of money," as Abbey put it.[8] The hotel opened onto an inner courtyard; witnesses called the police—who were seen running down the hallway with machine guns drawn. Pickett was arrested and carted off to jail, and Baxter left the tour.

The singer's ire was further provoked by the fact that Sam Moore, who during the "Double Dynamite" heyday of Sam & Dave had put on one of the only soul revues to rival that of Wilson Pickett, was becoming the star of the show once again. Pickett "would get upset if he was headlining a program and he was the star," said Moore. "He wanted to dictate how many songs you sing. 'Cause if someone told him you had a good show, you can rest assured you're going to hear from him. I know a lot of people said they'd sooner not do a show with Pickett 'cause of how he could get inside your head and intimidate you from doing a good performance."

Notably he never tried it on with his former Falcon, Eddie Floyd. "He's an extremely nice man; but he's probably not somebody you pick a fight with," said Abbey of Floyd, who he described as acting like a "sheriff" on the tour. "And I got the feeling that Pickett knew that."[9] Nor did Pickett take out his frustrations on Carla Thomas, who "stood up to him," said Sam Moore. "She said, 'My contract says so-and-so, and he's not [the one] paying me, and I'm going to do my show.' She did her show, and he was very upset. So, he came after me."

"Sam was doing a great job; he was adding so much to the show," said Abbey. "And Pickett spent so much time goading and aggravating Sam." When the group checked into one particular hotel, which had four wings emerging from the central reception, Pickett somehow climbed into the false ceiling. "When Sam came by, [Pickett] jumped out of the ceiling on to him," said Abbey. "It was just unbelievable."

Moore was not hurt, but in Lisbon, Pickett's envy turned into fury. "Sam got over and had an incredible show," said Joyce McRae. "Pickett was knocked and he was looking for us, 'cause he wanted to fuck Sam up. He really wanted to attack Sam. He was running through the halls, pounding people's doors: 'I will find you motherfucker Sam Moore, you aren't going to hide from me.' We're scared shitless. I call downstairs, they send a Portuguese policeman to sit at the vestibule of our hotel room, with a pistol pointed at the door all night, so that if Pickett broke down the door he would have shot him."

But Pickett was not always like this. Joyce McRae was out with her daughter when she ran into Pickett on the street in Barcelona. He asked for their help: Saphan had just been born, her mother was getting the baby's ears pierced, and Wilson wanted assistance picking out something appropriate. "He was absolutely as cordial and pleasant and as nice as any psychotic would be when they're on the good side of their behavior," said McRae. "Whatever his true diagnosis was, he really did present both people."

Shortly thereafter everyone assembled for the flight to Paris, and "by the time we get to the airport, he is fucked up," said McRae. "He must have been drinking and he probably dropped some drugs."

This was not a marginal observation. "The minute you saw the vodka come out, you knew that cocaine was right behind it," said John Abbey, "and once he mixed the vodka and the cocaine, that's when the crazy shit started."

On the plane to Paris, Pickett again turned on the Moore entourage, hitting on McRae's fifteen-year-old daughter, asking Sam Moore, as McRae recalled it, "Are you getting some of that … ? If you don't want it, I sure do. I'm getting what I want 'cause I'm in the mafia." The confrontation was eventually de-escalated by Crusher Green and the plane's captain, but upon disembarking the Moores checked into a different hotel for their own protection. At the Paris show, at a rock club on the Champs-Elysees, Sam Moore went on first, to get in and out of the venue before Pickett could show up. Once the headliner arrived, he was in a worse mood than ever. "I think he just wanted to go home," said Marc Ribot. "We did Carla's set; Wilson wasn't there. The show was two hours late, it was packed to the rafters. Wilson delayed. People were getting heavy. Finally, Wilson came on, did one tune—and split. Walked out the back door, got in a car, and drove away. This is a formula for starting a riot—and it worked. I had the forethought to grab my pedals and guitar offstage, and we just hid in the basement while people tore the club apart."

John Abbey recalled that Pickett "did ten or twelve minutes and then walked off," but the consequences were the same. "Obviously the promoter was angry; the audience was angry. At that point, and it was my call, I felt that Pickett had reached the point where you didn't know what was going to come next. I said, 'the tour ends here.'" Shows in England and the Netherlands were canceled.[10]

"Wilson summoned everyone to the hotel room," said Ribot. "I remember he went out on the trumpet player, whacking him around, and nobody did anything about it because . . . the bodyguard was there? Because he had our passports? Because we were a week behind in our pay? He accused the trumpet player of conspiring with the promoters to do something bad to Wilson . . . My impression was that [Wilson] was paranoid." The following morning Pickett got on a plane from Paris to Miami, and straight on to Guyana. His band went home without being paid for the final, abandoned week of the tour.

For Ribot, who would on go to an acclaimed career as a writer, recording artist, performer, and collaborator, his sole outing with Wilson Pickett was a particularly egregious example of a notably nonunionized business. "If you are in a community where there is such huge unemployment in general, and among musicians in particular, you can get away with murder if you're handing out jobs," he said. "It seemed to be that a lot of the musicians who were on the tour had a really rough time. But those who needed the gig went out on the next one, even though it wasn't physically safe. It's what happens when there's no organization to push back. It's what happens in a situation where people don't have a lot of work, and some people are giving out work. It's natural that they acquire a lot of power, and it's human nature that some people abuse that power."

Twelve years later, at a festival in Belgium, Pickett would seek out Sam and Joyce Moore and apologize to them for his behavior on that 1982 tour. Similarly, when he ran into John Abbey on a New York City street around the same time, he almost broke down as he apologized for his actions. In the meantime, though, his aggressive behavior would continue, off and on, for many years to come.

"Crusher wasn't going out of the house for about three weeks after one of those tours because he had been badly beaten," said Ribot. "He said to me, 'Well I showed him I'm no punching bag,' because he had gotten in a few licks too. But I'm sorry, when you're fighting with your employer it's not a fight, it's abuse. And I'm sure that Crusher didn't start it. And I'm sure the other people I saw him terrorize didn't start it. You can write about all the extenuating circumstances, and maybe it needs to be put in historical context, but . . . You know why guys beat women? Because they fucking can. And it's abuse. That's why employers beat employees, when they can. I've worked with black bandleaders and white bandleaders who are respectful, courteous and generous human beings—and then I've worked with Wilson Pickett."

CHAPTER 25

If you see Wilson in a restaurant, go to another restaurant. If he's in the hotel bar, go to another bar, anywhere but where he is. You can have a very pleasant evening.
David Akers, trumpet player, Midnight Movers

Without a label of his own, Wilson Pickett jumped at an invitation in 1981 to record with a brand-new independent company—as the supporting half of a duet with Jackie Moore, another of the former soul stars down on their luck. He was only invited to do so because Moore's first choice, Johnnie Taylor, serving a five-year probationary sentence for cocaine possession, had lost the gig after Moore rejected his vocals.

Pickett and Moore were brought back together by Bobby Eli, the guitarist and songwriter who had worked on *In Philadelphia* and *Mr. Magic Man*. Eli had become Moore's producer during her more lucrative years at Columbia, and was continuing in that role alongside Moore's former A&R man, Richard Mack, at Mack's newly established Catawba label (named for its North Carolina base). By the time Pickett joined the project, Eli had already recorded the backing tracks for the single—a remake of Moore's 1971 hit "Precious, Precious" and a song called "Seconds." As performed by the group Pockets (another former Columbia connection), "Seconds" had a sharp crispness that very much reflected the mood of the newly emerging electro-funk dance floor; this was not the disco of old.

The vocal sessions in a midtown Manhattan studio were chaotic. "Jackie and him both had bottles of liquor," said Eli. "There might have been three or four different types on the desk in the studio—plus some other white substance laying around." Events played out accordingly. "Pickett says, 'My main man Bobby Eli, so glad we're back working together.' Then he goes into the bathroom, comes back out, and says, 'You Jew motherfuckers, us niggers can't cop a break, you Jews taking all our records . . .' Half an hour later, he comes back and says, 'Bobby Eli, you my main motherfucker, I love you man,' and a half hour later we've taken all his money again! I guess if you do a lot of blow, you have a tendency to be a little schizophrenic, paranoid."

Regardless, Pickett could still turn it on in front of the microphone. "He was screaming, screaming, *screaming*," said Eli. When the producer suggested he tone it down a little, he was curtly informed: "Motherfucker, I'm the Wicked Pickett, this is what I do."

His vocal performance was stronger than probably anything on his last couple of albums. "Seconds," Pickett's most contemporary dance record in a long time (albeit one on which he received second billing) was released, with an instrumental version on its flip, by Catawba late in 1982 and in Europe through various other independent labels. It succeeded in the clubs but failed to take off beyond that. The recording of "Precious, Precious" never made it to disc. It didn't help that Mack and Moore were injured in a car crash while out promoting it, and that Pickett did not join them on such gigs in the first place. Luck did not seem to be on Pickett's side.

Fortune had not been kind to various Midnight Movers either, several of whom returned to Pickett over the course of the 1980s. Among them were guitarist Skip Pitts, drummer Woody Woodson, and Curtis Pope. Despite playing with Chuck Brown's Soul Searchers, the prime proponents of the DC funk subgenre known as go-go, Pope had hit rock bottom by the point that he returned. Pickett "had to nurse me back from the ghetto," Pope said. "He put up with me. Didn't care what I did, he would back me. Because he knew I would back him." For those who had enjoyed the halcyon days with Pickett, there remained a deep loyalty and respect on both sides. Pope eventually revived his reputation as a trumpet player, the name of the Midnight Movers with it, and moved into the role of Pickett's bandleader, a position he maintained for almost fifteen years.

The musicians Pope assembled were mostly from the Washington, DC area, and although the drummer changed frequently—Woodson, Crusher Green, and Robert "Mousey" Thompson—the rest of the new-look Midnight Movers were relatively stable. Alongside Pope and, on occasion, Pitts, there was David "Weasel" Akers on trumpet, Artie Sherman on keyboards, Vernon "Chico" Jordan on sax, Theodore "Teddy Bear" Jones on second guitar, and Kevin "Plucker" Walker on bass. Born in 1965—the year of "Midnight Hour"—Walker was gigging by the age of thirteen, covering the classic sixties material in a band with Curtis Pope's brother. When invited to fill in as a last-minute replacement for an early 1980s Pickett gig in Texas, he already had the necessary confidence. "I knew the music," he said, "and didn't have to practice." Soon, he was playing with Pickett whenever possible. "Once I got this gig," he said, "it was such a big deal for me there was no ways I was going back to being normal."

The circuit for the new Midnight Movers was varied. Pickett enjoyed playing the clubs, where the people could dance: in May 1983, he shared the bill at New York's fashionable Peppermint Lounge with an up-and-coming Madonna. Private and corporate shows brought in the money, theater concerts the prestige, and there was a bread-and-butter circuit of other oldies acts to play alongside, from Chubby Checker to the Staple Singers—and Little Richard, with whom Pickett formed a strong friendship. Increasingly, Pickett also doubled up on concert bills with James Brown, which "was very intense," said Walker, "because those guys would always get into some type of *something*, at every gig. They loved each other, but it was a love-hate relationship, down to which dressing rooms and who would go on first."

In the mid-1980s the role of lead guitarist fell to Ronnie Hinton, who was about the same age as Walker and shared in enjoying preferential treatment with the bassist. Early in his employment, following a couple of rehearsals in Englewood, Pickett "gave me a Yamaha dirt bike he had up at his house," said Hinton. "It was in great shape. He said he had bought it for his son, and his son never used it." Michael Pickett had by then gone into the military, and on the occasions they did meet, he and his father were continually at odds.

Pickett's temperament ensured no lack of drama. Thompson and Akers each recalled a situation backstage at a New York club where the promoter's wife walked in to the office while Pickett was demanding preshow payment, and admiringly touched his current girlfriend Jean Cusseaux's fur coat. Pickett swore at the woman, according to Thompson, and "slapped her across the face," in Akers's memory. Yet the show went ahead and, said Thompson, "Two months later we were back in that club again."

"People loved Pickett so much that they took it as 'Hey, I just got cussed out by Wilson Pickett, this is a great thing,'" said Kevin Walker. "He was such a legend that people automatically thought they had done something wrong to deserve it."

Not everyone backed off, however. In 1982 the singer attended a Bobby Womack show at the Ritz in New York City, where both he and Ronnie Wood of the Rolling Stones joined Womack onstage. Afterward, Pickett got in an argument backstage with a Hell's Angel and was stabbed in the hand. The incident was reported in *Billboard*, and a Pickett concert at the midtown venue Bond's was canceled.[1] When he showed up at Bond's for his show the next night, he offered author Gerri Hirshey, then busy researching her soul music book *Nowhere to Run*, a succinct explanation as he examined his bandaged hand: "So, I fucked up again."[2]

In Florida, a young man came to a venue with a tell-all book he wanted Pickett to sign. "Pickett takes this book, realizes that he didn't authorize this author to do the book, and he decides he's going to take the book away from this guy," said Walker.[3] "Well this guy had some friends who happened to be a champion kickboxing team, about eight of them. Pickett decides he's not going to let these guys take this book no matter what. So he pulls out his knife. 'Nobody's going to take this book . . . anyone come over here, I'm going to cut you.' And he was serious. That gives you an idea of what kind of guy he was . . . someone looking under every rock for a royalty check."

In 1986, Wilson Pickett and Bonnie Covington finally divorced, almost a quarter-century after they originally parted ways. That same year, his father passed away. Wilson Pickett Sr. had married Helen Walker in 1974 and gave up drinking four years later. But he never fully reconciled with his son. Wilson Pickett Jr. "took care of every last one of his brothers and sisters," according to daughter Veda. "He did that on his own, and a lot of people don't realize that. The only person he really didn't care for was his father—but he cried when he heard his father had passed away. It hurt his heart because he never really did what he should have done for his father. That really haunted him. (Because) his father did so much for *him*."

Throughout these difficult times, Pickett kept up efforts to cut another record. He reached out to André Perry in Quebec; Perry declined. On the Bill Boggs show in the spring of 1984 Pickett told the TV audience that he was negotiating a deal with Elektra, but nothing more was heard of it. He nonetheless tried to impress on his live band that better times were just around the corner, and in 1987, his promises came true. Berry Gordy caught wind of a particularly strong demo of a ballad titled "Don't Turn Away," and Pickett signed with Motown. "I figured if Gordy wanted it, there must be something going on," said Pickett in the subsequent press release. "He doesn't let too many fishes get away."[4]

Gordy's sudden indulgence was no exercise in whimsy. That was not how Motown had made its fortune, nor why Gordy had moved his operations out to California and set himself up in a Beverly Hills mansion to mingle with the Hollywood big shots. Given the right material, the right delivery, and the right breaks, Gordy may have seen an opportunity to revive the career of Wilson Pickett. Along with his long-standing VP Ewart Abner, Gordy hired Robert Margouleff, the man behind Stevie Wonder's transformation from 1960s child superstar to 1970s soul singer. Margouleff had programed the synthesizers on Pickett's 1975 album *Join Me and Let's Be*

Free; in later years he had applied his programming and production talents to a wide range of artists, including new wave acts Devo and Depeche Mode.

Margouleff and his studio partner of ten years, the arranger Robert Martin, sat down with Pickett and the Motown brass to decide on songs. The opportunity to once again record for a major label after an absence of six years was for Pickett tempered by the methodology of the process; he found he was essentially at the whims of the producers and their synthesizers and computers. While Margouleff and Martin did employ a backing band, the album was constructed in the fashion of big budget albums of the 1980s—piece by piece, each instrument recording separately. Without the opportunity to inspire the musicians around him, to stomp his feet and bring them up to his level, Pickett had no focus. And a Wilson Pickett without focus, especially on location, as André Perry could attest, was a recipe for trouble.

"Wilson really made tremendous demands on the record company," said Margouleff, mentioning the singer's demand for a white suit to wear to the studio, and a chauffeur-driven car every day. "And not to diminish his singing ability, but he came into the studio loaded once or twice. And I said to him 'Wilson, you have to make a decision. You can either drink and party, or you can work in the studio. But you can't drink in the studio.'" The condition seemingly fell on deaf ears. "He did like to drink some wine," confirmed Robert Martin. "It was definitely not the kind of thing where he always waited until five o'clock in the afternoon."

"If you let him get away with something in the studio, he'd get away with it, he'd party," said Margouleff. "And he was constantly fighting with his wife," that being Jean Cusseaux (Pickett generally referred to any of his steady partners as his "wife"). At one point, he even disappeared for a couple of days; "it turned out that he had gone to San Francisco to deal with some kind of domestic issue," recalled Martin. And yet "when he opened his mouth in front of a microphone that always was magic," said Margouleff. "And it did not come from someone supereducated, going to Emerson or Juilliard or anything like that; he was a true folk singer."

The producers' task, then, was to reign in Pickett as best they could, mediate tensions with the record company, and deliver the best possible record. They were helped by a team that included composers Larry Weiss ("Hi Ho Silver Lining" and "Rhinestone Cowboy") and Jerry Lynn Williams (recent hits for Eric Clapton and Bonnie Raitt), who contributed compelling songs such as "A Thing Called Love," "A Man of Value," and "When Your Heart Speaks," which joined the epic "Don't Turn Away" on the finished album as among the strongest compositions Pickett had been offered in fifteen years. Nonetheless, *American Soul Man*, as the record was titled, shrieked of its time and place, mid-1980s Los Angeles, and never more so than on the exhausting six-minute reworking of "In the Midnight Hour," which was drowned in reverberating drums, "Eye of the Tiger"-style synthesizers, and wailing guitar solos, with Pickett responding in kind with a series of overly enthusiastic vocal interpolations.

Margouleff and Martin sensed from the moment that they handed *American Soul Man* in to Motown that the label might not fully promote it. "Abner and he did not get along very well," said Margouleff, recalling Pickett charging in and threatening to turn the VP's desk over at one point. "And he did not get along very well with (the other) people at the record company. I think they wanted to be away from Wilson as soon as they possibly could do so."

Ultimately, Margouleff saw a deeply troubled Wilson Pickett. "His life was chaotic," he recalled. "He was an alcoholic. Really was. Not in control of his own role. And that's the reason he didn't make records for years. I had to reach really hard to get what I got." And yet "he never really sang badly, and he never really sang out of tune. He just wanted to be called an *American Soul Man*, 'cause that's what he was. Right out of the dirt, right out of the field, he was a real *American Soul Man*, one of the few real genuine articles, and with all the wrinkles and stuff that came along with it. That's who he was."

Despite the producers' reservations, Motown did initially get behind *American Soul Man*. The single "Don't Turn Away" and the album itself each entered what *Billboard* now referred to as the "Black Music" chart in late 1987, and the remake of "In the Midnight Hour" was released as a single all over the world, in seven-inch and twelve-inch formats with multiple mixes. This gave Pickett his first (minor) UK chart hit in years. A major televised concert at the Forum in Los Angeles showed the singer to still be in fine voice, but no longer in the best of physical health—his face looked puffy, his eyes glazed, his body bloated.

The band, for its own part, reflected the era's tendency toward overindulgent playing. Guitarist Ronnie Hinton and bass player Kevin Walker filled nearly every half-beat on classic soul songs otherwise known for their sense of space. Walker in particular was singled out by the media for his virtuosic "slapping"—the technique made popular by Larry Graham of Sly and the Family Stone and now prevalent in the 1980s jazz-funk scene.

The band went to Europe in late 1987 to promote *American Soul Man* (though the live show hardly featured any new songs from the album). When they arrived in Hamburg for a day off, Pickett promptly hit the hotel bar, where Curtis Pope heard him giving an interview, saying of his bass player, "That boy, he thinks he's the star of the band."

"Pickett was completely insane," said David Akers of the singer that day. "And he was yelling at Jean, and she looked to be beaten up, and he walked out of the room and ordered more vodka, and came back and slapped the desk clerk and was just going *off*. He was on the rampage." Walker confirmed that "Wilson had gotten into something with Jean," and recalled Pickett had already "beat up the promoter" by this point in the evening. "He wanted the whole band to come downstairs to the lobby. Because she had our passports, and he thought that maybe somebody in the band was hiding his wife." Pickett decided that "somebody" must have been Kevin Walker.

The musicians mostly took the verbal assault with familiar aplomb, seeking to walk away from it at the first opportunity. David Akers recalled that "we went to get on the elevator, and as the doors were closing, [Pickett] leaned in and hit Kevin. For no good reason. I guess he was going to hit whoever he could reach." Pope said, "Pickett pulled the boy out of the elevator, 'cause he was the closest to the door."

"He was out of his mind," said Walker. "Out of his *mind*. I'm instantly looking over for the band members to come and grab him, because they knew him, they'd been there. They didn't do anything." Curtis Pope's response, as bandleader, was always to let Pickett's anger blow over rather than risk escalating it. "We were saying, 'Pickett didn't mean nothing,'" Pope recalled of his actions as the singer stormed off and Walker rejoined the group in the elevator. "I said, 'Man, go to your room, go to sleep, tomorrow it will all be forgotten.'"

Walker did not sleep it off or forget all about it. "I was the kid in the band," he said. "I didn't do anything wrong. So I didn't deserve to be attacked. And I didn't understand why he attacked me . . . I mean, he was crazy, but he'd never been coming out physical like that. I got really angry, I'm embarrassed, I can't believe this guy put his hands on me, so I thought about it, and I came back downstairs to confront him." And he did so with his bathroom towel rack in his hands. "He pulled it out of the wall," said Hinton, his roommate. "I watched him."

"He saw me coming downstairs," recalled Walker of Pickett, "and I was using every curse word you could think of . . . 'If you ever lay your hands on me again I'm going to beat you so-and-so . . .'"

"Pickett was going forwards towards Walker," recalled Hinton, "saying 'What are you going to do, what's your problem?' And I think Kevin was afraid and was excited, and was hurt and angry, and swung the towel rack without thinking about it."

"He started charging at me just like a bull," said Walker. "Just coming at me. And right before he was getting ready to hit me, that's when I came around."

"Pickett came from behind the bar," said Pope, "and the boy clonked him with that thing." The towel rack caught Pickett directly in his left eye, breaking the bone behind it, throwing the singer to the floor. Most of the other musicians were in their rooms. "Someone came up and told us that Wilson had gotten hit upside the head," recalled Woody Woodson. "So I rushed back down and they had him going to hospital. Blood was everywhere."

Walker ran away for hours. "The promoter ended up finding me after I got back. When he saw me, he said, 'Oh my God, man, thank you so much for kicking his ass.' And then he started crying, which was horrible, because he had put a lot of money into the tour." In an attempt to stem that promoter's losses as well as their own, the band honored the remaining shows without their singer. Pickett himself spent the next several days in the hospital, the doctors trying to save his sight.

Not surprisingly, these would be the last dates that Kevin Walker ever played in the name of Wilson Pickett—although the singer did not press charges. "I wish it had never happened," said Walker of the fight, noting that he tried to apologize through Curtis Pope but was never sure if word got through. "It's not something I'm really proud of. But it's not something I think *deserved* to have happened . . . I wasn't the initiator." The incident may have in fact jump-started his career. Back in the States, Walker was recruited by Patti LaBelle, who had seen him at the televised Forum show in Los Angeles. Soon enough Walker was playing with Prince, and earning a reputation as perhaps the best young bass player in all of American R&B.

When Pickett got out of the hospital he started wearing glasses to protect his eye, and never fully regained his vision. As for *American Soul Man*, one can imagine the reaction at Motown's office in California when they heard that Wilson Pickett's European tour had just been abandoned following an internal fight that nearly blinded the singer. They'd had enough trouble with him just making the record, and it wasn't as if anyone was raving wildly about the results. Pickett was dropped. He didn't make another album for a decade, and it seemed to many that he never would.

CHAPTER 26

Sure there's a lot of different music you can get off on but soul is more than that. It takes you somewhere else. It grabs you by the balls and lifts you above the shite.

Jimmy Rabbitte, band manager, *The Commitments*, 1991

"I went into a great depression," Wilson Pickett told Ted Drozdowski of the *Boston Phoenix* in 1999. "I said, 'To hell with it.' I was getting nowhere. I was sinking my own money into recording projects and never getting my money back out of it. So I thought I might as well relax with this. I didn't relax, though. I got very depressed. I went into my house and didn't come out for about ten years. I just went to the grocery store or the post office. Sometimes I'd sneak out and go fishing. People thought I was dead or something. They would drive by and try to peek to see if they could see Wilson Pickett. They'd ring the bell, but I didn't answer. I didn't want to talk to nobody."[1]

Such candor and introspection were admirable from a man who eventually came to recognize his failings, though his self-isolation may have been a bit exaggerated. There certainly were periods over the decade following *American Soul Man* when he would hole up in the Englewood house, but he also spent plenty of these years on the stage. He had a lifestyle to maintain, an ego to uphold, and a musical reputation that, with that ever-powerful voice, he could still preserve.

There was also the occasional burst of mainstream attention, as when Dan Aykroyd, in his *Blues Brothers* alter ego Jake Elwood, invited Pickett to rerecord "Land of 1000 Dances" for his latest movie, *The Great Outdoors*. The studio rendition of the old hit song was bizarre—a lightweight hip-hop reworking—and in the movie's unsettling promo video, Pickett wore the Blues Brothers' pork-pie hat and dark shades, performing in a fictional barn of a club, the movie's cast hamming it up.

On the eve of the film's release, on May 18, 1988, Aykroyd and Pickett teamed up to perform the song at the Atlantic Records 40th Anniversary Concert, held at New York's Madison Square Garden, backed by the Blues Brothers band. That put Pickett on a stage with Steve Cropper and Donald "Duck" Dunn for the first time since Watts in 1965. Accusations over song-writing splits from those Stax sessions had frequently appeared in the press over the years, and that night Cropper had braced himself for an argument. Instead, he recalled, Pickett greeted him "like long lost brothers." The singer, after all, could no longer afford to make enemies of those who admired him in the first place.

Pickett's manager Jimmy Evans had passed away in 1983, and without his gatekeeper of two decades' standing Pickett found himself booked by any number of competing agents, who were subcontracting artists to each other for the various oldies packages requested by promoters of varying reputations. Pickett's inevitable cancelations and no-shows further damaged the singer's reputation and lowered his fee. Clearly, he needed someone to replace Evans—not only to book him exclusively but also to look out for him.

He found that person in Margo Lewis, former keyboard player with sixties rock girl group Goldie and the Gingerbreads, now representing rhythm and blues musicians at her own agency, Talent Consultants International. Lewis was Bo Diddley's personal manager, and she represented Eddie Kendricks and David Ruffin. "I respect musicians and I respect what they have to go through, and I respect people who have been in the business for a while," she said. "Especially people like Wilson who have been at the top and are now no longer there—where just the slightest thing can go wrong in a day that can set you off and your show is going to be awful." Her first bookings for him went through an intermediary. "He was barely working. He was not feeling good about the way he was being responded to, the type of gigs he was getting, the money he was getting. He was paranoid. We started with a very low [fee], which we doubled very quickly—but that's because we delivered."

Dealing with Pickett was never simple. "Occasionally a woman would get on the phone—whoever was his woman that month or that year—which meant that he was indisposed or not able to talk, but that he wanted to make sure we stayed cool. And then the next day, he would call us—when he was sober." From experience, Lewis learned to navigate his mood swings. "He was charming when he wasn't resorting to drink or drugs. But when he was, he was absolutely obnoxious. And when he was that way, he was very disrespectful to women." At those times, she would end the conversation, "because I refused to be insulted by him—and I knew that he was drunk." Pickett came to trust Lewis, who, in addition to acting as his agent, took on the role of manager.

Validation of Wilson Pickett's influence and ongoing legacy arrived at the moment he may most have needed it. In late 1990 the announcement went out that he was to be inducted into the Rock and Roll Hall of Fame, in only his third year of eligibility (an artist is considered eligible twenty-five years after their first record, and Pickett received the nod ahead of Johnny Cash, Bobby Bland, the Isley Brothers, and Booker T. and the M.G.s, each of whom had released key records before him). The Induction Ceremony was held January 16, 1991 in the ballroom of midtown Manhattan's Waldorf-Astoria hotel. Pickett was to be inducted in the performer category, alongside John Lee Hooker, LaVern Baker, the Impressions, Jimmy Reed, Ike and Tina Turner, and the Byrds. Some of these artists were dead, others were incapacitated (Ike Turner was serving a lengthy jail sentence for cocaine possession), and it was uncertain whether the Byrds could put aside their differences long enough to play together. Pickett was therefore billed as a star attraction, lined up to provide one of the night's intended musical highlights: singing "Mustang Sally" alongside Bruce Springsteen.

When the moment arrived, however, Chaka Khan (initially hired to play the role of the absent Tina Turner on "Proud Mary") stepped up to sing his part. And by the time Pickett was formally inducted, it was obvious something was amiss. Ahmet Ertegun gave the introduction speech that offered a mea culpa for Atlantic's rejection of "I Found a Love" all those years ago, and then Bobby Brown, the "New Jack Swing" R&B star many saw as a modern version of Pickett, and who was charged with providing the official induction speech, was forced to finish it with the news that "Mr. Wilson Pickett couldn't be here with us this evening."

Ertegun then resumed his role as Master of Ceremonies to wrap up the evening, wearing the expression of a man not used to being snubbed. "Wilson Pickett was supposed to be here tonight," he said to the crowd. "And he might be hiding somewhere in the back." There were no cries of confirmation. "But I don't think so," he concluded, and that was that.

Where *was* Pickett? "The limo driver couldn't get him to come out of his house," said Margo Lewis. Pickett's nervous anxiety, amplified on this occasion, was such that "two days before the event, he'd start to drink. And start to do his little blow. And then he'd make himself crazy—and he would actually go a little bit out of his mind." In this particular case, "when the car came, he was barricaded in the house, waiting for someone to come through the front doors. He could have shot somebody if they tried to come in."

Pickett's longstanding fondness for guns was about to get him into more serious trouble. On May 7 that same year, at four o'clock in the morning, he drove across the lawn of his next-door neighbor, Donald Aronson, who just happened to be the mayor of Englewood. "After shouting threats about killing the Mayor," the *New York Times* reported, "Mr. Pickett drove the wrong way down a one-way street and encountered police officers, who arrested him for drunk driving, weapons possession and other charges."[2] He spent the rest of the day in jail, before being released on $2,500 bail on the charge of "simple assault and making terroristic threats."[3] For unlike Pickett's victims of domestic abuse, the mayor appeared fully intent on letting the police pursue charges. The incident made its way across the wires, where it offered subeditors easy headlines about "the midnight hour" and did little to rescue Pickett's sinking artistic reputation.

That rescue would come from a surprise hit movie out of Ireland, *The Commitments*. When Roddy Doyle self-published his novel of that name in 1997, about the struggles of an Irish soul music covers band, he did not mention Wilson Pickett. But when screenwriters Dick Clement and Ian La Frenais and director Alan Parker were hired to turn the book into a movie, they decided to introduce a real soul singer into the plot. Pickett was an obvious candidate, in part because the fictional Commitments auditioned their singer with "Mustang Sally," but more so because Pickett was the only male soul singer of the era who was alive, still performing, and, of necessity for how the plot would unravel, still known to be wildly unpredictable. Who better to announce a Dublin date in the midst of the group's comedic rags-to-near-riches tale than the Wicked Pickett himself?

The Commitments promoted sixties soul as the universal music of the downtrodden, regardless of creed or color—an important historic reinterpretation some quarter-century after the likes of Pickett first came onto the black American music scene. His fictional Dublin concert was central to the resolution of the plot, and in a penultimate scene a character presumed to be Pickett was heard—but not seen—from the back of his limousine, playing upon (and perhaps adding to) his aura as a mysterious superstar in real life. But it wasn't actually Pickett in the back seat. It remains a perfect irony that the greatest movie Wilson Pickett ever "appeared" in was one he *never* actually appeared in.

Advance buzz on *The Commitments* led to its release in the States ahead of Ireland and the United Kingdom, and the fictional group, fronted by a gruff seventeen-year-old called Andrew Strong who, in the movie, gave Pickett a run for his once-youthful money in both voice and ego, agreed to play for real at the American premiere parties. Margo Lewis quickly got involved, and Pickett turned up as a "surprise" guest onstage with the Commitments in New York, Los Angeles, and elsewhere.

In the space of eight months, then, Wilson Pickett had been given two enormous boosts to his legacy and reputation, even if he had infamously slighted the first of them. Yet though the quality of bookings started to pick up again for him—he played at the Super Bowl build-up festivities in Minneapolis in January 1992—Pickett simply could not stay out of trouble. On April 15 of that year, he was arrested again. According to a media report, it was Pickett who called the police, "to say he had been in a fight with his girlfriend and warn officers not to come to his house."[4] They did so anyway, upon which Jean Cusseaux informed them he had thrown a bottle at her and made threats against her and her family; she moved to a women's shelter and filed assault charges against Pickett.[5]

Nine days later Pickett was arrested yet again, this time for drunken driving. He had struck an eighty-six-year-old pedestrian, Pepe Ruiz, with his car in Englewood, sending the elderly man to the hospital. Pickett was clearly spiraling out of control, a danger not only to those in his own house but also to the public at large.

On May 4 Pickett went before Superior Court in Hackensack, where Cusseaux dropped the assault charges as part of an agreement. Pickett would enter an alcohol rehabilitation program, pay $3,500 to the battered woman's shelter, and additionally pay Cusseaux's legal fees—along with her moving expenses back to California.[6] The next day, Pickett was at Englewood Municipal Court on the drunk driving charges. Prosecutor Leopold Monaco noted that Pickett's blood alcohol level had been over twice the legal limit at the time of his arrest and sought to have Pickett's license revoked, stating that "him still being out there . . . is like a loaded gun." Judge Joseph Clark nonetheless allowed Pickett to keep his license and released him on his own recognizance until the full case could be heard. The judge noted the agreement from the Superior Court the previous day, in which Pickett would be entering rehab after returning from a tour of Australia.[7]

The Australian tour passed without incident. But while he was away Jean Cusseaux filed a lawsuit in Hackensack Superior Court, seeking "punitive and compensatory damages for personal and emotional injuries." In doing so, she listed five specific dates when she was "physically assaulted by plaintiff's fists" between 1986 and 1992.[8] She noted that on at least one of those dates her nose was broken, and that she had sought treatment at three different hospitals for three different attacks. The case noted additional dates when she had been struck with a heavy kitchen pot, a large baking dish, and a gallon container of bleach. The singer publicly denied all charges.[9]

Pickett's travails continued to play out in public over the subsequent year. In February 1993 Donald Aronson, the Englewood mayor, agreed to drop his charges against Pickett in exchange for the singer performing a concert on behalf of the Englewood Community Chest.[10] Pickett was back in court almost immediately on the earlier drunk driving charges, and given the extent of the damages suffered by Ruiz (who had been hospitalized for several months with head injuries), and the fact that Pickett had a previous driving conviction, he did not fare so well. Between March and October his lawyers negotiated a plea bargain, but that could not prevent him from going to prison. On October 1, 1993, Judge Arthur Minuskin sentenced Wilson Pickett to a year in jail, five years additional probation, two hundred hours of community service, a $5,000 fine, and continuation of treatment for alcohol abuse.[11] At the start of the following year, having already completed the inpatient alcohol rehabilitation program, Pickett began serving his sentence.[12]

He was hardly the only soul legend to have fallen so hard. James Brown went to prison for three years in 1988 after leading the police on an interstate car chase; Brown was suffering from an addiction to PCP.[13] Ike Turner had missed his own Rock and Roll Hall of Fame Induction due to imprisonment on various cocaine charges. Johnnie Taylor, Etta James, Ray Charles, and Bobby Womack were just some of the other soul greats who also had highly publicized drug addictions. And others had begun to pass away from a range of ailments. Joe Tex had died of a heart attack at the age of just forty-seven, back in 1982; Pickett, Don Covay, and Ben E. King were among his pallbearers. In 1992 Covay suffered a serious stroke himself, effectively ending his career.

Pickett did not spend a full year in jail; he was out and performing live again by the end of July. But his legal problems were far from over. A month after his release, Judge Andrew P. Napolitano of State Superior Court in Bergen County ruled that Jean Cusseaux could use battered woman's syndrome as grounds in her claim for civil damages. Napolitano noted a 1980 case when it was successfully used as a defense argument against murder charges; the Cusseaux case represented the first time in New Jersey that battered women's syndrome was used in a civil filing.[14] Pickett and his lawyers ultimately settled out of court.

As he attempted to resume his professional career, Pickett at least had one reliable presence by his side: Chris Tuthill, fresh out of college and newly employed at Margo Lewis' TCI. Tuthill's first show with Pickett, at New York's Tramps, was the usual baptism by fire: "He got in a rage backstage about something, but I got through it," recalled Tuthill. "And the next day, even though he had screamed at me, I had been told that I was 'alright.'" When no one else wanted to accompany Pickett in December 1994 to the Diamond Awards Festival in Belgium, Tuthill went as tour manager.

The Antwerp event marked the first time in years that Pickett employed a white person in his band. Bobby Manriquez had grown up in Washington, DC in an almost exclusively black neighborhood; he'd also grown up listening to and then playing British Invasion music and classic American soul.

Manriquez, whom the singer christened "Wheat Cracker," was not used to a structure like Pickett's, where the singer communicated to the musicians through his bandleader. He was similarly taken aback by what he saw as the group's lack of discipline. "Wilson Pickett was incredible," said Manriquez. "He was one of these musicians who could ad-lib with the best of them; the problem was that the band wasn't tight enough to follow his ad-libs. His ideas would often unfold during the performance, which is what happens when bands or artists have their stuff together; you ad-lib. Those guys had been doing it for a long time, so I don't know exactly what their excuse was. But it was not a tight band; that's all there is to it."

Manriquez quit after a few months, replaced by another white guitarist from DC, David Panzer (promptly nicknamed "Wheat Bread"), who also found the band wanting, though more from stale playing than sloppy ad-libbing. As a thirteen-year-old, "really serious about soul music," Panzer had taught himself Dennis Coffey's lines on "Don't Knock My Love." Prior to his first show, in St. Paul in June 1995, he made a point of listening to the other intricacies of Pickett's litany of studio guitarists—"and got on stage and realized I needn't have bothered."

He was particularly disappointed by the approach to "Mustang Sally." "That song has been so abused, and I thought, 'Well, now I'm going to get to hear it played right.'" Instead, when he played the chromatic guitar lick that appears several times in the song, he was rebuffed. "Wilson Pickett said, 'Don't do that shit!' So, basically it was a bar band doing Wilson Pickett. Apparently, he didn't care, or that's what he wanted. And I have to think that it's what he wanted, because every song was too fast, every song was way too loud, and every part was too busy." And Pickett would never perform a moment longer than contractually required, which meant frequently eschewing an encore. "He would always give each song his all," said Tuthill. "But he'd start to try and cheat. He'd do the revue thing and go off stage in the middle so the band could do a couple of songs. And the band would do a long intro."

"We played the lamest caricature of soul music that you could imagine," said Panzer of that introduction. "Something that would probably have been too cheesy for Las Vegas. It was a medley of every obvious hit soul record, mostly sung by David Akers, but the whole thing was just over the top, choreographed, like a soul revue—here's a history of soul music in ten minutes."

For those around him, off-stage as well as in his band, Pickett's work ethic was a source of constant frustration. "The potential for his career, even in the mid-nineties onward," said Tuthill, "was still huge, if he had been able to pull himself together. That was the biggest disappointment for me, just knowing how good he was and how much better he could be, and how much more he could do for himself if he put himself out there a little bit more and promoted himself more, and didn't expect to be paid a certain amount of money to leave the house."

Still, other musicians in the band had fond memories of this period, especially of a trip taken to Brazil in May 1995, in between Panzer's and Manriquez's individual tenures, for which Skip Pitts returned to the fold.

Of a show from São Paolo that was televised, David Akers recalled, "That night there was magic in the air. A huge crowd. Pickett was on rare form. It was just beautiful." Pitts appeared once more in his element, his patent grin having lost none of its magnetism, his lead guitar work—as requested mid-song by Pickett—neither flashy nor clichéd. Perhaps what Pickett really needed was someone who knew how to kick *his* ass.

Throughout this period, Pickett's violence toward women, despite the intended lesson of jail time, continued unabated. Margo Lewis recalled of Jean Cusseaux that "her face would have these things on them from where he hit her so many times." In the summer of 1995, on a plane to Europe for a major tour of Jazz and Blues festivals, she witnessed Wilson's new girlfriend receive the same treatment: "We were in first class. Bo Diddley is sitting behind Wilson, and [she] is sitting on the inside, and we see him . . . actually hitting her with his fists. And finally the pilot or copilot came out and with some stewards they took her away. Bo was so upset . . . It just ruins the whole thing."

In April 1996, a thirty-three-year-old Elizabeth Trapp came running out of the Englewood house partially clad and bleeding; when confronted by police, she claimed that Pickett had beat her. Police raided the house and allegedly found two grams of cocaine in a bedroom nightstand. Trapp subsequently withdrew her story, claiming that she fell on a glass table. The police still prosecuted Pickett for the cocaine possession.[15] On July 1, 1996, Pickett pleaded guilty to two counts of being under the influence of cocaine and was offered the choice of professional help or eighteen months in the Bergen County Jail. He opted for the former, and the *New York Daily News* reported that he would be voluntarily checking into a drug rehabilitation center in the Catskills. This may have been a PR ruse to paper over the harsh reality of what was to come, for in September 1996, he returned to the Bergen County Jail to begin a new custodial sentence. Ten years after his last album, Pickett had reached rock bottom.[16]

PART III

Redemption 1997–2006

CHAPTER 27

He could be woken from a deep sleep and do one of those screams. It was just physically the most amazing voice I ever heard. And to hear that live, next to your ear, on stage, with no studio effects . . .

David Panzer, guitarist, Midnight Movers, 1990s

Wilson Pickett would remain an active alcoholic for the rest of his life. Nonetheless, he underwent a positive change as a result of his second stint at the Bergen County Jail. The term included a mandatory month in its Drug Rehabilitation Center, during which time, according to a fellow musician inside, he was a model prisoner.[1] When he emerged from prison, it was with a sense of moderation; if there was cocaine use over the remaining years of his life, it was kept well hidden. "He did, in his own way, quiet down," said agent Chris Tuthill.

Casino engagements became an increasingly steady part of his income. "He would fly in, hole up in his suite and you wouldn't see him until the next day," said Tuthill. "I think he did that as a self-imposed thing. And then he would go to the gig, party a little in the dressing room before the gig, party a little after the gig and then get out the next morning and go back home." He would have a beer at that airport in the morning, which his manager Margo Lewis considered relatively "benign." His entourage only grew concerned when he drank hard liquor.

Lewis and Tuthill booked Pickett straight on to the summer 1997 circuit of blues and jazz festivals once he was released, shows that took him to continental Europe as well as across the United States; in September, at the American Music Festival on Virginia Beach, he performed once more alongside the Commitments, now touring as a fully fledged soul covers group.

He also filmed his proper debut movie appearance that year. As long on contrivance as it was short on laughs, *Blues Brothers 2000* felt more like a remake of the 1980 original than a sequel, down to Aretha Franklin singing "R-E-S-P-E-C-T" under almost identical circumstances to her show-stopping performance of "Think" from a decade earlier. The odds were always stacked against such a venture: back in 1982 John Belushi had died from an overdose of cocaine and heroin at the age of thirty-three, and rather than rely solely on Belushi's cinematic replacement John Goodman to accompany Dan Aykroyd, child actor J. Evan Bonifant was added, reducing the plot to a noticeably more juvenile level. Stilted dialogue delivered by Steve Cropper, Donald "Duck" Dunn, B. B. King, Eric Clapton, and others, kept the gulf wide between excellent musicianship and the equivalent in acting.

Pickett's role was to appear alongside Eddie Floyd in a cameo performance of "634-5789." The phone number of the title now referenced "Ed's Love Exchange," a sex line staffed by bored middle-aged women in nighties and curlers. And the otherwise noble attempt to breathe some genuine soul into the elaborately choreographed song-and-dance number (recorded in advance, in a Toronto studio, with Paul Schaffer as producer) was nullified when hot young white blues guitarist du jour, Jonny Lang, was wheeled across set on a dolly cart by Dan Aykroyd, for a horrendously overstated solo. Lang then sang—and crucified—the final verse. Audiences sensed a turkey; in stark contrast to the lasting, runaway success of the original film, *Blues Brothers 2000* barely made back its production costs.

Still, when the movie was released in early 1998, Pickett and Floyd were invited to perform "634-5789" on *Late Night with David Letterman*. Cropper and Dunn were on guitar and bass, Schaffer on piano, and Matt "Guitar" Murphy took the Jonny Lang role. Aykroyd, Goodman, and Bonifant wisely stood in the lead duo's shadows, and the two former Falcons absolutely killed it with a call-and-response performance that confirmed not only their continued star power but the ongoing might of soul as an incomparable live musical form. Pickett appeared in finer voice than for many, *many* years, ascending into an impressive falsetto on his first line, reviving it on the last verse, and resorting to familiar screams and squalls at the song's conclusion.

The Midnight Movers had long been renting themselves out as an independent unit, earning good money by playing private events. But their increased bookings eventually began to clash with Pickett's schedule. A politician who had hired the Midnight Movers for a private event threatened legal action over one such conflict, so Curtis Pope and David Panzer both stayed back from the start of the 1997 European summer tour, catching up with the rest of the group a few days later. This did not sit well with Wilson Pickett.

And it did not sit well with Pope that he and the band were left out of the recording process for *Blues Brothers 2000*. "I panicked," said Pope. "I said, 'If I don't do this movie with Wilson Pickett I'll never do anything with him.'" Egos were bruised on both sides, and after a festival in Tuscaloosa, Alabama in early September 1997, the pair agreed to part ways. "Pickett gave me his blessing," said Pope. "I called him, told him I loved him. He said, 'You don't love me.' I said, 'Yes, I do!'" Crusher Green took over the role of bandleader, putting together a new group out of New York. Pope would keep the Midnight Movers as its own group down in Washington, DC. It turned out they had split from the singer who gave them their name at the very moment he got his career back on track.

If Pickett hoped that his appearance in *Blues Brothers 2000* would entice record labels to beat a path back to his door, he was mistaken. To make another record while he still had his voice, then to quote his newly revived hit, he would have to pick up the telephone. He soon did just that, dialing one Jon Tiven.

Tiven's involvement with the soul scene went far back. As an aspiring twenty-one-year-old all-rounder, relocating to Memphis from New York in 1976 to produce an album for ex-Box Tops singer Alex Chilton, he had found himself signed to East/Memphis Music, the newly bankrupt Stax label's publishing arm, which appointed Eddie Floyd as his mentor. Floyd had in turned introduced Tiven to Sir Mack Rice; the mentorship, recalled Tiven, consisted largely of getting together at a local bar. Over the years that followed Tiven struck up a productive friendship with Don Covay, brought Arthur Alexander out of retirement, and wrote for or produced B. B. King, Donnie Fritts, Syl Johnson, and more. After he produced a new album for Sir Mack Rice, titled *This What I Do*, Rice encouraged him to send an advance copy Pickett's way. Shortly thereafter, in early 1998, Pickett called him, eager to commission a similarly professional production.

Tiven and Pickett hit it off immediately. "He was very humble and very nice," said Tiven of their first meeting, echoing most initial impressions of late 1990s Wilson Pickett. "He really just wanted to get back in the studio. He had the eye of the tiger; he wanted to go at it again. He figured he'd give it another shot."

Tiven could write, produce, play guitar and keyboards; his wife Sally could play bass, and Tiven had sufficient industry experience that he could help place the finished record. He also understood how to keep the album relevant. "I was keenly aware that the marketplace in America for black people making music over the age of fifty was mainly going to be a blues audience," he said. "So the more we could do to blend the Memphis soul with the blues on the record, the easier time we would have."

Pickett's audience was now predominantly white, and they viewed him as a legacy artist, a man of specific time and place. Rather than pretend that the singer could compete under contemporary chart conditions, with all its modern production techniques, an agreement was immediately reached that the album would, as it eventually stated in large letters on the CD sleeve, be "Certified Organic," meaning "no samples, loops or digital instruments" and as "performed by actual musicians in real time without click tracks."

The first songs to the table formed the core of the subsequent record. "It's Harder Now," a mid-tempo blues written by Tiven, was easily construed as a reference to life's rocky physical and emotional road, though on closer listen the lyrics revealed themselves as pertaining to a one-on-one (business) relationship. "Soul Survivor," which the Tivens had written with the now veteran Fame and American studios singer, songwriter, and musician Dan Penn, offered a valedictory stroll through Penn's southern soul experience with musical and lyrical references alike to Don Covay, Otis, Solomon Burke, Aretha, Bobby Womack, Joe Tex, and Sam & Dave, as well as the Wicked Pickett. Opening with an approximation of the "In the Midnight Hour" motif and playing similar tricks with signature songs as it referenced each singer in turn, as well as the studios of Memphis and Muscle Shoals, "Soul Survivor" was consistently clever but never corny, as demonstrated by the line "I remember 1965, everybody was still alive."

Soul Survivor was first choice for the album title, but given that Bobby Womack had used it in the 1980s, Tiven and Pickett settled on *It's Harder Now*. The initial recording sessions in New York involved just Jon and Sally Tiven and their regular drummer Todd Snare, with whom Pickett also hit it off. Pickett had apparently learned to moderate his drinking: "He wouldn't have a drop until we were finished with all the work" for the day, said Tiven. "I never saw him sloshed, even tipsy. I think it was just something to take the edge off after the day in the studio."

The positive mood was further enhanced when Sky "King" Williams stopped by. Tiven had played most keyboards on the initial tracks, but Williams was brought in on the playing, songwriting, and arrangements of the second set of songs. He was joined in the band by Tiven's friend Simon Kirke, the renowned rock drummer who had played with Bad Company and before that Free, in which capacity he had cut the original "Fire and Water."

For this second session, Tiven and Pickett (and then Williams too) sat down to write together. Immediately, Pickett's irascible nature came to

the fore. "He had all these lines in his head for a song, 'All about Sex,'"
said Tiven of a particularly upbeat and apparently autobiographical number. Tiven and Pickett soon doubled their take with the self-explanatory
cowrite "What's Under That Dress?" and the subject matter was further
emphasized with a recording of Tiven's cocomposition with Alabama songwriting veteran Charlie Feldman, "Taxi Love."

Placing two of these three up front in the running order—after the
excellent Pickett-Tiven-Williams opener "Outskirts of Town"—seemed
somewhat tawdry in retrospect, given Pickett's age. Still, it was true to
type, and Pickett was only being honest when he opened "What's Under
That Dress?" by confessing "I used up all my best lines in my own youth/All
I got to give you, girl, is the honest truth."

When the record was completed, Tiven and Pickett, with Sky Williams
in tow, took a car trip downtown to Canal Street to meet with the heads
of Capricorn Records, the label Jerry Wexler had helped set up in Macon,
Georgia a quarter century ago. The meeting was a bust. "He had trouble
keeping food down," said Tiven of Pickett's noticeable gastrointestinal
problems, which unnerved the executives. "He kept sipping on cokes, burp-
ing, throwing up. Stress and depression was just winding him up beyond
belief. When there were these things involving business and music, he had
a really tough time with it." Pickett admitted as much on the album's finale,
"Stone Cold Crazy," singing, in lyrics written for him by Tiven and Williams,
"I'm trying to mellow out, decompress, sometimes I just can't deal with this
stress," before regaling listeners with the madness of his lifelong travels.

The finished album, rounded out by the addition of the Uptown Horns
and male and female backing singers and mixed by the veteran rock engineer Eddie Kramer, was something of a revelation. As per Tiven's game
plan, it was more firmly anchored in the modern blues than in sixties soul,
and it was indeed organic, played and sung with evident depth of feeling.
Even the meandering six-minute "Stomp" served a purpose. By avoiding
the trends, *It's Harder Now* actually sounded relevant.

When he started shopping the finished record, Tiven found that "the
majors couldn't care less." But that should not have been surprising; with
its organic nature, it had not been made for them in the first place. He
eventually secured a deal with Rounder Records, a considerable distribution force in roots music as well as a highly reputable imprint in its own
right. Margo Lewis negotiated the terms; Pickett paid Tiven $15,000 for his
production work on top of the other studio fees. In assigning the artist to
its Bullseye Blues & Jazz imprint, hiring a highly credible independent publicity firm, and promising tour support if necessary, the Massachusetts-
based Rounder signaled its intent to treat Pickett's return to the racks as a

major event. The label even hired famed photographer Mick Rock to shoot the album sleeve. Wilson Pickett, true to form, showed up in a brand-new, full-length, $6,000 Prada silk jacket purchased especially for the occasion. He also arrived by plane from his new home in Virginia.

The house was in Ashburn, just thirty miles northwest of Washington, DC, conveniently close to that city's international airport and part of a new development like those rapidly springing up all across formerly rural, newly suburban America. It wasn't especially exclusive; it wasn't the natural domain of a rock star; there were none of the famous neighbors that Englewood had. But all of that was to his long-term advantage. "He got his life back when he moved to Virginia," said his daughter Saphan. "He was a big kid in a candy store. He got land. He got to decorate for himself."

There wasn't a lot of time for that decoration; the pieces were busy falling back into place in Pickett's professional career. On January 29, 1999 he was inducted into the Alabama Music Hall of Fame, in a ceremony held in the hall's ten-year-old Tuscumbia home. The house band for the ceremony, which also featured Percy Sledge, was the Swampers, the former Fame rhythm section, and that meant Pickett needed to mend a few fences. He seemed eager to do so, especially as Jimmy Johnson, whom he had so gravely hurt over two decades earlier, was set to present him with his official induction award. "I was glad to do it," said Johnson. "And it put us back together." Still, when Pickett and the Swampers performed "Mustang Sally," the musicians found themselves disappointed by the singer's performance, just like guitarist David Panzer had. "We wanted to do it as it was on the record," said bass player David Hood. "He wanted to do it as he did live. We were trying to capture the feeling from the records that made him famous, not the shows that nobody saw."

The national Rock and Roll Hall of Fame Induction Ceremony was still being held at the Waldorf Astoria in Manhattan, even though a purpose-built museum had finally opened in Cleveland in 1995. That ceremony had grown considerably in merit and prestige over the years, the highlights now broadcast as a special concert on VH-1. The 1999 event proved particularly star-studded: Paul McCartney, Bruce Springsteen, Billy Joel, and the Staple Singers all attended for their inductions. Sadly, fellow inductees Dusty Springfield and Charles Brown had died shortly beforehand, while Curtis Mayfield, paralyzed when hit by stage equipment at a 1990 performance, proved too ill to attend. Their absence were partially compensated by the fact that Ray Charles, Bono, Neil Young, and Lauryn Hill were among those conducting the ceremonies, and that the E Street Band joined their former employer Bruce Springsteen on stage for the first time in a decade.

Alongside such illustrious company, Wilson Pickett was invited back—eight years after standing up the Boss in the same room for the same event, to "kick his ass," as Pickett put it in a scripted intro to their duet of "In the Midnight Hour." Billy Joel joined in on additional piano; Paul Schaffer conducted the band. Pickett near enough tore the house down. He had finally redeemed himself for his earlier no-show.

Pickett had by now found a new girlfriend on one of the seafaring musical cruises that formed a significant part of his performing income. Gail Webb was considerably older than his previous partners, a divorced mother not much younger than Pickett, and she was at the end of a three-decade-long career at Ford in Detroit. She owned her own house, had an income, and enjoyed independence, none of which she was inclined to give up. And so, as Pickett settled into his new house in the not-quite-countryside near DC, Webb would visit every couple of weeks before returning to her own life in Detroit.

Webb was there when Pickett celebrated his career revival and domestic relocation by hosting a family reunion at the end of July. The fortunes of his children had waned in recent years. Lynderrick was in prison, as was his own son, Lynderrick Jr. Michael Pickett, living in Philadelphia, was wrestling with his own demons, some bequeathed directly by his father. Veda was coming out of an abusive marriage and was currently living out of her car with her two children. Saphan was still in high school in New Jersey. Two of Wilson's brothers had battled alcoholism in their own lives, and his younger ones constantly felt the pull of their older brother's fame. Only Maxwell, with a job at AT&T in Georgia, was solidly in the professional middle class. All things considered the reunion went off relatively well, but Wilson started drinking heavily as it wound down, and the family, with the exceptions of Saphan and Gail Webb, were quickly dispatched.

Webb was also present when Pickett flew in to Newark Airport for the *It's Harder Now* photo session with Mick Rock. He was met there also by a film crew: husband-and-wife directors D. A. Pennebaker and Chris Hegedus, and producer Roger Friedman. Pennebaker was renowned for the music documentaries *Don't Look Back* and *Monterey Pop*. Friedman was an entertainment journalist and soul fan who had looked at the music's dwindling number of legends and decided, "If I don't film these guys soon, they're not going to be around." Friedman had fortuitously run into Miramax Films executive Harvey Weinstein, who had just attended the 1999 Rock and Roll Hall of Fame ceremony, and who said he would provide financing and distribution, "If you can get Wilson Pickett to do it." Friedman then reached out to Margo Lewis, and recalled being told, "If you can find him, you can keep him."

Friedman set out on his debut cinematic venture, titled *Only the Strong Survive*, by treating the artists with the respect they deserved. Pickett, Sam Moore, Jerry Butler, Mary Wilson, Isaac Hayes, Carla and Rufus Thomas, and Ann Peebles all received advances both from Miramax and from Koch Records, which was compiling the soundtrack. Pickett couldn't help pegging the producer for being Jewish, a reference that was included in the finished movie. "I don't know if it was Jerry Wexler he was thinking of," said Friedman. "He never explained it to me." He didn't need to; it was part of Pickett's way of unsettling people to gain control. Nonetheless, as he did with Jon Tiven, Pickett formed a firm friendship with Roger Friedman that extended beyond their period of professional engagement. "I showed an interest in him," was Friedman's simple explanation for how he got behind the singer's protective veil. "And despite the fact that he was really a piece of work, he was so much fun. And we enjoyed each other."

Increasingly, then, Pickett was surrounding himself with a team of younger professionals, working with him in part because they were doing their job and following their own aspirations, but also because they cared for Pickett and the other soul singers—wanted to see them not just survive, as Friedman's movie put it, but thrive. At last, Wilson Pickett had reasons to look up once more.

CHAPTER 28

We were lucky to know him. He was a great artist. Like a poet, painter, writer. He was who he was all the time.

Wayne Jackson, trumpet, the Memphis Horns

On the surface, *It's Harder Now* allowed Wilson Pickett what Jon Tiven called "a victory lap." It received more reviews than any album of his in decades. It brought him back to *Late Night with David Letterman*, where he delivered a powerful performance of "Soul Survivor" backed in tandem by his own band and that of Paul Schaffer. It helped fuel his show-stealing appearance in *Only the Strong Survive* as the sole singer in the movie actively promoting a new record. It engaged him in a hefty bout of press interviews. "I don't go out partying after gigs like I used to do," he told *the Boston Phoenix*. "You know, you grab four or five chicks and go party all night long. I don't have that kind of energy anymore." Writer Ted Drozdowski responded to this by asking whether Pickett was "not as 'wicked' as [he] used to be," and the singer laughed. "Hey, if you call that wicked! . . . I sure did love it!"[1]

In another interview, this one with *Blues on Stage*, he expressed his desire for more permanent recognition. "I've never been broke," he said. "I'm not broke now. I have a beautiful home in Virginia. I have cars, I have one car that's worth over $100,000 . . . But what I would like to do is walk up and get a Grammy. That's it."[2]

In February of 2000, he nearly got his wish. *It's Harder Now* was nominated in the category of Best Traditional R&B Vocal Performance, alongside albums by Barry White, Smokey Robinson, Aaron Neville, and Peabo Bryson.[3] Although he lost to Barry White, he could be consoled by the fact that three of his competitors were on major labels, which may have given them an edge. And just two months later, he collected all three trophies for which he was nominated at the W. C. Handy Blues Awards, hosted by the Blues Foundation in Memphis: Soul/Blues Male Artist of the Year, Soul/Blues Album of the Year, and Comeback Blues Album of the Year.

Pickett received yet further validation—and the opportunity for an important reconciliation—after Jerry Wexler reached out to Jon Tiven to express his admiration for *It's Harder Now,* citing it, in Tiven's recollection, as "the best contemporary soul record that anybody had done in years." That September, Wexler received a "brass note" embedded into Memphis's Beale Street, the ceremony followed by a party at the city's House of Blues. "Suddenly here comes Wilson into the club, without advance notice and totally unexpected," recalled Wexler in 2007, just a year before he passed away. "It was instant high-fives and warm embraces." Pickett was playing a casino gig just over the Mississippi border, and Wexler was especially touched that he had driven up, "because Wilson was never known for sentimental displays of affection," noting, somewhat sadly, "We had never truly bonded."[4]

Saphan watched her father fluctuate between moments of great joy and melancholy. "I don't know if it's that he wanted the recognition for himself," she said. "I think he just wanted the accomplishment of that period to be recognized. Because he would count it down: 'There's only five of us left, there's only four of us left.' He was very, very aware of his own mortality and he was aware, if it's right to say, of the mortality of the music, 'cause there was no more would be created."

This would never have been more apparent to Pickett than on April 19, 2000, when he drove to Rockville, Maryland, where Don Covay was now living. Despite his stroke, Covay had assured the Tivens that he was capable of recording a new album, but when they arrived to start work on it, recalled Jon, "we quickly realized his synapses were not firing quickly enough for him to get the words out in time with the band." The record was duly named *Ad-Lib,* relying heavily on vocal partners recruited for the occasion, such as Paul Rodgers, Ann Peebles, and Huey Lewis—but Pickett stole the show. "This was Wilson's finest hour," said Tiven. "He was like the welcome wagon. He was there to cheer up his old buddy. He'd visited with Don, he knew the state Don was in, but he wanted to do everything he could to give Don *his* chance at a victory lap."

The two soul survivors gathered around a pair of microphones for Pickett to rally Covay through his "Three Time Loser," immortalized years earlier by Pickett on the B-side of "Mustang Sally." From there, Pickett helped Covay and the Tivens finish the song "Nine Times a Man." With acoustic guitar, organ, and a soft drumbeat, it revealed a humble side of Pickett, for "Nine Times a Man" was very much Wilson Pickett's performance. "It was basically Wilson carrying Don on his shoulders," said Tiven of a song that became "a huge hit on beach radio shortly thereafter."

As with "Three Times a Loser," which opened with a spoken reminiscence of their old songwriting sessions, "Nine Times a Man" kicked off with fond memories. "Hey," said Pickett, "You remember our slogan?" To which Covay joined in as they recounted it: "Give me some juice, turn me loose, let me hang out like a wild-necked goose . . . Hey!"

It was to be Wilson Pickett's last co-composition, and his final time in the recording studio.

Wilson Pickett did not feel fully redeemed by his comeback. "It's very difficult to get somebody who's been to the top of the mountain to accept that they're living on the hillside," said Jon Tiven. But Pickett's own attitude and misconceptions helped keep him tethered halfway up that hill—his limited success a self-fulfilling prophecy. Failing to understand the nature of modern promotion, Pickett refused to tour nationally behind *It's Harder Now*. He feared that if he took a lower fee to tour and the record didn't sell, he'd never get his price back up again. After a New York City club show celebrating the album's release, he resumed the usual circuit of casinos and legacy festivals, plus lucrative one-offs like "the Ultimate Midnight Hour" at the Rock and Roll Hall of Fame in Cleveland for the Millennium New Year.

Rounder sought to push *It's Harder Now* beyond its core blues market by commissioning an "urban radio" remix of "What's Under That Dress?" According to Tiven, Pickett's A&R man went on vacation prior to release; the label couldn't find the master recording and sent out the album version instead; the programmers at modern R&B (urban) radio weren't impressed, and the single did not get played. Having now spent its promotional budget, Rounder lost interest. "We were very optimistic about how the record would do," said Tiven, "and critically it did as well as we could possibly have hoped. [But] he didn't have a tour to go with it and we didn't have real exposure to help translate it into what you would call a hit record."

Had Wilson Pickett won the Grammy, it might have been a different story—but when he was passed over for Barry White he took it badly, skipping out on the postawards parties and returning to his Los Angeles hotel suite with his partner Gail, presumably to drown his sorrows.

Jon Tiven could only watch on as his new friend essentially gave up on himself. "I would have loved to have been able to do something to get Wilson healthier," he said. "But that was not part of the job description. He wanted me to help him make a great record. I did that. I loved the guy. I wish I could have helped him out of the hole, but he had dug himself too deep. He just had too high expectations of what having a record would do for him, so when it didn't live up to that, it just made everything worse."

Pickett's disappointment was unreasonable. For a singer who had served as many jail terms in nearly two decades as he had released albums, and who had not seen any substantial chart success for a quarter century, *It's Harder Now* was nothing short of a triumph. His career facing forward once more, he only had to initiate the next step. A duets album? He would have reveled in the competition. That long-awaited gospel record? It would have been the perfect moment. A set of soul classics he hadn't yet recorded? His audience would have loved it. A series of classic rock anthems, a la "Hey Jude" and "Fire and Water"? A guaranteed attention-grabber. Or just another record of new material, to prove that *It's Harder Now* was but an opening act in a full-fledged Pickett revival?

None of it came to pass. Pickett continued with his part-time perfor-mance schedule, which kept him financially secure and in contact with his audience. A final core group coalesced around Crusher Green as bandleader with fellow veterans Sky Williams (keys) and Wayne Cobham (trumpet), joined by Paul Zunno and Victor "Boots" Jeffries on Guitar, Zerrick Foster on bass, Mike Lewis on trumpet, and Dan Cipriano on sax. "We would go on tour for two, three weeks," said Cipriano, who observed that those who fell afoul of Pickett's temper generally did something to instigate it. "And from the moment we got to the airport to the moment we got back it was just one big constant laugh."

Cipriano, who played with Pickett from 1999 through 2004, marveled at the magic of Pickett's voice. "Let's say I played 'Midnight Hour' with him 250 times: he never sang the first line the same way, ever. He'd start on a higher note, a lower note—and everyone knows how it starts on the record. And maybe he did that once."

"There's a certain element of black singers who grew up in the church down south," Cipriano continued. "They have an element where they can play with the time. And Wilson Pickett was really great at laying behind the beat, and just kind of following it. I talked to him about it once, and he didn't know what I was talking about. He couldn't analyze it; he didn't even realize he was doing it. There are a lot of talented guys out there but there are a select few and Wilson Pickett is one of them. They just have it. They don't have to study it, they don't have to work at it; he was just one of those people. Every night I would turn and I would look and would think, 'Goddamn, it's Wilson Pickett.'"

Still, times had changed. The communal on-stage dances during "Mustang Sally" no longer qualified as stage invasions. These days Pickett would often select the heaviest or oddest-looking audience members for security to bring onstage for a lascivious bump-and-grind. On at least one occasion, according to Chris Tuthill at TCI, he became so engrossed watching the dancers that he forgot to sing the song. And the night Pickett saw Little Richard pull up a chair by the side of the stage, Cipriano recalled that he skipped entirely the routine of inviting audience members to sing—typically out of tune—part of "I'm in Love." Pickett did not want to show any musical weakness, least of all in front of a fellow legend.

All the same, there were some prominent appearances during these final years, perhaps none more so than the star-studded opening of the Mohegan Sun Casino in Connecticut on June 21, 2002. Ray Charles opened for Aretha Franklin in the main room, and Dan Aykroyd hosted a free Blues Brothers show in the Wolf Den—that doubled as Aykroyd's surprise fiftieth birthday party celebration. Pickett performed for the party alongside Sam Moore, among a cast that included Ashford and Simpson, Steven Tyler of Aerosmith, and Peter Wolf of the J. Geils Band. Former President Bill Clinton was in attendance for the Casino's ribbon-cutting ceremony, and Pickett implored him to come on stage and play saxophone during "Land of 1000 Dances." Clinton declined—that was not a solo easily replicated—but Pickett kept at him, begging on bended knee, and Clinton finally joined Pickett and Moore for "Soul Man."[5]

Gradually, it became apparent that Pickett wasn't going to make another record. He was now dealing with failing health and he was not the only one. Crusher Green collapsed on stage one night in Europe. He was diagnosed with pancreatic cancer and, upon return to the States, withdrew from the band. The role of bandleader fell to Wayne Cobham, and that of drums to Wally "Gator" Watson, who had played with Pickett at the Soul To Soul concert in Ghana. Crusher Green died in January 2002, at the age of fifty-seven; Pickett did not attend the funeral.

Watson was on drums in July 2002 when, in the heat of a steamy New York summer, a sixty-one-year-old Pickett played a free outdoor lunchtime concert as part of the Brooklyn Academy of Music's annual concerts program. The event served as a massive reunion. From the stage, Pickett pointed out a former school friend from Alabama (bringing her onstage to dance with him), his driver from forty-five years back (as he claimed), members of the Chi-Lites, and Lance Finney, the guitarist from the Falcons. Eddie Jacobs was in attendance, too. So was daughter Saphan, whom Pickett insisted join him on stage, where he threatened to "kick her butt" if she stepped out of line at college. He then rapped dirty to the middle-aged women he invited to come dance with him—ad libbing "lift up your dress, show me your mess" in "What's Under That Dress?" The following night, Pickett headlined B. B. King's in Time's Square, at a concert to celebrate the release of *Only the Strong Survive*. A live performance of "Soul Survivor" appropriately led off the soundtrack.

Pickett returned to Australia early in 2003, and also had a brief European tour that summer. "He actually stayed in the Courvoisier Estate, where I think there were thousands of Courvoisiers in the bar," said Lewis. "And for some reason, he sat in his room and didn't cause any problems, and put on a great show." At home in Virginia, "He had his Budweiser," said daughter Saphan of what she saw from her visits, "and every once in a while, he had me drive to the store and get him a fifth of something." Though it was against doctor's orders, she acquiesced. "He gave his life to the world; who cares if he has a drink? Do what makes you happy. You worked hard; enjoy yourself. Don't overindulge—and he never did. He never got to that point where he was drunk in the house. I never got to see that." Gail Webb nonetheless recalled many times when an inebriated Pickett tried to strike her, but that she easily evaded him by running up the stairs. Pickett was no longer strong enough to give chase.

In 2003 Wilson's mother Lena passed away, at eighty-five. Her large brood gathered for her funeral in Louisville, Kentucky, where her coffin was placed in a mausoleum in the Evergreen Cemetery. Some of the siblings expected Wilson to pay for the mausoleum on their behalf, and he insisted that he was but one of her eleven children. His own child, Michael Pickett, recalled that his father wouldn't even talk to him at the funeral.

Time was running out for family estrangements, whether or not the singer was willing to admit it. Roger Friedman drove to see Pickett perform at a private engagement on Long Island, and was taken aback by his friend's appearance. "He was gaunt," Friedman recollected. "He was really drinking, that was definitely a problem. He was not eating properly. He had some real young girl shacked up, and he was not well." Friedman had sought to document the soul survivors and ended up watching several soul singers he treasured fade before his eyes. To Pickett, he said, "'I can take you to my doctor, I can bring you to someone in New York if you want to do that.' But he wasn't interested and I couldn't force him." Friedman drew conclusions beyond Pickett's alcoholism. "A lot of these people are very private and don't want to talk about their health. If the word gets out that you are sick, you're not going to get the dates. 'Cause the money was from these gigs, and you had to keep touring."

But those days were coming to an end. In August 2004 Pickett flew to Canada to play the Calgary Blues and Roots Festival alongside Sam Moore, Joan Osborne, and others. Americans with criminal records often had difficulty crossing into Canada, and Pickett paid the necessary administrative fee to ensure his performance went ahead. His tour manager, however, was held back due to his own criminal record. For forty years Pickett had had people navigate his transportation, fill out his paperwork, and even pack and unpack his suitcases. At the Calgary Airport after the festival he found himself lost, and he approached Sam Moore and his wife for help. "He had no idea how to leave the country," recalled Joyce McRae-Moore. "He looked terrible and it was really scary. He looked at me and said, 'I don't know how to fill this paperwork out. I need a little help, I can't see real well.'"

This was true, but so was the fact that he had trouble reading the paperwork to begin with. A similar truth had gradually dawned on his band members over the years when they would bring him positive press to read on an airplane and he'd plead: *read it to me, I'm tired*. In the airport that day, McRae, having been around professional R&B musicians all her life, sensed the reality and said nothing. "I helped him get him through customs, get him his plane ticket, get him to the right gate, because left to himself, he probably would have died in Calgary." McRae and Moore noted that Pickett was sickly, not alert: "You could tell that he was failing."

Pickett played the Ford Gala in Detroit the following week, surrounded by Mustangs. He brought his daughter Veda and her own daughters on stage to sing with him. It was the first time Veda had ever seen him perform. It would also be the last. There were three more shows in September, and that was it. His last public performance was at the Emerald Queen Casino in Tacoma, Washington, on September 25, 2004.

Wilson Pickett spent most of 2005 shuffling the few miles back and forth from his home in Ashburn, Virginia, to Inova Loudoun hospital in nearby Leesburg. His list of ailments was long: bulimia, diabetes, and kidney disease, his body destroyed from the years of hard living. The alcohol he persisted with until the end, but "We didn't think that he was into drugs," said Saphan. "Usually his temper was an indication of that."

Gail Webb became his gatekeeper, which made his siblings and children increasingly uncomfortable. "It got to the point where she was so insistent on marrying him that he figured, 'Let me just buy her a ring,'" said Saphan, "and that's when he told me that he would never ever get married again. It was just to make her happy. She'd come down from Detroit any time he called her, so why the heck not?"

He became increasingly dependent on his prescriptions and on physical assistance. On the occasions that Gail was back in Detroit, Wilson's immediate family assumed that there would still be someone—a housekeeper or the occasional young secretary—watching over him. But they were mistaken. In late 2005, neither Veda nor Saphan could get anyone to pick up the phone for several days. The younger daughter called the police, who had to break in through a downstairs window to reach their father.

"They found him on the floor," Veda wrote in her memoir, *I Never Had a Golden Spoon*. "He had been lying there for three days, too weak to move. He had lain in his own urine for three days." Veda and Gail ended up on the same flight to Washington, DC—but did not speak to each other. Saphan picked up Veda at the airport; Gail was left to take a cab. Once at the Ashburn house, Veda saw immediately where her father had fallen. "There was a stain on the carpet, and it smelled bad. It smelled like death."[6]

As Wilson was nursed back to some degree of health, his daughters told him they were disappointed they hadn't been able to reach him to offer ongoing help. They later said that their father had been equally distressed to learn they had been told to stay away. "When he found out about it he was very hurt," said Veda. "But there was nothing he could really do about because he was sick and weak, and Gail knew it."

"That's when [Gail] started getting real nasty," said Saphan. "She started trying to get him to sign power of attorney." Wilson refused. He called for his brother Maxwell to visit and become his coexecutor alongside Gail. Maxwell accepted, but was recovering from quadruple bypass surgery and was unable to be on hand regularly. It became apparent that time was running out, and his older sisters came from Louisville, along with his older brother James.

"Gail wanted to get some papers signed, 'cause she was trying to get some money transferred from Wilson's account to some other account," said sister Bertha. "They all went out to the desk, so it left only me with Wilson. Wilson told me, 'Bert, go out there with them, Gail's trying to take all my money.' I said, 'Maybe she's not doing that, maybe it's just some business,' and he said, 'No, Bert, she's trying to take all my money.'" The family members accompanied Gail to the bank. "They told Gail his attorneys had to be there. They couldn't transfer nothing unless it was signed by Mr. Pickett and his attorneys had to be present. So Gail got a little upset . . . and so did I." Later at the house, Bertha heard Gail on the phone with attorneys. "She wasn't mentioning none of his children, I told her I didn't like it," she said. "I asked her why she was trying to transfer money over when Wilson was in the bed, sick, and she didn't like what I was saying. We really got heated up, and I was ready to fight her."

The ongoing drama did nothing to help Wilson's health. "He couldn't walk," wrote Veda. "He couldn't hold down his food. He'd simply throw it back up again. Some of it was worry. He was so stressed out that he just could not rest, could not let his body heal. He knew that the vultures were gathering."[7] And his oldest sister, Catherine Williams, said, "He was nothing but skin and bones. He had a lot of gastro problems. And the drinking didn't help him." The sisters returned to Kentucky, and Wilson Pickett was released from hospital in time to go "home" for Christmas, his favorite holiday. By Christmas night, he had fallen again, and was back in the hospital. He had left his house for the final time.

On January 6, 2006, Lou Rawls passed away from cancer, at the age of seventy-two, and the newspapers and music media mourned the passing of one of the great gospel and soul singers—a man who had spanned the generations, having sung with Sam Cooke *and* at Monterey. Meantime, Wilson Pickett was moved out of the Loudoun hospital and into Sunrise Assisted Living in nearby Reston. There the staff insisted someone sit with him from seven in the morning until eleven at night. Gail took on that duty, hiring a private nurse to join her, and the Pickett family sensed that they were now on a death watch.

Bertha called Dovie Hall in Michigan, suggesting she might want to travel to Virginia if she wished to see Wilson once more. "I'm sorry I didn't go," Dovie later said. "But I didn't think that was right. If Gail had asked me to come then I would have gone. But Gail didn't ask me to come. To me, that's disrespecting Gail. I wouldn't want anyone to do me that way. And I wouldn't *let* anyone do me that way." Somewhere toward the end, Wilson did speak with his ex-wife Bonnie Covington. "He told her to take care of herself," said Veda, "and I think that was a way of him mending, because he was sorry about the relationship."

On January 18 Gail took Wilson to get a haircut at Sunrise, "got his mustache shaped and got him looking the way he needed to look."[8] Later that day, Wilson managed some dinner. Gail recalled saying the Lord's Prayer with him, after which she and the private nurse left, close to the eleven o'clock curfew.

Wilson Pickett had a heart attack shortly thereafter and died, alone. The date of death was given as Thursday, January 19, 2006. He was sixty-four years old.

Epilogue

We've lost a giant, we've lost a legend, we've lost a man who created his own charisma and made it work around the world.

Solomon Burke[1]

The obituaries for Wilson Pickett—and they were everywhere— inevitably balanced the good with the wicked. The *Guardian* in the United Kingdom described him, accurately, as the "singer who revolution- ised the sound of 60s soul."[2] Just about every paper of record made some reference to his troubled 1990s, his jail terms, or what the *Washington Post* referred to simply as his "volatile personality."[3] Aretha Franklin was among the surviving soul stars who paid tribute. "One of the greatest soul singers of all time," she said, a simple statement of which there could be surely no dispute.[4]

The *Washington Post* was one of the many papers to report that Pickett was survived by "his fiancée, Gail Webb." His family felt otherwise about that description. Gail moved out of the Ashburn house and into a nearby hotel prior to a private service held at the Loudoun Funeral Chapel on January 21. Among the attendees that day were many of the musicians who had played under the name of the Midnight Movers; Margo Lewis and Chris Tuthill; Bo Diddley, who had become good friends with Pickett over the years of sharing stages and hotels and airplanes with him; and Don Covay.

Wilson Pickett's body was transported to Louisville, Kentucky. There, at the Canaan Christian Church, on January 28, hundreds gathered to pay respects and mourn his passing. The service proved memorable: sister Emily Jean led a rousing gospel tribute in honor of those Sunday morning walks through the Prattville backwoods en route to Jericho Baptist, and brother Maxwell offered measured words of comfort that recognized both Wilson's brilliance and his difficulties. Stephanie Harper read from the scriptures. Dovie Hall sat quietly in the pews. Sir Mack Rice and Willie Schofield of the Falcons, with guitarist Lance Finnie, paid tribute, and although Aretha Franklin and Solomon Burke, each listed on the printed program, did not in fact attend, the mourners received an impromptu, show-business eulogy from a sequin-clad Little Richard.

"Wilson, he's an innovator, an emancipator," said Richard. "He's *supposed* to be in the Hall of Fame; he's one of the ones that paved the way for all these people you see, like Puff Daddy, and Will Smith, and Eminem, and Kanye West. If it weren't for him, they wouldn't be there."

The official eulogy was delivered by the Reverend Steve Owens, imported from Maxwell Pickett's home church in Decatur, Georgia. Maxwell and Owens had become good friends once it was discovered that the preacher had played in a soul band prior to taking up the church—and that he had, of course, covered many a Wilson Pickett song in his day. As Owens reached the climax of his eulogy, he sang the refrain from "Land of 1000 Dances." Soon enough he had the whole church chanting a joyous last hurrah: "Na, na-na-na-na, *na-na-na-na-na-na-na-na-na-na* . . ."

At the conclusion of the service Wilson Pickett's casket was taken to the mausoleum in the Evergreen Cemetery, close to his mother, per his request. His eternal resting place was engraved with an image of his face in its prime and inscribed with the Lord's Prayer.

There were to be further tributes over coming weeks and months, including a public memorial concert at B. B. King's in New York. And family drama resumed. Gail Webb was bought out from her position as coexecutor, and Maxwell Pickett was left to administer a Wilson Pickett Jr. Legacy company with an associated scholarship fund. A trust fund was established for Wilson's four children, the only family members to benefit directly from his wealth; part of Michael Pickett's quarterly inheritance would make its way directly to Dovie Hall, who had served as his mother throughout his formative years.

Barely a week after he was interred, Wilson Pickett was honored at the Staples Center in Los Angeles, where he finally received the recognition from the Grammys that he had always sought. The subdued awards ceremony focused largely on the devastation wrought the New Orleans musical community by Hurricane Katrina the previous summer, but at the conclusion of the evening a one-off supergroup assembled to play the soul anthem to eclipse them all: "In the Midnight Hour." The lineup included Dr. John on piano, The Edge of U2 and Elvis Costello on guitars, and Bonnie Raitt, Yolanda Adams, and Patti Scialfa on backing vocals. Singing lead was one of the last remaining great voices of Pickett's generation, Sam Moore, who delivered a stirring, heartfelt rendition of the first verse. He was joined for the second verse by Bruce Springsteen and for the finale by the Soul Queen of New Orleans, Irma Thomas.

For all the hundreds of times that "In the Midnight Hour" had been performed on television—and for the hundreds of *thousands* of times that it had been covered in bars, clubs, theaters, concert halls, and stadiums around the world—this was an especially spirited, emotionally evocative rendition. "This is for the Wicked Pickett," roared Springsteen as the second verse gave way to the famous horn instrumental, and it was evident that he was doing so not just on behalf of the musicians on stage, but on behalf of every soul fan who had ever been touched by one of the greatest voices and, yes, one of the most volatile personalities of the last fifty years.

Wilson Pickett had gone on home. Lord, have mercy.

NOTES

All quotes in the text are from the author's own interviews (see Acknowledgments for full list), except as referenced below.

CHAPTER 1
1. "Where progress and preservation go hand in hand" is the official slogan of Prattville, as promoted prominently on www.prattvilleal.gov.
2. "Albert James Pickett, Alabama's First Historian," *Alabama Historical Quarterly*, Spring 1930, 113–14.
3. Jeff Benton, "Historian's Work Now Discounted," *Montgomery Advertiser*, March 2, 2011, 3C.
4. Retrieved from 1860 US Federal Census Slave Schedules results for Pickett, http://search.ancestry.com/cgi-bin/sse.dll?_phsrc=MxP3&_phstart=successSource&usePUBJs=true&db=1860slaveschedules&gss=angs-d&new=1&rank=1&gsln=PIckett&gsln_x=0&msrpn__ftp=Montgomery%20County,%20Alabama,%20USA&MSAV=0&uidh=000&gl=&gst=&hc=20&msrpn__ftp_x=XO
   http://search.ancestry.com/cgibin/sse.dll?db=1860slaveschedules&gss=sfs28_ms_r_db&new=1&rank=1&gsln=PIckett&gsln_x=0&msrpn__ftp=Autauga%20County%2C%20Alabama%2C%20USA&msrpn__ftp_x=1&MSAV=0&uidh=000
5. Alabama total and slave population 1860 as on permanent exhibit at the National Civil Rights Museum, Memphis; total American black population of 4.5 million from Kempton, *Boogaloo*, 9.
6. Kenneth E. Phillips, "Sharecropping and Tenant Farming in Alabama," Encyclopedia of Alabama, July 28, 2008, www.encyclopediaofalabama.org/article/h-1613.
7. Kenneth E. Phillips and Janet Roberts, "Cotton," Encyclopedia of Alabama, March 14, 2008, www.encyclopediaofalabama.org/article/h-1491.
8. All birth years, some of them officially approximate, retrieved from www.ancestry.com.
   http://search.ancestry.com/cgi-bin/sse.dll?gl=allgs&gss=sfs28_ms_r_f-2_s&new=1&rank=1&gsfn=Major&gsfn_x=1&gsln=Pickett&gsln_x=1&msypn__ftp=Autauga%20County%2C%20Alabama%2C%20USA&msypn=211&msypn_PInfo=7-%7C0%7C1652393%7C0%7C2%7C3246%7C3%7C0%7C211%7C0%7C0%7C&msbdy_x=1&MSAV=0&msbdy=1893&cp=0&catbucket=rstp&uidh=000 and http://search.ancestry.com/cgi-bin/sse.dll?gl=allgs&gss=sfs28_ms_r_f-2_s&new= 1&rank=1&gsfn=Minnie&gsfn_x=1&gsln=Pickett&gsln_x=1&msypn__ftp=Autauga%20County%2C%20Alabama%2C%20USA&msypn=211&msypn_PInfo=7-%7C0%7C1652393%7C0%7C2%7C3246%7C3%7C0%7C211%7C0%7C0%7C&msbdy_x=1&msbdp=2&MSAV=0&msbdy=1891&cp=0&catbucket=rstp&uidh=000&msypn__ftp_x=1&msypn_x=XO

9. Major Pickett lived until 1969. One of his daughters, Honeymoon, born around 1923, was still living in Prattville at the time of writing.

10. Kempton, *Boogaloo*, 75.

11. Detroit's ten-year population would peak in 1950 at 1,850,000, before entering a steady decline; in 2010, it was back at the 1910 level of 700,000. The percentage of blacks within that population continued to increase due to white flight, however, so that by 2010 blacks accounted for over 80 percent of the total population, as compared to barely 1 percent a century earlier.

CHAPTER 2

1. Of slight build compared to his siblings, Hezekiah would develop a reputation for humility and comedy, later changing his name to Hercules as a reflection of both his physical size and inner strength. There were some noted weaknesses that, in the modern era, according to his brother Maxwell, would have been classified as "special needs."

2. George, *The Death of Rhythm and Blues*, xiii.

3. Hirshey, *Nowhere to Run*, 44.

4. Pickett-New, *Don't Let the Green Grass Fool You*, loc. 438.

5. David Llorens, "Soulin' with 'Wicked' Pickett," *Ebony*, October 1968, 134.

6. DeNeen L. Brown, "A Good Whuppin'? Adrian Peterson Child Abuse Case Revives Debate," *Washington Post*, September 13, 2014, www.washingtonpost.com/blogs/she-the-people/wp/2014/09/13/a-good-whuppin-adrian-peterson-child-abuse-case-raises-old-debate/.

7. Pickett-New, *Don't Let The Green Grass Fool You*, loc. 470.

8. Nick Kent, "Land of a Thousand Libels," *New Musical Express*, November 10, 1979.

9. Hirshey, *Nowhere to Run*, 45.

10. There is some uncertainty regarding the name of the quartet: I was offered both the Jericho Hummingbirds and the Union Gospel Singers.

11. Pickett-New, *Don't Let The Green Grass Fool You*, loc. 588.

12. "The Life and Times of Wilson Pickett," BBC 6 Music, March 2012.

13. The four specific h's stood for head, heart, hands, and health.

14. Young, *Woke Me Up This Morning*, 149–50.

15. Hirshey, *Nowhere to Run*, 47.

16. Kempton, *Boogaloo*, 84.

17. As the Original Blind Boys, Brownlee's group had one of the few spiritual songs to be included in the R&B chart, a vocal rendition of the Lord's Prayer, "Our Father (Which Art In Heaven)," which was a major hit over Christmas 1950.

18. Cheeks quotes from Heilbut, *The Gospel Sound*, 122–24.

19. Llorens, "Soulin' with 'Wicked' Pickett," 134.

20. Ibid.

21. In 1959, shortly before he died, Brownlee came out of hospital to join the Original Blind Boys on a program with the Sensational Nightingales in New Orleans. His rendition of "Leave You In the Hands of the Lord" was such that, as Cheeks recalled, "I woke up in the dressing room. That's the first and only time I ever fell out" (Heilbut, *The Gospel Sound*, 124–25.)

CHAPTER 3

1. Of the prodigious Fortune catalog, special attention is due the singles "So Strange" and "Harmony of Love" by the Five Dollars, each of which eschewed all use of lyrics or a chorus, capturing instead a vocal purity of almost folk art proportions.

2. Ritz, *Respect*, 17.
3. Hirshey, *Nowhere to Run*, 47.
4. Pickett-New, *Don't Let the Green Grass Fool You*, loc. 750–51.
5. Hirshey, *Nowhere to Run*, 46.
6. A *Gotham Gospel* compilation CD on which this session is included makes no mention of Pickett, but his presence on the one track is generally supported by those around at the time, along with Pickett's own frequent statement of a sole recording session for Battle that went unreleased.
7. At the point of writing, a "new" CD purporting to package Pickett's "Early years 1957–1962" includes the Spiritual 5 single. The producer of the set was not able to offer any proof of Pickett's presence on the record, only that "it has always been accepted that it is him."
8. Jim Delehant, "Official Sound Report," *Hit Parader*, April 1967.
9. Interview with Sue C. Clark, September 1969. Rock and Roll Hall of Fame and Museum Library and Archives, Cleveland, Ohio.

CHAPTER 4

1. Eddie Floyd quote from http://silentstereorecords.blogspot.com/2006/01/in-memoriam-wilson-pickett.html.
2. "Given the times, it wasn't all that unusual for a man to brutalize a woman," James Cleveland told David Ritz in *Respect*, 41.
3. Interview with Michael Lydon, "Return of the Wicked Pickett," *New York Times* (full audio recording version), 1977
4. Lydon interview (full audio version).
5. On June 10, 1959, in Chattanooga, Tennessee, the Falcons appeared on the same bill as Sam Cooke, Jackie Wilson, Hank Ballard and the Midnighters, Marv Johnson, (Gladys Knight and) the Pips, Johnny Guitar Watson, Baby Washington, and half a dozen others.
6. Pickett sounded very much at home on the twelve-bar blues of "Anna," but he struggled with the meandering, James Brown-like vocal approach to "(I Don't Want No) Part Time Love," despite being listed as a cocomposer, and also with the overt commerciality of "Billy the Kid," written by the prolific Sax Kari. Robert West later released "Anna" and "Billy the Kid" across two A-sides, in 1965 and 1967 respectively, as Wilson Pickett and the Falcons. These and other recordings by the Falcons, including some beautifully raw demos featuring Pickett or Stubbs singing lead accompanied only by voices and piano, appear on the 115-track, four-CD compilation *The Definitive Falcons Collection*, released in 2014.
7. Pickett-New, *Don't Let the Green Grass Fool You*, loc. 1117–18.
8. Rick Whitesell, audiocassette interview with Wilson Pickett, recorded December 3, 1980, archived at New York Public Library for the Recording Arts, Music Division, Lincoln Center, NY.
9. Pickett-New, *Don't Let the Green Grass Fool You*, 1145.
10. Lydon interview (full audio version).
11. The writing credits for "I Found a Love" were shared between Pickett, Willie Schofield, and Robert West, the latter a source of considerable discontent for the singer. "When I wrote 'I Found a Love,' I didn't know nothing about BMI," he told Michael Lydon, referring to the songwriters' agency. "So my manager says, 'Well, you know, you're not a BMI writer, so I'll have to sign.'" Such scenarios were not uncommon at the time. Schofield additionally complained of not seeing his share of the publishing.

12. Wexler and Ritz, *Rhythm and the Blues*, 150.
13. Ertegun's speech ran as follows: "In the early 1960s, a producer in Detroit contacted us about a group he wanted to record. Jerry and I decided to finance the sessions but when we heard the finished recordings we found they weren't strong enough to release. So we gave them the masters back. Several months later we heard about a record that was breaking in the Detroit area, and become a regional hit, by a group called the Falcons. It was called 'I Found a Love.' What we didn't realize was that it was one of the songs we had turned down in the first place. So in an ironic twist we went back and reacquired the masters that we'd originally paid for."

It is highly unlikely that Atlantic reacquired those original masters. Atlantic studio logs show that West rerecorded the songs in Detroit, and Detroit soul archivist Keith Rylatt notes that the Atlantic recording of B-side "Swim" is substantially "thinner" than what was officially released. This suggests that the later tapes were used. The existence of two separate recordings would also indicate why Schofield recalled being at the "I Found a Love" session with the Ohio Untouchables in Cincinnati, yet his replacement, Ben Knight, is heard singing on the single. A Detroit recording would also explain Don Juan Mancha's insistence that he played piano on the track.

14. Pickett's billing for the opening of the Twenty Grand on October 27, 1961 contained the comical lie that he had played New York's esteemed, elite Copacabana.
15. It has been suggested that the Supremes sang on Pickett's Correc-tone recordings. Under their original name of the Primettes, the Supremes were indeed managed by Bob West, who cut a single on them for his Kudo label, although it went unreleased at the time. And in her autobiography *Dreamgirl*, Mary Wilson writes of seeing Pickett at the Forrest Street studio during the Primettes' first session around 1960, calling him "a real street guy." But once they signed to Tamla, and especially given his intentions on Diana Ross, Berry Gordy was not about to let them moonlight. The fact that the Adantes often covered for the Supremes in the studio down the line might help explain this historical inaccuracy.
16. Among the 110 recordings collected on the exhaustive and exhausting *Definitive Falcons Collection* is a demo of the Fabulous Playboys singing "I Found a Love" accompanied only by an upright piano; taken at a slower pace than the original Falcons hit, its gospel roots are that much more evident. Also included on this set, indicating that they were produced or released by Bob West, is a version by Maxine Davis from 1963 and an extended rendition by Joe Woods, who put as much of his soul into it as did Pickett. The song was later covered by Johnnie Taylor, Etta James, and others. Sam Cooke borrowed from it wholesale for his 1963 composition for the Sims Twins, "That's Where It's At," though he took sole songwriting credit nonetheless.

CHAPTER 5

1. "Detroit Label Releases Disk by Ex-Falcon Star," *Jet*, April 26, 1962.
2. "Correc-tone: Pickett," *Soulful Detroit*, http://soulfuldetroit.com/web16-correc-tone/05-05-Pickett.htm.
3. Wexler and Ritz, *Rhythm and the Blues*, 156.
4. "Correc-tone: Pickett," *Soulful Detroit*.
5. Ibid.
6. Price, *Sumdumhonky*, loc. 1592.
7. Montague, *Burn, Baby! BURN!*, 23.

8. Ibid., 93.
9. Ibid., 92.
10. "Stone smash" from Wexler and Ritz, *Rhythm and the Blues*, 157.

CHAPTER 6

1. From transcript of Tom Thurman interview, as archived under Immaculate Funk Collection, Rock and Roll Hall of Fame and Museum Library and Archives, Cleveland, Ohio. Interviews conducted 1996-1999 for Immaculate Funk: The Jerry Wexler Story, FBN Productions, d: Tom Thurman, 2000.
2. Wexler and Ritz, *Rhythm and the Blues*, 147.
3. Burke quotes from Thurman, Immaculate Funk Collection, Rock and Roll Hall of Fame and Museum Library and Archives, Cleveland, Ohio. Pickett quotes from "The Wicked Pickett: The Life and Times of Wilson Pickett," BBC 6 Music, March 2012.
4. Confirmation of the recording details from "Correc-tone: Pickett," *Soulful Detroit*, http://soulfuldetroit.com/web16-correctone/05/05-Pickett.htm in which Robert Bateman confirmed that "It's Too Late" was cut at Bell Sound.
5. Montague, *Burn, Baby! BURN!*, 90.
6. For more about the decision to postpone "A Change is Gonna Come," see Peter Guralnick's Sam Cooke biography *Dream Boogie*. In his memoir My Story, Bobby Womack, Cooke's guitarist and confidante at the time, recounts Cooke's fears of releasing the song.
7. Dovie Hall confirmed the basics of the incident. Don Juan Mancha's colorful recollections are recollected in Rob Moss, "Don Juan Mancha: The Story," *Soul Source*, February 19, 2013, www.soul-source.co.uk/articles/artist-articles/don-juan-mancha-the-story-r2652/.
8. Pickett believed that he had paid for at least one session in Detroit, a claim substantiated by Don Juan Mancha, who said that Pickett did so because Golden had run out of money. Some songs for the *It's Too Late* LP originated from the Motor City. But others came out of New York, and while the Funky Midnight Mover box set lists United Sound in Detroit as the location for all of Pickett's pre-Atlantic solo recordings, this runs counter to many other accounts, including those of producer and writer Robert Bateman, that had them recording at the Correc-Tone studio in Detroit and then Bell Sound in New York. It is almost certain that the singles "It's Too Late" and "I'm Down to My Last Heartbreak" were recorded at Bell Sound on Double L's budget.
9. Michael Lydon, "Return of the Wicked Pickett." *New York Times* (full audio version), 1977.
10. Lydon interview (full audio version)
11. Wexler and Ritz, *Rhythm and the Blues*, 156.
12. Gordon, *Respect Yourself*, 106.
13. Abbey, "Jerry Wexler: Aretha, She's Just Unbelievable." *Blues & Soul*, January 1971.
14. Thurman, transcript of interview as archived under Immaculate Funk Collection 40, Rock and Roll Hall of Fame and Museum Library and Archives, Cleveland, Ohio.
15. The circumstances of their first meeting, and Pickett's greeting, recalled by Don Covay in interview with the author.
16. The single's failure to make the R&B charts can be excused by the fact that one was not published in 1964, which was *Billboard's* perverse reaction to so many

black-oriented singles crossing over to the pop charts. The R&B chart was eventually reinstated under pressure from those putting out the records, who had come to rely on it both to measure the rise of new artists and to follow the status of records that did not have commensurate success on the pop charts.

17. Bert Berns cut a separate session on Tami Lynn, in which she recorded his "I'm Gonna Run Away From You." A flop at the time, it was revived on the English "northern soul" circuit in 1971 and became a top ten British hit.

CHAPTER 7

1. In McPhatter's sole performance, the former Dominoes and Drifters star was called "pitiful" by the *New Amsterdam News'* "Theatrical News" column, May 8, 1965.
2. "'Mustang Sally' by Wilson Pickett," *Song Facts*, www.songfacts.com/detail.php?id=5798.
3. Rick Whitesell, audiocassette interview.
4. Gordon, *Respect Yourself*, 106.
5. Wexler had been making noises about selling the label, assuming he could get Ertegun on board, and Stewart wanted a "key man" clause, meaning that if Wexler was no longer part of Atlantic, Stax would be free to pursue other distributors.
6. At the National Civil Rights Museum, established within Memphis's Lorraine Motel, which in the 1960s was an essentially black hotel where the Stax musicians often socialized by day, and where Martin Luther King Jr. was shot dead in 1968, it is claimed as part of a permanent exhibit that "In the Midnight Hour" was written on those premises. It was not. The Holiday Inn chain had fully cooperated with recent laws regarding integration; it was the one place that both Pickett and Wexler could each receive appropriate respect and comfort.
7. Kempton, *Boogaloo*, 235.
8. Cropper's oft-stated comment that the Stax musicians were unfamiliar with the Jerk seems unlikely given that it was already all over American Bandstand as well as the charts, and even more so given that Pickett referenced it in the other hit they recorded that day at Stax, singing "You do the jerk, you do the twine" on "Don't Fight It." He and Cropper had supposedly written that song just the night before.
9. At Pickett's Apollo residency of March 1965, there was an audience "jerk and twine" contest; the singer may have picked up the reference here.
10. "Watts Riots," Civil Rights Digital Library, http://crdl.usg.edu/events/watts_riots/.
11. Magnificent Montague was forced to retire his catchphrase. He introduced "Have Mercy" instead, from the chorus of the Don Covay single he'd released on his own label. It would not have the same effect.

CHAPTER 8

1. Delehant, "Official Sound Report." That accent on the beat may have been due to the fact that Atlantic engineer Tom Dowd, according to Cropper, "flew Al Jackson up and overdubbed more snare drum on some cuts."
2. Bowman, *Soulsville, U.S.A.*, p. 63.
3. Ibid.
4. For more about Memphis race relations in the midst of the Stax era, read Gordon's *Respect Yourself*.

5. Like Covay's *See-Saw* LP, *Otis Blue* featured a white girl on the cover; it sold over a quarter of a million copies while Pickett's picture on *In the Midnight Hour* languished in the R&B racks.
6. Interview with Sue C. Clark, September 1969. Rock and Roll Hall of Fame and Museum Library and Archives, Cleveland, Ohio.
7. Lydon interview (full audio version), 1977.
8. Ray Stiles, "Interview with Wilson Pickett," *Blues on Stage*, August 13, 1999, www.mnblues.com/review/pickett-interview.html.
9. Joyce McRae, manager and wife of Sam Moore and a former board member of the Rhythm & Blues Foundation, stated as follows in an interview with the author: "What they all used to do, Berry Gordy or Ahmet Ertegun or Morris Levy and all these guys, would be to put their names on a record. Stewart didn't want take a chance of putting his name on anything because everyone would have figured it wouldn't have been him. But Cropper was Jim Stewart's boy, so Cropper was designated to put his name on everything. Steve Cropper and David Porter were the guys that were in the position to write and fill out and file the material for the copyright office. Period, end of story, full story."
10. Cropper has consistently said that he heard Pickett using the phrase "in the midnight hour" on an old gospel record, but those did not exist. It had to be one of the two commercial releases mentioned.
11. "Respect," *Rock & Roll*, WGBH/BBC, 1995. From transcript of interviews dated 1987–88, archived at Rock and Roll Hall of Fame Library and Archives, Cleveland, Ohio.
12. Cropper was not immune from facing the same kind of dilemma. In 1995 Janet Jackson asked to cover one of his less successful cowrites from 1967, "What'll I Do." But there was a condition: "The only way you get on a Janet Jackson album is if you give half your royalties away," he said. He agreed to do so and came out considerably better off: "She sold 16,000,000 CDs."
13. By the time of Pickett's second session at Stax, Atlantic's own engineer Tom Dowd had flown down to Memphis and attached a stereo separator, allowing Stewart and Cropper to continue recording the way they knew how, in mono, but for Atlantic to offer a stereo option as was becoming increasingly popular for LPs. In the studio itself, it remained business as usual: record everything to tape in a single take, with no overdubs.

CHAPTER 9
1. Chapter epigraph from "Wilson Pickett Biography," Rock & Roll Hall of Fame, https://rockhall.com/inductees/wilson-pickett/bio/.
2. *Muscle Shoals*, directed by Greg Camalier, Magnolia Pictures, 2014.
3. Thurman, *Immaculate Funk Collection* 7. Rock and Roll Hall of Fame and Museum Library and Archives.
4. Ibid.
5. *Muscle Shoals*, Camalier.
6. Clark interview, 1969.
7. Thurman, *Immaculate Funk Collection*.
8. Hall, *The Man from Muscle Shoals*, loc 377.
9. Jones, *Memphis Boys: The Story of American Studios*, 28.
10. Thurman, *Immaculate Funk Collection*.
11. There is some uncertainty as to who eventually played the bass line. Rick Hall has it that Tommy Cogbill stepped in, dipping his hands in Vaseline to loosen

the strings, but while Cogbill took over on bass in October, by most accounts it appears that Lowe saw out this three-day session. That raises the question of whether Cogbill made any significant contributions at Fame for Pickett's first visitation; it is hard to discern a third guitar to confirm his presence other than as an observer. Hall writes and talks of "flying in" the choral response to Pickett's "na-na-na-na," which would have meant mixing mono to mono, something he would do only sparingly, not least because of audio degradation.

12. *Muscle Shoals*, Camalier.
13. Only one of the ten cuts from this monumental Fame session did not find its way on to record: "When a Man Loves a Woman." Pickett was unimpressed by Sledge, who was not the world's greatest singer. He may also have felt threatened by him—commercially, that is. Physically, Pickett almost pummeled Sledge at Fame, when Sledge compared Pickett's voice to James Brown's.
14. Fame finally made the leap from mono to three-track late in 1966, almost certainly after the second Pickett session.
15. The official Atlantic logs—as subsequently used for the liner notes of the *Funky Midnight Mover* box set—record the presence of sax players Andrew Love, Floyd Newman, and Charlie Chalmers, and trumpeter Wayne Jackson, on the May 1966 Fame session, along with John Peck on "unknown" instrument; this could only refer to the one-armed trumpet player "Jack" Peck. For the second session at Fame, Chalmers, Logan, and Caple are listed on sax, and "Bowlegs" Miller on trumpet player. However, the back of the *Exciting Wilson Pickett* LP, which was drawn exclusively from the first two Fame sessions, makes no mention of Peck, Jackson, or Love—and adds a credit for Ben Cauley on trumpet. Contacted by the author, Cauley, eighteen at the time of those sessions and just starting to acquire a reputation around Memphis, insisted he played on both sessions. Anything is possible, including the presence of two or more trumpets, or indeed, different players on different days. The discrepancy between the credits on the *Exciting Wilson Pickett* and those of the official studio logs most likely reflects Atlantic's unwillingness to list salaried Stax employees on a non-Stax LP.
16. Thurman, Immaculate Funk Collection.

CHAPTER 10
1. Clark, 1969.
2. Gordon, *Respect Yourself*, 105.
3. Womack, *My Story*, 133.
4. Kent, *Land of a Thousand Libels*.
5. "Respect," interview transcript.
6. Walter Rossi quotes from interview with Ryan Sparks, Classic Rock Revisited, January 2005, as archived at www.walterrossi.net/Net%20interviews/Interview%20With %20Walter%20Rossi.htm.
7. Lydon interview (full audio version).
8. Robinson argument with Murray per Don Lehnoff as recollected at Are U On Something http://www.areuonsomething.com/print_pickett.html.
9. Townshend quote as archived at Are U On Something http://www.areuonsomething.com/print_pickett.html.
10. Account of Pickett's generosity from Are U On Something http://www.areuonsomething.com/print_pickett.html.

11. Miles played on the Hendrix LP Electric Ladyland, formed the group the Electric Flag that debuted at Monterey Pop, launched the Buddy Miles Express, with Rossi on board, and then teamed up with Hendrix full time in the Band of Gypsys.

CHAPTER 11

1. Womack, *My Story*, p. 115.
2. "Bobby Womack's Regrets Over Wilson Pickett Snub," *The Express*, December 4, 2012, http://www.express.co.uk/celebrity-news/362564/Bobby-Womack-s-regrets-over-Wilson-Pickett-snub.
3. Whitesell, audiocassette interview.
4. Womack, *My Story*, 130–31.
5. See the documentary *Bobby Womack: Across 110th Street*, directed by James Maycock, BBC TV, 2014.
6. According to Peter Guralnick's biography Dream Boogie, Cooke had supposedly sought to release "Yeah, Man" as an A-side but was convinced to shelve the song by his new business manager, Allen Klein. It showed up on his posthumous LP *Shake*, the jubilant arrangement, highlighted by a swinging horn line, indicating that his instincts were correct. The lyrics, however, and his jokey delivery, delightfully revealing though they are, suggest that he would need to have returned to the studio to rerecord his vocals.
7. See the "*Billboard* Year-End Hot 100 Singles of 1967," *Billboard*, Dec 30, 1967, 42. Proof of soul music's dominance that year can be indicated by the presence of Sam & Dave, Aretha Franklin, Arthur Conley, the Soul Survivors and Stevie Wonder all in the top 20 of this list, along with blue-eyed soul boys the Box Tops and the Young Rascals.
8. Ostensibly, the musicians were brought to New York to work on a King Curtis session. As a sidenote, while those Fame musicians interviewed for this book were happy to reminisce fondly about their sessions with Wilson Pickett, it was difficult to stop them going off on a tangent about their work with Aretha, which was evidently (and often stated as such) the professional highlight of their lives.
9. "Respect," interview transcript.
10. Ibid.

CHAPTER 12

1. Bobby Emmons quotes from Jones, *Memphis Boys*, 84 (on Womack), 88 (on Curtis).
2. Womack, *My Story*, 130.
3. "The Story of Wilson Pickett," *Unsung*, TV One, September 2014.
4. Thurman, *Immaculate Funk Collection*.
5. "The Life and Times of Wilson Pickett," BBC 6 Music.
6. Harold Logan was found shot dead in his office of the Turntable nightclub, which he had opened with Lloyd Price in May 1969. The murder was never solved, though it was tracked back to feuds with the black Mafia. In an interview with Mark Jacobson of *New York* magazine in the year 2000, Frank Lucas, the convicted Harlem drug dealer and killer and model for the movie *American Gangster*, credited the murder as follows: "Logan got his. Two bullets in the same hole smack between the eyes. Bang. Bang." Lloyd Price closed up the Turntable soon after. See Mark Jacobson, "Footnotes to an Obit: The Wild Life of Howard Tate, the Greatest Lost Soul Man," *Vulture*, December 9, 2011, www.vulture.com/2011/12/footnotes-to-an-obit-soul-great-howard-tate.html.

7. Four of Pickett's bandmembers cited an anecdote surrounding legendary dice hustler C. B. Atkins, who by then was Sarah Vaughan's ex-husband. While Pickett would often exclude his own band members as the stakes rose, it was often for their protection, and if he played against his own musicians exclusively, he rarely called in the debt.

8. George-Warren, *A Man Called Destruction*, 62.

9. "The Life and Times of Wilson Pickett," BBC 6 Music.

10. Those two songs were "Remember, I Been Good To You," and "It's A Groove," neither of which Womack claimed to have written on his own.

11. *Bobby Womack: Across 110th Street*.

12. Pickett attempted to claim Young's share for himself, changing the credits on releases beyond the original 45 to read Womack-Pickett; the BMI registration, however, is still in the name of Womack and Young, who insists that he gets his royalties.

13. As detailed in his own memoir, Bobby Womack had an affair with his stepdaughter Linda, who would go on to marry Bobby's brother Cecil.

CHAPTER 13

1. Cauley, the sole survivor, was the only member of Redding's fated entourage who had recorded with Wilson Pickett.

2. When industry publication *Cashbox* calculated its poll for Top R&B Male Vocalist of 1967, based on chart positions, it could not distinguish between Brown, Redding, and Pickett, and gave them equal number one status.

3. Hirshey, *Nowhere to Run*, 329.

4. Wexler and Ritz, *Rhythm and the Blues*, 201.

5. Guralnick, *Sweet Soul Music*, 276.

6. Ibid.

7. Thurman, *Immaculate Funk Collection*, Rock and Roll Hall of Fame and Museum Library and Archives.

8. Guralnick, *Sweet Soul Music*, 275.

9. The compilation was released as *Beg Scream & Shout*, Rhino Records, 1997.

10. Thurman, *Immaculate Funk Collection*, Rock and Roll Hall of Fame and Museum Library and Archives.

11. Wexler and Ritz, *Rhythm and the Blues*, 186.

12. Gordon, *Respect Yourself*, 175.

13. Founded in 1951, the Sanremo Music Festival (Festival della canzone italiana di Sanremo) is an annual song contest that takes place in the coastal Liguarian town of Sanremo. Drawing huge crowds every year, the festival continues to this day, and was an inspiration for the more famous Eurovision Song Contest.

14. "The Life and Times of Wilson Pickett," BBC 6 Music. Womack was open about his cocaine use, writing freely about it in his memoir and talking about it during multiple interviews, including an official BBC TV documentary shot shortly before his death in 2014.

CHAPTER 14

1. Black soldiers had complained in letters to *Soul* and *Jet* that they couldn't hear the likes of James Brown, Aretha Franklin, and Wilson Pickett on their radio stations; USO tours by the likes of Roy Rogers and Wayne Newton were hardly likely to compensate (Smith, *The One*, 194–216). Also see Smith for more about James Brown and the Black Panthers.

2. Wexler and Ritz, *Rhythm and the Blues*, 227–29.
3. George, *The Death of Rhythm and Blues*, 98–115.
4. Haralambos, *Soul Music*, ch. 3.
5. Shaw, *The World of Soul*, 213–14.
6. Womack, *My Story*, 136.
7. Shaw, *The World of Soul*, 214.
8. Clark interview, 1969.
9. Thurman, *Immaculate Funk Collection* transcript.
10. Clark interview, 1969.
11. Another interview appeared to indicate that it was the water cooler that Allman spiked, which may have been enough to do similar damage to the session.
12. The exact date of this session is difficult to state with complete certainty; November 27 is that which most closely adheres to studio logs and various memories of events.
13. Other than the enforced rendition of the Young Rascals' "Love Is a Beautiful Thing," Pickett had stayed clear of covering white artists since heading down south to record.
14. According to legend, Pickett was so unfamiliar with the song that he thought it was called "Hey Jew" and sang it accordingly, but Pickett never confessed to this. It seems extraordinarily unlikely he would mistake the name of the year's single biggest song.
15. Clark interview, 1969.
16. Lydon interview (full audio version), 1977.
17. Wexler's reported response does beg the question as to whether he had heard Allman's astounding contribution to Clarence Carter's "The End of the Road" from a month earlier—and if so, why he hadn't asked exactly the same question back then.
18. Ben E. King was among those who cited it to the author as his favorite Pickett performance.

CHAPTER 15

1. In 1972, as Alder Ray Black, she recorded a single fronting the Fame Gang in Muscle Shoals: "Just Because the Package's Been Unwrapped and Opened (Doesn't Mean the Merchandise is Spoiled)." Pickett's opening act and confidant Danny White is not to be confused with the recorded soul singer of the same name.
2. Chris Lowe attended the session but felt conflicted by loyalty to Pickett, whom he had been with longer than the others, and left before its completion. Ernest Smith also attended, but found sixteen-year-old Ernie Isley making his debut on bass instead. Along with Claston Higgins, Smith and Lowe stayed with Pickett—for now.
3. Clark interview, 1969.
4. Ibid.
5. *Billboard*, August 23, 1969, 5; R&B Now Soul.

CHAPTER 16

1. Trailer for *Sigma Sound: The Sound Heard Round The World*, directed by Bill Nicoletti, Visual Innovations, 2016, aired at https://vimeo.com/129463478#at=0
2. Abbey, "Jerry Wexler: Aretha, She's Just Unbelievable."
3. "Wilson Pickett Inks $150,000-A-Year Recording Pact," *Jet*, February 5, 1970, 54.

4. Interview with Sue C. Clark, 1973. Rock and Roll Hall of Fame and Museum Library and Archives, Cleveland, Ohio.
5. "Respect," interview transcript.
6. Ibid.
7. Sigler was not credited with playing on the LP, but insisted to the author on his hands-on involvement with "Days Go By," the song he wrote with Eugene Dozier. "If it's going to sound like it's going to sound, I have to play on it. There was a lot of things I worked on that I didn't get credit for."
8. "Respect," interview transcript .
9. "Funky Broadway" (in 1968) and "Get Me Back On Time, Engine Number 9" (1971) were both nominated in the category of Best Male R&B Vocal Performance. Pickett lost to Lou Rawls's "Dead End Street" and B. B. King's "the Thrill is Gone," respectively.

CHAPTER 17

1. Jerry Wexler quote in chapter epigraph from "Jerry Wexler: Aretha, She's Just Unbelievable," John Abbey, Blues & Soul, January 1971.
2. Pickett-New, *Don't Let the Green Grass Fool You*, loc. 2058.
3. Pickett quote of $100,000 from "Respect," interview transcript. The $60,000 referenced by Bobby Eli is from author's interview and other published sources.
4. Pickett quotes about Gamble and Huff/In Philadelphia from "Respect," interview transcript.
5. Bill Dahl, sleevenotes to *Wilson Pickett, Funky Midnight Mover: The Atlantic Studio Recordings (1962-1978)*, Rhino Handmade, 2010.

CHAPTER 18

1. Rob Bowman, sleeve notes, *Soul To Soul*, Rhino DVD/CD, 2004.
2. Ibid.
3. Audio commentary, *Soul To Soul*, Rhino DVD/CD, 2004
4. According to Ingrid Monson in *Freedom Sounds*, 128–30, Louis Armstrong had been greeted by a crowd of ten thousand on his arrival in 1956.
5. It apparently pained Pickett that he was referred to by the Ghanaians as "Soul Brother Number Two," with the clear implication that he was still second to James Brown.
6. Lydon interview (full audio version).
7. Monson, *Freedom Sounds*, 152.
8. Ibid., 129.
9. Bowman's sleeve notes cite a briefly contentious comment en route to Ghana, when someone noted that the black musicians had been brought to America by "whitey" on a slave ship, and were being brought back to Africa on a chartered plane.
10. Audio commentary, *Soul To Soul*, Rhino DVD/CD, 2004.
11. Roger St. Pierre, "Wilson Pickett on African Soul." *New Musical Express*, May 13, 1972.
12. St. Pierre, "Wilson Pickett on African Soul."
13. Bowman, liner notes, *Soul To Soul*, Rhino, DVD/CD, 2004 .
14. Phyl Garland, "Soul To Soul," *Ebony*, June 1971, 79.
15. Audience estimation from Bowman, *Soul To Soul* liner notes.
16. St. Pierre, "Wilson Pickett on African Soul."
17. Audio commentary, *Soul To Soul*, Rhino, DVD/CD, 2004.

CHAPTER 19

1. Clark interview, 1969.
2. Bowman, liner notes, *Soul To Soul*. Rhino DVD/CD, 2004,
3. "New York Beat," *Jet*, March 9, 1972, 57.
4. "Talent In Action," *Billboard*, February 26, 1972, 15.
5. John Abbey, "Wilson Pickett/Jackie Moore: Copacabana," *Blues and Soul*, March 1972.
6. Clark interview, 1973.
7. Lydon interview (full audio version).
8. Ibid.
9. Ibid.
10. Clark interview, 1973.
11. Greenfield, *The Last Sultan*, chapter 14 header.
12. Clark interview, 1973.
13. The pop market was never as impressed with Pickett's covers of white hits as the R&B/soul audience was, and Atlantic by now should have known as much.
14. Clark interview, 1973.
15. Wexler and Ritz, *Rhythm and the Blues*, 263.
16. "From the music capitols of the world," *Billboard*, January 6, 1973, 4.

CHAPTER 20

1. In his memoir, Wexler was unapologetic about this kind of behavior. "It's traditional—and certainly legal—for the ex-label to repackage records by recently departed acts" (Wexler and Ritz, *Rhythm and the Blues*, 263).
2. "Executive Turntable," *Billboard*, August 11, 1971, 4.
3. Clark interview, 1973.
4. Cliff White, Wilson Pickett – Join Me and Let's Be Free, *New Musical Express*, July 26, 1975.
5. Pickett quotes from Lydon interview (full audio version).
6. Fong-Torres, *Becoming Almost Famous*, 64.
7. John Abbey, "The Wicked One," *Blues and Soul*, 1976. www.soulmusic.com/index.asp?S=3&T=3&ART=2872.
8. Ibid.
9. John Abbey, "Wicked As Ever," *Blues and Soul*, August 1974. http://www.soulmusic.com/index.asp?S=3&T=3&ART=2871
10. Lydon (full audio version).

CHAPTER 21

1. Newfield, *The Life and Crimes of Don King*, 33–41.
2. Pickett-New, *Don't Let the Green Grass Fool You*, loc. 932.
3. Pickett-New, *Don't Let the Green Grass Fool You*, loc. 2038–39.
4. "Billy Rowe's Notebook," *New Amsterdam News*, February 2, 1974, A10.
5. "Wilson Pickett pays $500 Bail," *Jet*, December 12, 1974, 60.
6. "Billy Rowe's Notebook," *New Amsterdam News*, March 23, 1974, A11. A somewhat lackluster double LP recorded on the tour of Japan was released in parts of Europe, the United Kingdom included, but was not issued in the United States, proof that Pickett's relationship with RCA was rapidly deteriorating at the time.
7. McWilliams walked right into the band of Fats Domino, who was also performing there at the time, with whom he stayed for the next fourteen years.
8. "They called her the Lady Wilson Pickett," said Shapiro of Jackson.

9. Criteria was not listed on the LP credits, although given the use of T. K.'s in-house string arranger Mike Lewis, and the additional writing credit of Albhy Galuten, it's highly likely they spent some time there.
10. John Abbey, "Wilson Pickett: The Wicked One."
11. Lydon interview (full audio version).

CHAPTER 22
1. Chapter epigraph from TV One, "Unsung" documentary on Wilson Pickett, 2014.
2. "Wilson Pickett Tells of Hard Luck in South Africa," *Jet*, April 22, 1976, 62.
3. For more on the bankruptcy of Stax and the scapegoating of Al Bell, see Robert Gordon's book *Respect Yourself*, and the documentary that preceded it, *Respect Yourself: The Stax Records Story*, codirected by Gordon and Neville Morgan, Stax, 2007.

CHAPTER 23
1. Nick Kent, "Wilson Pickett: Land of a Thousand Libels."

CHAPTER 24
1. Pickett-New, *Don't Let the Green Grass Fool You*, loc. 2083–95.
2. Ibid., 2083–95.
3. Eddie Jacobs, Joyce McRae, and Jon Tiven were among the interviewees who suggested that Pickett would have benefited from a professional medical diagnosis.
4. "Soumaya is not his kid, by DNA," said Saphan in a 2015 interview with the author. "Proven."
5. Hirshey, *Nowhere to Run*, 327.
6. Robert Palmer, "A Reunion of Soul Clan at the Savoy Tonight." *New York Times*, July 24, 1981.
7. Adam White, "Talent in Action," *Billboard*, Aug 8, 1981, 41.
8. Of the accusation in question, John Abbey insisted, "I had no knowledge one way or another."
9. Floyd claimed not to remember much of this tour during an interview with the author; it may just have been that he preferred not to speak ill of his former friend and partner.
10. Pickett would perform a tour of England's chain of Dingwall's clubs in 1983.

CHAPTER 25
1. "Talent Talk." *Billboard*, March 6, 1982.
2. Hirshey, *Nowhere to Run*, 313.
3. The book was almost certainly Sue C. Clark's *The Superstars: In Their Own Words*, for which Pickett had personally cussed out the author when she next interviewed him.
4. Biography of Wilson Pickett, Motown Records publicity department, 1987.

CHAPTER 26
1. Ted Drozdowski, "Still Wicked: Wilson Pickett's Raw Return," *Boston Phoenix*, October 18, 1999.
2. Nadine Brozan, "Chronicle," New York Times, May 5, 1992, www.nytimes.com/1992/05/05/style/chronicle-683492.html.
3. "Singer Wilson Pickett Faces Charges of Beating Girlfriend," *Jet*, May 4, 1992, 54.
4. Ibid.
5. Brozan, "Chronicle."
6. Ibid.
7. "Wilson Pickett Pleads Innocent," *Sun Journal*, May 6, 1992, 28.

8. "Pickett Hit With Suit by Former Girlfriend," *Jet*, June 22, 1992, 59.

9. Cusseaux vs. Pickett, 279 N.J. Super 335, decided August 4, 1994, www.leagle.com/decision/1994614279NJSuper335_1586.xml/CUSSEAUX%20v.%20PICKETT.

10. The case had been moved to Teaneck given that Aronson appointed the judges in Englewood. "Pickett to Perform in Concert to Settle Dispute with Mayor," *Jet*, March 15, 1993, 60.

11. "Singer is Sentenced to Jail," *New York Times*, October 2, 1993, www.nytimes.com/1993/10/02/nyregion/singer-is-sentenced-to-jail.html.

12. "New Jersey Sheriff says Wilson Pickett Is Treated as Just Another Number in His Jail," *Jet*, Jan 24, 1994, 36.

13. Michael Goldberg, "James Brown Addicted to PCP," *Rolling Stone*, November 17, 1989.

14. Cusseaux vs. Pickett; "Court Victory Seen for Battered Women," *New York Times*, August 7, 1994, www.nytimes.com/1994/08/07/nyregion/court-victory-seen-for-battered-women.html?ref=topics.

15. "New Jersey Police Look Into Charges Famed Singer Wilson Pickett Beat His Girlfriend," *Jet*, April 29, 1996, 53.

16. Francesca Chapman, "Celebs Get Tongue-Lashing from Madonna," September 18, 1996, http://articles.philly.com/1996-09-18/news/25633034_1_madonna-cuts-maternal-girl-marriage; Corky Siemaszko, "Wilson Picks Rehab Over Pokey," *New York Daily News*, August 7, 1996, www.nydailynews.com/archives/news/wilson-picks-rehab-pokey-article-1.744641.

CHAPTER 27

1. The musician wished to remain anonymous.

CHAPTER 28

1. Drozdowski, "Still Wicked."

2. Ray Stiles, interview with Wilson Pickett, Blues on Stage, August 13, 1999, www.mnblues.com/review/pickett-interview.html.

3. In 1999, Pickett's original recording of "In the Midnight Hour" was inducted into the Grammy Hall of Fame; in 2000 the same honor was bestowed upon his rendition of "Mustang Sally."

4. Sleeve notes, Funky Midnight Mover: The Atlantic Studio Recordings (1962-1978), *Rhino*, 2010.

5. "Bill Clinton, SNL Stars Surprise Dan Aykroyd," June 24, 2002, www.foxnews.com/story/2002/06/24/bill-clinton-snl-stars-surprise-dan-aykroyd.html.

6. Pickett-Neal, *Don't Let the Green Grass Fool You*, 77.

7. Ibid.

8. Pickett-New, *Don't Let the Green Grass Fool You*, loc. 3097.

EPILOGUE

1. Aretha Franklin and Solomon Burke statements, "Soul Singer Wilson Pickett Dies," http://news.bbc.co.uk/2/hi/entertainment/4630184.stm.

2. "Wilson Pickett: Singer Who Revolutionised Soul," *The Guardian*, January 2006. www.theguardian.com/culture/2006/jan/20/usa.world.

3. Matt Schudel, "'Midnight Hour,' 'Mustang Sally' R&B Singer Wilson Pickett, 64." *Washington Post*, January 19, 2006. http://www.washingtonpost.com/wp-dyn/content/article/2006/01/19/AR2006011903266.html.

4. "Soul Singer Wilson Pickett Dies." January 20, 2006. http://news.bbc.co.uk/2/hi/entertainment/4630184.stm.

BIBILIOGRAPHY

Agee, James. *Cotton Tenants: Three Families*. Brooklyn: Melville House, 2014.

Bjorn, Lars, with Jim Gallert. *Before Motown: A History Of Jazz In Detroit, 1920–1960*. Ann Arbor: University of Michigan Press, 2001.

Boland, S. R., and Marilyn Bond. *The Birth of the Detroit Sound: 1940–64*. Chicago: Arcadia, 2002.

Borden, Ernest H. *Detroit's Paradise Valley*. Chicago: Arcadia, 2003.

Boyd, Herb. *Black Detroit: A People's History*. Unpublished.

Buskin, Richard. *Inside Tracks: A First-Hand History of Popular Music from the World's Greatest Record Producers and Engineers*. New York: Spike, 1999.

Bowman, Robert. *Soulsville, U.S.A.: The Story of Stax Records*. New York: Schirmer, 2003.

Coffey, Dennis. *Guitars, Bars, and Motown Superstars*. Ann Arbor: University of Michigan Press, 2009.

Dobkin, Matt. *I Never Loved A Man the Way I Love You: Aretha Franklin, Respect, and the Making of a Soul Music Masterpiece*. New York: St. Martin's, 2004.

Evans, Curt J. *The Conquest of Labor: Daniel Pratt and Southern Industrialization*. Baton Rouge: Louisiana State University Press, 2001.

Fong-Torres, Ben. *Becoming Almost Famous: My Back Pages in Music, Writing, and Life*. New York: Hal Leonard, 2006.

Garland, Phyl. *The Sound of Soul*. Chicago: Henry Regnery, 1969.

George, Nelson. *The Death of Rhythm and Blues*. London: Omnibus, 1988.

George-Warren, Holly. *A Man Called Destruction: The Life and Music of Alex Chilton, from Box Tops to Big Star to Backdoor Man*. New York: Viking, 2014.

Gordon, Robert. *Respect Yourself: Stax Records and the Soul Explosion*. New York: Bloomsbury, 2013.

Gordy, Berry. *To Be Loved: The Music, the Magic, the Memories of Motown*. New York: Warner Books, 1994.

Greenfield, Robert. *The Last Sultan: The Life and Times of Ahmet Ertegun*. New York: Simon & Schuster, 2011.

Guralnick, Peter. *Dream Boogie: The Triumph of Sam Cooke*. New York: Little, Brown, 2005.

——. *Last Train To Memphis: The Rise of Elvis Presley*. New York: Little, Brown, 1994.

——. *Sweet Soul Music: Rhythm and Blues and the Southern Dream of Freedom*. New York: Harper & Row, 1986.

Haralambos, Michael. *Soul Music: The Birth of a Sound in Black America*. New York: Da Capo, 1985.

Hall, Rick. *The Man from Muscle Shoals: My Journey from Shame to Fame*. Heritage Builders (Kindle Edition), 2015.

Heilbut, Anthony. *The Fan Who Knew Too Much: Aretha Franklin, the Rise of the Soap Opera, Children of the Gospel Church, and Other Meditations*. New York: Knopf, 2012.

The Gospel Sound: Good News and Bad Times. New York: Hal Leonard Corporation, 1975.

Henson, Stanley Jr. *In The Midnight Hours: The Movie Book*. Woodbridge, VA: EOMP, 2006.

Hirshey, Gerri. *Nowhere to Run: The Story of Soul Music*. London: Pan, 1984.

Hughes, Charles L. *Country Soul: The Southern Recording Industry and The Making of Race in the United States, 1960–1980*. Chapel Hill: University of North Carolina Press, 2015.

Jackson, John A. *A House on Fire: The Rise and Fall of Philadelphia Soul*. New York: Oxford University Press, 2004.

Jackson, Wayne, and Amy Jackson. *In My Wildest Dreams—Take 1*. Wayne and Amy Jackson (Kindle Edition), 2012.

Jones, Roben. *Memphis Boys: The Story of American Studios*. Jackson: University of Mississippi Press, 2010.

Kempton, Arthur. *Boogaloo: The Quintessence of American Popular Music*. New York: Pantheon, 2003.

Koloko, Leonard. *Zambian Music Legends*. Lulu.com, 2012.

Lavette, Bettye, with David Ritz. *A Woman Like Me: A Memoir*. New York: Plume, 2013.

Lornell, Kip. *From Jubilee to Hop Hop: Readings in African American Music*. New York: Routledge, 2009.

Marsh, Dave, and Sam Moore. *Sam and Dave: An Oral History*. New York: Avon, 1998.

Milan, Jon. *Detroit Ragtime and the Jazz Age (Images of America)*. Chicago: Arcadia, 2009.

Monson, Ingrid. *Freedom Sounds: Civil Rights Call Out to Jazz and Africa*. New York: Oxford University Press, 2007.

Montague, Magnificent, with Bob Baker. *Burn, Baby! BURN! The Autobiography of Magnificent Montague*. Urbana: University of Illinois Press, 2003.

Neal, Mark Anthony. *What The Music Said: Black Popular Music and Black Public Culture*. New York: Routledge, 1998.

Newfield, Jack. *The Life and Crimes of Don King: The Shame of Boxing in America*. Sag Harbor, NY: Harbor Electronic Publishing, 2003.

Pickett, Albert J. *History of Alabama: And Incidentally of Georgia and Mississippi, from the Earliest Period*. Baltimore, MD: Genealogical Publishing, 2000.

Pickett Neal, Veda. *I Never Had a Golden Spoon: Veda Pickett Neal, Daughter of Legendary Soul Singer Wilson Pickett, Tells Her Survivor's Story*. Bloomington, IN: iUniverse, 2009.

Pickett-New, Louella. *Don't Let the Green Grass Fool You: A Sibling's Memoir about Legendary Soul Singer Wilson Pickett*. Xlibris (Kindle Edition), 2014.

Poe, Randy, *Skydog: The Duane Allman Story*. New York: Hal Leonard, 2008.

Price, Lloyd. *Sumdumhonky*. Cool Titles (Kindle Edition), 2015.

Ribowsky, Mark. *Ain't Too Proud To Beg: The Troubled Lives and Enduring Soul of the Temptations*. New York: Wiley, 2001.

Signed, Sealed, and Delivered: The Soulful Journey of Stevie Wonder. New York: Wiley, 2010.

The Supremes: A Saga of Motown Dreams, Success, and Betrayal. New York: Da Capo, 2010.

Riedel, Johannes. *Soul Music, Black and White: The Influence of Black Music on the Churches*. St. Paul, MN: Augsburg, 1975.

Ritz, David. *Respect: The Life of Aretha Franklin*. New York: Little, Brown, 2014.

Rosengarten, Theodore. *All God's Dangers: The Life of Nate Shaw*. New York: Knopf, 2013.

Rylatt, Keith. *Groovesville USA: The Detroit Soul & R&B Index*. Stuart Russell (Kindle Edition), 2014.

Savage, Jon. *1966: The Year The Decade Exploded*. London: Faber & Faber, 2015.

Selvin, Joel. *Here Comes The Night: The Dark Soul of Bert Berns and the Dirty Business of Rhythm and Blues*. Berkeley, CA: Counterpoint, 2014.

Shaw, Arnold. *The World of Soul: Black America's Contribution to the Pop Music Scene*. New York: Cowles, 1970.

Smith, R. J. *The One: The Life and Music of James Brown*. New York: Gotham Books, 2012.

Smith, Suzanne E. *Dancing in the Street: Motown and the Cultural Politics of Detroit*. Cambridge, MA: Harvard University Press, 2001.

Werner, Craig. *A Change Is Gonna Come: Music, Race & the Soul of America*. Ann Arbor: University of Michigan Press, 2006.

Higher Ground: Stevie Wonder, Aretha Franklin, Curtis Mayfield, and the Rise and Fall of American Soul. New York: Crown, 2007.

Wexler, Jerry, and David Ritz. *Rhythm and the Blues: A Life in American Music*. New York: St. Martin's, 1993.

Whitburn, Joel. *Top 40 R&B and Hip-Hop Hits*. New York: Billboard Books, 2006.

Top 40 Hits. New York: Billboard Books, 1996.

Rhythm & Blues Top R&B Albums. Menomee Falls, WI: Record Research Inc., 1999.

The Billboard Book of Top 40 Albums. New York: Billboard Books, 1991.

Williams, Jerry. *Detroit: The Black Bottom Community (Images of America)*. Chicago: Arcadia, 2009.

Williams, Otis, and Patricia Romanowski. *Temptations*. New York: Cooper Square, 2002.

Wilson, Mary. *Dream Girl: My Life as a Supreme*. New York: St. Martin's, 1986.

Womack, Bobby, with Robert Ashton. *My Story, 1944–2014*. London: John Blake, 2014.

Young, Alan. *Woke Me Up This Morning: Black Gospel Singers and the Gospel Life*. Jackson: University of Mississippi Press, 1997.

INDEX